T0326627

L'Europe méditerranéenne

Mediterranean Europe

P.I.E. Peter Lang

Bruxelles · Bern · Berlin · Frankfurt am Main · New York · Oxford · Wien

L'Europe et les Europes
(19e et 20e siècles)

Construire l'Europe, ce n'est pas seulement élargir l'Union ou doter les institutions communes de nouvelles compétences. C'est aussi promouvoir l'Europe dans la diversité de ses cultures et de ses passés qui participent tous à la conscience que les peuples européens ont de leur destin commun. Préparer l'avenir de l'Union demande donc de se souvenir de ce passé. Car la connaissance de l'histoire contribue à maîtriser la mémoire collective.

La collection *L'Europe et les Europes* se donne comme objectif de publier des travaux historiques consacrés aux États et aux nations européennes, à leurs relations, entre eux et avec l'ensemble du monde. Elle privilégie l'étude des crises internationales, la démarche comparative et l'histoire de l'histoire. Si le politique, qu'il s'agisse d'institutions, de doctrines ou de mentalités occupe une place de choix, la collection est également ouverte aux sciences sociales et humaines, en souhaitant refléter ainsi les activités de l'Association internationale d'histoire contemporaine de l'Europe.

Directeur de collection :
L'Association internationale
d'histoire contemporaine de l'Europe

représentée par :
Jacques Bariéty
Président de l'AIHCE

et Christine Manigand
Responsable scientifique de la collection

Marta PETRICIOLI (éd)

L'Europe méditerranéenne

Mediterranean Europe

L'Europe et les Europes
No. 8

Soutien financier pour la publication/Financial support for publication: Dipartimento di Studi sullo Stato and Cassa di Risparmio di Firenze.

© P.I.E. PETER LANG S.A.

Éditions scientifiques internationales

Bruxelles / Brussels, 2008

1 avenue Maurice, B-1050 Bruxelles, Belgique

www.peterlang.com ; info@peterlang.com

ISSN 1422-9846
ISBN 978-90-5201-354-1
D/2008/5678/28

Ouvrage imprimé en Allemagne / Printed in Germany

Information bibliographique publiée par « Die Deutsche Bibliothek »

« Die Deutsche Bibliothek » répertorie cette publication dans la « Deutsche National-bibliografie » ; les données bibliographiques détaillées sont disponibles sur le site http://dnb.ddb.de.

Bibliographic information published by "Die Deutsche Bibliothek"

"Die Deutsche Bibliothek" lists this publication in the "Deutsche National-bibliografie"; detailed bibliographic data is available in the Internet at <http://dnb.ddb.de>.

CIP available from the British Library, GB and the Library of Congress, USA.

Table des matières/Contents

Introduction

Marta PETRICIOLI

Università di Firenze

Mediterranean Europe occupies a very different time and space from the other areas of Europe (north, Atlantic and central-eastern) into which the continent has been divided for the research project, coordinated by the Institut Pierre Renouvin, *"Espaces et temps de l'Europe"*.

First let us take a look at its space. In the south it is limited by the coastline and extends to various islands, large and small; to the north its limits are less distinct: it includes the Pyrenees, the Alps and the Balkan mountains, but it slices France into two halves; to the west it includes Portugal, because the country belongs in cultural terms to the rest of the Iberian peninsula, even though, like Galicia, it is bathed by the Atlantic. Its eastern limits are even more uncertain, because it involves the very concept of Europe, in which some feel it embraces Turkey, while others do not. Besides, this area includes the Orthodox fault line and several Muslim groups, in Bosnia, Kossovo and Albania.

However, this space becomes more homogeneous in terms of land-scape, since the climate is by and large the same; oranges, olives, vines and cereals are the main crops, and there is a liberal scattering of ar-chaeological remains of a shared culture that goes from the Phoenicians to the Etruscans, and from the Greeks and Romans to the Byzantines. For some scholars, such as Pedrag Matvejevic, the Mediterranean landscape ends with the last olive tree; for Takis Theodoropoulos *"il s'arrête là où je vois se dresser la dernière colonne dans le paysage nu, en partant de Baalbek au Liban jusqu'au Volubilis au Maroc"*, the presence of columns being characteristic of all countries in Mediterra-nean Europe from Greece to Italy, and from France to Spain. As Theo-doropoulos tells us *"Les ruines du passé, qu'elles soient glorieuses ou honteuses, petites ou grandioses, sont des existences actuelles"*[1].

---

[1] Takis Theodoropoulos, *La Méditerranée grecque*, Paris, Maisonneuve & Larose, 2000, pp. 26-27.

The time span is also very different from that of the rest of Europe, both because its history goes further back, and because of the differing times in which the various states of Mediterranean Europe joined the European Union. Beside the founding members, Italy and France, Greece and Spain joined later and some countries, such as Malta and Cyprus are very recent additions, while others, such as Croatia and Turkey, are still standing awaiting entry, and others have not even begun accession talks. Yet another difference is the late arrival of a fully democratic process in some Mediterranean states.

The sea itself is perceived differently. Whereas the inhabitants of central, northern and Atlantic Europe see the Mediterranean as the southern limit to the continent, a place for pleasuring and relaxation[2], a sort of cultural Club Méditerranée, a safari towards difference on the shores of the *Grand Bleu*, where the rich of the north congregate. For the people of the Mediterranean the sea is not a border but a medium linking three continents; on the shores of this sea "civilization was born", or rather a few of the great civilizations of the world. Its very name, *in medias terras*, proves this to be true. The Greeks have several words for sea: *thalassa*, a general term containing the idea of womb from which all things came, *pelagos*, or an expanse of water, but also *pontos*, which transforms this expanse into a connecting link[3]. This connecting function is underlined by Hegel:

> These three continents are not separate but connected by the Mediterranean, around which they are situated. By nature North Africa belongs to Europe right up to its desert sands; the inhabitants of this part of Africa [...] are related to the Europeans. The whole of Asia Minor is also part of Europe; the real Asiatic race inhabits East Asia.

In the classical and romantic periods the Mediterranean was seen as a spiritual motherland. For example, Goethe links his inner journey to an external trip southwards; he flees the north to travel round the Mediterranean, writing:

> Herrlich ist der Orient
> Übers Mittelmeer gedrungen;
> Nur wer Hafis liebt und kennt,
> Weiß, was Calderon gesungen[4].

---

[2] See, for example, John Pemble, *La passione del sud. Viaggi mediterranei nell'Ottocento*, Bologna, Il Mulino, 1998, or Paul Fussel, *All'estero. Viaggiatori inglesi tra le due guerre*, Bologna, Il Mulino, 1988.

[3] Bertand Westphal, "Leggere il Mediterraneo", in *Abitare il Mediterraneo*, Firenze, 2004, p. 54; Pedrag Matjevic, *Il Mediterraneo e l'Europa. Lezioni al Collège de France*, Milano, Garzanti, 1998.

[4] Georg Meiering, *La Méditerranée allemande*, Paris, Maisonneuve & Larose, 2000, pp. 49-51.

Despite the contrasts that have arisen in history (east/west, north/south, Christianity/Islam) the Mediterranean basin has been the scene of contacts and exchanges, of products both cultural and material. Furthermore, after the vanquished had been enslaved, the victors had raped their women, people had been kidnapped by pirates, and others forcibly converted, after *devshirme*, Mediterranean genes are far more pluralistic than its religions or its nationalisms. For this reason Mediterranean Europe is an ideal place in which to study such phenomena as adaptability, borrowings, appropriation and transformation, all important aspects of social creativity. For instance, here we can study relationships and family units, forms of social and political organization, or investigate why, in countries such as Greece, Italy or Spain, relations between a local community and state institutions bring to the fore a local potentate and have relations of clientele connecting a village to the country's state institutions, or how the state relates to local realities[5]. All this is a great help in understanding those who live on the opposite shores of the Mediterranean.

Yet the Mediterranean is not just one whole. It is a multiple reality. If one tries to limit the Mediterranean identity one is forced, as one is usually in dealing with identity, to proceed by exclusion. As Edgar Morin has written this is a:

> paradoxe que ne peut comprendre, ni la pensée qui ne voit que l'unité et occulte la diversité, ni la pensée qui ne voit qu'un catalogue de diversité sans percevoir l'unité. Pour concevoir la Méditerranée il faut concevoir à la fois l'unité, la diversité et les conflictualités; il faut une pensée qui ne soit pas linéaire, une pensée dialogique qui saisisse à la fois complémentarités et antagonismes. Oui la Méditerranée est la mer de la communication et du conflit, la mer des polythéismes et des monothéismes, la mer du fanatisme et de la tolérance, et, ô merveille, la mer où le conflit, enfin policé dans la petite Athènes du Ve siècle, est devenu débat démocratique et débat philosophique[6].

Today it would be really dangerous for Europe to shut herself in; to become a fortress controlling those within and those without its walls. The risk is all the greater because identity is constructed in opposition to something else, to alterity. The more Europe withdraws, the more the Arab and Muslim world will build itself an identity beyond regional and national realities; it will become a community in which religion is its

---

[5] Dionigi Albera, Anton Blok & Christian Bromberger (eds.), *L'anthropologie de la Méditerranée*, Paris, Maisonneuve et Larose, 2001, pp. 277-359; Luciano Li Causi, "Un punto di vista antropologico", in *Abitare il Mediterraneo, op. cit.*, pp. 77-83.

[6] Edgard Morin, "Introduzione", in Baltasar Porcel, *Méditerraneé. Tumultes de la houle*, Actes Sud, 1998, pp. XII-XIII.

main, its strongest form of identity, in opposition to an European Union that emphasizes the Judeo-Christian nature of its roots.

The great historical and cosmopolitan oases, that were multiethnic and multi religious: Alexandria, Granada and the Sicily of Frederick II, all disappeared years ago. More recently from Turkey, Egypt and the Balkans; others still exist, precariously, in Lebanon and Palestine. These are the examples Europe should choose if it is to regenerate communication between the three continents, to bring back the quintessence of the Mediterranean world: openness, communication, tolerance and rationality. To quote Theodoropoulos again:

> outre le temps de l'histoire, Hérodote découvre aussi les personnages du drame, ou plutôt pour reprendre les termes du Ve siècle, les personnages de la tragédie. Car, de même que dans la mise en scène de Sophocle tout le monde a raison, aussi bien Créon qu'Antigone, de même, dans celle d'Hérodote, les Barbares, tout comme les Grecs, ont raison. Car les deux camps partagent le même lot, celui que fixe la part divine de l'existence, toute envie et fureur. Car la surface bleue de la Méditerranée possède encore ce divin attribut : en te révélant le visage de l'autre elle te révèle aussi que ce visage ne diffère guère du tien. La mer elle-même ne devient au-delà des langages, au delà des coutumes, le véritable catalyseur d'une existence qui dépasse tes propres limites[7].

Placing the accent on Mediterranean Europe could serve to avoid the risk, for the whole of Europe, as the geophilosopher Caterina Resta has expressed it:

> of becoming part and parcel of the West, the land of the setting sun, on which the night of darkness descends, making everything indistinct and uniform.

Resta is convinced that Europe should interrogate her history, which began on the shores of the Mediterranean, to which Zeus had first kidnapped and then taken her.

> Just as crossing the sea tells us about the youthful beauty of Europe, whose history belongs to the shores of the Mediterranean, so her fatal attraction for the West and yearning for the Ocean remind us of her inevitable decline, of her crazy voyage beyond the limits of the Mediterranean, in pursuit of the setting sun. The seductive attraction of the Ocean – she thinks – has led to the westernization of the world. From the experience of its homogeneous and empty spaces was born western reason [...] which, in the name of the West, has been imposed on the terrestrial and watery *orbe*, unifying all in the name of globalization. A potent reduction *ad unum*, this process ploughs through cultures, languages, landscapes, as if the world were an indistinct

---

[7] T. Theodoropoulos, *op. cit.*, p. 14.

ocean surface, stamping it everywhere with the same seal, the same hall-mark, obliterating differences, originality, specificity and making everything perfectly homogeneous, monochromatic, like the area between sea and sky.

On the other hand, the Mediterranean, according to Caterina Resta

is an experience, absolutely unique, of the meeting of sky and sea, a shared space which separates and divides, but also connects and unites, encouraging exchanges between identities, which, in a never ending dialogue, wish to remain different. Its many borders and frontiers have been the scene of conflict, but also of extraordinary encounters and never ending confrontation with the other, preventing, moderating any form of reduction ad unum. Europe was born of this sea of differences, an irreducible 'pluriverse' of peoples and languages, forced into dialogue, forced into the unceasing burden of translating while maintaining their distance. Can this ancient sea, surrounded by so many countries – wonders the author – still represent a model for a structure that is not a universe, but a 'pluriverse'? Will we all be able to become, and not just us Europeans, Mediterraneans once again and rediscover at last a new nomos, a new balance between sky and earth and sea?[8]

The contrast between the Europe facing the Mediterranean and the Europe facing the Atlantic suppresses the fact that the European population is made up of people who have come from three cardinal points, different in appearance and culture, who have fused and overlapped during the *millenia*. Whole communities of men, women and children with their few possessions and their precious herds have for centuries moved over vast territories in search of fresh pastures and better opportunities. They were attracted above all by green Europe and its high rainfall; its rivers, woods and green fields. What historians once called invasions, (of Huns, Goths, Vandals, Longobards, Franks and Saxons) were merely huge migrations. The last great wave, which changed the political map of Europe just after the millennium, was that of the Normans, who sailed down form Scandinavia and settled in Normandy, England and on the coasts of Puglia, Calabria and Sicily, at the very centre of the Mediterranean. Here, in the space of a century they founded a flourishing and stable kingdom where people spoke many languages and followed their own customs, where the Latin Church was predominant, but the Greek Church, Islam and Judaism continued freely to practice their faith.

From a geopolitical point of view a line can be drawn through the Mediterranean dividing the developed world, rich industrialized Europe, from the poor world which is still searching for development, and is

---

[8]   http://www.geofilosofia.it/pelagos7Resta_rimini4.html.

beset by violence, a visible expression of this poverty[9]. According to Robert Ilbert and Gérard Chastagneret the Mediterranean is no longer just a landlocked lake, but it is once again a sea, almost a *cordon sanitaire*[10]. On a much smaller scale it reproduces the disproportion that exists between north and south throughout the world; yet the history of the sea, so replete with economic, human and cultural exchanges, can be read in a positive vein, as an example worth following and perfecting, as a model for cooperation. The route followed by the EEC and then by the EU has everything to gain from the contribution of its Mediterranean states, based on history and past experience.

Although the peoples who inhabit the shores of this sea do not recognise the existence of a Mediterranean identity[11], perceived as an artificial category, based on the nostalgic dream of exceptional historical moments – typical of northern intellectuals, of the ideologues of impossible encounters or of rootless travellers – yet they recognise the existence of a certain "family resemblance". The Mediterranean world is divided in terms of language, religion, politics and economics, but there is no better place than these sea shores in which to observe "the fluid limits and living frontiers" along which contrasting cultural habits and an antagonistic sense of community live side by side. Only the Roman Empire managed to give political unity to this world, with its history of wars, invasions, schisms and opposing blocs. Precisely these conquests, these forced proximities, the coastal trade of goods and ideas, migrations, similar ecologies and even a common faith in the same God, lend that "family resemblance" to Mediterranean societies.

Christian Bromberger and Jean-Yves Durand see the coherence of the Mediterranean area as deriving from the fact that here, more than anywhere else, each individual is defined in contrast with another, a mirror game of differing customs, behaviour and convictions. In the Mediterranean world "the other" has a specific status: shared religious ideas (stemming back to Abraham), the backdrop of a common background, and a sheaf of differences that can only be understood as part of a game of clashes between "blood relations". Take, for example, food

---

[9] Marc Augé, *L'antropologia del mondo contemporaneo*, Milano, Eleuthera, 2006.

[10] G. Chastagneret, R. Ilbert, "Quelle Méditerranée ?", *Vingtième siècle*, 32, pp. 3-5.

[11] Though one can deny the existence of a real identity, there is a virtual identity in which images and words are based on a few 'strong' stereotypes, consisting in domestic goods, tourism and foodstuffs. The Mediterranean diet, though it is an "invention" of the Anglo Saxon consumer, is an identity forged elsewhere, based on certain territorial and cultural elements, that were not seen as part of a collective identity within the Mediterranean world, but merely as part of everyday life, see Alessandro Cavalieri, "L'Identità mediterranea nella prospettiva del mercato globale", in *Abitare*, *op. cit.*, p. 33.

taboos. According to these two authors, the food taboos of the various cultures, which are neither too close nor too distant, defines the specific character of the Mediterranean world. Three animals, they assert, are symbolic of three concepts of this world according to whether the emphasis falls on a breach, on distant common ancestry or on shared values. There is the pig, whose consumption traces a frontier crossed only by the odd poacher. The bull, which takes us back to the origins of the Mediterranean world, that of Sumerian, Babylonian and Egyptian cults. The lamb, a symbol on which all Mediterranean cultures agree, whether it is the sacrificial lamb or the Lamb of God[12].

This short premise is intended to underscore the importance of studying Mediterranean Europe, a task the research group of the Universities of Florence and Perugia initiated a few years back as part of the project, launched in 1989 by the late René Girault, and under the present direction of Robert Frank and Gérard Bossuat. During the first phase our group published a volume on *The seas as Europe's external borders*, in which we dealt with the Atlantic, but focussed specifically on the Mediterranean and on its history during the nineteenth and twentieth centuries. It is a history of conflict between various Mediterranean states, between France and Italy, Italy and Greece, and the hiatus of the Second World War, when Europe lost its central role in the Mediterranean to the advantage of the United States and the Soviet Union.

However, though the Mediterranean then became an arena for a vaster confrontation, not all the states involved interpreted this in the same way. Italy, for instance, having shed the burden of her colonial past, suggested the Mediterranean should become an area of dialogue, of a *tête-à-tête* among civilizations, an attitude that was adopted also by De Gaulle, in opposition to the attitude of the IVth Republic. Within this context the Mediterranean became both the southern frontier of the western system, a bulwark against Soviet expansion, and also one of the privileged areas of European presence beyond Europe, in which the Mediterranean united the two continents within the concept of "Eurafrica"[13].

During the second phase, in which we dealt with the borders of Europe as a whole, we again studied the Mediterranean, together with the Channel, the Atlantic and the continent's terrestrial frontiers. In this instance we studied not only the history of international relations but also cultural, social, economic relations and demography. Scholars from

---

[12] C. Bromberger, J.-Y. Durand, "Faut-il jeter la Méditerranée avec l'eau du bain ?", in Dionigi Albera, Anton Blok, Christian Bromberger (eds.), *op. cit.*, pp. 733-747.

[13] M. Petricioli and A. Varsori (eds.), *The Seas as Europe's External Borders and their Role in Shaping a European Identity*, London, Lothian Foundation Press, 1999.

various areas tried to outline how the idea of Europe is perceived in non European countries, both by analysing certain European communities living in non European countries, in an attempt to measure their awareness of being European, and also by looking at the perception of European reality as reflected in the works of travellers and writers who are not European. Nor did we ignore the more recent phenomenon of the complex relations between Europeans and immigrants from other continents. The overall picture that emerges from these studies is one of light and shadow, especially in relations between Europe and the Mediterranean. Emblematic were the opinions of Arab travellers and writers, who admired Europe's scientific progress and political institutions, but condemned the loose behaviour of its citizens and the role of women. A very different experience was that of European communities living on the southern shores of the Mediterranean, well integrated and participating actively in local reality, but then forced to pack their belongings and go home because of the growing nationalism of the Arab states and peoples[14].

Our new project, as presented in this volume, concentrates on Mediterranean Europe and is the result of a conference held in Florence in 2004. On the basis of the guidelines set out at the organizing meetings for the project *"Espaces et temps de l'Europe"*, our group, coordinated by Xosé Nunez, Procopis Papastratis, Marta Petricioli and Luciano Tosi, divided its work into four headings: "Representations, Common Features, Identity and External relations of the Mediterranean Region" and invited a group of scholars from various branches of learning to examine the subject. Not all the papers presented at the conference became essays, while that of Alexis Wieck was added to this volume although it had not been presented at the Florence conference.

On the whole the area covered by these essays is wide-ranging and stimulating, particularly so because it is seen from very different methodological points of view. Besides the purely historical essays, there are others by politologists, demographers, anthropologists, economists and on international, cultural and political relations.

In the first section we wanted to show how historians, geographers, politologists describe the Mediterranean area and how these descriptions are influenced by certain strong ideas with ancient roots, or by situations that have arisen in more recent times. The essays contained in this book only satisfy this ambition in part, because certain areas of the original project have not been covered, but they are thought provoking. In the

---

[14] Luciano Tosi (ed.), *Europe, Its Borders and the Others*, Naples, Edizioni Scientifiche Italiane, 2000.

first section, for example, we get a vision of the Mediterranean area that historians refuse to limit to its geographical confines, since in various periods it expanded to include other and more distant worlds. It is an area that in the imagination of its coastal states spreads from *Mare Nostrum* to the *Megali Idea* and includes the concept, dear to the French Enlightenment, of links with ancient and glorious civilizations. An area traversed by ideas, men and women, goods and technologies.

The second section is a variegated picture of the characteristics that bring the countries on either side of the Mediterranean together, both through mutual influence due to the presence and the activities of men, and to the conditions imposed by nature. One aspect is the importance of the Jewish diaspora that, from Leghorn in Tuscany, linked all the main coastal ports in an exchange of men, goods and ideas; another is the Masonic lodges that help to spread the ideas of the Enlightenment, such as social openness and tolerance, which then took root in countries outside Europe, in spite of social and religious differences. Links and similarities can also be found in the essays of political, demographic and economic analysis, both on the political development of states on the northern shore of the sea, and also on recent changes in demography. The influence of the new concept of agricultural space, not seen merely as the production of food, but as a mixture of ecological tourism and the defence and rehabilitation of a territory, has spread from continental Europe to the Mediterranean area, and may even cross that sea. A very different panorama emerges in the world of labour, in which the gap between the north and the south of the continent continues to be huge, while on the other shores of the Mediterranean this becomes such a chasm as to provoke vast migrations northwards.

In the third section the accent is on a comparison between the minorities within the various states of Mediterranean Europe. Our original project contained studies of interesting realities such as Occitania, Corsica and Macedonia; yet the regions studied here (Catalonia, Sicily, Sardinia, Malta, Cyprus) offer a variegated and interesting picture of their various attitudes to the central states, as well as differing perceptions of how their Mediterranean nature relates to their respective identities. At present Europe's ties to the Mediterranean are weak, but this could in future prove to be a useful trump to play in the global card game.

The fourth section has a twofold objective: to show how the development of a common foreign policy for all EU member states could be based on two important levers: one economic and the other cultural. A balanced and careful application of these two levers have, in the past and perhaps even more so in the future, contributed to projects of stabilization and development of countries and areas close to the Union. However, an analysis of the force of the economic lever in dealing with countries close to Europe reveals both the strength and the limits of such a macro-economic approach, seen from the point of view of the development and maintenance of inner stability within the Mediterranean area.

From a cultural point of view our objective was to compare American and European attempts at "winning the hearts and minds" of the peoples on the southern side of the Mediterranean. From the 1950s on, American cultural diplomacy concentrated on proving the distance that separates the social and political model of the 'free world' from that of the Soviet Union. In that same period the European states (France, Great Britain and Italy) were still under the thrall of nationalism and an enduring competition with other western states. The European Union should overcome this traditional competition and make use of the cultural lever to reduce the chasm that seems to separate the two shores of the Mediterranean. As the EU turns increasingly to financing projects with a strong symbolic content (such as the reconstruction of the bridge at Mostar, or the opening of the Library in Alexandria) we can appreciate the beginning of a new approach to relations across the Mediterranean, as seen by the EU and by single member states in recent times. Part of the same approach is the new leading role played by local authorities and non-governmental organizations in their use of *paradiplomacy*[15].

---

[15] André Lacours, "When Regions go Abroad: Globalization and Nationalism and Federalism", paper for the Conference "Globalization, Multilevel Governance and Democracy: Continental, Comparative and Global Perspectives", Queen's University, 3-4 May 2002.

Première partie

Représentations
de l'espace méditerranéen

Part I

Representations
of the Mediterranean Region

Histoires et historiens
de la région méditerranéenne

Salvatore BONO

Emeritus Università di Perugia

Le discours politique et historique sur la Méditerranée – plus abondant et diversifié ces dix dernières années – apparaît souvent rhétorique et répétitif, et à la fois plutôt vague. On peut en particulier se plaindre d'une lacune de définitions, du moins de quelques précisions et éclaircissements de la part des auteurs, sur les divers termes employés, du plus générique et général « Méditerranée » à d'autres comme « pays côtiers », pays méditerranéens, « espace euroméditerranéen », monde méditerranéen et ainsi de suite. Pour nous, maintenant, il s'agit d'expliquer ce que nous entendons par « région méditerranéenne ». Celle-ci va certainement au-delà de la mer méditerranéenne proprement dite et même au-delà des ports et des implantations maritimes, des plages et des localités balnéaires, etc. Il s'agira, en tous les cas, de préciser si nous entendons la région méditerranéenne européenne ou bien celle « non européenne », ou bien encore la région toute entière (Nord et Sud, comme on le dit plus communément, mais aussi plutôt sommairement).

Par cohérence avec la définition et le thème général du congrès, nous nous en tenons à un discours sur la « région méditerranéenne européenne ». Si nous n'étions pas insérés dans ce contexte, préétabli de façon univoque et légitime, le terme de « région méditerranéenne » serait communément entendu dans son ensemble, c'est-à-dire « région méditerranéenne » comprenant une partie européenne et une « non européenne ». Nous notons immédiatement que, pour la première, nous avons naturellement trouvé un adjectif significatif et précis et que, pour l'autre, nous restons dans la négation (non européenne) ou bien on recourt à des termes géographiques génériques (le Sud ou le Sud-Est).

Écoutons tout d'abord les géographes, prémisse d'autant plus raisonnable que la Méditerranée est avant tout, et ainsi a-t-elle été reconnue, une réalité géographique ; en outre, les observations qui découlent de la géographie conduisent, à notre avis, dans la même direction que celles géopolitiques et historiques. Pour les géographes, la région méditerranéenne est délimitée par la culture de l'olivier, dont la présence en marque la limite septentrionale (mais aussi vers les zones plus élevées des pays du Sud, par exemple en Italie, la partie centrale des Apennins, pourtant étrangère à la région climatique). Nous considérons que si nous appliquons les critères proprement dits géographiques, seuls deux États européens sont intégralement méditerranéens, Malte et Chypre. Tous les autres, même ceux qui dans notre imaginaire commun sont par excellence considérés méditerranéens, ne le sont en réalité que pour des parties plus ou moins amples de leur territoire ; il en est ainsi pour la France, l'Espagne et même pour l'Italie et la Grèce. Cela vaut aussi pour la rive sud : beaucoup plus méditerranéennes la Tunisie et l'Algérie, moins le Maroc et l'Égypte, paradoxalement encore moins la Libye, qui pourtant s'ouvre amplement sur la mer intérieure. Nous rappelons, au hasard, entre le Nord et le Sud, la Galice et la Vallée d'Aoste, l'Atlas marocain ou la chaîne slovène des Caravanche, sans parler de la plus grande partie du territoire de la Libye appartenant au désert saharien.

Par rapport à cette région méditerranéenne ainsi définie, quelle histoire peut-on faire ? Certainement une histoire de ses ports, de l'urbanisme de ses cités maritimes, de la pêche, des techniques de navigation, d'activités et de productions, agricoles ou d'autre nature (tel le tourisme) propre de ses zones côtières, et ainsi d'autres aspects et phénomènes comme ceux analysables dans une vue anthropologique ou folklorique, et classifiables comme « méditerranéens ». Mais tout cet ensemble de recherches et de reconstructions historiographiques – déjà bien riche – ne constitue pas une « histoire de la région méditerranéenne » ; cette limite géographique ne confère à l'espace qu'elle délimite aucun sens d'un point de vue politico-social et, encore moins, de civilisation. Les géographes ont, en vérité, proposé des variantes ou même suggéré des critères tout à fait différents, toutefois encore moins significatifs d'un point de vue géopolitique et historique. Ajoutons que ces nettes réserves envers toute définition géographique de la région méditerranéenne valent pareillement que l'on observe la « région européenne » ou celle « du Sud », si nous voulons l'appeler ainsi.

Laissons donc la géographie qui, semble-t-il, ne nous aide que bien peu pour une analyse historico-politique d'un certain espace méditerranéen délimité. Passons au critère géopolitique plus généralement adopté et communément perçu non seulement comme raisonnable, mais même comme évident : considérer comme méditerranéens les États qui donnent sur le bassin de la mer intérieure. Le critère est net et ne permet aucun doute ; il est donc facile d'énumérer les pays méditerranéens du Nord autant que ceux du Sud. Il n'y a rien à contester ; il faut cependant toujours rappeler la déjà citée « partialité », ou le différent « degré », de méditerranéité géographique pour presque toutes ces nations.

Non sans motifs, le géographe Jacques Bethemont – auteur d'un des plus récents et meilleurs livres sur la Méditerranée – a conclu : « De toute évidence, la définition de l'espace méditerranéen implique souplesse et même subjectivité : telle région peut être totalement intégrée à l'espace méditerranéen, telle autre région ou tel pays ne le sera que dans telle ou telle perspective économique, sociale ou politique »[1]. Ceci comporte qu'à l'intérieur d'un même pays on puisse trouver situations, sensibilités, intérêts divers par rapport à telle ou telle question, forme de coopération, ligne politique méditerranéenne. Il suffit de penser, par exemple, au fort et profitable engagement méditerranéen de la Catalogne et aux initiatives, globalement prioritaires dans le temps, de la Sicile et de la Sardaigne, qui se sont concrétisées cependant en des résultats politiques ou socio-économiques bien moins importants.

Au sein d'une réflexion principalement historique comme la nôtre et concernant en premier lieu la région méditerranéenne européenne, il est opportun d'observer que même le caractère géographique côtier d'un État n'est pas une donnée absolue. Il existe deux cas de « méditerranéité » conventionnelle pour ainsi dire, le Portugal, au Nord, et la Jordanie au Sud. Pour le Portugal, valent son appartenance à la péninsule ibérique, qui peut être considérée méditerranéenne dans son ensemble, et surtout sa réalité historique globale, même si le destin plus haut et plus original du royaume portugais a été marqué par sa projection océanique. Pour la Jordanie – éloignons-nous un instant de la région européenne –, son actuelle réalité politique, outre l'histoire, la lie aux autres pays arabes méditerranéens (la considération devrait cependant valoir aussi pour l'Irak, centre du monde arabe durant un demi-millénaire).

Dans un discours historique, une certaine complication – nous ne disons pas objection – à distinguer les pays côtiers et les autres est due aux multiples variations intervenues au cours du temps. Dans l'Antiquité, le monde méditerranéen constituait en soi une totalité, les autres « mondes » étant tout à fait séparés ou inconnus ou seulement en vague relation avec celui de la mer intérieure. Et dans cette totalité, avant et après la constitution de l'empire romain, il y a eu diverses entités de nations donnant sur la Méditerranée et territorialement ouvertes vers différentes directions continentales (exceptionnel, sur de nombreux aspects, l'empire d'Alexandre le Macédonien, méditerranéen dans sa genèse et dans son centre du pouvoir mais qui s'étend jusqu'à l'Indus). Durant le Haut Moyen-Âge, l'empire carolingien s'est ouvert sur la mer intérieure par

---

[1]   Jacques Bethemont, p. 10.

les côtes françaises et celles de la moitié septentrionale de la péninsule italienne, même si son noyau fort franco-germanique était marquant et tendait à détacher l'Europe naissante de la mer de ses origines. Pareillement de l'autre côté, dans le monde arabo-islamique, l'empire abbasside fut pendant un demi-millénaire tout autant méditerranéen, avec sa capitale Bagdad, la ville des *Mille et une nuits*. Les exemples deviennent peut-être plus significatifs à partir du Bas Moyen-Âge : vers la fin du XIe siècle, la Hongrie déboucha sur l'Adriatique par la conquête de la Dalmatie septentrionale et resta méditerranéenne jusqu'à la Première Guerre mondiale, même sous diverses formes. L'Autriche à son tour s'était ouverte sur la Méditerranée dès le XIVe siècle avec le contrôle de Trieste, qui se développa à partir du XVIIIe siècle, puis de toute la Vénétie, de 1799 à 1866, et de la Dalmatie. On peut en outre rappeler la possession autrichienne, qui ne dura guère mais non négligeable pour autant historiquement, de la Sardaigne (1713-1720) et de la Sicile (1720-1737).

Quant à des exemples plus récents, nous pensons à la Yougoslavie, aux États qui la composaient, tous d'une certaine manière liés à la « méditerranéité », alors qu'après sa dissolution ne sont plus strictement « méditerranéennes » que la Macédoine et la Serbie. On pourrait proposer de nombreux autres exemples d'États européens s'ouvrant sur la mer intérieure, soit de manière souveraine soit par le biais de possessions à divers titres et ayant duré plus ou moins longtemps : le plus éclairant à l'heure actuelle est celui de l'Angleterre (Gibraltar, encore en sa possession, Minorque, Malte, les îles ioniennes, Chypre, l'Égypte).

La définition des pays européens côtiers pose également un problème concernant ceux qui donnent sur la mer Noire. Il faut considérer celle-ci comme une mer à part, différente de la Méditerranée, ou peut-elle être vue comme une des mers à travers lesquelles se définit la mer intérieure dans son ensemble ? L'alternative apparaît raisonnable et a de fait ses partisans respectifs. Géographiquement, il est clair que la mer Noire se différencie de l'ensemble de la Méditerranée : ses eaux sont plus froides et moins denses ; elle est alimentée par le débit des grands fleuves qui y affluent, provenant de l'Europe continentale (le Danube en premier lieu, le plus grand fleuve européen, et certains grands fleuves russes). Du reste, il y a une forte connexion géographique de la Méditerranée avec la mer Noire ; la grande mer ne survivrait pas si elle n'était constamment alimentée par un flux de courant marin provenant, plutôt en profondeur, de la mer Noire (dans l'ensemble, l'évaporation des eaux méditerranéennes est sensiblement supérieure à la masse aqueuse qu'elles reçoivent ; seul, le Nil est comparable aux grands fleuves de la mer Noire, pas même le Rhône et le Pô, et certainement pas les autres).

L'incertitude sur la « méditerranéité » de la mer Noire provoque parfois de curieuses incohérences : certains articles d'encyclopédies, par exemple, indiquent que l'étendue de la Méditerranée est de 3 millions de km², sans préciser que cette mesure inclut la mer Noire ; dans d'autres cas par contre, on mentionne que la superficie de la Méditerranée est de 2 millions 500 000 km², mais par erreur on y compte l'antique Pont-Euxin. La « méditerranéité » de la mer Noire, la plupart du temps exclue par les géographes, se reflète, quand elle est admise, sur la Bulgarie, dont l'aspiration à une ouverture sur la Méditerranée ne se réalisa qu'entre 1913 et 1920, et la Roumanie, où des motifs géographico-historiques se font jour dans ces deux pays (l'appartenance à la péninsule balkanique, par analogie à ce que l'on affirme pour le Portugal, en considérant son appartenance à la péninsule ibérique ; demeure enfin, et nous y reviendrons, la prospective historique).

Le fait de donner sur la mer Noire pourrait également poser la question de la méditerranéité de l'Ukraine, de la Russie et de la Géorgie. Mais pour ces dernières, il semble que n'entre en jeu qu'une donnée géographique extrinsèque, alors qu'il est certain que ces trois pays sont beaucoup moins intégrés au reste de l'Europe (la Géorgie se situe du reste conventionnellement en Asie). De toutes façons, notre intention n'est pas – et ce serait une sotte prétention pour quiconque – de résoudre définitivement la ou les appartenances à la Méditerranée ; il nous apparaît seulement intéressant de montrer combien peuvent être variés et complexes les critères et les considérations.

Sans aller outre dans l'analyse, encore incomplète, des divers espaces méditerranéens, nous voudrions pour le moment tirer une conclusion sur la possibilité de faire l'histoire de la « région méditerranéenne européenne » dans son acception plus limitée (pays latins, Grèce, Chypre et Malte, tous compris désormais dans l'Union européenne), ou bien plus étendue, en y ajoutant tous les pays adriatiques, ainsi que la Bulgarie et la Roumanie. À notre avis, la définition de cette région méditerranéenne côtière peut être fonctionnelle à l'une ou l'autre finalité d'organisation, de coopération au niveau technique ou politique, ou autre, mais elle ne semble pas offrir en tant qu'espace d'ensemble une « cohérence historique » suffisante et significative à partir de laquelle il est possible de suivre le fil d'une reconstruction historiographique. Une nouvelle démonstration de cette affirmation peut être constituée par le manque, de fait, d'œuvres historiques concernant une « région méditerranéenne », délimitée d'une façon ou d'une autre ; le titre des œuvres se rapporte toujours à la Méditerranée et concrètement, parfois même sans que leurs auteurs s'en rendent compte, il déborde vers un espace bien plus étendu qu'une quelconque « région méditerranéenne ».

Pour clarifier, nous affirmons explicitement que la précédente exclusion n'entend pas nier ce qui appartient à la logique de la réalité géographique ; autrement dit, les pays européens côtiers de la Méditerranée ont eu dans leur ensemble, au cours des siècles, des rapports plus constants et intenses, et même pour beaucoup d'entre eux avec des pays côtiers non européens – au-delà du type de rapports qu'ils aient pu entretenir au cours du temps. Les événements historiques et la production historiographique confirment avec évidence ce que nous avons affirmé. Une autre analyse historiographique est celle qui compare les histoires de chaque pays, ou de régions, ou d'autres entités « méditerranéennes » ; ces entités peuvent encore exister ou bien être dépassées par le cours des événements.

Une question analogue – s'il est possible d'en faire une histoire unitaire – peut se poser à propos des pays de la région « Sud », disons du Maroc à la Turquie, au moins à partir de leur islamisation. La réflexion porte rapidement à une réponse tout autant négative si l'on entend se limiter rigoureusement aux pays côtiers. Quel sens y aurait-il à exclure la péninsule arabique, ainsi liée aux autres pays arabes dans l'histoire de l'expansion de l'empire arabe, et par la suite dans l'histoire des deux derniers siècles ? Il en est de même pour une prétendue exclusion de l'Irak. La Turquie en revanche devrait rester exclue de la considération historiographique unitaire tant qu'elle fut gréco-byzantine (et donc non islamique). Une fois cet aspect précisé, une histoire du monde arabo-islamique méditerranéen peut bien se faire et, en effet, elle fut amplement et diversement reconstruite, au moins du point de vue européen, tant qu'elle trouverait son unité dans le fait d'être « l'autre », c'est-à-dire un ensemble territorial caractérisé par la civilisation islamique (même si en son sein on peut distinguer, au moment voulu, les événements de l'empire abbasside, du califat de Cordoue et de celui fatimide d'Égypte, etc.). À partir du XVIe et jusqu'au début du siècle dernier, le monde arabe fit d'une certaine façon partie (à part le Maroc) de l'empire ottoman. Cet empire eut une évidente unité, qui impliqua cependant l'exigence, sur l'aspect historiographique, de faire place, dans une certaine mesure, aux pays balkaniques, différemment soumis à la souveraineté ou au contrôle ottoman. À partir du siècle dernier, une histoire de la région « Sud » doit tenir compte, évidemment, de la genèse et de la constitution effective de l'État d'Israël et de ses conflits avec les pays arabes.

Notre réflexion doit désormais s'orienter sur l'ensemble de la région côtière méditerranéenne, du « Nord » et du « Sud », c'est-à-dire euro-péo-chrétienne et arabo-ottomane. Avec quelques extensions vers le Sud (dans les directions déjà soulignées) et le Nord (au fur et à mesure des nécessités), l'histoire de cette région méditerranéenne a été faite et comprise comme « histoire de la Méditerranée ». Le fil conducteur et unitaire a été trouvé – et il ne pouvait en être autrement – durant le long processus historique de juxtaposition – parfois de conflits, parfois de cohabitation et même de collaboration dans l'espace méditerranéen, dans l'immense variété d'échanges, d'influences, de transferts réciproques de culture matérielle et de patrimoine intellectuel.

Depuis une décennie, lorsque l'on parle du rapport entre l'Europe et les pays de la rive « sud » de la Méditerranée, on fait référence, plus ou moins consciemment et explicitement, au partenariat euro-méditerranéen, processus politico-institutionnel de coopération dans le cadre méditerranéen engagé par l'Union européenne avec la Déclaration de Barcelone du 24 novembre 1995. Le partenariat a créé en quelque sorte une autre aire, à laquelle on donne souvent aussi le nom de Méditerranée : l'ensemble des « pays tiers », c'est-à-dire ne faisant pas partie de l'Union européenne, adhérents au partenariat. Avec l'accord de 1995, les quinze pays, alors membres de l'Union européenne, invitèrent douze « pays tiers » (Turquie, Malte, Chypre, Israël et huit pays arabes, dont sept côtiers, outre la Jordanie). On peut aussi bien de façon légitime considérer comme une zone à part l'ensemble des pays, européens et « tiers », participant au partenariat (devenus 35 depuis 2004, 25 européens, comme on le sait, et dix « tiers » ; Malte et Chypre sont entrés dans l'Union).

Cependant, on peut se rendre compte aisément que des deux éléments du partenariat, l'un, l'Union européenne, est une réalité bien structurée et consolidée, avec de forts liens en son sein. Il n'en va pas de même pour les autres « pays tiers » (douze ou dix), qui de plus se trouvent depuis 2004 en nette minorité par rapport aux européens (passés de 12 face à 15 à 10 face à 25). En ce qui concerne notre démonstration, on relève l'hétérogénéité de cette aire euro-méditerranéenne, dont on parle, souvent mais improprement, comme d'Europe et de Méditerranée. À l'aire du partenariat appartiennent en effet la Finlande et la Pologne, mais pas la Croatie et l'Albanie ; la Tunisie et la Syrie, mais pas la Libye et l'Irak, et l'on pourrait continuer ainsi avec d'autres incohérences (qui ont évidement des motivations précises). Par ailleurs, c'est une zone mouvante ; en 2004, elle s'est remarquablement élargie avec huit nouveaux pays européens, alors que deux pays, avant membres « tiers », sont entrés dans l'Union. Des élargissements sont déjà prévus, à travers l'admission dans l'Union européenne d'autres pays ; l'entrée de la Turquie apparaît prévisible, même si elle n'est pas imminente, et certainement de grande importance.

Notre réflexion sur l'histoire de la région méditerranéenne nous conduit maintenant à poser la question de savoir si l'aire du partenariat peut être l'objet d'histoire. Oui, certainement, concernant le processus même de développement du partenariat de 1995 à aujourd'hui, mais aussi légitimement pour ses précédents : la politique de l'Europe institutionnelle, donc de la Communauté économique européenne depuis 1957, envers les pays « non européens » de la Méditerranée. Depuis le début, en effet, l'Europe eut l'exigence de régler ses relations avec les pays particulièrement proches et en conditions d'interdépendance avec elle. Les vicissitudes du partenariat et des rapports de l'Europe unitaire avec les pays du bassin méditerranéen ont déjà eu, en effet, leurs historiens, souvent même interprètes des options et des prévisions pour l'avenir.

L'histoire du partenariat peut donc évidement appartenir à l'histoire de la Méditerranée mais, dans une prospective à long terme, cette dernière ne peut être qu'une histoire étendue au-delà de toute délimitation partielle de la Méditerranée, que ce soit la région géographique ou les pays côtiers ou d'autres. Une histoire de la Méditerranée est une histoire qui se déroule dans un vaste espace, qui converge géographiquement vers la mer intérieure, même s'il n'est pas homogène. Il s'agit d'une histoire qui se constitue dans son essence par la rencontre entre les peuples et les pays de cultures et civilisations différentes, dont les vicissitudes ont été marquées par une interdépendance profonde et constante. Cette histoire a pour scénario et pour « personnage » – comma l'a dit Braudel – le monde méditerranéen.

Cette nécessité de l'extension du regard de l'historien du monde méditerranéen apparaît de façon toujours plus évidente, au fur et à mesure que l'on passe d'un aspect de l'histoire à un autre. L'histoire du commerce méditerranéen n'est pas seulement, et peut-être pas même principalement, une histoire d'échanges entre les régions côtières, mais au contraire elle est, sinon plus encore, une histoire de médiation, d'échanges de productions, « méditerranéenne » et non méditerranéenne, d'une rive à l'autre, et vers des régions et des pays plus lointains, créant ainsi un bien plus vaste monde qui gravite constamment, plus ou moins directement, autour de la mer intérieure.

Est d'autant forte l'essentielle connexion des événements politico-militaires de la région côtière avec le reste du monde méditerranéen. Pour s'en rendre compte, il suffit de parcourir à nouveau l'histoire antique, où culminent des phases dans l'expansion et dans la crise de l'empire romain, puis dans celle de notre « Moyen-Âge », de l'expansion arabo-islamique à la constante projection des royaumes « barbares », et dans l'empire germanique vers la région méditerranéenne. Ces phases sont par exemple symbolisées par Théodoric et les Vandales, Fréderic Barberousse, les Normands, Frédéric II. Et si, d'une part, la grande « reconquête » et l'expansion commerciale et territoriale européenne au détriment de l'Islam est l'œuvre prédominante des États, des régions, des cités maritimes (de Amalfi à Pise, de Gênes à la Catalogne, etc.), comment pourrait-on reconstruire et interpréter les croisades sans considérer les souverains, les seigneurs féodaux et les gens de l'Europe continentale ?

Et l'histoire de la Méditerranée, du rapport entre deux parties et même entre deux mondes, au cours des XVIᵉ-XVIIIᵉ siècles ne peut se reconstruire et s'expliquer si l'on ne considère que les événements maritimes et de la région côtière – de Tripoli (1510) à Rhodes (1522), à Tunis (1535), Prevesa (1535), Alger (1541), et ainsi de suite jusqu'à l'assaut de Malte et à la bataille de Lépante (1571) –, sans envisager conjointement les scénarios continentaux, de l'Égypte (1517) à Mohacs (1526), dans la plaine hongroise, et puis de Candia (1644-1669) à Vienne (1683), jusqu'à la « question d'Orient », puis le début et l'expansion des conquêtes coloniales européennes, de l'Algérie (1830) à l'Égypte (1882), en passant par l'affaire du canal de Suez, dans laquelle des pays moins méditerranéens, comme la France et l'Autriche, eurent des rôles certainement plus importants que ceux de l'Espagne et de la Grèce.

Au-delà de chaque époque, des événements spécifiques et des aspects politico-économiques, l'unité historique du monde méditerranéen se manifeste clairement dans toute sa portée, dans l'histoire religieuse, philosophique, intellectuelle et artistique des pays de la région européenne, prise dans son ensemble. Comment pouvons-nous scinder les événements religieux ou bien distinguer les valeurs fondamentales de la vie politique, du droit, de la société de l'Italie, de la Grèce, de Malte, de la Croatie, de ceux de la France, de la Hollande, de la Suède, de l'Autriche ou de la Hongrie ? Les différences et les oppositions qui se sont créées parmi les gens et les pays de l'Europe méditerranéenne et ceux de l'Europe germanique, et nous pouvons ajouter slave, n'ont pas à nos yeux l'importance qui leur fut attribuée par certains dans le passé.

Toujours sur le plan des civilisations et dans une prospective d'ensemble – dans sa dimension la plus ample (l'Europe qui aujourd'hui s'identifie en grande partie avec l'Union européenne, effective et potentielle) –, comment peut-on dans le discours historique poser des limites entre celui-ci et celui-là, entre les uns et les autres pays d'Europe d'un côté, et de l'autre ceux qui aujourd'hui sont marqués par d'autres civilisations, avant tout, évidemment, par celle arabo-islamique, plus étendue territorialement et caractérisée par une relation plus « critique » avec l'Europe ? Cette implication de l'Europe toute entière dans l'histoire globale du monde méditerranéen est concrétisée de fait dans toutes les différentes synthèses historiographiques qui ont pour objet la Méditerranée. Dans cette prospective, nous avons déjà analysé certaines « histoires de la Méditerranée ».

Mais l'œuvre historique dans laquelle le monde méditerranéen trouve sa dimension la plus juste est le célèbre ouvrage de Fernand Braudel, *La Méditerranée et le monde méditerranéen à l'époque de Philippe II*[2], alors que dans la traduction italienne (*Civiltà e imperi del Mediterraneo nell'età di Filippo II*, Turin, 1953) on a perdu la double indication à la mer et à un vaste espace, d'un monde autour d'elle. Toute l'œuvre du grand historien lorrain converge en vérité dans l'élargissement du cadre géographique et historique considéré. Le premier tome trace un cadre géographique ou mieux « du milieu ». Mais on ne commence pas avec la mer, au contraire *Avant tout les montagnes*[3], puis les hauts plateaux, les collines, les plaines ; seulement plus loin, on arrive *Au cœur de la Méditerranée : mers et littoraux*[4]. Mais tout de suite après, on tente – et peut-être faut-il rester au niveau de la tentative – de supposer, ne disons pas tracer, des « limites » de la Méditerranée. Braudel se rend compte du vaste horizon qui s'ouvre grâce à lui et il a presque une certaine crainte à proposer « un agrandissement apparemment excessif du champ d'observation »[5], dépassant l'une après l'autre les limites non seulement géographiques mais aussi celles des « géologues et biographes ». « De la mer Méditerranée, cœur de ce vaste espace-mouvement, on va jusqu'à la frontière successive [...], cent frontières : à la mesure pour les unes de la politique, pour les autres de l'économie ou de la "civilisation"[6] ; se trace ainsi une "Méditerranée aux dimensions de l'histoire" ».

Cette Méditerranée met en jeu l'Europe elle-même. Dans la réflexion de Braudel, la conception de la Méditerranée met en cause inévitablement la relation entre l'Europe et la Méditerranée[7] ; Braudel poursuit le rayonnement de la Méditerranée, en particulier dans le parcours de ses produits et de ses civilisations, loin des rives, mais il va jusqu'à voir l'Europe comme quelque chose qui s'oppose à la Méditerranée. Il ressent fortement le potentiel dialectique de ce rapport, qui unit les deux termes d'une manière intime et durable, mais en même temps il les distingue et les oppose. Il nous semble qu'il faille regarder vers un vaste espace, à l'intérieur duquel l'Europe se retrouve incluse, dans son identité multiple et dans son unité, si l'on veut, mais alors en tant que

---

[2]   Paris, Armand Colin, 1949.
[3]   *Ibid.*, pp. 9-37.
[4]   *Ibid.*, pp. 94-165.
[5]   *Ibid.*, pp. 166.
[6]   *Ibid.*, p. 168.
[7]   *Ibid.*, p. 229.

partie d'un ensemble plus grand – que l'on pourrait dénommer Méditerranée continent – dans lequel à ses côtés, avec la même dignité, se situeraient les territoires du monde arabe, Israël, la péninsule anatolienne.

Note bibliographique

Nous donnons une liste restreinte d'œuvres, choisies avec un critère extrêmement sélectif et seulement d'orientation, par rapport à la vaste bibliographie concernant les espaces géographiques, les évènements historiques et les questions d'actualité politique auxquels nous nous sommes référés. Certains titres de l'auteur ont été mentionnés, non pas pour son intrinsèque importance, mais parce qu'ils contiennent d'autres considérations et arguments sur la même ligne des considérations exprimées ici, et qui peuvent ainsi constituer une intégration.

AA. VV., *Conditions du développement et stratégies politiques en Méditerranée*, Arles, 1997.

AA. VV., *Il Mediterraneo e l'Europa*, Roma, 2001.

ABDI N. (dir.), *Aire régionale méditerranéenne*, Paris, 2001.

ABULAFIA D. (dir.), *Méditerranée. Berceau de l'histoire*, préface de Emmanuel Le Roy Ladurie, Paris, 2005.

ALIBONI R. (a cura di), *Partenariato nel Mediterraneo. Percezioni, politiche, istituzioni*, Milano, 1997.

AMOROSO B., *Europa e Mediterraneo. Le sfide del futuro*, Bari, 2000.

ATTINA' F., LONGO F. (a cura di), *Unione Europea e Mediterraneo fra globalizzazione e frammentazione*, Bari, 1996.

AUBARELL G., *Las políticas mediterráneas. Nuevos escenarios de cooperación*, Barcelona, 1999.

BALARD M., DUCELLIER A. (dir.), *Le partage du monde. Echanges et colonisation dans la Méditerranée médiévale*, Paris, 1998.

BALTA P. (dir.), *La Méditerranée réinventée. Réalités et espoirs de la coopération*, Paris, 1992.

BARCELLONA Pietro, CIARAMELLI Fabio (a cura di), *La frontiera mediterranea. Tradizioni culturali e sviluppo locale*, Bari, 2006.

BENDO-SOUPOU Dominique (dir.), *Géopolitique méditerranéenne*, Paris, 2005.

BETHEMONT J. (dir.), *Le monde méditerranéen. Thèmes et problèmes géographiques*, 2001.

BISTOLFI R. (dir.), *Euro-Méditerranée. Une région à construire*, Paris, 1995.

BONO S., *Il Mediterraneo. Da Lepanto a Barcellona*, Perugia, 1999.

BRAUDEL, *La Méditerranée et le monde méditerranéen à l'époque de Philippe II*, Paris, 1982 (1re éd. 1949 ; ed. ital. Torino, 1986).

CARPENTIER J., LEBRUN F (dir.), *Histoire de la Méditerranée*, Paris, 1998.

CHALLIAND G., RAGEAU J.-P., *Atlas historique du monde méditerranéen*, Paris, 1995, Szeged, 1998.

CROUZATIER J.-M., *Géopolitique de la Méditerranée*, Paris, 1988.

DAGUZAN J.-F., GIRARDET R., *La Méditerranée. Nouveaux défis, nouveaux risques*, Paris, 1995.

DUMOULIN M., DUCHENNE G. (dir.), *L'Europe et la Méditerranée*, Bruxelles, 2001.

G. DUBY, *Gli ideali del Mediterraneo*, Messina, 2000.

GIZARD X. (dir.), *La Méditerranée inquiète*, Paris, 1993.

HADHRI M. (dir.), *Dialogue de civilisations en Méditerranée*, Tunis, 1997.

HADHRI M., *La Méditerranée et le Monde arabo-méditerranéen aux portes du XXI⁰ siècle. Choc de cultures ou dialogue de civilisations?*, Tunis, 2004.

ID., *Géographie de la Méditerranée. Du mythe unitaire à l'espace fragmenté*, Paris, 2000.

ID., "L'histoire dans la construction du partenariat euroméditerranéen", in Lehners J.-P., Bento J. P. (dir.), *L'Islam et l'espace euro-méditerranéen*, Luxembourg, 2001.

ID., "Il 'Mediterraneo' in un mondo globale", in Anna Baldinetti (a cura di), *Società globale e Africa musulmana*, Soveria Mannelli, Rubbettino, 2004.

ID., *Il Mediterraneo e l'Europa. Lezioni al Collège de France*, Milano, 1998.

ID., *La Méditerranée. L'Espace et l'Histoire*, Paris, 1977 (trad. ital. Milano, 1992)

ID., "Réflexions sur l'histoire et l'avenir de la Méditerranée", in *Mediterrán Tanulmanyok. Etudes sur la région méditerranéenne*, XI, Szeged, 2002.

ID., "Un Mediterraneo troppo italiano di Pietro Silva", in Antonioli M., Moioli A. (a cura di), *Saggi storici in onore di Romain H. Rainero*, Milano, 2005.

ID., "Una nueva historia para construir puentes en el Mediterraneo", in Toledo Jordán J.M. (ed.), *Mediterránneo. Puentes para una nueva vecinidad*, Sevilla, 2005.

İHSANOĞLU Ekmeleddin (ed.), *Cultural contacts in building a universal civilisation: islamic contributions*, Istanbul, O.I.C. Research Centre for Islamic History, Art and Culture (IRCICA), 2005.

JEHEL G., *La Méditerranée médiévale de 350 à 1450*, Paris, 1992.

KERDOUN Azzouz, NEMOUCHI Farouk (dir.), *Euro-Méditerranée. Le processus de Barcelone en question*, Costantina, Université de Costantina, 2004.

KHADER B., *L'Europe et la Méditerranée. Géopolitique de la proximité*, Paris, 1994.

LIAUZU C., *Histoire des migrations en Méditerranée occidentale*, Bruxelles, 1996.

MARQUINA A. (dir.), *Perceptions mutuelles dans la Méditerranée. Unité et diversité*, Paris, 1998.

MASALA C., *Der Mittelmeerraum. Brücke oder Grenze ?*, Baden-Baden, 2002.

MATVEJEVIC P., *Mediterraneo. Un nuovo breviario*, Milano, 1996.

MICHEAU F., *Les relations des pays d'Islam avec le monde latin du milieu du Xe siècle au milieu du XIIIe siècle*, Paris, 2000.

PACE M., SCHUMACHER T., "Conceptualizing Cultural and Social Dialogue in the Euro-Mediterranean Area: A European Perspective", *Mediterranean Politics*, vol. 10, No. 3, November 2005.

RAGIONIERI R., SCHMIDT DI FRIEDBERG (a cura di), *Culture e conflitti nel Mediterraneo*, Trieste 2003.

REYNAUD C., SID AHMED A. (dir.), *L'avenir de l'espace méditerranéen*, Paris, 1991.

RIBEIRO O., *Il Mediterraneo. Ambiente e tradizione*, Milano, 1983.

ROSEN K., *Das Mittelmeer – Die Wiege der Europäischen Kultur*, Bonn, 1998.

ROTHER K., *Der Mittelmeerraum: ein geographischer Überblick*, Stuttgart, 1993.

TOLEDO JORDAN J.-M., *Mediterráneo.Puentes para una nueva vecindad/ Méditerranée. Des Ponts vers un nouveau voisinage*, Sevilla, 2005.

VIDAL-BENEITO J., DE PUIMEGE G. (dir.), *La Méditerranée: modernité plurielle*, Paris, 2000.

Mediterranean Geopolitics

Rodolfo RAGIONIERI

Università di Sassari

The reader may ask whether another essay with a title containing two much used word (Mediterranean and geopolitics) is even worth a glance. The use of the word *geopolitics* sometimes intends to give some "scientific" flavour to otherwise methodologically questionable considerations. It is only a catchall word that points to a rough realist discourse using some more or less refined ideas drawing on historical and/or political geography.

In a way in some sense analogous, the word *Mediterranean* is the pretext for many different rhetorical exercises and redundant logomachies. A typical example of rhetorical exercise can be provided by the juxtaposition of dialogue vs. clash of civilisations (as though dialogue and clash, in the same way as conflict and co-operation, were not two different dimensions of the relations between different areas)[1]. Common representations of the Mediterranean can so swing between postcards of Club Méditerranée to images of the eschatological battle of Armageddon[2].

---

[1] The expression clash of civilisations is obviously derived from Samuel P. Huntington, *The Clash of Civilizations and the Remaking of World Order*, New York, Simon & Schuster, 1996. A typical example of the rhetorical juxtaposition dialogue vs. clash is the title of the 18th Conference of the International Peace Research Association, held in Tampere on August 5-9, 2000: *Challenges for Peace Research in the 21st Century. A Dialogue of Civilisations*.

[2] The word Armageddon derives from Har Megiddo (the mount of Megiddo). Megiddo is an ancient town on the Eastern slopes of the Carmel, where many battles have been fought. The first one took place in 1481 BC between the Egyptians lead by the pharaoh Tuthmose III and an alliance lead by the king of Qadesh. The Egyptians won the battle, took by force the city and imposed their hegemony up to the Euphrates. Another battle was fought in Megiddo in 609 BC between Josia, king of Judea, and the pharaoh Necao, who was the winner.

If we want to give a precise meaning to our title, we have to assess the meaning (or at least an acceptable meaning) of the word *geopolitics*: it is an approach that emphasises the importance of *space* in international politics[3]. Thus, the general theoretical question is: what are the different views of space in international politics? Our specific question is: is there a shared view or many conflicting representations of the Mediterranean political space?

I. Geopolitics

What is geopolitics? The definition depends much upon the author, the group of authors, the school of thought and, the historical situation. Geopolitical analysis is often understood as dealing with the relations of territory and space. More precisely, Yves Lacoste writes that "a geopolitical situation is defined, at a given moment of an historical evolution, by power rivalries of a smaller or larger scope, and by relations between powers that are on different parts of the concerned territory"[4].

For a long time after World War II the word *geopolitics* and the related way of thinking about international politics was almost a taboo. The roots of the discredit that had fallen upon geopolitics were not only political, but also intellectual. It was a kind of conventional wisdom in and around the discipline of International Relations that the word became unspeakable after World War II because of the connection between the German school of geopolitics and the National Socialist regime[5]. The link was obviously Karl Haushofer's *Geopolitik*. However, together with that, the deeper cause was that different geopolitical intellectual traditions (German, Anglo-Saxon, etc.) tried, sometimes effectively, to give an "objective" expression to current problems in the grand strategy of a given major power: the defence of the British Empire and the fear of its decline for Sir Halford Mackinder, the rise to global power of the United States for Alfred T. Mahan, the creation of a secured German area of influence in Europe (Ratzel) or in the Euro-African area (Haushofer). With the resurrection of geopolitics in the 1980s and 1990s, its ideological flavour has not at all disappeared. For example, Zbigniew Brzezinsky's global chessboard[6] is neither more nor less than a manifesto for American hegemony in the Post Cold War era.

---

[3] See Y. Lacoste (ed.), *Dictionnaire de géopolitique*, Paris, Flammarion, 1993.

[4] Lacoste, *op. cit.*, p. 3.

[5] On the German school of geopolitics see Rainer Sprengel, *Kritik der Geopolitik. Ein deutscher Diskurs*, Berlin, Akademie Verlag, 1996.

[6] Zbigniew Brzezinsky, *The Grand Chessboard: American Primacy and Its Geostrategic Imperatives*, New York, Basic Books, 1997.

Huntington's clash of civilisations is a geo-cultural theory that tries to find the "new enemies" of the West in civilisations that are deemed to be incompatible with a liberal international order[7].

A really geopolitical approach should not pretend to be universal and objective, but rather try to compare different approaches. Thus, geopolitics can be defined as "a global method of geographical analysis of concrete socio-political situations taken into consideration as far as they are localised, and of usual representation describing them"[8]. When we talk about space in international politics, there is always a double aspect. As far as it is a space that can be dealt with in the context of physical geography, it has objectivity (in the sense of natural sciences). From this point of view, it can be defined and measured, and its characteristics, from the perspective of other natural sciences like ecology or climatology, are well assessed. However, when we consider space from the point of view of the social sciences, we deal with approaches, interpretations, discourses. In a certain sense, the relation between space in physical geography and geopolitics is analogous to the relation between language and identity. Languages can be the object of linguistics, which has its own methodology. However, a language, or a group of languages[9], can or cannot be a relevant element in political identity, within different historical settings.

Space in international politics cannot be an objective category. It can appear objective because in a world of territorial states[10] it is divided into many distinct and non-intersecting territories. However, different visions of geopolitical space as environment, stake and theatre[11] of

---

[7] Samuel P. Huntington, *The Clash of Civilisations and the Remaking of World Order*, New York, Simon & Schuster, 1996. See also Samuel P. Huntington, *The Third Way: Democratization in the Late Twentieth Century*, Norman, University of Oklahoma Press, 1993.

[8] Michel Foucher, *Fronts et frontières*, Paris, Fayard, 1991, quoted in Lacoste, *op. cit.*, pp. 10-11.

[9] From the strictly scientific point of view, it does not make sense to make a difference between language and dialect.

[10] Everybody should keep in mind that the universalisation of the modern territorial (or nation) state, i.e. the extension of the European state system to the whole planet dates back only to the Fifties and the Sixties, with the process of decolonisation, see Bertrand Badie, *L'État importé : essai sur l'occidentalisation de l'ordre politique*, Paris, Fayard, 1994. The paradoxical necessary implication (and this is not an oxymoron) was the ultimate end of the order that had regulated relations between European powers for at least two centuries, see Carl Schmitt, *Der Nomos der Erde im Völkerrecht des Jus Publicum Europaeum*, Berlin, Duncker & Humblot, 1988.

[11] See Raymond Aron, *Paix et guerre entre les nations*, Paris, Calman Levy, 1962, pp. 187-189.

international politics is constructed in ways depending on the position in space and time of the different individuals and communities.

In this context, I am interested in the critical comparison of different points of view on spaces and flows in, around and through the Mediterranean area.

II. Borders and flows

I start from a polarity: space can be seen as a place that is well defined and separated from other parts of space. In this case, borders are lines or areas that are considered to be delimiting two non-intersecting areas[12]. This line is strongly intersubjective (that is, almost objective) when it divides two areas, subjected in an unambiguous way to different political authorities that acknowledge each other implicitly or explicitly. Obviously, this is the case of most modern borders, but it is not the case, for example, of Israeli borders. Moreover, there is a modernist one-sidedness in the uncritical application of our concept of State for every situation in space and time.

As we shall see below, the Roman Empire constructed, both conceptually and – partially – materially, a line dividing "Us" from "Them", the *Limes*[13]. The same was achieved, even earlier, by the Chinese Empire, which since its establishment wanted not only to secure its Northern borders, but also to show with an impressive achievement the separation between the "Empire of the Centre" and the barbarian nomadic populations.

However, since border is related to territory, in many situations it is not univocally defined. For example, for a long time it was tribes that gave their allegiance to empires or kingdoms. The suzerain did not control (indirectly) a territory, but a population. Thus, there was often ambiguity with respect to the real suzerain of the territories where there was a sparse nomadic population, as it was the case for the Ottoman Empire and its northern border (between the Khanate of Crimea) and some part of its southern (Arabian peninsula) or eastern border (what can be called eastern Kurdistan)[14]. Moreover, spaces can have different or disputed borders: physical (mountains, rivers), linguistic, "historical"

---

[12] On borders see for example M. Foucher, *op. cit.*; Marta Petricioli and Vittore Collina (eds.), *I confini nel 20° Secolo : barriera o incontro ?*, Milano, Mimesis, 2000.

[13] Limes has become such a "geopolitical" word that in Italy *Limes* is the journal representing geopolitics' renaissance.

[14] Kurdish chieftains often shifted their loyalties from the Ottoman Empire to Persia and back, see David McDowall, *A Modern History of the Kurds*, London, I.B. Tauris, 1997.

borders are typical conflict originating borders. Sometimes borders are curiously overlapping, as is the case of greater Armenia and greater Kurdistan. The problem is that space is differently constructed and represented in different national, religious, cultural traditions and discourses. The only possibility is to try to show how the different discourses are related to each other and if they are compatible, i.e. if there is a possible dialogical approach to space.

Space can be seen as a space of flow. We can have flows of goods, people and information. In a sense here we have the same problem that I tried to outline with regard to borders. Flows obviously have an objective, material, measurable aspect. You can measure, in principle, how many people in one year visit one country from another country, how many emigrate from one country into another. You can measure how much of a certain commodity was exported or imported. Even in this case, it is relevant how the actors look at these flows in their construction of political and social space. A typical example is represented by migration, which can be seen, according to different historical contingencies and points of view, as a routine element of transnational relations, opportunities or threats (and, especially if this is the case, they become a part of a biased geopolitical representation).

III. The borders of the Mediterranean or the Mediterranean as a border?

One first approach is to try to fix the Mediterranean as a geographical (geopolitical, geohistorical) space. In this case, I have to delimit this area, i.e. to state what the borders of this region are. This is by no means easy. There is no single answer to this question.

Let us begin with a more general question. What is the Mediterranean Sea? There are many Mediterranean Seas, but not every sea that is surrounded by land is a Mediterranean[15]. The ones we are dealing with here are the three Mediterraneans surrounded by Europe, Asia and Africa, or the Euro-Arab Mediterranean, the Asiatic Mediterranean, between the Asiatic continent and the archipelagos of Japan, the Philippines and Indonesia, and the American Mediterranean, between North America, Central America, South America and the Caribbean Islands. On the contrary, the Arctic Ocean is surrounded by the northernmost parts of three continents (Asia, Europe, America), but it is not the fourth Mediterranean, because it does not have, for its riparian countries, the function of a connection or channel of (conflict-ridden or friendly, advantageous or disadvantageous) relations.

---

[15] See Lacoste, *op. cit.*, pp. 990-997.

For the Arabs what we call the Mediterranean is one of the three seas that "stay in the middle". In Arabic the name of the sea is *al-bahr al-abiad al-mutawassit* (the white sea that stays in the middle). The two other *mutawassit* are the Red and the Black Seas.

If you start from the point of view of physical geography, there is an obvious and seemingly straightforward answer: it is the area whose waters flow into the Mediterranean Sea. However, this definition implies a paradox, and an ambiguity. The paradox is that a huge area of Africa (Nile) would be a part of the so-defined Mediterranean. The other problem is that one is not certain whether the Black Sea is or not is a part of the Mediterranean. If this were the case, the "Mediterranean" would include not only parts of Ethiopia, Uganda and Rwanda (the sources of Nile-Akagera!), but also the large areas of Russia and the Ukraine included in the drainage area of Don, Dnepr Donec, Dnester etc., and a large part of Europe pouring its water into the Danube. Even though this definition of "Mediterranean" seems to be quite bizarre, it is true that any international or transnational policy concerning the ecosystem of the Mediterranean as a sea has to take into consideration the condition of all the rivers and their drainage areas.

Another answer could be that the (fuzzier) borders of the Mediterranean are defined by the borders of a certain ecosystem or of a family of ecosystems. To the south and the east, the borders would be identified by the transition to desert, to the north it is more difficult to clarify. This definition, with respect to a region deeply transformed by human activity, cannot be separated from agricultural areas. From this point of view, we are brought back to Fernand Braudel's first definition of the Mediterranean as the olive tree area[16].

Another simple answer could be that the borders of the "Mediterranean" are the borders of the states surrounding the sea. This definition, as simple as it seems, leads to strange consequences. If you consider the EU as a unity, the "borders of the Mediterranean" would reach as far as northern Finland and Sweden!

There was a long era in history when the Mediterranean Sea was the centre of a political and economic space with clearly defined borders. This era was that of the Roman Empire. Rome rose in an incredibly short period (from an historical perspective) from one of the political units struggling for hegemony in a relatively peripheral area, central Italy, to achieving a hegemonic role in the Mediterranean. The battle in Sentinum (295 BC), where the Roman army defeated a coalition of

---

[16] Fernand Braudel, *La Méditerranée et le monde méditerranéen à l'époque de Philippe II*, Paris, Armand Colin, 1976.

Samnites, Etruscans etc., decided the struggle for hegemony in Central Italy. After a century of victorious wars, against the Greek city states in Southern continental Italy (280-271 BC), twice against Carthage (264-241 BC and 218-202 BC), twice against Macedonia (208 and 200-187 BC) and finally against the Seleucide Empire with the battle in Magnesia (190 BC), Roman influence extended to the whole area and in a sense defined the Mediterranean, which the Romans called *Mare nostrum*. The sea was *nostrum* for the Romans not only because Rome had full control of the areas around it, but also, I argue, because they had developed the space as a unitary space, by means of conquest and organisation.

The Mediterranean (political, economic and even cultural) space was coextensive with the empire, and attempts to extend the empire itself in regions outside that space, like Germany or Mesopotamia, failed, with the notable exception of Britain.

However, this co-extension of the area around the sea with an area that centred on the sea itself was a specific characteristic of the long Roman age. For example, the Achemenid Empire, though certainly the major power on the Mediterranean shores for two centuries, was not a Mediterranean power, not only because the political centre of the empire was located in the plateaus of Iran, but because it was a land power, from a political, military and economic point of view. As the Roman Empire did not manage to extend its reach beyond the periphery of the Mediterranean area, the Achemenid Empire could not become in any sense a Mediterranean power, even though it tried twice to take control of Greece and had intentions to contend to Carthage the hegemony on the central and western part of the sea.

According to the Belgian historian Henri Pirenne, that unity was not broken by the so-called Barbarian Invasions (perhaps better defined by the German word *Völkerwanderungen*) and the split of the Western Roman Empire into many different kingdoms, but by the rise of Islam and the expansion of the caliphs' empire into the Mediterranean area, starting with the battle of the Yarmuk (336 A.D.) and the conquest of Syria, up to Spain and Sicily[17]. However, this change did not bring about a new Mediterranean unity because the caliphs' armies were not able to take over all the lands surrounding the sea and because the Mediterranean was not the political, cultural and economic centre of gravity of the new empire: "The Islamic expansion could not incorporate the whole Mediterranean. It could encircle it in the East, South and West; but it could not consolidate in the North. The old Roman sea became the

---

[17]   See Henri Pirenne, *Mahomet et Charlemagne*, Paris, PUF, 1992.

border between Islam and Christianity. All the old Roman Mediterranean provinces conquered by the Muslims gravitated by this time towards Baghdad"[18].

With the rise of Islam as a religion and a civilisation, the Mediterranean has been at the centre of great strategic rivalries between European "Christian" powers and "Islamic" powers, but often as a struggle for the hegemony between those same Christian powers, as it was in the case of Venice and the Byzantine Empire under the Comnens during the twelfth century, or the so-called Mediterranean Hundred Years' War.

In the sixteenth century, and above all in the second half of that century, it was the site of disputes between the two greatest empires of that period, the Ottoman and Habsburg Empires[19]. This was a clash of empires rather than civilisations, as some recent trends would have us believe: the imperial negotiations with Khayr ed-Din Barbarossa, the alliance between Francis of Valois and Suleiman the Magnificent (an alliance that allowed the Berber fleet to winter in Toulon between 1543 and 1544) prove this clearly enough. At the end of the century, after Lepanto and the final clashes over Cyprus and Tunis, the Mediterranean "exits world history"[20]. Neither would the last Ottoman offensive be able to bring it back. This offensive started with the Candian War (1645-1669), when an Ottoman army landed on the island of Crete (at that time under the control of Venice) and laid siege to the fortress of Candia, which was finally taken in 1669. However, this attempt reached its climax with the failed siege of Vienna (1683) and was disastrously concluded for the Sublime Porte by Eugene of Savoy's campaigns in Hungary and Serbia, and the Karlowitz Treaty (1699)[21].

The Mediterranean returned, however, to play a role in world history with the decline of the Ottoman Empire. The Balkans and the Eastern part of the basin became one of the main theatres for the so-called Great Game, i.e. the challenge between Great Britain and Russia for domination in an immense area that stretched from the European confines of the Sublime Porte dominion, at this time in obvious decline, to Persia and Afghanistan.

A geographic area that was not totally dissimilar to this historical area was affected by the rivalry between the Great Powers in the bipolar

---

[18] Pirenne, *op. cit.*, p. 177.
[19] See F. Braudel, *op. cit.*, pp. 225-468.
[20] *Ibid.*, pp. 469-514.
[21] The last big Ottoman attempt to expand in the Mediterranean and in Central Europe, and its eventual failure and reverse, is brightly described by E. Eickhoff, *Wien und die Osmanen. Umbruch in Südosteuropa 1645-1700*, Stuttgart, Ernst Klett, 1988.

period (with its various phases) that lasted from the end of the Second World War until the beginning of the 1990s. In the bipolar system the position of the Mediterranean was quite clear in as much as it was the southern side of the front between the two blocks and the strategic hinge between two areas that were vital to the two superpowers in different ways: as an area of energy supplies and important routes of communication for the United States and a front of security for the Soviet Union. This strategic role and the importance of naval power enlarged the Mediterranean to cover an area whose borders were represented by some choke-points, like Gibraltar, the Turkish Straits, Bab al-Mandab and the Straits of Hormuz, i.e. extending as far as the Gulf and the Red Sea. From a general point of view, the same was true for the Mediterranean as was for the rest of the planet, that is that the global security structure was a given, and polarised the regional and internal dynamics of individual countries, without however being able to completely eliminate them.

This historical summary shows how, in recent centuries, the area in question has at times been at the centre of attention or a target for the powers that were struggling for supremacy in the world (or in the part of the world that includes this area, which is the system of European states). On the contrary it is definitely not possible to say that the enlarged Mediterranean is currently outside the interests of the major powers, as is clearly shown in the concerns originated by the Gulf Wars[22], the activism of outside powers in the Israel-Palestine peace process, the anxiety aroused by the Algerian conflict and the interventions in the Balkans. It is, on the other hand, true that with the end of the Cold War it is no longer easy to identify a formula that can generally outline the conflict in this area.

If it is difficult to draw the borders of Mediterranean, it is even more difficult to see it as a univocal border between two distinct areas: Christian Europe and the *dar al-islam*. The idea of Mediterranean as a border between two confronting civilisation areas was implied in Samuel Huntington's ideas of the clash of civilisations. To be more precise, in Huntingtonian terms, the Mediterranean should be seen as the border between three areas of civilisation, Western, Orthodox and Islamic. However, from this point of view, problems arise because we have a "torn country" and the difficulty of defining the borders between "Western" and "Orthodox" civilisation.

---

[22]   The First Gulf War (1980-88) is the Iran-Iraq war; the Second Gulf War (1990-91) is the war initiated by Iraq's invasion of Kuwayt and ended with Iraq's crushing defeat at the hands of the US-lead and UN-legitimated alliance; the Third Gulf War (2003 or 2003 - ?) was or has been the war for Iraq.

The torn country is Turkey[23], where an overwhelming part of the economic and political elite wants to be "European", which means avoiding the quagmire of Middle Eastern politics and gaining a full membership in the EU. However, parts of the elite and public opinion do not want to repudiate their Islamic identity. Paradoxically, from the point of view of population, the secularised republic of Turkey is much more "Islamic" than the corresponding area under Ottoman rule in the 19th century[24].

Moreover, there is an overlapping between the "West" and the Orthodox civilisation. If we think that the European Union is perceived, both internally and externally, to be one of the contemporary constituent parts of the "West" together with the US, we have not only Greece as a part of both areas, but also largely Orthodox countries like Bulgaria and Romania as EU members. Other countries, like Serbia and Montenegro and Macedonia[25] (and possibly the Ukraine and Moldova), intend to detach themselves from the Russian-Orthodox area to become part of the EU.

The revealing metaphor that Huntington uses to describe the borders between civilisations is the *fault line*. In geology a fault line is the area along which two plates come together. This metaphor bears in it two ideas. The first is that cultures are like tectonic plates: they change only very slowly, but do not mix together. They clash with each other, caus-

---

[23] Another country that could be considered a torn country is Albania. However, even if we accept a civilisational approach, it seems to be more attracted to the geopolitical European area than to the Islamic one. First, religion is not a major identity factor. In the Ottoman Empire Albanians were an important part of the military and administrative elite, but were neither particularly orthodox, nor pious, and communism eradicated much of what was left of Islam. Second, Albania is geographically strongly embedded in Europe and attracted by countries such Italy or Germany.

[24] During the most part of the Ottoman rule relations between the Porta and the two major Christian communities (the Greek Orthodox and the Armenian Orthodox) were not bad, and the Armenians were called *milliyet siddiqi*. The big demographic change during the 20th century was caused not only by the deportation and extermination of the Armenians during the First World War and by the expulsion of the Anatolian Greeks, mostly with the so-called exchange of population negotiated and decided with the Lausanne Treaty (1923), but also by the immigration of Muslims from former Ottoman areas. This process obviously started during the 18th century with the beginning of the territorial contraction of the empire, in the Balkans and in Southern Ukraine and Crimea, and assumed more dramatic proportions in the 19th century, when millions of Muslims of Balkan origin emigrated to the remaining Ottoman territories. Even after the Second World War Albanians from Yugoslavia, Turks and Pomaks from Bulgaria emigrated to Turkey, see Xavier de Planhol, *Les nations du prophète*, Paris, Fayard, 1993. For example, there are presently in Turkey around six million people claiming Albanian origin.

[25] Officially FYROM (Former Yugoslavian Republic of Macedonia).

ing earthquakes (violent conflicts). Often, one of the two plates is subjected to subduction, i.e. is pushed down by the other. Usually the oldest plate is pushed down. In terms of clash of civilisations, this would imply a strongly pseudo-darwinian approach, where the less modern civilisation should give way to modernity.

As we have seen, the definition of the Mediterranean by means of the word "border" raises more problems than provides solution.

IV. Mediterranean flows

From an historical point of view, the first possible knowledge of the existence of the Mediterranean was probably provided by Phoenician and Greek colonisations. There were certainly peoples that sailed the Mediterranean Sea before the Phoenicians created a network of [empori], like the Egyptians, or the sea peoples (the Shardanas, for somebody the ancestors of the Sardinians, the Philistines, etc.), but the Phoenicians were certainly the first that created the Mediterranean as a space of trade and exchange. This is well proven by the network of cities that their city states purposely created. The same is true for the process of Greek colonisation in the Eastern and Western Mediterranean.

We have seen in the previous paragraph that the Roman Empire and the Mediterranean world, to a large extent, coincided. We could say that, the victory of a land power over a sea power in the long struggle between Rome and Carthage was also the victory of a conception that gave the precedence to territories and domination over territories, i.e. borders against flows.

A basic factor in the picture of the enlarged Mediterranean area in the last decades has been the production and transit of raw energy materials. Although in the aftermath of the Second Gulf War the issue of energy-security seems to play a less relevant role, due to the low price of oil and the perceived absence of threats to the security of production and shipment of oil, this element will remain one of the basic factors in the geopolitical picture of the Mediterranean. The oil of the Gulf will for decades remain one of the main sources of raw energy materials in the world, and transport lines will pass through the straits of Hormuz, Bab al-Mandab, Suez and Gibraltar, or through pipelines connecting oil fields with harbours in this area. It is possible that the importance of the enlarged Mediterranean area will be increased in the future, because of the establishment of pipelines shipping oil and gas from Central Asia and the Caucasus region in the direction of European and Mediterranean countries.

If it is assumed that the Mediterranean is a space of flows and not a space to be determined by means of borders, a deeper study of this representation must be made. We have basically flow of goods and people. The main types of goods flowing through the Mediterranean are row energy materials, i.e. oil and gas. However, if one takes into consideration these flows, it is difficult to limit one's view to the physical Mediterranean. This has become even more true after the big change in the years 1989-91 and the opening of the oil-producing areas in the Caucasus (and central Asia) to the international market. Supply lines of oil and gas from the Persian Gulf, the Red Sea, North Africa and the Caucasus are heavily conditioned by physical and political geography: for example, sea lines in transit from the Persian Gulf have to go across Hormuz and Bab al-Mandab.

There are, moreover, pipelines and gaslines that transport these materials from the areas of production to the Mediterranean. The diplomatic and economic competition for the creation and control of these lines is so important that sometimes it has been overestimated. All the conflicts between the Caucasus and central Asia have been connected with competition for this or that pipeline.

V. Mediterranean polarities

"The Mediterranean is a set of land and sea routes connected with each other, and then of towns that all hold hands, streets and streets, i. e. a system of circulation"[26]. I argue that in the case of the Mediterranean the polarity, intrinsic to any geopolitical approach, between marking borders, analysing flows, is even more evident. However, in our case, there are many other polarities that contribute to giving an appropriate picture. For example, we have seen that one way to look at the Mediterranean as a border is to represent it as the "fault line" between Western, Orthodox and Islamic civilisations. This representation, even though it captures some historical aspects, fails to take into consideration the important dialogical relationship between Mediterranean cultures and civilisations.

Only the proper appreciation and discussion of the many different polarities in all their aspects can contribute critical historical understanding of what the Mediterranean has represented for people around and beyond its coasts.

---

[26] Fernand Braudel, "La mer", in Fernand Braudel (ed.), *La Méditerranée*, Paris, Arts et métiers graphiques, 1986.

From *Pax Romana* to *Pax Americana*, 1789-1995

The Idea of the Mediterranean in the French Imaginary between Orientalism and Altermondialism

Alexis WIECK

History Department, Columbia University, New York

> Ici vers l'an 600 avant J.-C. des marins grecs ont abordé venant de Phocée, cité grecque d'Asie Mineure. Ils fondèrent Marseille d'où rayonna en Occident la civilisation.
>
> Bronze Plaque on the Lacydon (Vieux Port), Marseille[1]

> L'Islam vis-à-vis de l'Occident, c'est le chat vis-à-vis du chien. On pourrait dire un Contre-Occident, avec les ambiguïtés que comporte toute opposition profonde qui est à la fois rivalité, hostilité et emprunt... Il est, à lui seul, l'« autre » Méditerranée, la Contre-Méditerranée prolongée par le désert.
>
> Fernand Braudel[2]

In the case of France, the Mediterranean has long constituted a fount of intimate identity, external expansion and alien threat. This is confirmed by both historical events and their representation in French literature, fictional and academic. From the Napoleonic ambitions of re-

---

[1]   I would like to thank Raphael Botiveau for bringing this reference to my attention.
[2]   Cited in Jean-Louis Triaud, "L'Islam vu par les Historiens Français", *Esprit*, October, 1998, p. 113.

49

creating an imperial '*mare nostrum*' to the Barcelona Process of Euro-Mediterranean cooperation, from Bory de Saint-Vincent's commentaries on the scientific expeditions on the Mediterranean shores of Morea to Michel Cahen's recent eulogy of the Roman empire as a model for European integration, passing through the colonization of Algeria and Braudel's famous masterpiece, the Mediterranean has played a central role in the formation of the modern French state and identity.

In this paper, I shall examine the major phases of the representation of the Mediterranean in French imaginary, as *both* an external *and* an internal object of policy *and* identity. In other words, the interpellation of the Mediterranean as a symbolic notion by a French intellectual implied an encounter with both Self and Other, familiarity and radical otherness. A quick look at the geography of the country and the region allows one to grasp this tension emerging from the sea: the third largest city of France, and arguably its most important port, Marseilles, is proudly established on the Mediterranean, and Algeria itself was long considered in the Métropole to be an integral *département* of the nation; yet the evocation of the Mediterranean also signified a border separating France from a radical enemy, and the crushing majority of the population of Algeria always remained second-class citizens. Nothing perhaps evokes this contradiction as powerfully as the slogan of the imperialist and racist colonial circles of nineteenth century France: "La Méditer-ranée traverse la France comme la Seine traverse Paris"[3]. The representations of the Mediterranean thus intimately engage the theme of contact between France and the Arab world, Islam, and more generally, 'the Orient'. The debt of my analysis to Edward Said's classic study is obvious – my conclusions differ in their detail, however, precisely due to the dual motion of the Mediterranean discourse in France as a source of both active Self and determinant Other.

We thus intend here to unravel the plural genealogies of the construction of the idea of 'the Mediterranean' in the French imaginary, as it appears historically and publicly. Sources on which this study was based consist mainly of works drawn from the French human and natural sciences – although these terms are not meant in a strict discipli-nary or institutional sense, but should be understood as a loose identifi-cation of intellectual works that have played a role in the constitution of the scientific fields of knowledge production. Travel literature, for example, although not 'scientific' in and of itself, held a crucial place in the modalities of scientific inquiry, especially in relation to non-traditional spaces of history, for "[à] la fin du XVIIIᵉ siècle, le voyage

---

[3]   Asher Kaufman, "Phoenicianism: The Formation of an Identity in Lebanon in 1920", *Middle Eastern Studies*, 37, January 2001, p. 175.

savant apparaît à la fois comme la forme par excellence du voyage et comme un mode privilégié de recueil de l'information scientifique"[4]. Moreover, as Anne Ruel suggests, the modern idea of the Mediterranean and its construction as a scientific subject, is the product of complex processes that conjure up, at one and the same time, "cultures intellectuelles et scientifiques, affirmations nationales et enchantements des imaginaires"[5]. It is inevitable then, that the lines of its genealogies should be multiple. The specific focus on the human and natural sciences, and the discipline of history within them, is due to the striking fact that the idea of the Mediterranean in France developed over the past two centuries as a *scientific* subject of inquiry. This is not unique to this particular region, of course – it corresponds, rather, to the larger intellectual framework that became hegemonic at the end of the 18th century, and rested on a universalistic and systematizing understanding of knowledge, grounded in the conviction that there exists a fundamental, secular *order* of nature and (potentially) of society. This order, logically, depended on a specific set of laws that were identifiable and intelligible through observation, experimentation and measurement. "[D]ans ce processus de rationalisation du savoir sur le monde", concludes Marie-Noëlle Bourguet, "la collecte des "curiosités", "merveilles" et autres "singularités" locales se trouve délaissée au profit de la quête de données homogènes et cumulatives, de la recherche de régularités"[6].

Following Thierry Fabre, it is important to insist on the plurality and the essential incoherence of these genealogies, without denying their poignancy and power in the structure of the French imaginary[7]. There is no such thing as a singular, uniform line of inheritance of a stable, fixed 'idea of the Mediterranean'. There is, rather, a discourse formed by an amorphous, fluid and yet ordered set of dominant tropes regarding the idea of the Mediterranean as it appears in the formation and crystallization of disciplinary knowledge in France following the modernizing national and imperial project of Napoleon Bonaparte. An important conclusion of this quest for the representation of the Mediterranean is its fundamentally *dynamic* nature – it is not stable within a fixed frame-

---

[4] Serge Briffaud, "L'Expédition Scientifique de Morée et le Paysage Méditerranéen", in Marie-Noëlle Bourguet, Bernard Lepetit, Daniel Nordman, Maroula Sinarellis (eds.), *L'Invention scientifique de la Méditerranée – Égypte, Morée, Algérie*, Paris, 1998, p. 290.

[5] Anne Ruel, "L'Invention de la Méditerranée", *Vingtième Siècle*, October-December 1991.

[6] Marie-Noëlle Bourguet, "De la Méditerranée", in *id. et al.* (eds.), *L'Invention scientifique de la Méditerranée, op. cit.*, p. 9.

[7] Thierry Fabre, "La France et la Méditerranée : Généalogies et Représentations", in Thierry Fabre and Robert Ilbert (eds.), *La Méditerranée Française*, Paris, 2000.

work, but evolves over time, in accordance with its geopolitical, social and intellectual environment. Three general periods can be identified in the scientific construction of the idea of the Mediterranean in France. This classification is of course schematic – the boundaries and weight of periodization are never rigid, all the less so in the case of a genealogical elaboration. The temporal categories and their thematic attributes are neither absolute nor impermeable; they do, however, indicate dominant trends in the elaborations of discourse and highlight their shifting contours. The first major period of the genealogies of the Mediterranean, starting symbolically with the invasion of Egypt which we will call, using Anne Ruel's evocative terminology, 'the invention of the Mediterranean', coincides with the imposition of Napoleon's new order. Visions of imperial grandeur, along with the systematization and institutionalization of the scientific disciplines, evoked the Mediterranean in the French imaginary as an encroaching Orient, crashing its waves of mysterious and violent passion onto the shores of a civilized (North-)West, which desperately called for the intervention of an Enlightenment-inspired *mission civilisatrice*. This phase was rapidly contested and it gradually declined in the face of repeated blows to France's confidence that saw the rise of its neighbours, primarily England and Prussia, to the status of hegemonic powers, a process that culminated in the humiliating defeat at the hands of Prussia in the war of 1870. The second period, which extends from 1870 to the final demise of the French colonial empire with the independence of Algeria witnessed a reshaping of France's shattered self-image around the representation of a stable and enduring French personality attached to the Mediterranean, in southern contrast to its north-eastern Germanic and north-western Anglo-American domineering neighbors. It is, then, the phase of "the consolidation of the Mediterranean". The third and last period is that of a post-colonial France coinciding with the imposition of a neo-liberal *Pax Americana* over Europe and the globe. In this, the current phase, the French imaginary increasingly tends to look to the Mediterranean as a site of resistance and alternative collective identity in defiance to the increasing hegemony of the United States and its socio-economic model in world affairs. It signals the 'death of the Mediterranean', and, perhaps, the 'birth of the Mediterraneans'.

A warning is in order – the coverage and linkage of state policy, social science, and identity is not intended to indicate any particular and strict relation between these domains of public and private existence (this would have to be done on a more case by case basis, whereby the life and work of a person can be associated with a political scheme). It is simply meant to point to the coexistence and interdependence of these fields of knowledge, power and identity: a dominant narrative is inevitably and intimately, although intricately, entangled in the production of policy, science, and identity, as will become clear throughout this essay.

The Invention of the Mediterranean

The idea of the Mediterranean as a unitary, coherent and intelligible analytical tool did not appear *ex nihilo* in the nineteenth-century – much to the contrary, it has a long history that harkens back to ancient times. The Greeks, the Phoenicians and the Romans entertained a life-style and developed a world-view in which the Mediterranean Sea was the beating heart. As the authors of the original and amply researched *The Corrupting Sea – A Study in Mediterranean History* suggest:

> In the ancient geographical tradition the sea shapes the land, not the other way about [...]. A specialized terminology of land – (or sea-) forms was elaborated, a Mediterranean topographical expertise that has displayed striking continuity over the centuries. [...] From the time of Plato and Aristotle, the Greeks referred to the Mediterranean as the 'Sea over by Us'; the Romans more simply came to regard it as *Mare Nostrum*, 'Our Sea'[8].

With Napoleon's rise to power in France and the launching of ambitious national and imperial re-orderings, which included both the systematization and institutionalization of the scientific disciplines in France and their projection onto colonized territories, a new, 'scientific', idea of the Mediterranean emerged. This is what prompted Anne Ruel to assert provocatively in the opening lines of her landmark article: "Ce n'est finalement qu'au début du XIXe siècle que l'on peut parler d'une Méditerranée"[9].

It was in the wake of the treaty of Campoformio in October 1797, and in order to capitalize on the glories of his victories in Belgium, Holland and Italy, that Napoleon, on behalf of the Directory, invaded Egypt, thereby 'inventing' the Mediterranean, the Orient and the very idea of the 'expedition' itself as a mission to open, enlighten, analyze and organize uncivilized lands with glorious pasts[10]. The reasons for Bonaparte's interest in Egypt were clear: the ancient nation represented the idealized form of the fallen great civilization, the present decadence of which pleaded for a French intervention to recover its past glory. Classical themes and references were omnipresent in the expedition – in

---

[8] Peregrine Horden and Nicholas Purcell, *The Corrupting Sea – A Study of Mediterranean History*, Oxford, 2000, p. 11.

[9] Ruel, "L'Invention de la Méditerranée", *op. cit.*, p. 7.

[10] Emma Spary, "L'Invention de l'expédition scientifique – L'Histoire Naturelle, Bonaparte et l'Égypte", in Marie-Noëlle Bourguet *et al.* (eds.), *L'Invention scientifique de la Méditerranée, op. cit.*, p. 127.

its preparation, execution and conclusions. Aboard the ships that took them to Egypt, the excited scientists read their counterparts from Antiquity (geographers in particular, as they sought to identify and give rebirth to the local sites of classical reference), in addition to the travel accounts of their adventurous contemporaries (the famous Volney in particular)[11]. More generally, their education and culture were deeply attached to the classics, in both form and content[12]. They were thus concerned with the glorious past of Egyptian Antiquity, rejecting its 'barbaric' present and affirming France's *mission civilisatrice* and the Western constitution of knowledge. As the article on 'Egypt' in the *Encyclopédie* confirms with simple eloquence: "C'était jadis un pays d'admiration, c'en est un aujourd'hui à étudier"[13].

The Egyptian expedition rested on a republican and neo-classical vocabulary, itself anchored in classical metaphors suggesting an essential and singular tradition linking an idealized Mediterranean identity and a celebrated imperial European (and especially French) present; it therefore also likened the Corsican general to the great conquerors of classical Antiquity[14]. This retro-projection of modern France as the extension of the glorious path of the greatness of classical Antiquity is a central theme in representations of the idea of the Mediterranean during the phase of imperial grandeur. It is based on a teleological understanding of historical development couched in evolutionary terminologies (most expressively represented by the common metaphors of the infant-like qualities of certain peoples). This is precisely the framework that nurtures the dynamics of the three 'scientific expeditions' (Egypt, Morea, Algeria), important in terms of scope, ambition and consequence, which all took place in the Mediterranean and in the first half of the nineteenth century. Bernard Lepetit rightly insists on the differences between these expeditions in order to highlight the subtle modalities of their articulation with military ventures[15]. We are however concerned here with their

---

11   Bourguet, "De la Méditerranée", *op. cit.*, p. 10.

12   Annie Forgeau, "Les Repérages des Sites de l'Égypte Pharaonique par les Membres de la Commission des Sciences et des Arts", in Marie-Noëlle Bourguet *et al.* (eds.), *L'Invention scientifique de la Méditerranée, op. cit.*, p. 34.

13   Cited in Bernard Lepetit, "Missions Scientifiques et Expéditions Militaires : Remarques sur leurs Modalités d'Articulation", in Marie-Noëlle Bourguet *et al.* (eds.), *L'Invention Scientifique de la Méditerranée, op. cit.*, p. 99.

14   Spary, "L'Invention de l'Expédition Scientifique", *op. cit.*, p. 126.

15   "Trois entreprises se succèdent donc. La première, en Égypte, associe projet des Lumières, forte d'agressivité de l'environnement guerrier et communauté affichée des savants et des militaires. La seconde, en Morée, est plus détachée des buts locaux spécifiques d'aménagement et est menée dans un environnement pacifique. La troisième, en Algérie, requiert la science pour soutenir une entreprise de contrôle territo-

similarities, for it is precisely their approximate conjunction in space and in time that was the source of the original construction of the Mediterranean as a unitary and coherent analytical concept, in which the repeated perception of the physical resemblances between both shores of the sea was confronted with the effort to affirm the differences between their peoples. Thus, while the conclusions of the observations and analyses in the natural sciences – geology and botany in particular – affirmed the unity of the region (including southern Europe, and the French Midi), those of the medical and social sciences suggested the contrary. The botanist Augustin Pyramus de Candolle helped develop his new discipline by postulating the division of spatial units in relation to categories of homogenous floral entities and was probably the first to speak, in 1820, of the "Mediterranean region" as a climatic and bio-geographical unity "qui comprend tout le bassin géographique de la Méditerranée; à savoir la partie d'Afrique en deçà du Sahara, et la partie d'Europe qui est abritée du Nord par une chaîne plus ou moins continue de montagnes"[16]. Bory de Saint-Vincent, in the opening pages of the first volume of the physical sciences section of the *Expédition Scientifique de Morée* which he edited, underscores the constitution of a 'Mediterranean landscape' (although the noun is not used as such) by relating his feeling of estrangement in the South of France, while observing the fortress of the city of Hyères:

La position du fort que j'y trouvai, les matériaux employés pour sa construction, son état de délabrement, l'aridité des monts où s'arrête la vue lorsque l'on est parvenu au faîte des tours en ruine, la nature des rochers et la constitution géologique du lieu, la campagne un peu sèche, au loin la mer semée d'îles noirâtres du côté du sud, les plans assez doucement inclinés ou les brusques escarpements par lesquels on s'est élevé, de grands murs d'enceinte, le fossé à demi-comblé, régnant où la défense naturelle n'a pas été jugée suffisante, la teinte de la végétation, les espèces de coquillages terrestres collés par leur bouche contre la pierre, et les insectes qui commençaient à bruisser dans l'air, tout avait autour de moi un aspect où n'existait presque plus rien de celui que présentent les autres parties, même tempérées, de la France. C'était celui qu'on peut appeler méditerranéen, mais renforcé s'il est permis d'employer cette expression ; c'était déjà celui du pays que

---

rial, se développe sous la menace des armes et dans une atmosphère de suspicion des militaires à l'égard des civils de la Commission scientifique. Ainsi, la diversité des contextes idéologiques et des contraintes de la conjoncture militaire empêche de rabattre sur une explication univoque, dans l'un ou l'autre registre, les modalités de production du savoir." Lepetit, "Missions Scientifiques et Expéditions Militaires : Remarques sur leurs Modalités d'Articulation.", pp. 103-4.

[16] Cited in Jean-Marc Drouin, "Bory de Saint-Vincent et la Géographie Botanique", in Marie-Noëlle Bourguet *et al.* (eds.), *L'Invention scientifique de la Méditerranée, op. cit.*, p. 152. See also Bourguet, "De la Méditerranée", p. 22.

j'allais visiter ; il y avait plus de Péloponnèse encore que de Provence dans la physionomie de tout ce qui m'environnait[17].

From one surprising discovery of geographical and botanical similarities to another, the idea of a coherent and intelligible 'Mediterranean region' uniting all shores of the sea came to dominate the perspectives of the French imaginary. Simultaneously, theories were developed, drawn primarily from the work of the medical and social science dimensions of the Expeditions, relating to the *anthropological* differences between the shores of the Mediterranean, focusing primarily on the ancient glories of the region, 'interrupted' by the alien and destructive intrusion of Islam. Bory de Saint-Vincent, for example, chooses in his racial taxonomies to oppose the peoples of the European shores of the sea to its southern and eastern neighbors. Although he affirms the family relation of the ancient Mediterranean races descended from a lost Atlantis, of which there were remnants in the indigenous populations of North Africa, the Arab invasions damaged this ethnological unity, brutally dividing it along east-west and north-south lines of confrontation[18]. This myth of the common ancestry of the indigenous people of North Africa and the peoples of western Europe would in fact become a trademark of French colonialist writings on the Mediterranean in an attempt to solidify the justifications of conquest through a vague sense of underlying racial identity, whereby the "recuperation" of these "Auvergnats d'Afrique" was envisioned "à la condition, toutefois, qu'on investisse sur eux tout le travail d'éducation, de civilisation que nécessite l'évolution de ces "sauvages" (de bonne nature et de bonne disposition) pour les rendre effectivement semblables en tous points à leurs modèles !"[19]

In similar contrast to the naturalist discourse, the medical scientists highlighted the differences that the Expeditions confronted in the new lands, and the disorientations and dangers that accompanied them. As Michael Osborne affirms:

les impressions de similarité avec l'Europe que l'on peut glaner dans la littérature botanique française sur la Morée et l'Algérie n'ont pas d'équivalent dans les écrits médicaux sur l'Algérie. Car si les botanistes qui accompagnaient les expéditions scientifiques en Égypte et en Algérie se sentaient en

---

[17] Cited in Briffaud, "L'Expédition Scientifique de Morée et le Paysage Méditerranéen.", p. 296. For a discussion of the role of Bory de Saint-Vincent in the formation of the discipline of 'botanical geography', see Drouin, "Bory de Saint-Vincent et la Géographie Botanique", *op. cit.*

[18] Bourguet, "De la Méditerranée", p. 24.

[19] Abdelmalek Sayad, "Minorité et Rapport à l'État dans le Monde Méditerranéen : État et 'Minorités' en Algérie, le 'Mythe Kabyle'", in *Connaissances de l'Islam*, Paris, 1992, p. 144.

terrain scientifique familier, les médecins français en Algérie étaient à la fois intellectuellement et mentalement désorientés, ou, pour utiliser la terminologie contemporaine, "déracinés"[20].

Again, the same Bory de Saint-Vincent, while relating the natural contours of the French maritime landscape to its eastern counterpart, simultaneously describes Greece as a place of decay, inhabited by degenerate and miserable people, something illustrated by the health torments that faced the Expedition[21]. Although he does compare the regions of southern Europe to the eastern and southern shores of the sea in general medical terms, the internal partition of the Mediterranean in different anthropological spaces is evident; and it is clearly defined in moral terms, with the idea that the oriental basin of the sea was infested with problems of health and hygiene that called for the intervention of French civilization. "En bref", Osborne continues in his examination of the French perceptions of their southern subjects,

les Algériens avaient besoin des Français et de leurs institutions civilisées, en particulier de leur science dans le domaine de l'agriculture et de la médecine. Il incombe à la France, écrivait Périer, de relever l'Algérie de sa chute, et de lui rendre sa gloire ancienne [...] [l]'hygiène signale les sources du mal : que l'administration supérieure ne néglige rien pour hâter les progrès de l'assainissement[22].

From its very inception, then, the idea of the Mediterranean found itself internally pitted between its (south)-eastern and (north)-western parts. United in nature and landscape, the Mediterranean remained a space plagued by divisions and confrontations at the social level. These themes based on contradictory simultaneous pressures of unity and diversity are most expressively represented in the archaeological dimensions of the Expeditions that gave the newly constructed Mediterranean the depth of 'great history'. The quasi-obsessive interest of all three Expeditions with the recovery and cataloging of the ruins of Antiquity, Roman in particular, inscribed the idea of the Mediterranean in a linear civilizational frame, the *telos* of which culminated in the French imperial project in the region. It is unnecessary to dwell on the recurrent focus on the Roman presence in the *Mare Nostrum*. The ideological function of such "pure clichés"[23] is clear: they trumpet the inevitable

---

[20] Michael A. Osborne, "La Renaissance d'Hippocrate – L'Hygiène et les Expéditions Scientifiques en Égypte, en Morée et en Algérie", in Marie-Noëlle Bourguet *et al.* (eds.), *L'Invention scientifique de la Méditerranée, op. cit.*, p. 189.

[21] *Ibid.*, p. 198.

[22] *Ibid.*, p. 200. Périer was a prime member of the Algerian expedition.

[23] Forgeau, "Les Repérages des Sites de l'Égypte Pharaonique par les Membres de la Commission des Sciences et des Arts", p. 49. Confirming the essentially ideological

identification between Napoleon and Caesar, the French army and the Roman army, the French Empire and the Roman Empire, and, most importantly, French (and 'Western') civilization and Roman (and 'Hellenic') civilization. In Egypt, Greece, and, most meaningfully, in Algeria, the French scientists evoked the past glories of the Ancient civilizations that had once flourished in those lands that were now barren and decadent in the stultifying chains of Arab, and more largely 'Muslim', despotism. They thus participated in the construction of a 'Mediterranean space' that united France to its southern and eastern neighbors, but one revolving around romantic notions of remnants of the past[24]. The Muslim epoch ('Arab' or more recently 'Turkish') was meant to be a simple parenthesis between the glorious hegemonies of 'Western civilization', whether in its ancient, Roman-Hellenic or its present, French form[25]. This thought process found its culmination in Algeria, where the traces of the Roman presence provided both an example to be followed and a justification for the conquest, since they imposed the duty to reintroduce a unitary classical civilization to the various Mediterranean lands[26]. In the words of Nélia Dias:

> Qualifiée d'acte de libération à la fois à l'égard du "joug des Mamelouks" et d'un "autre fléau, l'ignorance", l'expédition d'Égypte représentait aux yeux de Jomard le combat des Lumières contre les ténèbres : les membres de cette expédition, "Argonautes" des temps modernes, au lieu d'aller à la recherche de l'or [...] allaient porter à une nation épuisée par l'oppression, le fanatisme et l'ignorance, le trésor de la civilisation"[27].

Renaissance-inspired Classicism and Orientalism thus went hand in hand in the construction of a simultaneously intimate and alien space that was meant to be domesticated by Western civilization. From its

---

nature of the archaeological focus on Roman ruins, Forgeau adds that the work of the same scholars on the sites associated with the ancient Hebrews was "more scientific".

[24] Monique Dondin-Payre, "La Production d'Images sur l'Espace Méditerranéen dans la Commission d'Exploration Scientifique d'Algérie – Les Dessins du Capitaine Delamare", in Marie-Noëlle Bourguet *et al.* (eds.), *L'Invention scientifique de la Méditerranée, op. cit.*, p. 236.

[25] It is interesting to note in this context that in Renaissance classicism the European Middle (or 'Dark') Ages, the imaginary of which is intimately associated with *Northern* scenery, are also understood as a negligible parenthesis to be overcome by a relinking with Ancient greatness. It would be fascinating to pursue a comparison along these lines of the theme of the civilizational 'parenthesis' in the classical tradition.

[26] Dondin-Payre, "La Production d'Images sur l'Espace Méditerranéen dans la Commission d'Exploration Scientifique d'Algérie – Les Dessins du Capitaine Delamare", p. 236.

[27] Nélia Dias, "Une Science Nouvelle ? La Géo-Ethnographie de Jomard", in Marie-Noëlle Bourguet *et al.* (eds.), *L'Invention scientifique de la Méditerranée, op. cit.*, p. 162.

very creation, then, and in all three Expeditions, the idea of the Mediterranean was constructed in opposition to the allegedly existing negative model of oriental despotism (associated with Islam), which attributed to French science and power an essential project of civilizational (re)-vitalization.

The Consolidation of the Mediterranean

As the phase of 'imperial grandeur' rapidly waned, culminating in the traumatizing defeat by Prussia in 1870, it was this historical-civilizational dimension in particular that would hold the attention of the French imaginary. On the psychological, ideological and cultural levels, this process contested and shattered France's self-confident national-imperial identity. On the political level, it reoriented the country's objectives away from the continent and into the Mediterranean, Asian and African worlds, since "[t]he French colonial myth concerning its 'mission civilisatrice' gained even more importance as France failed to make the principles of the French revolution a reality within Europe."[28]

The writings of Ernest Renan, perhaps more than anyone else's, express the general lines of this gradual shift of the idea of the Mediterranean. The renowned philologist reinforced the traditional idea of the existing decrepitude of the cultures of the Mediterranean, in particular on its southern and eastern shores, couched in deeply negative 'orientalizing' vocabulary. His dislike of Islamic culture is well-known[29], but he was also appalled by the primitive religiosity and the "servility" of the people of Naples, which he saw as "la Porte de l'Orient." This contrasts with his unbounded admiration for Northern Italy, starting from Rome, "temple de la pensée"[30]. His veneration of Greece as the culmination of pure Reason is of course entirely related to classical Antiquity and is not concerned with its contemporary inhabitants, whom he also saw as primitive and servile. In 1860, Renan was sent to the Levant by Emperor Napoleon III to lead an expedition sent specifically to recover the traces

---

[28]   Kaufman, "Phoenicianism: The Formation of an Identity in Lebanon in 1920", p. 175.

[29]   Hichem Djaït, for example, summarizes Renan's vision as follows (the quotes are from Renan himself): "En lui-même, 'ce monde dégradé' [de l'Islam] ne mérite pas qu'on lui apporte 'les mêmes soins qu'aux nobles restes du génie de la Grèce, de l'Inde antique, de la Judée', mais il fait partie de la tradition de l'homme dont 'les plus tristes pages demandent aussi des interprètes'. Les sociétés théocratiques dont l'Islam est le modèle le plus largement répandu [...] sont la négation de l'épanouissement de l'intelligence, un coup d'arrêt donné à la raison, donc un mal historique". Hichem Djaït, *L'Europe et l'Islam*, Paris, 1978, p. 49.

[30]   Cited in Marcel-Henri Jaspar, *Le Génie Libéral de la France : Essai sur Renan*, New York, 1942, p. 61-65.

of Phoenician culture, in an attempt, yet again, to link the French civilizational project to its classical precedents. His massive *Mission en Phénicie*, relating the findings of the archaeological expedition, barely referred to the contemporary state of the region. Although of clear scientific intent and value[31], this study is best understood within the ideological and socio-political context of its production, where history was increasingly appropriated as a fount of exclusive spiritual heritage and of justification for national and colonial projects. "This exposure to the past", Kaufman asserts in relation to Renan's Mediterranean expedition, "covered in its European wrapping of the day, reflected the dream of the present and proved in the eyes of the Europeans, the technological and cultural superiority of the West, and specifically, which concerns us, of France"[32]. Renan's interest in the Levant was linked to its ancient past – and apart from his archaeological findings on the great classical civilization, he expressed admiration for the Biblical scenery that surrounded him. The region, he wrote, "a un charme grandiose, un reste du parfum qu'il avait au temps de Jésus"[33]. Both geography and history, however, carry new subtleties of meaning in his vision. As Anne Ruel shows, for the northerner Renan, the discovery of 'the Mediterranean' was significant:

> Elle touche au sentiment de la nature et plonge dans les racines de la civilisation. Renan en témoigne, tout comme, un peu plus tard, Nietzsche. […] Le climat est donc interprété par l'homme du Nord comme un attribut, voire une condition de la civilisation. La Méditerranée est pensée comme un nature d'exception, chargée de culture et d'histoire, elle s'élève au rang de civilisation[34].

In parallel, Kaufman notes another change in the character of the European travels and research in the classical and biblical past that he associates with Renan: they become increasingly embedded in a *national* perspective[35]. On a larger metaphysical scale, these shifts are symptomatic of Renan's referential framework based on Hegelian rationalism, through which he understood 'le progrès rationnel' to be all-important and "picture[d] human progress as the acting out of a grandiose providential drama in which perfection becomes incarnate"[36].

---

[31] See H. W. Wardman, *Ernest Renan – A Critical Biography*, London, 1964, p. 83.

[32] Kaufman, "Phoenicianism: The Formation of an Identity in Lebanon in 1920", p. 175.

[33] Cited in Jaspar, *Le Génie Libéral de la France : Essai sur Renan*, p. 67.

[34] Ruel, "L'Invention de la Méditerranée", p. 10.

[35] Kaufman, "Phoenicianism: The Formation of an Identity in Lebanon in 1920", p. 175.

[36] Wardman, *Ernest Renan – A Critical Biography*, p. 48.

It is with the anarchist geographer Elisée Reclus that the idea of the Mediterranean finds its explicit and compact consecration as a unitary category of analysis, since he was the first geographer to consider the Mediterranean as an *autonomous* object of study. "Par cette analyse visionnaire", Ruel suggests,

> Elisée Reclus accomplit un saut scientifique majeur : avec lui, la Méditerranée devient une valeur. [...] Avec lui, nous pénétrons dans un autre monde, qui trouve son unité dans une communauté de traits partagés par le Nord comme par le Sud[37].

His monumental *Nouvelle Géographie Universelle*, the first volume of which appeared shortly following the defeat of 1870, devoted an entire independent chapter to "the Mediterranean", drawing on the earlier inspiration of Candolle regarding the existence of such a region defined by the sea. Reclus' "Mediterranean", however, is no longer the inert object of a geographical reality; it is a (if not *the*) dynamic civilizational *subject* of history[38]. In the development of his theory of human geography, famously relating natural features (such as landscape and climate) to the formation of cultural identities, Reclus intimately linked the idea of the Mediterranean to the source of 'Western' civilization. In his own words:

> La Grèce et son cortège d'îles prouvent que les flots incertains de la Méditerranée ont eu sur le développement de l'histoire plus d'importance que la terre même sur laquelle l'homme a vécu. Jamais la civilisation occidentale ne serait née si la Méditerranée ne lavait les rivages de l'Égypte, de la Phénicie, de l'Asie Mineure, de l'Hellade, de l'Italie, de l'Espagne et de Carthage[39].

The Mediterranean becomes here the matrix of Civilization and majestically enters the self-definition of French identity. The affirmation of the specifically *Mediterranean* source of western civilization would have a powerful and enduring life; and Reclus played a particularly important role in the establishment of the hypothesis that the Phoenicians had laid the foundations of classical and therefore European civilization[40]. This essential linkage of France to the shores of the Levant served in many ways to justify the spiritual superiority and colonial ambitions of the former over the latter. In Kaufman's words:

---

[37] Ruel, "L'Invention de la Méditerranée", p. 9.

[38] Fabre, "La France et la Méditerranée : Généalogies et Représentations", p. 44.

[39] Cited in *Ibid.*, p. 44.

[40] Kaufman, "Phoenicianism: The Formation of an Identity in Lebanon in 1920", pp. 184-5.

La montagne du Liban n'atteint pas les hautes altitudes – wrote Gabriel Hanotaux, the French foreign minister in 1894-98, who acted emphatically to revive French attention to colonialism – mais c'est une des cimes les plus élevées de l'histoire universelle. De Salomon jusqu'à Renan la sagesse humaine s'est assise à l'ombre des cèdres séculaires.

From Biblical times to Hanotaux, a direct line was drawn which connected the eras and emphasized the cultural heritage of France. Hanotaux's words were not written in a vacuum, but rather on the stable foundation of France's clear awareness of the Mediterranean Sea and its cultures that the French considered as their personal heritage[41].

As in the previous phase, and despite the difference in nature noted above, in spatial, intellectual and civilizational terms, the consolidated idea of the Mediterranean was primarily, and more or less explicitly depending on the author, opposed to a fantasized and vilified Islamic 'Orient'. This 'Orient' may have been more (Reclus) or less (Renan) integrated into the framework of cultural analysis attached to the Mediterranean, as Anne Ruel insists[42] – it nonetheless remained alien to a march of historical progress and civilization that was postulated as fundamentally *occidental* and *Christian* in its dynamic present. This thematic found its most condensed expression in Henri Pirenne's groundbreaking historical thesis, as he brought the consolidations of both the 'Mediterranean Self' and the 'Islamic Other' to their culminations[43]. The conventional narrative of the decline and fall of the Roman Empire in the West saw in the 'Barbarian invasions' of the 5th century a cataclysmic transformation from an idealized and romanticized classical 'state of nature' of the Mediterranean anchored in socio-political unity and civilizational greatness to the politically divided and culturally stagnant 'Dark Ages'. In an article entitled "Mahomet et Charlemagne" first published in 1922, and then developed into a book of the same name, Pirenne asserted that the Germanic invasions had not in the least affected the essential dynamics of the coherent Roman Mediterranean, as evidenced by the economic-financial unity and cultural-spiritual homogeneity of the region. This idyllic situation was only shattered, Pirenne continued, with the Arab-Islamic invasions of the 7th century that fractured the coherence of the sea: "the classic tradition was shattered, because Islam had destroyed the ancient unity of the Mediterranean"[44].

---

[41]   *Ibid.*, pp. 175-176.

[42]   Ruel, "L'Invention de la Méditerranée", p. 11.

[43]   Although Pirenne is of course Belgian by nationality, he played an important role in the French historical field, and can be readily integrated in France's imaginary.

[44]   Henri Pirenne, *Muhammad and Charlemagne*, Bernard Miall trans., London, 1958 [1939], p. 185.

The Mediterranean is thus at the very heart of the historian's analysis: its unity created greatness, and its division, doom. Indeed, "[o]f all the features of that wonderful human structure, the Roman Empire, the most striking and also the most essential was its Mediterranean character."[45] With the establishment of Christianity as the state religion and despite the political disintegration of the empire, the unity of the *Mare Nostrum* was preserved, with commerce, culture and intellect remaining Roman, and spirits becoming Christian. In fact, "the Mediterranean was the home of a living Christianity" and the church was "the most striking example of the continuity of Romanism"[46]. Moreover, he continued,

> There is yet another fact which hitherto has hardly been noted, yet it constitutes a final proof that society, after the invasions, was precisely what it had been before them: namely, the secular character of that society[47].

In this way, the fundamental basics of 'Western civilization', grounded in a Mediterranean Self (Classical, Christian, Secular) were well established in Pirenne's account, against which was pitted a radically alien Arab-Islamic Other. In complete contrast to the idealized Western society articulated by a secular political system, imbued with Christian values and organized along classical norms of intellect came the wave of the Arab-Islamic invasions of the 7th century. With almost perfect symmetry, Arab-Islamic society is portrayed as having had "practically no dealings" with the Roman world before the invasions; its people are described as "the servants of God"; and its faith is seen as considering it "intolerable [...] that any influence should escape the control of Allah"[48]. Islam was thus a non-classical, anti-Christian, and essentially religious – in a word, non-Mediterranean – Other.

The radical otherness of the traditional alter-ego is confirmed by the apocalyptic undertones of the vocabulary used to describe the intrusion ("a religion which it would presently cast upon the world, while imposing its own dominion"; "the peril which was to manifest itself in so overwhelming a fashion"; "the expansion of Islam was due to chance"; "the lightning-like rapidity of its diffusion was a veritable miracle"[49]). All of these factors culminate in a profession of faith of sorts that guides the linear projection to contemporary times:

> There was a clean cut: a complete break with the past. Wherever his power was effective, it was intolerable to the new master that any influence should

---

[45] *Ibid.*, p. 17.

[46] *Ibid.*, pp. 127 and 124.

[47] *Ibid.*, p. 136.

[48] *Ibid.*, pp. 147, 150 and 152.

[49] *Ibid.*, pp. 148-149.

escape the control of Allah. His law, derived from the Koran, was substituted for Roman Law, and his language for Greek and Roman. When it was converted to Christianity the Empire, so to speak, underwent a change of soul; when it was converted to Islam, both its soul and its body were transformed. The change was as great in civil as in religious society. With Islam a new world was established on those Mediterranean shores which had formerly known the syncretism of the Roman civilization. A complete break was made, which was to continue even to our own day. Henceforth two different and hostile civilizations existed on the shores of Mare Nostrum. And although in our own days the European has subjected the Asiatic, he has not assimilated him. The sea which had hitherto been the center of Christianity became its frontier. The Mediterranean unity was shattered[50].

The difference between the Germanic and the Arab-Islamic invasions was clear to Pirenne: it was "of the moral order", an opposition between "Islam and Christendom, or one may say, between East and West"[51]. This was the primary contradiction of History, the origin of the gulf that destroyed the ancient Mediterranean unity, which created 'the West' and forced it (temporarily) to recuperate and regenerate in its northern continental bastions, cut off from the sea[52].

Drawing on a long tradition, Pirenne thus created a framework of analysis of European history, in which the Mediterranean is somehow both Self (in its *authentic*, classical and Christian manifestation) and Other (in its more recent, parenthetical, and profoundly alien, Islamic representation). Similarly and contemporaneously, the celebrated French historian of North Africa É.-F. Gautier accuses the Arabs of breaking the otherwise linear and compact continuity of North Africa (just as they had broken the continuity of European history in Pirenne's perspective), thereby completing arguments in the trial to which Islam was being subjected in the writing of European history. For Gautier, it is France, "nouvelle Rome en Afrique du Nord", that brings the return of History to the region[53].

This rejection of Islam would become something of a leitmotiv in the French imaginary, particularly in the historical discipline as recently shown by Jean-Louis Triaud:

> [L]e modèle de Pirenne [l'idée d'une frontière irréductible et dangereuse à travers la Méditerranée, d'une sort de "rideau de fer" avant la lettre] continue, d'une manière ou d'une autre, à hanter les mémoires. En brisant la Méditerranée, l'Islam a ainsi rempli la seule fonction historique qui lui est re-

---

[50] *Ibid.*, pp. 152-153.
[51] *Ibid.*, pp. 150 and 174.
[52] *Ibid.*, p. 185.
[53] See Triaud, "L'Islam Vu par les Historiens Français.", p. 123.

connue. Pour le reste, l'Histoire se détourne vers d'autres cieux, laissant le monde arabo-musulman et ottoman dans une situation de marginalité ou d'immobilité hors du temps, du seul temps qui compte, celui du Progrès[54].

Before it could be transcended, however, the line of argumentation had to be drawn out to its logical conclusion, especially with regard to the idea of 'Mediterranean unity'. This it found in the classic works on the question by Fernand Braudel, whose debt to Pirenne and Gautier is acknowledged by all, not least Braudel himself. In a rare autobiographical testimony, he recounted his passionate attraction to the Belgian historian's vision: "In 1931, Henri Pirenne spoke at Algiers about his ideas on the closure of the Mediterranean after the Moslem invasions. His lectures seemed prodigious to me; his hand opened and shut, and the entire Mediterranean was by turns free and locked in!"[55]. As for Gautier, Braudel cites him in unequivocal simplicity as an "historien génial"[56]. The literature on Braudel is considerable – most of it focuses on his celebrated dissertation (first published in 1949 under the title of *La Méditerranée et le Monde Méditerranéen au Temps de Philippe II* and repeatedly re-edited since then) and most of it is of great quality[57]. This is not the appropriate arena for a serious engagement with Braudel's long and complex oeuvre – what we are interested in here is the explicit and implicit intellectual imaginary that moulds his writings.

It is clear that Braudel's 'Mediterranean', and not only in terms of the methodology and theory of history, was deeply embedded in the framework established by his predecessors. It has even been said that "it inscribes itself in the continuity of the inspiration of Pirenne"[58]. Unquestionably, his approach to the historical role of Islam in the region is similar: already in his *La Méditerranée et le Monde Méditerranéen au Temps de Philippe II*, drawing upon the typically Orientalistic works of Xavier de Planhol, he described the Arab and Turkish invasions as "the

---

[54] *Ibid.*, pp. 112-114.

[55] Fernand Braudel, "Personal Testimony", *The Journal of Modern History* 44, December, 1972, p. 452.

[56] Fernand Braudel, Les *Mémoires de la Méditerranée*, Paris, 1998, p. 221.

[57] For a recent compilation of (parts) of the principal critical essays on Braudel, see Jacques Revel (ed.), *Fernand Braudel et l'Histoire*, Paris, 1999. For the most complete and convincing analysis devoted to Braudel, both humorous and yet profound and well-researched, see J. H. Hexter, "Fernand Braudel and the Monde Braudellien", *The Journal of Modern History* 44, 1972. For an important discussion of Braudel's notions of 'structure', see Samuel Kinser, "Annalist Paradigm? The Geohistorical Structuralism of Fernand Braudel", *The American Historical Review* 86 February, 1981

[58] Erato Paris cited by Fabre, "La France et la Méditerranée : Généalogies et Représentations", p. 107.

two gaping holes" ("les deux coupures béantes") in Mediterranean history[59]. Later, in *La Méditerranée – L'Espace et l'Histoire*, a simplified and shortened version of his *magnus opus* meant to appeal to a larger public, Braudel went even further by elevating the ethno-civilizational divisions of the Mediterranean between three irreconcilable partners (Islam and the two Christianities) to a "quasi structural and theatrical dimension"[60]. He thus categorically proclaims, in the lyrical and passionate style that is his specialty:

> L'Islam vis-à-vis de l'Occident, c'est le chat vis-à-vis du chien. On pourrait dire un Contre-Occident, avec les ambiguïtés que comporte toute opposition profonde qui est à la fois rivalité, hostilité et emprunt... Il est, à lui seul, l'"autre" Méditerranée, la Contre-Méditerranée prolongée par le désert[61].

In parallel to the traditional rejection of Islam, Braudel also reiterates the conventional master-narrative of the linear teleological continuum of 'Western civilization', from classical Antiquity to the "us" of his present, by concluding his posthumously published volume on the ancient Mediterranean by the solemn proclamation:

> [L]a religion chrétienne ne devient pas religion d'État sans avoir composé avec la politique, la société, la civilisation même de Rome. Cette civilisation de la Méditerranée romaine est prise en charge par la jeunesse du christianisme. Il en résulte pour lui des compromis multiples, fondamentaux, structurels. Et c'est avec ce visage, ce message, que la civilisation antique est venue jusqu'à nous[62].

It is in the definition of his subject of study that Braudel innovates. The heir, as we have seen, of a long tradition of affirmation of the unity and autonomy of the Mediterranean entity, Braudel extracts it from its classical chains and places it in the famous 'longue durée'. Moulded in the framework of the innovative historical geography of Paul Vidal de la Blache and geographical history of the founders of the *Annales* school, Lucien Fèbvre and Marc Bloch, Braudel's 'Mediterranean' is one throughout the ages – and this, not through the political genius of Roman generals or the spiritual values of a state religion, but in fact *despite* the 'histoire évènementielle' that he so denigrates. How this type of confident geographical 'determinism' is supposed to accord with the fierce declarations regarding 'gaping holes' provoked by political events such as those noted above, or with the ur-'évènementielle' Pirenne

---

[59] Fernand Braudel, *La Méditerranée et le Monde Méditerranéen au Temps de Philippe II*, 6th ed., 3 vols., Vol. 1, Paris, 1985 [1949], p. 86.

[60] Triaud, "L'Islam Vu par les Historiens Français", p. 113.

[61] Cited in *Ibid.*, p. 113.

[62] Braudel, *Les Mémoires de la Méditerranée*, p. 350.

thesis (in which a *single* event, the Arab-Islamic invasions, can wreak so much structural damage) is unclear. While positing the unity of the Mediterranean as a stable and autonomous historical actor – the originality of which is perhaps best represented by the title's reversal of the traditional distribution of roles between human subject and inanimate object, whereby a non-state liquid entity takes on the primary active role – Braudel simultaneously suggests its plurality. The Mediterranean is, he recurrently repeats, a 'complex of seas' that extends, through geographical and human networks, over Africa, Northern Europe and Asia, and over other bodies of water such as the Red Sea and the Atlantic Ocean. "Le pluriel toujours l'emporte sur le singulier : il y a dix, vingt, cent Méditerranées et chacune d'elles se divise à son tour", he affirms before adding, as if to confirm the primary binary oppositions between Orient and Occident, Islam and Christianity:

> En outre, de grands contrastes brisent l'image une de la mer : le Nord n'est pas, ne peut pas être le Sud ; plus encore l'Ouest n'est pas l'Est. La Méditerranée s'allonge trop selon les parallèles et le seuil de la Sicile la casse en deux plus encore qu'il n'en réunit les morceaux. [...] Nord contre Sud, c'est Rome contre Carthage ; Est contre Ouest, c'est l'Orient contre l'Occident, l'Islam à l'assaut de la Chrétienté. [...] La mer finalement les a toujours obligés à vivre ensemble, mais ce sont des *frères ennemis, opposés en tout*[63].

It is precisely in its inconsistencies and incoherencies that Braudel's work is so revealing for the purposes of the present research. His greatest achievement, perhaps paradoxically, is the opening of the way for the deconstruction of the dominant idea of the Mediterranean, first by assuming and positing with such self-confidence its *unity* and then by demonstrating its *plurality* and internal inconsistencies. After Braudel, 'the Mediterranean' becomes so real and self-evident in the French consciousness that it can, it must, be demystified (rather than recurrently magnified as it had been until then). With Braudel, to follow Thierry Fabre in borrowing Rancière's concept, 'the Mediterranean' becomes 'écriture'[64] – but a particularly *French* écriture. To parody Voltaire about God, 'si Braudel n'existait pas, il faudrait l'inventer.'

---

[63] *Ibid.*, pp. 32-33. Emphasis added.

[64] Cited in Fabre, "La France et la Méditerranée : Généalogies et Représentations", p. 111.

The Death of the Mediterranean:
Birth of the Mediterraneans?

The binary vision of the Mediterranean that opposes the unitary idea of a civilization of the sea (epitomized by the Roman Empire and to be resurrected by the French) to an Arab-Islamic Other has certainly not disappeared. In fact it has found a new vitality in the mediatic fixation on 'terrorist threats' allegedly lurking on the other sides of the sea, as the journalist Georges Suffert perfectly demonstrated in an editorial addressing the affair (that turned out to be spurious) of a supposed anti-Semitic aggression in a train in Paris (which the media was quick to turn into a spectacular compilation of accusations against the immigrant youth of the proletarianized suburbs of the capital[65]) by proclaiming that "La haine est en train de franchir la Méditerranée"[66]. In 1974, the respected French historian Pierre Chaunu was still echoing the traditional reasoning on Islam and the Mediterranean, explicitly referring back to the standard forefather :

> Henri Pirenne a quand même raison, la cassure entre chrétienté et islamité est extrêmement profonde. [...] En cassant les circuits d'échanges méditerranéens, en les obligeant à rebrousser sur la frontière islam-chrétienté, la vielle rivalité contraint la chrétienté à basculer vers le nord, puis à l'ouest et au sud, sur l'océan[67].

As Triaud argues, the break is now interpreted in positive terms, but it remains the unbridgeable contradiction of the history of the Mediterranean, whereby the historical function of Islam has been to fracture an otherwise compact 'Western tradition'. Even the recent (and otherwise interesting and novel) *Histoire de la Méditerranée* somewhat sustains the traditional vision by identifying the Arab-Islamic invasions as a profound fracture and contrasting the supposed Byzantine "*thalassocratie*" (defined in social and civilizational terms in relation to the sea) with the (ethnically defined) "*arabocratie*" of the lands of Islam[68]. However, as Braudel masterfully brought '*the* Mediterranean' to its paradoxical zenith and as the French imperial project was formally smashed by the persistent resistance of subjugated peoples culminating

---

[65] On this stunning case of media-induced frenzy, see the special issue of the brilliant satirical journal *Pour Lire Pas Lu* entitled "Les Affabulateurs : Médiatisation d'une Agression Imaginaire dans le RER D, juillet 2004", Marseilles, October 2004.

[66] Georges Suffert, "Il faut punir plus", *Le Figaro*, 12/07/2004, cited in *Pour Lire Pas Lu*, "Les Affabulateurs", p. 10.

[67] Cited in Fabre, "La France et la Méditerranée : Généalogies et Représentations.", p. 109.

[68] Jean and François Lebrun Carpentier (eds.), *Histoire de la Méditerranée*, Paris, 2001 [1998], pp. 125 and 157.

in the Algerian war of independence, a space was opened for the deconstruction of the master-narrative of the French imaginary on the Mediterranean, ringing in the phase of the 'death of *the* Mediterranean', and providing the opportunity for the 'birth of the *Mediterraneans'*. This pluralist discourse involves multiple lines of reasoning and heritage, and contests the exclusionary politics of the great tale of 'Western civilization' from classical antiquity to modern (north-western) Europe.

The distinguished intellectual historian Alain de Libera's analysis of the history of medieval French philosophy mark a significant break in the traditional French perspective on the Mediterranean by formulating a thesis that he explicitly defines as the *inverse* of Pirenne's conclusion in *Mahomet et Charlemagne*. He argues that

> loin de mettre fin à l'unité méditerranéenne, la conquête arabe a permis la naissance, puis le développement d'une culture arabo-latine qui, née dans ce que nous appellerions aujourd'hui le sud de l'Europe, en l'occurrence en Espagne à Tolède, et en Italie à Naples et à Salerne, a remonté ensuite vers le Nord, pour s'imposer, pendant deux siècles au moins, au cœur de la chrétienté intellectuelle, l'université de Paris, puis, à travers elle, dans le reste du monde latin[69].

In Libera's work, then, the vision that is anchored in the assumption of a primary contradiction between Orient and Occident, between Islam and 'the Mediterranean' (defined by its Latinity) is overturned and reinscribed into a pluralist perspective of the history of the region. 'The Arab' and 'Islam' are no longer defined in opposition to 'the Roman' and 'Christianity' – to the contrary, these lineages come together to form a *common* heritage of "*Arabo-Latin* culture" that was only subsequently and retrospectively appropriated to the exclusion of one of its founding elements as it spread northwards. In the same edited volume, Mohammed Arkoun argues for the reversal of the construction of Europe to the north-west, in favor of an approach that would include the multiple lines of ethnicity and culture of "le monde méditerranéen en tant qu'espace historique et culturel, où s'enracinent également les pensées juive, chrétienne, musulmane jusqu'au triomphe de l'Europe laïque et de l'Occident économique et monétaire"[70]. The "anthropological continuity of the Mediterranean space" that he postulates is thus one that is *ethnically* and *religiously* indistinct, although it has a common civilizational existence (as the "Mediterranean world" in which ideas circulated since Antiquity) that provides it with analytical coherence[71].

---

[69] Alain de Libera, "Comment l'Europe a Découvert l'Islam", in *Connaissances de l'Islam*, Paris, 1992, p. 48.

[70] Mohammed Arkoun, "Europe, Orient, Occident", in *ibid.*, p. 78.

[71] *Ibid.*, p. 86.

He concludes by explicitly placing his scientific intervention within the framework of the *political* project of the construction of Europe:

> J'espère avoir contribué par cette modeste et rapide intervention à éliminer quelques préjugés, corriger des connaissances fausses et promouvoir une vision neuve de l'histoire des cultures dans le monde méditerranéen. Car celui-ci devient un enjeu important dans la construction en cours de l'Europe[72].

More recently and in a somewhat similar, although more radical, vein, Michel Cahen categorically asserts, in a short article on the construction of the identity of the European Union, that "[u]ne definition européenne sur une base exclusive de culture religieuse est une aberration ethniciste[73]." This great historian of Mozambique and theorist of identity, son of an eminent historian of the Middle East, goes on to provide an original perspective on the civilizational nature of the Mediterranean basin that deconstructs and rearticulates not only the traditional account of the culture of the sea, but also the concept of 'Western civilization' itself:

> Avec évidemment des nuances selon les périodes et les contextes, le bassin méditerranéen est en réalité resté le grand bassin de la civilisation occidentale (et pas "européenne" !) comparable au sous-continent indien, aux aires sino-japonaises, etc. Au sein de cette aire civilisationnelle, le Nord ("européen") est devenu dominant, pendant que le Sud (berbéro-arabo-turc, mais aussi ibérique, sud-italien et hellénique) a subi un long déclin depuis le XVIIᵉ siècle. [...] [C]'est tout le bassin méditerranéen qui doit être politiquement, économiquement, socialement, reconstitué, après le long destin et la cassure coloniale. Ce n'est pas que de l'idéalisme, mais tout à l'inverse, la seule perspective réaliste à terme, qui devrait être annoncée dès aujourd'hui pour que le chemin puisse en être tracé : la nouvelle Europe, du Portugal à l'Ukraine, de l'Irlande au golfe arabo-persique. Bref, à peu de choses près, la reconstitution de l'Empire romain au moment de son expansion maximale. C'est réaliste et c'est une révolution hautement souhaitable : tout simplement, organiser raisonnablement notre bassin de vie. Vive l'empire romain ![74]

In this view, 'Western civilisation' is thus still defined in relation to the Mediterranean and its classical heritage, but it is separated from its exclusive *European* and *modern* characterization and transformed into an *inclusive* vision of the multiple cultures, peoples and lines of heritage of all the different shores of the sea. The idea of the Roman Empire, and

---

[72] *Ibid.*, p. 83.
[73] Michel Cahen, "Éloge de l'Empire Romain", *Le Passant Ordinaire*, February-March, 2003.
[74] *Ibid.*

therefore the epitome of 'Mediterranean civilization', takes the shape of a plural entity composed of multiple cultures and traditions, and *not* the precursor of the French imperial project. This Mediterranean paradigm insists on internal plurality and on incoherencies within a framework of commonality rather than on allegedly essential rifts and conflicts between an 'authentic' Mediterranean and alien intrusions. It is a world of 'Mediterraneans', not a world of 'the Mediterranean'.

These developments, as we have suggested, should be seen in conjunction with the new political distribution of forces that followed the end of the Second World War and the formal decline of the traditional European colonial empires. The rise to hegemony of the United States, culminating in the fall of the Soviet Union and the imposition of a neoliberal *Pax Americana* over the globe, and the process of decolonization of most of the 'Third-World' all had a role in "provincializing Europe" (to borrow the words of Dipesh Chakrabarty's title), in a way that subverted the self-confident appropriating projects of the old colonial metropoles. In the case of France, this geo-political shift led its public intellectuals to question the master-narrative of the idea of the Mediterranean, sometimes in explicit contrast to the North-American model of social existence. This is evident in both the political and scholarly spheres. The reorientation on the political level was spearheaded by Charles de Gaulle, as he explained to the journalist of *Le Monde* Paul Balta:

> Voyez-vous, il y a de l'autre côté de la Méditerranée, des pays en voie de développement. Mais il y a aussi chez eux une civilisation, une culture, un humanisme, un sens des rapports humains que nous avons tendance à perdre dans nos sociétés industrialisées et qu'un jour nous serons probablement très contents de retrouver chez eux. Eux et nous, chacun à notre rythme, avec nos possibilités et notre génie, nous avançons vers la société industrielle. Mais si nous voulons, autour de cette Méditerranée – accoucheuse de grandes civilisations – construire une civilisation industrielle qui ne passe pas par le modèle américain et dans laquelle l'homme sera une fin et non un moyen, alors il faut que nos cultures s'ouvrent très largement l'une à l'autre[75].

This political declaration of intent is echoed by works of a more scholarly nature that also envision in 'the Mediterranean' the seeds of a civilizational alternative. Bernard Ravenel, for example, concludes his study of the recent geopolitical history of the regions around the sea with a lyrical appeal for the realization of a "Mediterranean utopia":

---

[75] Cited in Fabre, "La France et la Méditerranée : Généalogies et Représentations", pp. 130-131.

À la logique de cassure et d'auto-destruction qui paraît dominer, il faut opposer une 'utopie méditerranéenne' c'est-à-dire des propositions qui vont dans le sens de la construction d'un projet pan-méditerranéen qui, renversant la tendance actuelle à la rupture, soit porteur d'un avenir de développement, de coopération, de tolérance et de paix, en un mot d'une espérance[76].

Similarly, although in a more sober tone, the recent *Histoire de la Méditerranée* concludes on a particularly revealing interrogative note:

Les sociétés méditerranéennes sont-elles condamnées à subir une mondialisation dominée par les flux de la modernité transatlantique et transpacifique ? Auront-elles la capacité d'inventer de nouvelles synthèses, en redéfinissant un espace commun, en reconnaissant et leurs similitudes et leur diversité ?[77]

Perhaps these scholars and politicians would have all identified with, if not participated in, Jacques Berque's project of constructing a new model of politics and society in the region, on the basis of a communal perspective on past, present and future. The name of this projected political entity – and it is difficult to see how it could have been chosen innocently – was to be the 'Mediterranean United States'[78].

There does not presently exist, to the best of my knowledge, an 'anti-Mediterraneanist' discourse in France, although such a movement has been attempted elsewhere, including notably in the Arab world[79]. The complex positioning of Arab intellectuals, particularly in the Mashreq, in relation to the Mediterranean idea, will not be treated here: it requires a comprehensive study of its own. In the West, it is especially in the historical and anthropological fields of the Anglo-American tradition that the most sustained critique of 'Mediterraneanism' can be found[80]. Horden and Purcell, for example, conclude in their masterful book – although their target here is primarily the 'orientalizing' tendencies of

---

[76] Bernard Ravenel, *Méditerranée – Le Nord contre le Sud ?*, Paris, 1990, p. 279.

[77] Carpentier (ed.), *Histoire de la Méditerranée*, p. 510.

[78] Jacques Berque, "Entretien avec Jean Daniel", *Le Nouvel Observateur*, 17 avril, 1978 ; cited in Fabre, "La France et la Méditerranée : Généalogies et Représentations", p. 144.

[79] For an interesting discussion of the historical rivalry between the construction of a 'Mediterranean' identity and an 'Arab' one in Lebanon, see Ahmad Beydoun, "Extrême Méditerranée – Le Libanisme Contemporain à l'Épreuve de la Mer", in *La Méditerranée Libanaise*, Paris, 2000.

[80] For a novel discussion of the problems and perspectives of an anthropology of the Mediterranean, see Dionigi Albera, Anton Blok, and Christian Bromberger (eds.), *Anthropology of the Mediterranean*, Paris, 2001.

'Mediterraneanism', neglecting its flip side, the classical vision of the Mediterranean origin and nature of 'Western civilization':

> The sin of 'Mediterraneanism', [...] similar to Orientalism, can be summarized under three headings. First, it involves exoticizing: the label 'Mediterranean' serves the interests of anthropologists studying southern Europe because they feel vulnerable to the charge of operating too close to home for discomfort – for the culture shock that is the supposed beginning of ethnographic wisdom. These anthropologists therefore have to defamiliarize their subjects, denying them their Europeanness, and thereby linking them with the less controversially 'exotic' Middle East. In order to create for themselves a respectable and distinct academic identity, and to justify their emphasis on field work in small and isolated communities, they emphasize all that is apparently archaic, culturally and politically primitive in southern Europe, implicitly contrasting (northern) European diversity and modernity with the inferior, atomized uniformities of the south[81].

João de Pina-Cabral has published the most distinct and impassioned plea for the rejection of the category of 'Mediterranean' as a tool for regional comparison. Although the author is Portuguese, he places himself in the framework of the Anglo-American academy and the essay was published in a North American journal. He argues, borrowing the words of Llobera and with a striking neglect of French lines of genealogy, that "it has been largely due to the needs of Anglo-Saxon anthropological departments that the idea of the "Mediterranean" as a culture area has been constituted"[82]. This academic plot has been compounded by the fact that "[t]he whole industry of tourism advertising cashes in on this ambiguity. From the Club Méditerranée to the latest Yugoslavian version of the Volkswagen Golf, called the "Mediterrean", the *dolce far niente* becomes a positive economic asset"[83]. The elaboration of the category of the Mediterranean becomes, under Pina-Cabral's disapproving gaze, a simple product of academic and economic prerogatives, and it reflects little if any reality of the terrain. In fact, "the notion of the Mediterranean Basin as a "culture area" is more useful as a means of distancing Anglo-American scholars from the populations they study than as a way of making sense of the cultural homogeneities and differences that characterize the region"[84]. This provocative critique of the category of 'the Mediterranean' from an anthropological perspective is stimulating in many ways. It should be added, however, that Pina-Cabral

---

[81] Horden, *The Corrupting Sea – A Study of Mediterranean History*, p. 486.

[82] João de Pina-Cabral, "The Mediterranean as a Category of Regional Comparison: A Critical View", *Current Anthropology* 30, June 1989, p. 399.

[83] *Ibid.*

[84] *Ibid.*

focuses most particularly on the North-American context, and his evident desire to detach the study of southern Europe from its Islamic neighbors itself smacks of Orientalism and makes one wonder what are the objectives underlying the interest of the author in contesting the unitary category of 'the Mediterranean' and what are the alternative that he presents. Nonetheless, such recent developments in the Anglo-American academy that seek to maintain a critical distance from essentializing cultural categories and deconstruct the unitary understanding of the Mediterranean are refreshing, especially in the context of the French tradition on the subject.

Considering the weight and particularity of the French idea of the Mediterranean, there is little probability that a categorical critique of the idea of the Mediterranean such as that of the Anglo-American tradition described above would emerge – and for a good reason: the idea of the Mediterranean *is*, or has become over the past two centuries, 'a reality' in France. Promising avenues of research could perhaps combine the borrowing of concepts and conclusions of other traditions (such as the Anglo-American one, or more importantly, the Arab and African ones), without attempting the impossible feat of the blanket denial of the existence and vigor of the French imaginary and identity. Moreover, in addition to its long list of intellectual genealogies of which we have attempted to illustrate the dominant examples here, the 'idea of the Mediterranean' has found a material, structural hold on the reality of the French imaginary with its institutionalization in the academic and cultural centers that have emerged over the past century throughout the country[85]. What is indubitable, however, is that the 'idea of the Mediterranean' can no longer, even in France, be understood as a unitary and coherent analytical concept, and that a sound, novel approach will have to recognize the dense intellectual baggage and old genealogies that the term carries with it.

---

[85] Of particular vigor and importance amongst the numerous institutions attached to the idea of the Mediterranean is the Maison Méditerranéenne des Sciences de l'Homme in Aix-en-Provence.

Megali idea and *Mare Nostrum*

Aspects of Greek and Italian Nationalism

Procopis PAPASTRATIS

Pantheion University, Athens

The aim of this paper is to examine aspects of Greek and Italian nationalisms that focus their attention on the Mediterranean Sea. This
focus forms an integral and characteristic part of the nationalism of
these two poulations, and influences the relations of the two countries.
Relations go centuries back. Following the final establishment of the
Ottoman rule, the harshness of the Venetian occupation receded to the
background. The image of the Italian peninsula as the nearest outlet
across the Ionian Sea to Christian and, apparently, civilized Europe
gradually prevailed, in the collective memory.

In the mid-19th century, nationalism was already affecting developments in the area. The constrained borders of the Greek kingdom provided the ideal excuse for the Greeks, an inherently imaginative people,
to cultivate a rampant nationalism.

In Italy the *Risorgimento* and the process of Unification gave a more
concrete form to nationalism. A variation of this nationalism included a
Greek and a Balkan dimension in its strategy. It is during this period,
extending to the end of the 19th century and within the context of nationalism, that Italy and Greece present certain common characteristics and
face certain common problems.

Both countries appear again in the Mediterranean Sea, this time as
the latest examples in state formation in the area. Both seek to play a
role in the Mediterranean, evoking their past presence in this sea. At the
same time, both Italy and Greece claim regions north of their borders
which are not clearly defined. Both feel, and certainly fear, pressure
from the north.

This distinct pressure from the north influences the respective foreign policies of Italy and Greece. As a result attention in Italy is drawn

on *Italia Irredenta* (Trentino, Veneto, Istria) while in Greece on Macedonia. In the case of Italy the front-line adversary is Austria but also Slav nationalism. For Greece it is Ottoman Turkey but mainly Slav and more specifically Bulgarian nationalism which threatens the Greek claims in this area. In addition, the developing Austrian pretensions regarding Thessaloniki and their involvement, along with Italy, in the Albanian question increase Greek apprehensions.

As a result the Macedonian Question and the Adriatic Problem appear almost simultaneously. They already preoccupy the Greek and Italian people respectively since the early 1860s at least. However, these two issues gain new impetus and acquire the status of an international problem as a result of the Treaty of San Stefano and the Congress of Berlin in 1878. The creation of Great Bulgaria and the permission to Austria to occupy Bosnia and Herzgovina arouse nationalism in Greece and Italy respectively to new heights. At the same time these two issues tested the ability of diplomats and statesmen and exercised the imagination and the endurance of the people involved, who habitually suffered the consequences. The attention on Thessaloniki and Trieste respecttively shows that apart from the employment of lofty historical and national ideas, more pedestrian but solid economic arguments were not neglected.

Nevertheless it is their conduct of foreign policy and the role assigned to them by the Great Powers – in the case of Greece much more evident than in the case of Italy – in conjunction with their own limitations, which underlines the successes and failures of Italy and Greece in the field of irredentism. Apart from the establishment of large commercial communities in Italian cities, the long connection between the two people developed further by the simultaneous presence of Greek students in Italian universities.

In the 1850s mutual influence and interdependence developed between the national movements of the two countries. The initiative and the stronger push came from Italy. This relationship refers to their common efforts to cooperate and attempts from the Italian side to use the Greek factor to accomplish their wider visions for the area. This approach must be seen within the wider foreign policy of the Kingdom of Piemonte, which on this issue aimed at supporting the national claims of the Balkan people in order to promote a more widespread revolution and thus undermine the position of Austria.

This policy formulates the views held by a number of revolutionaries, foremost among them Giuseppe Mazzini. In his wider plans for a European confederation he believed that the mission of Greece was to lead the Balkan federation in order to block the descent of Russia to the

Mediterranean and to civilize the East, continuing thus its classical tradition. The Greek state should be extended to include Epirus, Albania, Macedonia, Constantinople, Asia Minor up to Cilicia, and Cyprus. A few years later, in a similar plan, Mazzini suggested the creation of a Danubian and a Slavo-Hellenic federation on the ruins of the Austrian and Ottoman Empires. Constantinople would then become a free city and the federation would ally itself to Italy.

Cavour himself favourably viewed the future creation of a large Greek empire, which together with Italy and Spain would secure for the Greek-Latin people the domination of the Mediterranean and in this way block the descent of the Slavic and Germanic people to the sea[1]. In contemporary politics however, Cavour attributed limited importance to the Greek factor. He considers in 1860 that it is not worth worrying about the Greeks because they are unreliable, while the British instead are very sensitive on every issue concerning Greece[2]. It is obvious that Cavour could not afford jeopardizing relations with England for the sake of a vague plan with a country that has to abandon, as he believed, its grandiose plans and promote its economic development in order to attract the Christian peoples of the East. Two years later the Milanese newspaper "*La Perseveranza*" expressed views similar to Cavour's regarding a Mediterranean alliance with Greece, Italy and Spain. But in this case, it is the penetration of England and France that has to be eliminated.

The mission of Greece to civilize the East, a recurrent theme among Italian democrats at the time, and Mazzini's plan that Constantinople should be given to Greece, forms in fact the epitome of the Greek *Great Idea*. These ideas underline a connection between the national ideologies expressed at that time which coincide on a specific aspect, with the situation in the Balkans and the East. Despite the existing relations between Italian revolutionaries and Greek politicians, the idea of Greece expanding into the Balkans to include Constantinople developed separately within these circles in the two countries. In Greece it becomes a convenient panacea for every conceivable ill besieging the country and also the dominant factor in foreign policy. The short-lived elevation by the Italian revolutionaries of the Greek people into a position of prefer-

---

[1] A. Liakos, *The Italian Unification and the Great Idea*, Athens, Themelio, 1986, p. 36, [in Greek].

[2] *Ibid.*, pp. 37, 46. Cavour had a different attitude towards the Hungarian, Rumanian and Serbian national movements and on the eve of war with Austria he repeatedly he suggested common action by them against this country. L.S. Stavrianos, *Balkan Federation. A History of the Balkan Movement towards Balkan Unity in Modern Times*, Northampton, Mass., 1942.

ence among the Balkan people is based on a blend of philellenism, revolutionary idealism and political realism in order to replace the despotic Ottoman Empire and check the descent of Russia to the Mediterranean. Apart from romantic revolutionaries, cynical statesmen also entertain the idea of Greece expanding to Constantinople[3], motivated by the same logic of denying it to Russia. Napoleon III proposed it to the Emperors of Austria and Russia as part of his plan to dissolve the Ottoman Empire. It was obvious that Greece, which had experienced the benefit of gunboat diplomacy by a combined British-French fleet during the Crimean War, would be more amenable to pressure if it was permitted to have Constantinople.

The development of Italian national aims in connection with the aims of the Balkan people continued until the early years of the 1860s. In the broader plan of Italian unification, Greece holds a privileged position because of its own glorious past, but also as a Mediterranean state. Following the Unification, the international solidarity of the Italian revolutionaries withdrew to the background and attention naturally focused on the strengthening of the new state. Nevertheless, the Italian revolutionary tradition survived in the volunteers who participated in the Cretan Revolution of 1866-69, in the Greek Turkish War of 1897, a result of another Cretan Revolt the previous year, and along with the Greek Army in Epirus in the Balkan War of 1912.

In the Greek-Turkish War of 1897 approximately 1,000 volunteers under Riciotti Garibaldi, 300 volunteers under Colonel Berte and 78 under the leadership of Amilcare Cipriani[4] fought in the Greek mainland, while Italy together with Britain, France and Russia, imposed their solution to the Cretan Question by dispatching their fleets to blockade Crete under the leadership of Admiral Felice Napoleone Canevaro[5].

In Epirus, the strong Greek irredentism conflicted with Italian expansionist designs regarding the future status of Albania. The presence of Garibaldini fighting strenuously and suffering heavy losses in a Greek war of liberation that is contrary to the interests of the Italian state underlines, yet another time, the distance between the revolutionary ideals of the Risorgimento and an official foreign policy guided by the logic of imperialism. However, in the early 1870s, the Mazzinian ideals

---

[3]   A. Liakos, *The Italian Unification*, pp. 39-41. The dissolution of the Ottoman Empire would satisfy Russia in the Black Sea and especially Austria with Ottoman possessions in the Adriatic for the loss of Lombardy and Venice.

[4]   A. Liakos "1897 Socialists, Garibaldini and War", in *The War of 1897*, Athens, Society for the Study of Neohellenic Civilization and General Education, 1999, pp. 173-174.

[5]   The blockade was announced on March 1897.

continue to be proclaimed. *La Riforma* in 1871 argues that with the defeat of Napoleon III in the war with Prussia the previous year, a solution of the Eastern Question can be achieved in view of the forthcoming collapse of the Ottoman Empire. By integrating Greece and granting complete autonomy to the Albanians, Bulgarians, Serbs and Rumanians, a Confederation can be formed with a central government in Constantinople[6].

It is obvious that such plans aiming at the emancipation of the people involved could not supersede the interests of the European powers for the control of the area. Thus Disraeli, confronted with a strong Russian presence in the Balkans, as a result of the Treaty of San Stefano, advocates among other plans the construction of a Mediterranean League comprised of Italy, France, Austria and Germany to safeguard the trade communications of Europe with the East from the "overshadowing influence of Russia"[7].

The emergence of a unified Italy introduces a new factor in the Mediterranean and further increases its geographical importance in this area. Britain had anticipated and actively supported this development during the period of *Risorgimento.* As a result, a new and friendly presence along the Adriatic coast together with a friendly Greece to the south could allow Britain to check any Russian plans of descending to the Mediterranean through the Balkans. In Italy itself, within the context of emerging expansionism, the role of the country as a Mediterranean power had been argued with conviction since the early 1860s. It is there where its commercial future lay. Italians are destined to dominate the Mediterranean basin as their ancestors in antiquity and the Middle Ages did. It is also pointed out that Italy is the only liberal power, unlike despotic Russia or authoritarian France, that can help to emancipate without expecting a reward, the people under Ottoman rule. This help will secure for Italy the political hegemony of the area, to be followed by economic expansion in the markets of the countries which are liberated[8].

It must be noted that the phraseology is inevitably common with similar expansionist but conflicting movements. During the same period, the prominent Russian panslavist N. Danievskii argues that Greece, only by integrating into a strong Greco-Slavic union – "this unique form

---

[6] F. Chabod, *Storia della politica esteran italiana dal 1870 at 1896*, Roma, Laterza, 1990, p. 74.

[7] F. H. Hinsley (ed.), *The New Cambridge Modern History XV. Material Progress and World-Wide Problems, 1870-98*, Cambridge, Cambridge University Press, 1962, p. 571.

[8] A. Liakos, *The Italian Unification*, pp. 45-46, 63-64.

in which the Eastern Roman Empire can be born anew" – can become again the great sea power it was. Another panslavist, General R. Fadieev was more explicit; he warned the Greeks that their *Great Idea* of a resurrected Byzantine Empire was a "senseless chimera" which Russia cannot allow to be realized[9]. It is evident that the Russian panslavists could hardly conceal their strong nationalistic emotions when claiming Constantinople, which, however, they deny to the Greeks whose argument runs along the same lines but from their own point of view.

It is during this period that Mazzini changes his attitude regarding Greek possession of Constantinople, or any other nation-member of the Balkan Federation he had proposed, while the Vatican increases its already existing presence in this area[10]. It can be argued that this change underlines another passage from revolutionary idealism to a realistic policy, pursued in this case by the Catholic Church, which tries to reassert its position in an area beset with European conflicts and entangled nationalisms. In this policy which Leon XIII inaugurates when he becomes Pope in 1878, the political dimension is evident. Reinforcement of Catholicism in the East and unification of the Greek-orthodoxs with Rome, which Leon XIII is eager to promote, aims at the formation of a Catholic front against the expansion of panslavism. From the Vatican's point of view the intention behind the project to reactivate and reconciliate Rome with the Ecumenical Patriarcate is to remove the Greek-orthodoxy in Constantinople and the Middle East from the hegemony of Moscow, the "third Rome". In addition, in order to extend the bonds of the Balkan people to Rome, the Vatican is ready to sign the same agreements regarding religious matters with their countries as it had signed with the other European States[11].

---

[9] M. B. Petrovich, *The Emergence of Russian Panslavism 1856-1870*, New York, Columbia University Press, 1956, p. 275, including quotations.

[10] This presence was reinforced in the formative years of the Bulgarian Question. A pro-western group within the Bulgarian movement for independence decides in 1860 that the solution to their national question is to break completely with the Ecumenical Patriarchate and join with the Uniate Church. With the help of French diplomatic agents in Constantinople they officially enter, within the year, the Catholic Church. Bulgarian Uniate Archbishop is ordained in 1861. However very soon the Bulgarian national movement realises that in order to succeed it must not antagonise the Orthodox Church but instead declare itself as its most fervent defender. As a result the influence of the Bulgarian Uniate Church diminished quickly. P. Matalas, *Nation and Orthodoxy, from the Greek to the Bulgarian Schism*, Herakleion, University of Crete Press, 2002, pp. 184-189 [in Greek].

[11] G. Del Zanna, *Roma e l'Oriente, Leone XIII e l'Impero ottomano (1878-1903)*, Milano, Guerini e Associati, 2003, pp. 21, 288, 292. In a speech delivered in 1880, it was pointed out that the Vatican, under the direction of Leon XIII, who was sent by Providence to establish harmony among the mixed groups of people immersed in

Among the Balkan conflicting nationalisms only the Greek one proclaims its destiny to expand and civilize "Our East", as it is in fact
mentioned, throughout the period under examination, denoting the
strong feelings on this issue. In the case of Greece expanding to the East
inevitably involves crossing the sea. The Greek *Great Idea* however
avoids studiously any reference to the Mediterranean while at the same
time an extreme expression of this ideology claims an area extending
from Crete to the Danube. This omission is not due to the inherent
vagueness which characterizes many cases of nationalism. It is definitely the result of political and economic realism. Apart from the
weakness of the Greek state any claims to the Mediterranean would be
detrimental for the interests of the extensive Greek communities in
every major port and for their commercial fleet plying this sea.

The only time Greece tries to act as a Mediterranean power protesting on behalf of its citizens across the sea is during the nationalist
revolution of 1882 led by Arabi Pasha. Shortly after the arrival of the
Anglo-French squadron, the two biggest ships of the Greek fleet arrived
in Alexandria in order to participate in the operations. The British
admiral asked in a courteous letter that the Greek ships withdraw, while
the Greek Government's offer to send an expeditionary force of 7,000
men was refused. After this symbolic participation in an imperialist
intervention, dictated by internal politics, Greece did not again under-
take the role of a Mediterranean power until the Balkan Wars and the
First World War introduced the final act of the Eastern Question[12].

The Mediterranean remained at the centre of the interest for both the
Italians and Greeks as they were familiar with this area and, at a certain
time, were the main arbiters of this sea. Their quest for a dominant
presence over the area has developed into an ideological construct that,
as historic nations with glorious past but a weak present, they find
difficult to ignore, let alone forget. During this period, however, Greece
was increasingly immersed in the Bulgarian Crisis and the Macedonian
Question that followed. As a result, Greece's expectations in the Mediterranean were limited to increased relations with its wealthy communities there that attracted investment for the development of the country.
Italy, at the same time, sought recognition as a European power. In the

---

social chaos, "riprendere e continuare efficacemente la grand opera dei Santi Cirillo e
Metodio". Pietro Ressuti, *Il Papato e la civiltà degli slavi meridionali*. Discorso, letto
all'Accademia di religione cattolica, li 18 marzo 1880, Roma, Tipografia dei Fratelli
Monaldi, 1880, pp. 70-71.

[12] L. Louvi, "The Restoration on National Dignity: The Opportunity of Egypt" in
K. Aroni-Tsichli, L. Tricha (eds.), *Charilaos Trikoupis and his Times*, Athens, Pa-
pazisis, 2000, pp. 122-127.

1870s, there was general support for a prudent and loyal policy that avoided any spirit of adventure and underlined the advantage the Concert of Great Powers would gain from the presence and moral influence of the young Italian state[13].

The Congress of Berlin caused repercussions for the Mediterranean that changed the foreign policy of Italy. Britain increased its presence in the area with the acquisition of Cyprus, France was able to expand into North Africa, Austria through Bosnia-Herzegovina controlled the Adriatic, even Greece was allowed to annex Thessaly. The Triple Alliance with Germany and Austria – an attempt to exorcise the threat in the Adriatic through an alliance – and the two Mediterranean Agreements introduce Italy into the European and, more specifically, into the Mediterranean powers.

These alliances at least aimed to restore the confidence of the Italian Governments. The brutal remark made in 1881 by the Russian Ambassador in Rome that Italy should not be considered a great power and that it was accepted it in their midst only as a gesture of courtesy, and not because they considered indispensable its consent, underlined a painful reality. The lack of Italian intervention in Egypt in 1882 alongside the British was greatly deplored in Parliament and was even criticized as the greatest error in foreign policy made by the Italian Government[14]. Both Mediterranean Agreements were signed in 1887. The first Agreement, an exchange of notes between Italy and Britain, provides for joint consultation to preserve the *status quo* in the Mediterranean area and refers to the Aegean Sea, Bulgaria, Asia Minor and the Straits. The second one is a treaty between Britain, Italy and Austria-Hungary to prevent Turkey from surrendering its rights in the Balkans and in the Middle East[15]. Although both Agreements remain secret and the second one is allowed to lapse in 1892, they serve as a clear declaration of intent on the part of Italy to lay claims in the Eastern Mediterranean. This is an undisputed fact, which the other signatory powers acknowledge with their signature.

The area which Mazzini and his fellow contemporaries had incorporated into their revolutionary plans, Italy now as a state included in its imperialistic expansion. In the quest for supremacy in the Mediterranean, these Agreements inaugurate Italy's preference for the eastern Mediterranean, an area with more opportunities and Italian communities

---

[13] F. Chabod, *Storia della politica estera…*, p. 533.

[14] *Ibid.*, pp. 550-551, 544.

[15] In the first Agreement Spain and Austria-Hungary adhere too. Germany knows of these agreements and approves. A. J. P. Taylor, *The Struggle for Mastery in Europe 1848-1918*, Oxford, Oxford UP, 1971, pp. 320-322.

than in the western part of the sea where the presence of France and Spain was evident.

Asia Minor but also the eastern Mediterranean was of course the area involved in the Greek *Great Idea*. In this area and the Balkans as well, Italian expansionism and Greek irredentism openly clashed from the beginning of the 20th century. For the moment Italy pursued its Mediterranean policy, while Greece struggled to modernise the State and the economy. Within this context the Ch. Trikoupis Government inaugurated the work for the opening of the Corinth Canal in 1882. The same year he sent the Greek ships to participate in the operations in Alexandria[16].

The feeling expressed in Italy that the country sacrificed its interests in Egypt by not participating in this operation reinforces the conviction that its fair share in the Mediterranean is long overdue[17]. In this sense, the Italian Ambassador in London, acting on his own and not under instructions, as he stressed, refered to the division of the Ottoman Empire in a conversation with Salisbury in December 1895 and argued that Italy had a just claim to Albania, Tripoli and, possibly, Crete. However, Italy had to accept the solution the Concert of the European Powers imposed in 1897 on the Cretan Question – to grant autonomy to the island – and made, this time, its presence felt in the eastern Mediterranean by dispatching a squadron to participate alongside with the British, French and Russian ships in the blockade of Crete, and force the acceptance of this decision[18].

Apart from the fact that the time to divide Ottoman Turkey had not yet come, the advantages for Italy acquiring Tripoli, Albania and Crete are so obvious that these claims could not be accepted by any power with vital interests in the Mediterranean. In view of these claims, the Greek King argued in 1899 that Greece deserved to have Crete since Britain had seized Cyprus, Germany had taken Schleswig-Holstein, and Austria claimed Bosnia and Herzegovina. Britain did not find this claim

---

[16] The Canal opens in 1893 and faces immediately financial problems as the Austrian Lloyd and the Italian shipping companies refuse to use it. *The Great Greek Encyclopedia*, Vol. 14, Athens, Pyrsos 1930, pp. 898-899. Italian workers, mainly experienced miners from Bergamo and Piemonte, are the first to start working on the site. They number 400 out of a total of 1.200, E. Papagianopoulou, *The Corinth Canal*, Athens, National Bank of Industrial Development 1989, pp. 82-83.

[17] F. Chabod, *Storia de la politica estera*, p. 550.

[18] The leadership of this joint fleet is given for reasons of seniority to the Italian admiral Felice Napoleone Canevaro. The more frivolous activities of the admirals of these fleets, well beyond their call of duty are immortalized vividly by Nikos Kazantzakis in his novel "Alexis Zorbas".

totally unacceptable[19], especially as the Greek Government proposed a plebiscite to decide the issue. Of course, plebiscites were a commodity not much in demand in the Age of Imperialism, as they denote reason and thus weakness.

Independently of the Italian claim for Albania and Crete, which could not have been known to the Greeks at the time, the attitude of the Greek public opinion towards Italy had changed dramatically since the *Risorgimento*. After initially taking Italian support for granted, due to the legacy of the *Risorgimento* and past common national struggles, Greek public opinion experienced bitter disappointment when, following the Berlin Congress, Italy abandoned Greece's claims [regarding the annexation of Epirus] and chooses to support Albanian nationalism and, of course, its own expansion into Albania. Italy's adherence to the Triple Alliance and, even worse, her participation in 1886, together with the other Powers, in an escalation of pressure on Greece, culminating with an ultimatum and a naval blockade, created a sense of betrayal by a sister-country. It is interesting to note that this disappointed nationalism was also expressed by the prolification of satirical newspapers, where the European powers, including Italy, were the target of sarcastic articles[20].

As these events and reactions developed, the trajectory of two emerging nationalisms could be observed. The Italian one gaining momentum, reinforced by the successful conduct of Italian foreign policy, and Greek nationalism, at an impasse. The disappointment is also clearly shown in an article written by a well-known writer and journalist, a democrat and admirer of the *Risorgimento*, K. Triantafylos, the Greeks do not resemble their Italian brothers by crying out "*La Grecia farà da sé*" and proceed to do it[21].

The two nationalisms do not offer themselves up to comparison, to historians at least, as they developed within a different context and under different conditions.

Italy sougt to play, and was in fact granted, the role of a great power towards the end of the 19th century, while Greece was briefly elevated to the status of a peripheral power, with the time difference of a few decades, at the end of the First World War. For the purpose of this study, it

---

[19] Douglas Dakin, *The Unification of Greece 1770-1923*, London, Ernest Benn, 1972, p. 152.

[20] Lina Louvi, *The Laughable Kingdom. The Satirical Newspapers and the National Question (1875-1886)*, Athens, Estia, 2002, pp. 43, 142-43, 242, 269 [in Greek] Greece had mobilised to attack Turkey in the aftermath of the annexation of Eastern Roumelia by Bulgaria.

[21] L. Louvi, *The Laughable Kingdom*, p. 153.

suffices to point out that the origins of their open confrontation in the Mediterranean can be traced to the Italian decision to reinforce their position in the area by occupying Tripolis and extending their presence in the Aegean Sea using as a pretext the exigencies of war with Ottoman Turkey. With the French in Tunis, the British in Egypt and Cyprus, the Dodecanese Islands was the only area, within proximity of the Anatolian coast, where Italy could establish a presence in view of the forthcoming solution of the Eastern Question.

The occupation of Libya redresses the image of Italy as a colonial power, since its defeat in the Ethiopian town of Adowa in 1896, and the crisis it evoked[22]. In a Mediterranean context, the acquisition of Libya, long expected as the promised land of Italian expansion, gave vent to frustrated attempts to obtain it through diplomatic arrangements. More importantly, however, it was considered by Italy as maintaining an equilibrium in the Mediterranean. It is a welcome diversion, due to its successful conclusion, from the intricacies to maintain the *Equilibrio Adriatico* which increasingly worried the various Italian Governments during the closing decades of the 19th century. Sonnino argued in an article in 1881 that it would be an exaggeration of the principle of nationalities to claim Trieste. On the contrary, Trento was an uncontested Italian land necessary to the defense system of the country. However, Italian interests in the Trentino were very modest compared to those deriving from a sincere friendship with Austria[23]. When making this realistic assessment on the eve of Italy's adherence to the Triple Alliance, Sonnino was obviously well aware that the Adriatic Sea was dominated, until the end of the 18th century, by the peoples living in the Italian peninsula.

This *équilibre adriatique*, a neologism in diplomatic language, as a French writer observed in 1901 in a study criticizing the Italian policy in the Mediterranean[24], is bound to affect Greek irredentism upon the

---

[22] An example of the passionate debate regarding the presence of Italy in Ethiopia in the short polemical book written in the same year of this event by the member of the Italian Parliament Giorgio Giorgini, *L'ora presente e la questione d'Africa*, Roma-Firenze-Torino-Milano, Fratelli Bocca, 1886.

[23] C. Loiseau, *L'Equilibre Adriatique. L'Italie et la question d'Orient*, Paris, Perrinet Co., 1901, pp. 32-33.

[24] *Ibid.*, pp. 1-2. A leading British scholar who began studying the Eastern Question at the beginning of the century prefered the term "Adriatic problem", J. A. R. Marriott, *The Eastern Question. A Historical Study in European Diplomacy*, Oxford at the Clarendon Press, 1918. For Austro-Italian relations in the Adriatic at the time, see also D. J. Grange "Détroits, bases navales et flottes de guerre. Géopolitique de la Méditerranée à l'époque de l'impérialisme", in Rosario Villari (ed.), *Controllo degli stretti e insediamenti militari nel Mediterraneo*, Roma, Laterza, 2002, pp. 221-242.

entrance of the Adriatic Sea in the contested area of Albania. With Italy's presence in Libya, the Italian nationalists compared "*Mare Nostrum*" with the myth of "*lac latin*" developed by the French colonialists[25]. This aspect of nationalism evokes the names bestowed on the Mediterranean by a succession of dominant powers. The ancient Greeks named the sea in connection with either the ocean beyond the Columns of Hercules or the Greek colonies established along its coasts.

The Greek Stravon (Strabo), the leading geographer of antiquity as well as historian (65 BC-AD 24?) named the Mediterranean "*η ημετέρα θάλασσα*" – "our sea" – in his 3rd book published in 18 AD. The Romans called it "*mare nostrum*", "*mare magnum*", "*mare internum*" or simply "*mare*". Whether the Romans translated the term "our sea" introduced by Strabo into latin or, as it is most probable, the name "*mare nostrum*" resulted from their strong belief in their own imperium, is a matter open to debate. Be, as it may, the Roman writer Gaius Julius Solinus introduced the term "*mare Mediterraneum*" in the 3rd century because it divided Europe and Africa.

While the nationalist fever to cross *mare nostrum* and occupy Libya gains momentum in Italy, by extolling even the "Hellenic beauty" of Libya's coastal cities[26], in Greece, the first Venizelos Government of 1910 helps to erase the stigma from defeat of the war with Turkey in 1897 with concerted actions in the field of foreign policy. Thus nationalism in Greece acquired new impetus while the nationalists in Italy pushed to expand the war to other parts of the Ottoman Empire.

The Italian foreign minister, San Giuliano, announces the bombardments of Beirut and Smyrna and the dispatch of a fleet to the Red Sea. Among other projected actions during 1911 Italy, would seize Thessaloniki in the process of invading Macedonia, in order to signal the Balkan states to attack the Ottoman Empire[27]. This is, in fact, an ingenious excuse for a rather imaginative plan to pre-empt Austria and the Balkan States in their race for Thessaloniki. However, irrespective of whether or not these plans materialised, they show the influence of nationalism on Italian foreign policy at the time. The presence of the Italian navy in the Aegean Sea, the raid on the Straits and the occupation of the Dodecanese, across the coast of Asia Minor, so as "to initiate our Asiatic

---

[25] Daniel J. Grange, "Paris et Rome avant la Première Guerre mondiale", in M. Petricioli and A. Vasori (eds.), *The Seas as Europe's External Borders and their role in shaping an European Identity*, London, Lothian Foundation Press, 1999, p. 72.

[26] Ronald S. Cunsolo, "Libya, Nationalism and the Revolt against Giolitti", *The Journal of Modern History*, Vol. 37, No. 2 (June, 1965), p. 189.

[27] W. David Wrigley, "Germany and the Turco-Italian War 1911-1912", *International Journal of Middle East Studies*, Vol. 11, No. 3 (May 1980), p. 321.

future" [as the nationalists Corradini and Frenzi declared],[28] in addition to Italy's claims on Albania, was seen in Athens as a clear incursion into Greater Greece.

Greece reacted to the developments by approaching Britain. In December 1912, in a meeting with Venizelos in London, Churchill, First Lord of the Admiralty at the time, suggested that Argostoli on the island of Chefalonia in the Ionian Sea should be used as a base for the British fleet in the Mediterranean and in return Cyprus should be annexed to Greece. Lloyd George and Prince Sir. L. Battenberg, First Sea Lord, were in agreement. The Prime Minister Lord Asquith and Sir E. Grey had no objections either. The plan of action would be for the British Fleet to use Chefalonia and Malta to block the Austrian and part of the Italian fleet inside the Adriatic Sea, while the Greeks police the eastern Mediterranean and the islands with small rapid ships[29]. In the end, the plan did not materialise. Nevertheless, Venizelos, a keen supporter of the Greek Diaspora's extensive financial interests, gained the confidence of Lloyd George regarding his plans for a Great Greece. Within this context, Venizelos' visit to London laid the foundations for extensive propaganda to promote Greek irredentism, which culminated with the Allied decision to allow Greek troops to land in Smyrna in 1919[30].

The Italian plan as it gradually developed during the Balkan Wars, was to keep the Dodecanese, while using them to bargain for a favourable frontier line in southern Albania and economic concessions in Asia Minor[31]. This attitude clearly showed why the foreign policy of the two countries and their respective nationalism were intensely antagonistic. In addition, the ultimatum issued to Greece, the main winner of the Balkan Wars, by the Triple Alliance in December 1913 over continued troubles in Epirus[32], was clearly not designed to endear Italy to Greek public opinion. In spite of the pro-British feelings of Venizelos, as his party represented the rising bourgeois class and the influential Greek Dias-

---

[28] R. S. Cunsolo, "Libya, Nationalism and the Revolt against Giolitti", p. 195.

[29] M. Llwelyn-Smith, *Ionian Vision, Greece in Asia Minor 1919-1922*, London, Allen Lane, 1973, pp. 14-17.

[30] P. Papastratis "The Role of the Diaspora in the formation of Greek Foreign Policy", in S. Patoura-Spanou (ed.), *Diplomacy and Politics*, Athens, National Research Institute, 2005, pp. 340-341, 44-347.

[31] For a detailed analysis of the Dodecanese Question and the situation leading to the First World War see, Marta Petricioli, *L'Italia in Asia Ninore. Equilibrio mediterraneo e ambizioni imperialiste alla vigilia della prima Guerra mondiale*, Firenze, Sansoni, 1983, pp. 213-269.

[32] Richard Bosworth, "Britain and Italy's Acquisition of the Dodecanese 1912-1915", *The Historical Journal*, Vol. 13, No. 4, Dec. 1970.

pora, he was unable sway the British Government to favour the Greece's claims.

The First World War kept the open antagonism between Italy and Greece in the background. The intense civil strife in Greece, resulting from the decision of Venizelos to participate in the War with the Entente, did not allow him to bargain for post-war gains as Italy did with the Treaty of London of April 1915 and the St. Jean de Maurienne Agreement of 1917. These two documents contain the seeds of further discord with Greece, as Italy, apart from its Adriatic gains including Valona in Albania, is promised the Dodecanese, the Turkish provinces of Adalia, Aidin and Konya in Asia Minor, Smyrna and also the port of Mersina.

The Bolsheviks rendered, unintentionally of course, a great service to Venizelos by revealing and denouncing the contents of the Treaty of London, setting thus in motion a new round of diplomatic confrontations between Italy and Greece. It is beyond the scope of this paper to examine the development of these relations, which center on the Greek mandate for Smyrna[33]. An attempt to find an overall solution to the existing problems between Italy and Greece is the Venizelos-Tittoni Agreement signed in July 1919 and the Venizelos-Bonin Agreement which replaced it, signed in August 1920, the same day as the Treaty of Sevres[34].

The conflicting interests of the two countries continued throughout the Greek presence in Anatolia, while the two governments tried to maintain relations at an acceptable level[35]. This situation had direct repercussions on the development of national aspirations in both countries especially with Mussolini's advent to power. Throughout the second decade of the 20th century, both Italy and Greece experienced a series of political and military developments with corresponding repercussions upon the two populations.

---

[33]   The mild reaction of F. S. Nitti when he writes on this event three years later does not depict the depth of Italian disappointment felt at the time. F. Nitti, *The Decadence of Europe: The Path of Reconstruction*, London, T. Fisher Unwin, 1923, pp. 162-167.

[34]   For a detailed examination of this attempt, see M. Petricioli, "Il Patto Tittoni-Venizelos del 29 luglio 1919", Facoltà di Scienze Politiche, Università di Firenze, 1967, (unpublished thesis). In Greek historiography, a critical assessment of this Agreement is presented by D. Filippis, "Greek-Italian Relations 1919-1940 and the Involvement of Spain", Department of Political Science and History, Panteion University of Athens, 2005 (unpublished Ph.D. thesis), pp. 40-64.

[35]   M. Petricioli, "La Resa dei conti : Diplomazia e finanza di fronte alle aspirazioni italiane in Anatolia (1918-1923)", *Storia delle Relazioni Internazionali*, 1986, anno II, pp. 63-93. D. Filippis, *Greek-Italian Relations*, pp. 13-39.

From *Guerra vittoriosa* to *vittoria mutilata* and from the triumph of the *Great Idea* in the Balkan Wars to the *Disaster of Asia Minor*, as it is still commonly referred to by the Greeks, the two nations are driven from exaltation to disappointment. *Italia Irredenta* and *Greater Greece* did not materialise and the national susceptibilities of the two countries were deeply wounded. Their reaction, however, was different because of the magnitude of the events, and thus the repercussions were different. *Greater Greece* did not materialise at the cost of a military defeat and the influx of approximately 1.3 million refugees. Their arrival, in fact, was a blessing in disguise, although it was not seen as such at the time. As a result, Greek internal issues took precedence, while the expansionist foreign policy of Mussolini affected Greece directly.

The Corfu "incident", as diplomatic prudence insisted on naming the bombardment and occupation of the island, inaugurates in practice this new policy. With this clearly premeditated – and prearranged – operation, Italy underlined its intentions to apply the doctrine of *mare nostrum*[36]. Corfu, a Venetian possession for 400 years, a fact as Mussolini pointed out that the Greek Government did not appreciate, was at the center of Italian attention since Rome had realised the strategic importance of Albania.

It can be argued that the occupation of Corfu was at the time seen as a test of Italy's sincerity in applying *mare nostrum*. In an intricate arrangement to appease Mussolini in his first Mediterranean dynamic act, Britain and France arranged that Greece would be condemned by the Conference of Ambassadors, and significally not by the League of Nations, in order to satisfy Italy's injured honor by the assassination of General E. Tellini[37]. At the same time, Britain and France in a successful effort to undermine *mare nostrum* and reassert their dominant position in the Mediterranean, convinced Mussolini to evacuate Corfu.

The arguments on *spazio vitale* which Mussolini developed parallel to *mare nostrum* must be seen in connection to the ongoing discussion

---

[36] P. Papastratis, "Foreign Policy", in Ch. Hadjiiossif (ed.), *History of Greece in the 20th Century. The Interwar 1922-1940*, Vol. B2, Athens, Bibliorama, 2003, pp. 261-264 [in Greek]; D. Filippis, *Greek Italian Relations*, pp. 110-119.

[37] Tellini was the chief of the Italian Mission in the International Committee for the delineation of the Greek-Albanian frontier. All the men of his escort were also assassinated. The perpetrators were never found. The predominance of political expediency in international affairs is amply revealed by J. Barros in his two books *The Corfu Incident of 1923. Mussolini and the League of Nations*, Oxford, Oxford UP, 1965 and *The League of Nations and the Great Powers. The Greek-Bulgarian Incident, 1925*, Oxford, Clarendon Press, 1970. This is also true for his third book, *Britain, Greece and the Politics of Sanctions. Ethiopia 1935-1936*, London, Royal Historical Society, 1982.

on emigration in Europe, and in Italy and Greece in particular. But at the same time, his regime underlined the importance of emigration as a vehicle of fascist ideology[38]. Already in 1922, Mussolini declared that he wanted to turn the Mediterranean into an Italian lake[39]. Mussolini justified Italy's vast aspirations in the Mediterranean basin as a struggle for life and death. As a result, in 1923, he declared that Italian expansion would take on every possible form: moral, political, economic and demographic[40]. Historical traditions are also duly evoked. The heritage of Rome directed the forces of the New Italy to its historical birthplace "The Sea of Rome", in order for the third Italian universal civilization to commence[41]. A few years later, I. Metaxas is much more modest when he copies the fascist propaganda model and declares the onset of the Fourth Hellenic Civilization without referring to the Mediterranean at all[42].

In Greece, during the interwar period, a lively discussion was also held on the viability of the country and its ability to feed its population. Emigration towards the colonies in Asia and the Eastern Mediterranean was also seen as an inevitable solution. The desired direction of the emigration also had to do with the problem of assimilation, which, unlike Italy, did not officially worry the Greek state. Thus in the entire eastern Mediterranean and even Abyssinia, as it is specifically stated, Greek intellectual superiority and the ability for economic domination was taken for granted. It is certain, therefore, that the "moral Greek Idea" could not be endangered by a non-existent, superior, materialistic civilization[43]. These arguments with their strong nationalistic undertones formulated a part of the wider debate on the conditions of the country under the impact of the defeat by Turkey and its repercussions.

The *Great Idea* is revived during the interwar period, but in a different context and in conjunction with the attempt at Balkan cooperation in

---

[38]   N. Labanca, "Politica e propaganda : emigrazione e fasci all'estero", in E. Collotti (con la collaborazione di N. Labanca e T. Sala) *Fascismo e politica di potenza. Politica estera 1922-1939*, Milano, La Nuova Italia, 2000, pp. 137-172.

[39]   D. Rodogno, *Il nuovo ordine mediterraneo. Le politiche di occupazione dell'Italia fascista in Europa (1940-1943)* Torino, Bollati Boringhieri, 2003, pp. 72-73.

[40]   I. Tournakis, *International Emigration Movement and Emigration Policy*, Athens, 1930, p. 140 [in Greek].

[41]   Aristotle Kallis, *Fascist Ideology. Territory and Expansionism in Italy and Germany, 1922-1945*, London, Routledge, 2000, p. 50.

[42]   On this issue, see V. Aggelis's penetrating analysis, *Lessons of National Education and Metaxas Youth Propaganda*, Athens, Bibliorama, 2006.

[43]   P. Papastratis, "From the Great Idea to Balkan Union", in M. Sarafis and M. Eve (eds.), *Background to Contemporary Greece*, London, Merlin Press, 1990, pp. 168-169.

the early 1930s following the world economic crisis of 1929. This revival ran parallel with the successful attempt of Venizelos to reassert the position of Greece in the Balkans. The Greek-Italian Agreement of 1928 and a series of Agreements he signed with Turkey two years later form the basis of his foreign policy. Venizelos himself, the least expected to do so, attacked the *Great Idea* repeatedly and declared that the wars of national integration had ended. In addition he exhorted the younger generation to excel in the field of learning in the forthcoming closer cooperation between the peoples of the Near East. The public reaction to this radical approach to the basic tenet of Greek national ideology is strong, and during his visit to Turkey to sign the Agreements with Kemal Atatürk, Venizelos is accused of "clipping the wounded wings of the *Great Idea* which kept the Greek race upright for five centuries"[44].

Emphasis, however, was on economic penetration and eventually a strong presence in the areas in question, although this will never be openly admitted. In the initially successful attempt for Balkan economic cooperation, through the establishment of Balkan Conferences, the same attitude can be observed. In the proposed Balkan economic cooperation, Greece is envisaged as the industrial partner *par excellence*, distinguished by the innate and unchallenged qualities of its people as entrepreneurs and seafarers, as was commented at the time. Such a prestigious position implied Greek superiority in comparison with the neighbouring farming, stock-breeding and wood-cutting Balkan peoples, and further underpinned Greece's ambitions for a future strategic position in the Balkan economy.

The rise of Nazism to power and Germany's foreign policy radically altered the political and economic situation in the Balkans. Following the occupation of Greece May 1941, the King, his Government and the Greek armed forces reached Egypt to continue the war. In early July 1941, Mr. E. Tsouderos, an idle Prime Minister of a Government-in-exile, sailing the Red Sea on a passenger ship on its long way to London, composed an extended list of national revendications, stressing that Greece is primarily a Mediterranean country. Northern Epirus, the Dodecanese, Cyprus and the former enemy colonies in N. Africa figured prominently in his memorandum. Tsouderos referred to these territories as part of the Allied New Europe, while at the same time they were already a part of the Fascist and Nazi New Order[45]. He did not exclude

---

[44] As cited in P. Papastratis, "From the Great Idea to Balkan Union", p. 168.

[45] E. Collotti, *L'Europa Nazista. Il progetto di un nuovo ordine europeo (1939-1945)*, Firenze, Giunti, 2002. Y. Durand, *Il nuovo ordine europeo. La collaborazione nell'Europa tedesca (1938-1945)*, Bologna, Il Mulino, 2002. J. Freymond, *Le*

the possibility of Greece undertaking the administration of these colonies and of other countries occupied by Italy. Mr. Tsouderos insists, for the time being, on the right to free emigration and colonisation of Libya[46]. Thus only thirty years after its occupation by Italy, a Greek counterpart of Giolitti is planning to follow a similar course.

IIIe Reich et la réorganisation économique de l'Europe 1940-1942, Leiden, A. W. Sithoff, 1974.

[46] H. Venezis, *Emmanuel Tsouderos, the Prime Minister of the Battle of Crete*, Athens, 1966, pp. 240-245.

DEUXIÈME PARTIE

CARACTÉRISTIQUES COMMUNES DE L'ESPACE MÉDITERRANÉEN

PART II

COMMON FEATURES OF THE MEDITERRANEAN REGION

A Mediterranean Diaspora

Jews from Leghorn in the Second Half of the 19th Century

Liana E. FUNARO

When the Tunisian poet Mohammed-al Sanusi (1851-1900) en route to Mecca visited Leghorn in 1882 on one of the first trips to Europe by a Tunisian intellectual, he wrote a detailed and positive account of the city and was not all surprised at finding in the city a café "where", as he writes, "Tunisian Jews meet" (and we know the importance of a place such as the café in the Arab world, as a place of *sociabilité* and as a status symbol)[1]. Similarly, when the Leghorn-resident Isacco Coriat, an entrepreneur, travelled to Tunis on business in one of his frequent journeys to his native land, e.g. in 1874, he visited and stayed with Italian families, friends and relatives belonging to the affluent, Italian-Jewish community, but also displayed a deep understanding of all aspects of the country, Tunisia, where he had been born in 1820s. The letters he exchanged with his daughter during his journey of 1874, where Italian, French, Arabic and Hebrew words are intermingled, picture a country emerging from a condition of total backwardness, and reveal much on the culture and general attitudes of a Leghorn manufacturer in the second half of the 19th century. Coriat recalls ancient family remembrances while visiting his mother's grave; attends the Synagogue "non per devozione", as he writes, "ma per offrire qualcosa al ministro officiante, al povero *Sciamasc* [the Synagogue attendant]", though negatively impressed by the local congregation[2]. He also attended other ceremonies, such as the *Festa dello Statuto* and witnessed the contemporary attachment of the Leghorn-Jewish notables to the kingdom of Italy

---

[1] A. M. Medici, *Città italiane sulla via della Mecca. Storie di viaggiatori tunisini dell'Ottocento*, Torino, L'Harmattan Italia, 2001, p. 129. On the importance of the café see O. Carlier, "Sociabilité masculine et effervescence citoyenne (Algérie XVIIe-XXe siècles)", *Annales*, 45, 4, 1990, pp. 975-1003.

[2] "Mancò poco per rimanere asfissiati, un puzzo di *Handak* [local word for sewage] e un caldo *non plus ultra*", Isacco Coriata "Miei amati", June 4, 1874, courtesy of Mrs. Fortunée Franchetti Treves, to whom I am most grateful.

and to local politicians[3]. He was especially attentive to the value of the Tunisian coin and appreciated all sorts of progress made in the city environment, thus sharing the prevalent attitude of European 19th century observers[4].

From the end of the 18th century onwards, yearly calendars, sometimes compiled by rabbis, were printed in the celebrated Leghorn printing houses; they listed side by side Jewish, Christian and Muslim holidays for the benefit of common trade[5]. On African shores the modern press in Italian, French and Judeo-Arabic was mostly established by Italian pioneer journalists, who had sometimes been born in Leghorn; for example in Tripoli, Alexandria, Saloniki and Tunisia before and after the French colonization[6]. As early as 1857, Elia Benamozegh, the most

---

[3] Isacco Coriata, "Miei amati", June 4, 6 etc. 1874, *ibid.*

[4] "Alla marina [...] vidi il nuovo mercato dei cereali che trovai grandioso, magnifico, essendo fatto da ingegneri europei; la Marsa, la Goletta divenuto un paesotto con piazze con continuo concorso di Europei e indigeni, la fabbrica di diaccio artificiale a vapore, la Panetteria a Vapore" (June 7, 1874, *ibid.*).

[5] See e.g. *Almanacco Orientale Illustrato per l'anno 1852 Bisestile e dalla Creazione del Mondo 5612 avendo principiato il dì 27 settembre scorso il quale contiene le Feste, i Digiuni, Equinozi, e Sostizj secondo il computo degli Israeliti; nascite degl'I. e R. Sovrani di Toscana; Noviluni e Pleniluni di ogni mese; mese dei Turchi etc. La Tavola delle 23 per comodo delle feste del Sabato, ed altri avvisi per comodo dei SS. Negozianti, con le scadenze delle Cambiali Messo in ordine da Meldola*, Livorno, presso gli Eredi Ottolenghi, 1852; see Leghorn, Archivio di Stato [henceforth ASLi], *Governo di Livorno*, 380, 1433. As late as 1873 Leghorn official calendars such as the yearly *Indicatore generale del commercio delle arti, delle industrie della città di Livorno compilato da V. Meozzi* listed Christian and Jewish festivities, even the less solemn ones, side by side. Up to 1860 there were not any commercial transactions on Jewish festivities thanks to the so-called "feriato Israelitico", a previlege awarded by the Habsbourg-Lorraine Grandukes to the Leghorn Jewish Community in the 18th century and confirmed by the December 17, 1814 "Motuproprio".

[6] E. Bigiavi, "Elenco dei giornali italiani che si pubblicarono o si pubblicano attualmente in Egitto", in *Noi e l'Egitto*, Livorno, Belforte, 1911, p. 118; on the printing houses from Leghorn *ibidem*, p. 117; C. Poma, "Israeliti italo-levantini", *Rivista Coloniale*, VI, 1911, pp. 503-506; A. Milano, *Storia degli ebrei italiani nel Levante*, Firenze, Casa Ed. Israel, 1949, pp. 187-197; *id.*, "Un secolo di stampa periodica ebraica in Italia", *La Rassegna Mensile d'Israel* [thenceforth *RMI*], XII, 1938, pp. 96-136, p. 104; B. Di Porto, "La stampa periodica ebraica a Livorno", *Nuovi Studi Livornesi*, I, 1993, pp. 172-198, p. 183 and footnote 75 p. 178; M. Larbi Snoussi, "Les débuts de la presse écrite en caractères hébraiques en Tunisie coloniale (1884-1896)", *Mesogeios*, 15, 2002, pp. 25-80; P. Manduchi, "La presenza italiana in Tunisia e il suo ruolo nello sviluppo della stampa", *Africana*, 2000, pp. 133-147; M. al-Tahir al-Jarari, "L'istruzione in Libia prima e dopo il 1911", in *Un colonialismo, due sponde del Mediterraneo, Atti del Seminario di Studi Storici italo-libici* (N. Labanca, P. Venuta eds.), Pistoia, C.R.T., 2000, pp. 61-74, p. 69; M. J. Vilar, "El nacimiento de la prensa in Libia: l'"Investigateur Africain" de Tripoli", *Africa*, LIX, 2004, pp. 221-230.

prominent figure of the 19th century Leghorn rabbinical school, (himself born in a Moroccan family), asked the local government authorities for permission to publish regularly a paper to meet the request of his "corrispondenti dell'Egitto, della Persia e della Barberia tutti Israeliti". This paper, written in Hebrew, would be rich in information drawn from Italian papers, with no attention to politics, as Benamozegh carefully stated to prevent objections from the suspicious Granducal authorities[7]. No wonder a rabbi could plan such a compilation with secular contents. Leghorn rabbis travelled across the Mediterranean and corresponded regularly with colleagues from different communities both on religious and secular subjects. Their *responsa* settled legal disputes both in family and in business areas. In 1887 Benamozegh required the payment of a debt from a rabbi from Tripoli, while in another case his colleague Israel Costa pleaded on behalf of a Tunisian debtor[8]. Rabbi Yehuda Sitrug (1840?-1913) followed the celebrated Caid Nissim Semama in his fiction-like escape from Tunisia first to Paris, then to Leghorn, where he survived his friend and master[9]. Rabbis from Leghorn often were themselves printers and established therefore a commercial and cultural connection with Mediterranean colleagues. They were also responsible for the money collected by affluent Italian Jews for the benefit of the four holy communities of the so-called "Terrasanta", Safed, Hebron, Tiberias and Jerusalem. Here pious students of the Law could survive thanks to the charity of the European, especially of the Mediterranean Jewish communities[10]. The community of Leghorn could also count on a

---

[7] ASLi, *Governo di Livorno*, b. 558, fasc. 210, March 31, 1857. E. Benamozegh asked for permission to print in his own printing house "ogni mese o due alcuni Fascicoli di non più di due Fogli a stampa da inviare ai Correligionari dell'Egitto, della Persia e della Barberia che hanno manifestato il desiderio di conoscere". In Benamozegh's words the title of the paper should have been "Mebasser" [the story-teller]. The permission was awarded by the local authority L. Bargagli on March 25, 1857. On a business agreement between two rabbis concerning the printing of a Bible see *Patti concordati fra gli Ecc. Sigg. Haham Michele Allum e Haham Elia Benamozegh*, Leghorn, Archivio della Comunità Ebraica [henceforth ACELi], f. 29, June 29, 1856 listing the number of volumes sent to Syria, Tunis, Alexandria, Oran, Algiers, Morocco via Gibraltar. See also I. Costa to "Università Israelitica di Livorno", November 2, 1868, ACELi, f. 32.

[8] E. Benamozegh to A. De Gubernatis, Livourne 5 avril 1887, in L. E. Funaro, "Speculiamo, amiamo, combattiamo. Lettere inedite di Elia Benamozegh", *Nuovi Studi Livornesi*, X, 2002-2003, pp. 131-148, p. 141.

[9] ACELi, *Filze di Mandati*, 18 April 1871, 23 August 1880, 12 July 1881. See R. Attal, *Le Caid Nissim Semama mécène du livre*, Jerusalem, 1995, pp. 27-32, stating Semama's bequest to Y. Sitrug. On the ill-famous Semama legal case (1878-1883) see *id*, *Les Juifs d'Afrique du Nord. Bibliographie*, Jerusalem, 1973, 1993.

[10] ACELi, f. 28, aff. 214; f. 29, aff. 150, 168, 203; f. 30, aff. 126, 164 etc.; f. 31, September 28, 1862; April 7, 1865; f. 32, October 18, 1867, March 31, 1868; August

number of official interpreters for Greek and Turkish, but not for Arabic. Arabic in fact was in some way familiar to the Leghorn Jews, accustomed as they were to Judeo-Arabic[11]. When in Leghorn, Arab merchants were under the protection of an active Beylical consulate; they used to rent flats owned by Jews, who generally invested their capitals in buying houses in the very centre of the city[12]. As for the use of the Italian language as a language of communication and trade, it was a sort of *lingua franca* in the Mediterranean ports. Its diffusion could only be compared to French or Judeo-Spanish, both languages equally familiar to Jews all over the Mediterranean; private, official or business documents (birth, death or marriages certificates, commercial testimonials) are often signed in Spanish, later in Italian or Hebrew, but accompanied by Arab official translation and countersigned by Italian officials and local Jewish notables. In Egypt, Tunisia, Saloniki few official openings of any Jewish institution (it could be a school, a hospital or a synagogue, often supported by Leghorn charities) could take place without an official speech delivered in Italian[13]; the *"Festa dello Statuto"*, as we read in Coriat's letters for Tunis, was celebrated with constant pompousness in Corfù, Saloniki, Alexandria synagogues all over the second half of the 19th century: and it is often pictured in the contemporary Italian Jewish press, rich in descriptions of long rows of orphans, students, international businessmen, Italian consular officials, and of course local rabbis, attending a ceremony carefully supervised

---

17, September 19, November 1st 1870; *Opere Pie Denunzie Statistiche Prospetti Diversi*, f. 234. See *L'Educatore Israelita* [thenceforth *E. I.*], 1871, pp. 75-77. See A. Milano, *Storia degli ebrei nel Levante, op. cit.*, pp. 180-199.

[11] J. P. Filippini, *La Nazione Ebrea di Livorno, Storia d'Italia, Annali II, Gli Ebrei in Italia*, (C. Vivanti ed.), Torino, Einaudi, 1997, pp. 1047-1066; L. Levy, *La Nation Juive Portugaise Livourne Amsterdam Tunis 1591-1951*, Paris, L'Harmattan, 1998; I. Avrahami, "La contribution des sources internes hébraiques, judéo-arabes et arabes à l'histoire des Juifs livournais à Tunis", *RMI*, L, 1984, pp. 725-741. Some Arabic words were of common use in Jewish and Leghorn non-Jewish family language.

[12] On the Beylical consulate see A. M. Medici, *Città italiane sulla via della Mecca, op. cit.*, pp. 47, 147 note 182-183. On the socalled Jewish quarter see L. Frattarelli Fischer, "L'insediamento ebraico a Livorno dalle origini alla emancipazione", in *Le tre Sinagoghe. Edifici di culto e vita ebraica a Livorno dal Seicento al Novecento*, Livorno, Graphis Arte, 1991, pp. 33-45.

[13] *"Mosé" Antologia Israelitica, pubblicazione mensile per cura d'una Società d'amici della religione e del progresso* [thenceforth *"Mosé"*], Corfù, I., 1878, pp. 35-37, 38-39, etc.]; *Il Vessillo Israelitico* [*V. I.*], 1878, pp. 118, 160, 191-192, 200-201, 274-275, 281; 1879, pp. 126-127, 242-243, etc. Special private bequests to Leghorn community charities, some going back to the 17th century, were reserved for the assistance of Algiers, Tunis, Saloniki, Alexandria poor.

and deeply felt also in Leghorn[14]. As for business transactions, which were such a share of the mutual relationships all along the Mediterranean, they could not take place among Jewish entrepreneurs without taking into account the price of the "coupon tunisino", the Tunisian coin or the quotation of the Egyptian piastra, the British pound obviously serving as the reference currency in the background. As late as 1878, members of the Franchetti family, who around 1782 had moved from Tunisia to Leghorn to become in a few decades and all along the 19th century among the richest bankers in town, speculated for differences between the Tunisian and Italian coins, with special attention to the French stock exchange: reluctant to enter in the contemporary industrial – speculations, they preferred to stick to a century-long family tradition which balanced its capitals between different Mediterranean shores[15].

These examples – some among the many possible – suggest a circulation of people, commodities, ideas and a multilingualism all around the Mediterranean. Events which happened around the Mediterranean, and the place of the Jewish minorities in them provide an opportunity to study the development of mutual relationships among different religious communities, and to examine the interaction between diverse ethnic, linguistic and cultural traditions throughout the centuries. Leghorn as a city and as a Mediterranean port *par excellence*, and the role of the Jewish community inside it, further provide an ideal point of observation, from which to reinvestigate on all these questions[16]. My focus on

---

[14] ACELi, f. 133, [N. P. 16], 1872-1874, May 26, 1874. On the patriotic (often masonic) celebration of the 20th of September 1870 see "Il XX Settembre ad Alessandria", *Rivista Coloniale*, VI, 1911, p. 340. See I. Porciani, *La festa della Nazione, Rappresentazione dello Stato e spazi sociali nell'Italia unita*, Bologna, Il Mulino, 1997. See also *V. I.*, L, 1902, p. 209.

[15] F. Franchetti to A. Franchetti, Leghorn, April 23, 1877, December 26, 1877, January 1st, 17, 1878 etc., courtesy of Mrs. F. Franchetti Treves. On Leghorn merchants as middlemen between North African rulers, European and Levantine ports (16th-18th centuries) see R. Ayoun, "Les négociants juifs d'Afrique du Nord et la mer à l'époque moderne", *Revue Française d'Histoire d'Outre-Mer*, 87, 2000, pp. 109-125; B. Lewis, *Gli Ebrei nel mondo islamico*, Firenze, Sansoni, 1991 (ed. or. 1984); D.S. Landes, *Banchieri e Pascià. Finanza internazionale e imperialismo economico* Torino, Bollati Boringhieri, 1990 (ed. or. 1958, 1970); J. Ganiage, *La population européenne de Tunis au milieu du XIXe siècle*, Paris, PUF, 1959; J. Taieb, *Sociétes juives du Maghreb moderne* (1500-1900), *un monde en mouvement*, Paris, Maisonneuve et Larose, 2000.

[16] J. P. Filippini, *La Nazione Ebrea...*, *op. cit.*; S. Marzagalli, *Les boulevards de la fraude: le négoce maritime et le Blocus continental 1806-1813: Bordeaux, Hambourg, Livourne*, Villeneuve d'Ascq, 1999; D. G. Lo Romer, *Merchants and Reform in Livorno 1814-1868*, Berkeley, University of California Press, 1987; S. Fettah, "Temps et espaces des trafics portuaires en Méditerranée. Le cas du port franc de

those features, which were common between the various communities, implies a deliberate choice to leave on the background the condition of Jews in Arab lands, their condition of *dhimmi* before the *Tanzimat*; and in some areas, also after it. There existed in fact important differences between a receptive environment, such as the Turkish one, and a far less receptive welcome as Morocco or Yemen, where permanent discrimination lasted till the 20th century[17]. I have here deliberately omitted blood libels, the well-known Damascus affair (1840), the rivalries between arising nationalities, such as the Greek or the Armenian in Saloniki after 1880-1890 and later[18], the particular salience of the Dreyfus affair in the Middle East[19] or the total destruction of communities such as Rhodes or Saloniki in the 20th century, as well as the final departure of almost 900,000 Jews from Arab lands between 1958 and 1971[20]; a small number of them, as we shall see, sought and found shelter in Leghorn. In this paper I would like to consider the Jewish diaspora as a continent, a network of families and of economic structures interacting through generations. In this context, I have chosen to avoid the double danger of Jewish historiography, stressing alternatively antisemitism or peaceful coexistence; both in fact represent difficult categories of analysis which in some way also lead astray the core of this research.

The history of the Jewish community of Leghorn, its relation with other Mediterranean cities and its representatives abroad has been thoroughly investigated from its foundation to the first half of the 19th century. As for the second half of the same century, with the possible exception of *Ebrei di Livorno tra due censimenti* edited by Michele Luzzati in 1990, much is still to be studied, as research has in fact been limited to the period up to 1861, when the Kingdom of Italy completed

---

Livourne (XVII-XIX siècles)", *Ricerche Storiche*, 1998, pp. 243-273. As for previous centuries see A. Molho, "Ebrei e marrani fra Italia e Levante", *Storia d'Italia, Annali II, Gli Ebrei in Italia, op. cit.*, pp. 1011-1046.

[17] Bat Yeor, *Le Dhimmi. Profil de l'opprimé en Orient et dans l'Afrique du Nord depuis la conquête arabe*, Paris, 1980; B. Lewis, *Gli Ebrei nel mondo islamico, op. cit..*; Bat Yeor, *Juifs et Chrétiens sous l'Islam. Les dhimmis face au défi intégriste*, Berg Intern., 1994 ; R. Toledano Attias, "L'antisémitisme au Maroc du début du XIXe siècle. Une mémoire ignorée", *Pardés*, 34, 2003; *L'exclusion des Juifs des pays arabes; aux sources du conflit israélo-arabe sous la direction de* Shmuel Trigano, pp. 61-72.

[18] P. Dumont, "La structure sociale de la communauté juive de Salonique à la fin du dix-neuvième siècle", *Revue Historique*, 534, 1980, pp. 351-394 ; Y. Kerem, "The Multicultural Background of Greek Jewry ; Factors in their diversity and integration in modern Greece", *Mesogeoios*, 20-21, *Méditerranée*, pp. 57-80.; G. Veinstein (ed.), *Salonique, 1850-1918*, Paris, Autrement, 1992.

[19] E. Benbassa – A. Rodrigue, *Storia degli Ebrei sefarditi da Toledo a Salonicco*, Torino, Einaudi, 2004 (ed. or. 2002).

[20] See the whole number of *Pardes*, 34, *op. cit.*

its unification: it should be noted, too, that Leghorn Jews, more as individuals than as official representatives of the Jewish community, took an active part in the Italian *Risorgimento* in proportions superior to their number[21]. In spite of many and careful studies (let me quote at least the name of Jean-Pierre Filippini, but many other scholars could be mentioned in the French area, in Israel and on both sides of the Atlantic Ocean), there is still room for a reconsideration of the various factors which emerged during the second half of the 19th century: the circulation of political ideas which spread from Leghorn to the different African communities before and after the Italian *Risorgimento*, the mobility of Jewish families and individuals from Leghorn, the interchange (sometimes the clash) between Jewish and local cultures, the field of linguistics, the subtle sphere of conversions, the slave trade. The quantity of religious texts and prayer-books printed in Hebrew, Arabic, Spanish by the celebrated Leghorn publishing houses deserves special attention: they spread all over the Mediterranean communities schoolbooks, *catechismi*, books intended for use in all sorts of Jewish schools, which were often founded or supported by benefactors or residents in Leghorn. Most Hebrew and Judeo-Arabic printing in Alexandria, in Tunis, all depended on Italian publishers; sometimes, as is the case of Bagdad, the very printing-machinery came from Leghorn[22]. Conversely, the local Jewish press, such as the Leghorn minor paper *"L'Israelita"* (1866), often published news and reports from the so-called *Holy Land*, from Yemen, from Egypt[23]. In Saloniki, in Corfù, in Alexandria synagogues up to the 20th century religious services, music included, were sometimes a mere replica of the ritual hymns sung or composed in Leghorn by musicians such as Bolaffi, Garzia, or by local rabbis, such as Piperno[24].

---

[21] See "I laboratori della democrazia e del Risorgimento. La "repubblica" di Livorno, l'"altro" Granducato, il sogno italiano di rinnovamento", L. Dinelli, L. Bernardini (eds.), *Atti del Convegno Livorno 5-6 dicembre 2002*, Pisa, ETS, 2004; *ivi*, M. Vernassa, "Il Risorgimento livornese nell'emigrazione toscana in Levante", pp. 304-343.

[22] *Hebrew and Judeo-Arabic Printing in Bagdad. Rare Printed Books from the Valmadonna Trust Library*, London, 2004.

[23] "Un pellegrinaggio in Terra Santa. Letture israelitiche di Albert Cohn; Gli Ebrei di Gerusalemme; Sesto viaggio di Sir Moses Montefiore in Terrasanta (dal periodico *L'Israelita* di Magonza); Osservazioni intorno alle condizioni della Comunità Israelitica di Alessandria d'Egitto; Acque Termali di Tebarià; Gli Israeliti dello Yemen", *L'Israelita*, I, 1866, pp. 107-113, 113-115, 116-117, 232-239, 247-249, 364-367: News and reports from Corfù, Bagdad, Alexandria, Algeria, Jaffa, *E. I.*, 1871, pp. 63, 95, 123, 124, 209, 219, 273, 288 etc.

[24] On Michele Bolaffi (1768-1842) see *Jewish Encyclopedia*, 4, p. 1185. He was also active in Florence as a composer (Florence, Archivio della Comunità Ebraica,

As for Tunis, the Leghorn Jewish community, the so-called *Grana*, had been independent since 1710 and would remain in open contrast with the local Jewish community (the *Touansa*) up to 1888; in 1865 the so-called *Comunità Portoghese* or *Livornese* included eight firms owned by French Jews, seven by British and one by a Spanish Jew. However, of the sixty-two firms trading in Tunis twenty-two were owned by Italians, fifteen of whom were entrepreneurs from Leghorn[25]. The community of Marseilles had been founded and kept according to the Leghorn rules and on the Leghorn model since 1775 and it welcomed members of Tunisian and Comté Venaissin families: and a total number of more than one thousand Leghorn Jews, mostly of affluent economic condition, some in the branch of fashion trade, moved from Leghorn to the French port, as stated in the commercial correspondence, which still exists at the local *Chambre de Commerce*'[26]. In Alexandria an independent Leghorn-like community was founded in 1854, as reported with details by the Italian-Jewish contemporary press[27]. There is much to

---

Tribunale dei Massari, D. 1. 3 (August 11, 1822). On July 15, 1872 David Garzia wrote from Alexandria to the Leghorn Jewish authorities asking for his musical compositions to be sung at the official opening of the Alexandria *Menascè* Synagogue (ACELi, f. 133). On Garzia see *Indicatore del commercio, op. cit.*, 18. Abraham Baruch Piperno, a much esteemed rabbi of the mid 19th century Leghorn community, composed the hymn *Col Bené Israel* sung also on special non religious festivities and still in use in the present Leghorn community. The whole repertory of the hymns sung on religious service at the Leghorn community can be found in F. Consolo, *Libro dei canti d'Israele*, Firenze, 1891.

[25] R. Attal, "À propos de la dissension entre Touansa et Grana à Tunis", *Revue des Études Juives*, CXLI, 1982, pp. 223-235; I. Avrahami *Keillà Portugesis betunis oupinasak* (Heb.) (*The Jewish Community in Tunis and its Memorial*), Tel Aviv, Bar Ilan Press, 1981-82, Vol. 2 as reviewed by J. Taieb, "Annales", 40, 1885, pp. 535-537; L. Levy, *La Nation Juive, op. cit.*; E. Boccara, "La Comunità ebraica portoghese di Tunisi (1710-1914)", *RMI*, LXVI, 2000, pp. 25-98; M. Vernassa, "Presenze toscane nella reggenza di Tunisi (1843-1851)", in *Tunisia e Toscana*, Studi a cura di Vittorio A. Salvadorini, Pisa, Edistudio, 2002, pp. 433-484.

[26] L. Levy, *La Nation Juive, op. cit.*, p. 337; R. Caty – E. Richard, "Contribution à l'étude du monde du négoce marseillais de 1815 à 1870 l'apport des successions", *Revue Historique*, 536, 1980, pp. 337-360; S. Fettah, "Temps et espaces des trafics portuaires en Méditerranée. Le cas du port franc de Livourne (XVII-XIX siècles)", *Ricerche Storiche*, 1998, pp. 243-273; D. Pennacchio, "Ebrei fra Livorno e altri porti del Mediterraneo secondo i registri delle emigrazioni dell'Archivio Storico della Comunità Israelitica", in *Studi Mediterranei ed extraeuropei*, Pisa, Edistudio, 2002, pp. 221-246, pp. 240-242.

[27] D. Pennacchio, *op. cit.*, pp. 237-238, gives a number of 111 Jews leaving Leghorn for Alexandria in 1854, and a number of 133 for 1865 for a total number of 1370 with a large majority of professionals. On Alexandria we only refer to *Alexandrie 1860-1960, un modèle éphémère de convivialité. Communautés et identité cosmopolite*, (R. Ilbert, I. Yannakakis, J. Hassoun eds.), Paris, Autrement, 1992; D. Amicucci, "La Comunità italiana in Egitto attraverso i censimenti dal 1882 al 1947", in *Tradizione e*

explore about families and individuals coming to Leghorn before the 1841 census or leaving the city in the fifties, especially towards Egypt, or later, in the years of the opening of the Suez canal and of the closure of the *portofranco* in Leghorn. The files of the present Jewish community, as well as those of the *Archivio della Camera di Commercio*, of the Leghorn *Archivio di Stato* and *Archivio del Comune* provide material for investigating displacements or repeated travels of rabbis, entrepreneurs, "*négociants*", money-changers, speculators and jobbers, affluent bankers or simple craftsmen, retailers, importers, wholesale merchants or small "*négociants de nouveautés*" moving alone or with some members of their own families towards Tunis (but also Susa and Sfax), Algiers, Marseilles, Alexandria and Cairo. Fewer moved towards Gibraltar, Izmir, Saloniki and. Costantinople[28]. Before and after 1861 consular representatives in Aleppo, Algiers, Bordeaux, Bona, Frankfurt, Saloniki, Tunis and Cagliari were generally Leghorn Jews[29]. London, Amsterdam and Manchester, within the frame of a century-long Portuguese circulation, were reserved for coral, diamonds and cotton traders at the highest levels. The Francos, the De Medinas, the Mocattas, the De Castros, influent representatives of the London Sephardi community, had members of their families stationed in India, Marseilles, Amsterdam and Leghorn, as recorded in the East India Company books, where exports and imports of coral and diamonds were registered in the name of London, i.e. Livornese, agents[30]. The immigration of affluent Livornese Jews to London at the end of the 18th century produced a little known relation between the London community and the Leghorn rabbinical school: Leghorn rabbis in fact were in charge of the London Sephardi Bevis Marks Synagogue for more than two centuries[31]. Supported by

---

modernizzazione in Egitto, (P. Branca ed.), Milano, F. Angeli, 2000, pp. 81-94. As for migrations from other countries *cf.* Y. Kerem, "The Migration and Settlement of Jews from the Greek Peninsula in Egypt in the 19th and 20th centuries", *Conference Bar Ilan University*, January 2004; E. Ya'akov, "Yemenite Jews in Egypt", *ibid.*; on Aleppan or "Damascene Jews" from Syria see Y. Harel, "Identification of Syrian Jews in Egypt", *ibid.*

[28] D. Penacchio, who has mainly focused her research on the first half of the 19th century, gives smaller numbers for Gibraltar, Malta, Costantinople, Izmir, Saloniki.

[29] *Indicatore generale del commercio, delle arti, op. cit.*, 1858, p. 5. See also R. Ayoun, "Les Juifs livournais en Afrique du Nord", *RMI*, L, 1984, pp. 650-706.

[30] G. Yogev, *Diamonds and Coral. Anglo-Dutch Jews and Eighteenth Century Trade*, Leicester Univ. Press, 1978. On Sephardi merchants in Jamaica see M. Arbell, *Portuguese Jews of Jamaica*, Canoe Press Univ., Jamaica, 2002.

[31] C. Roth, "L'elemento italiano nell'ebraismo inglese", *RMI*, XI, 1938, pp. 137-144. Leghorn rabbis were often required as possible resident rabbis at the London Sephardi Synagogue; see. ACELi, f. 24, aff. 96 (1804); f. 28, aff. 59, London, July

family networks, by the so-called *capitolazioni*, the privileges awarded by foreign consuls in the Ottoman Empire, and often by masonic ties[32], Leghorn Jews moved around their sea on different reasons. Some had been followers of Mazzini and Garibaldi since 1840 and kept their republican ideas after 1871; most were successful *négociants* trading in iron mines (Sardinia), leather production and soap, tobacco, silk, coral, cotton and glass. Others were managers, impresarios (Egypt, Tunisia). All were confident and open to progress; they inclined to help local communities by means of schools and charitable and sanitary institutions in line with the century-long tradition of benevolence in the Leghorn community, whose first charities and schools go back to the end of the 17th century. Their journeys, either motivated by business, by need, or on account of new (or renewed) family ties (there were frequent marriages between bourgeois Tunisian girls and Leghorn-born young men, weddings which kept closer families and finance on both sides) are duly noted in the *Registro delle partenze* still available at the Jewish Community Archives; a bride was often chosen among Livornese girls by Alexandria or Costantinople – Leghorn-born residents[33]. After 1865, when Leghorn Jews, by now Italian citizens, asked the Italian local authorities for their passports, the *Mandati per Procure*, located at the Comune di Livorno Archives[34], provide a sort of general picture of the Jewish community abroad in its most affluent as well as in its humblest members: people, goods, commodities move to different destinations with apparent facility inside that Sephardi world, which has been studied with renewed impulse after 1992, five hundred years after the banishment of Jews from Spain.

The nineties mark a turning point as far as attention to the Sephardi heritage is concerned, as any bibliography on Sephardi history shows. The recovery of a rather mythical past in France, the more and more self-assertive presence of Israeli citizens of Sephardi origin in Israeli

---

25th, 1853; London, June 3rd, 5624 [1864] and *Bevis Marks Records*, Oxford-London 1949-1993, I-IV. In 1884 an Italian Hospital open to patients of all confessions, was opened in London thanks to awards from the Italian Ortelli, and members of the Rothschild, Allatini, Arbib, Erlanger, Mocatta, Montagu, Pavia families (see V:l:, XLII, 1894, p. 167).

32 See *infra* F. Conti, pp. 109 ff.

33 ACELi, *Registro dei Matrimoni*, 10 (1858-1863), nn. 23, 38, 42, 47, 50, 52, 53, 70, 108, 120, 121, 124, 125, 131, 158, 161, 174; 11, (1863-1865), 11, 5, 41, 54, 77, 78, 80 etc. See L. Levy, *La Nation Juive Portugaise, op. cit.*; E. Boccara, *La Comunità ebraica portoghese, op. cit.*

34 Leghorn, Archivio del Comune di Livorno [thenceforth ComuneLi], *Mandati per Procure* 5115 (1828-1840), February 15, March 5, June 6, 10, 11; July 9, 1832; Sept., 14, 1840; June 11, 1848; 5116 (1859-63), April 1st, 1846, October 12, 1866, etc.

politics and society, a reaction to the pervasiveness of a militant Islamic culture may have suggested this revival which is evident all over the world. In Italy, few studies in journals have dealt with this subject and a few university dissertations on this topic were defended at the university of Florence as well as at the European University Institute. But, as far as the second half of the 19th century is concerned, we can only refer to the essays of Masi, to the old studies of Michel, to the *Storia degli Ebrei nel Levante* by Attilio Milano or alternatively, to De Felice's *Ebrei in un paese arabo*[35]. The point is that Italian communities, with the exception of Leghorn and possibly of Ancona, are not always and not entirely of Sephardic origin[36] and this partially explains why studies devoted to Italian Jewry have only partially dealt with the specific Sephardi diaspora. We are still waiting for a whole issue of a journal, such as, the 2000 number of the *Revue Française d'Histoire d'Outre Mer* totally devoted to "Les Juifs et la mer" or to a collection of studies such as *La Méditerranée des Juifs*[37].

Our time has suggested the definition of "global diasporas" for the contemporary phenomenon of international migration – an event familiar to any reader of today's papers[38]. However, the diaspora of Jews from Leghorn, though remarkable in number, has nothing to do with today's mobilized and proletarian masses of migrants in search of political refuge or of economic advancement moving from one continent to another. The already mentioned *Registri delle partenze* portray a wide range of individuals leaving Leghorn; far beyond the mere figures, these documents allow us an insight into the religious, legal and family traditions within the community. We find young boys leaving the city, sometimes after their coming of age (at thirteen according to the tradi-

---

[35] C. Masi, "Il Granducato lorenese e i 'livornesi' in Tunisia", *Bollettino Storico Livornese*, I, 1937, pp. 227-256, 381-403; E. Michel, *Esuli italiani in Tunisia (1815-1861)*, Milano, ISPI, 1941; id., *Esuli italiani in Egitto (1815-1861)*, Pisa, Domus Mazziniana, 1985; M. Vernassa, *Il Risorgimento livornese, op. cit.*; A. Milano, *Storia degli Ebrei, op. cit.*; R. De Felice, *Ebrei in un paese arabo. Gli Ebrei nella Libia contemporanea tra colonialismo, nazionalismo arabo e sionismo (1835-1970)*, Bologna, Il Mulino, 1978. See also *RMI*, XLIX, 1983 and *Ebraismo e rapporti con le culture del Mediterraneo nei secoli XVIII-XIX* (M. Contu, N. Melis, G. Pinna eds.), Firenze, La Giuntina, 2003.

[36] R. Toaff, "Livorno, comunità sefardita", *RMI*, XXXVIII, 1972, pp. 203-209; Y. Colombo, "Nostalgia del Sefardismo livornese", *ivi*, pp. 210-216.

[37] *Revue Française d'Histoire d'Outre-Mer*, 87, 2000, 326-327; as reviewed by J. P. Filippini, 88, 2001, pp. 299-328; *La Méditerranée des Juifs. Exodes et Enracinements*, ed. by P. Balta, C. Dana, R. Dhoquois-Cohen, Paris, L'Harmattan, 2003.

[38] R. Cohen, *Global Diasporas. An Introduction*, Seattle, Wash, 1997; J. T. Shuval, "Diaspora Migration Definitional Ambiguities and a Theoretical Paradigm", *International Migration*, 38, 5, 2000, pp. 41-55.

tional Jewish law), sometimes with permission of their parents. They usually moved to find a job or to reach relatives with "casa aperta, famiglia e traffico" abroad[39]. We read of husbands leaving their families only with the consent of their own wives[40]. The Jewish women were given a certain degree of power inside their families according to religious and traditional law; bigamy was not unfrequent and in some cases permitted by rabbinical *responsa*, particularly in Leghorn, but women's rights were safeguarded[41]. We also come in touch with young lawyers or bank clerks, moving from Leghorn to Egypt or Istanbul in the wake of international banks, such as the Hambros or the Camondos; others were on their way to Saloniki and Corfù in connection with the many branches of the Allatini or Modiano, Morpurgo, Fernandes families and business[42]. We equally find carpenters, furniture dealers, workers in all branches leaving Leghorn with or without their own families. They were specially attracted by the great changes in the Egyptian economy and society of the fifties and sixties or they could also have been damaged by the closure of the *portofranco* (1868), a measure which slowly but persistently damaged the economy of the whole city, leading to the reduction of the Jewish presence in their numbers and in the influence they could exert: in 1901 there were 2636 Jews as opposed to about

---

[39] ACELi, *Registro ordinato per lettera delle partenze*, 200, June 15, 1829; 201, May 1st, 1836, May 23rd, 1843; 202, May 13th 1839, October 30, 1849, June 9, 1864; 203, May 9, 1857; *Filza di Mandati* 31, August 14, 1865. There are some cases of widows or single women "libere da vincoli matrimoniali per fatto di divorzio" moving to Alexandria with their children; other women reached their own husbands who had already settled abroad.

[40] ACELi, *Registro ordinato per lettera delle partenze*, 202, August 22 1833, May 13, 1839, June 9, 1864; *ivi*, f. 31, 14 agosto 1865.

[41] C. Galasso, "La moglie duplicata. Bigamia e levirato nella comunità ebraica di Livorno (secolo xvii)", in *Trasgressioni. Seduzione, concubinato, adulterio, bigamia (XIV-XVIII secoli)* (a cura di S. Seidel Menchi e D. Quaglioni), Bologna, Il Mulino, 2004, pp. 417-441. On the role of women in the Jewish family tradition see L. Allegra, *Alle origini del mito della Jewish Momie. Ruoli economici e ideali domestici delle ebree italiane nell'età moderna. Le donne delle minoranze : le ebree e le protestanti d'Italia* (C. E. Honess and V. R. Jones eds.), Torino, Claudiana, 1999, pp. 243-254. On the Sephardic family see J. Bahloul, *La famille sépharade dans la diaspora du XXe siècle*, *La société juive à travers l'histoire* (S. Trigano ed.), Paris, Fayard, 1992, Vol. 4; II, pp. 469-496.

[42] E. Benbassa-A. Rodrigue, *Storia degli Ebrei sefarditi, op. cit.*; P. Dumont, *La structure sociale, op. cit.*; D. S. Landes, *Banchieri e pascià, op. cit.*, pp. 87, 348. As for the Italian contemporary press see *V. I.*, 1880, p. 195; 1905, pp. 145, 195-197, 207, 424, 430, 480 and No. 12. On the displacements of Jews towards Egypt in the fifties and sixties from Makedonia and Greece see Y. Kerem, *The Migration and Settlement, op. cit.*; on the movings from Yemen towards Egypt see E. Ya'akov, *Yemenite Jews, op. cit.* On the shifting of poor Leghorn Jews to Tripoli about 1840 see D. Pennacchio, *op. cit.*

5000 during the 19th century. A special section of this diaspora is reserved to Leghorn doctors. Born in Leghorn, they usually graduated at Pisa or Siena Universities and left their city in the wake of the few pioneer Italian and Franch doctors, who had been active in Egypt and Tunisia since 1827. Together with chemists and some midwives they fought against extreme conditions of plague, poverty and distress in Tunisian poor quarters, in Egyptian hospitals and in Palestinian orphanages[43]. Confident in progress, open to modern French medical culture, Jewish doctors were excellent observers and organizers of sanitary institutions in Alexandria, in Tunis, in Corfù between 1860 and 1890, well before local Jews could attend French or Italian universities. At least eight of them were active in the Mediterranean area; one of them, Dr. Castelnuovo, was one of the personal doctors of the Bey and of the King of Italy. The *Ospedale Italiano* (later *Ospedale Garibaldi*) in Tunis (1895) was founded and directed by doctors coming from Leghorn, who assisted patients regardless of their faith, whether Christian, Muslim or Jewish; the Alexandria Hospital, as well as the Soloniki one, were renowned all over the Mediterranean[44]. Italian-Jewish doctors shared the humanitarian medical tendency of the 19th century. In this sense they were responsible for studies and remedies for a number of Mediterranean endemic diseases and could in this line cooperate with the teachers who left for Tunisia (1862), for Beirut, for Istanbul, for Egypt (1856), Corfu (1877), but also for Volo (Thessalia) (1880) or Saloniki (1873) from the sixties onwards[45]. Some were sent to found rabbinical, but also secular and practical schools, whose model were the celebrated *Scuole Pie* of the Leghorn community; some were employed in the schools of the *Alliance Israélite Universelle*, the great French scholarly institution present all over the Mediterranean after 1862; some, as Moisé Allatini (1809-1882) were in charge of local sections of the *Alliance* apart from being a doctor, a successful entrepreneur and a benefactor[46]. But

---

43 S. Speziale, *Oltre la peste. Sanità, popolazione e società in Tunisia e nel Maghreb (XVIII-XX secolo)*, Cosenza, L. Pellegrini, 1997.

44 E. Bigiavi, *Noi e l'Egitto, op. cit.*, pp. 78-81; L. Levy, *La Nation Juive, op. cit.*, pp. 45, 47; S. Speziale, *Oltre la peste, op. cit.*; *Alexandrie, op. cit.* On the Saloniki Hospital see *V. I.*, XLII, 1894, p. 366; *Corriere Israelitico*, XXIX, 1890, pp. 201-203.

45 M. G. Ottolenghi [a teacher from Leghorn leaving for Volo, Thessalia] to "Signori Amministratori e Deputati del Culto e Beneficenza dell'Università Israelitica di Livorno, Livorno, March 24, 1869, ACELi, f. 32, 1869.

46 A. Rodrigue, *De l'instruction à l'émancipation. Les enseignants de l'Alliance Israélite Universelle et les Juifs d'Orient, 1860-1937*, Paris, Calmann-Lévy, 1989; E. Benbassa-A. Rodrigue, *Storia degli Ebrei sefarditi, op. cit.* Moisé Allatini born in Saloniki, studied medicine at Pisa and Florence University. A doctor and a successful entrepreneur in his native country, he married in Leghorn in 1838, then moved back to Saloniki where he set a charity for poor boys, then a non-religious school. As a

whether doctors, teachers or successful traders abroad, and as ancient students assisted by the Leghorn Community charities in their youth, they never forgot the city and the community where they had been brought up. They always acted as potential mediators between the old and new countries throughout their life; they made frequent visits to their native city, subterranean links with the city and with the culture of their origins across generations.

The diaspora of Jews from Leghorn is in fact a multifaceted and a two-way diaspora. The Arbibs, the Franchettis, the Chayes had come to Leghorn at the end of the 18th century to establish a new branch for their trade and in a couple of generations they had become among the most powerful bankers in town[47]. However, after the closure of the *porto-franco* and the general crisis which followed, Leghorn was no longer a place for entrepreneurs or bold merchants and most of the affluent families had moved to Pisa, Florence and Milan. At the end of the 19th century relations with Saloniki became weaker, owing to the unrest of the local communities pressed by different and clashing nationalisms[48]. On African shores in the same years some Jews from Tunis or Alexandria could range between the local ruling classes and *élites*. They could afford sending their sons to the University of Pisa or, more frequently, to French institutions. They could rent villas around Leghorn; they used to leave Tunisia or Egypt on special family celebrations or during the recurrent epidemics, while their housekeepers kept an eye on their properties, safely placed in French, London or, sometimes, Egyptian banks.

---

general president of the local *Comité* of the *Alliance*, he also established schools destined to Saloniki young people, whether Jews, Greek or Turkish. He died in 1882 as an Italian subject: see "Cronica" 179, 2002 reproducing *Journal de l'Orient*, 1887. See also *V. I.*, 1879, p. 317; 1880, pp. 52, 158-160; 1883, pp. 289-291; on the *Alliance* schools in Saloniki. *V. I.*, 1880, pp. 122-124.

47 On the two-way diaspora see J. P. Filippini, *La Nazione ebrea, op. cit.* On the Arbib family, original of Tripoli, see B. Nunes Vais Arib, R. Ciorli, *Scali Manzoni 51* (A. Pecchioli Tomassi ed.), Pisa, Pacini, 1995; M. T. Lazzarini, *L'Oriente a Livorno nell'Ottocento, L'Orientalismo nell'architettura italiana tra Ottocento e Novecento* (M. A. Giusti, E. Godoli eds.), pp. 83-96; M. Sanacore, *Il percorso interrotto. Il pluralismo etnico, religioso e politico nel sistema industriale livornese. La storia e le immagini (1865-1940)*, Pisa, Sybel, 2003. On the Franchetti family see M. Scardozzi, "Una storia di famiglia : I Franchetti dalle coste del Mediterraneo all'Italia liberale", *Quaderni Storici*, 114, 2003, pp. 697-740. The Chayes had moved from Spain to Poland and later to Leghorn to become among the most important traders in coral; see E. Gelles, "Chief rabbis in the genes", *Manna*, 2000, pp. 34-36.

48 P. Dumont, *La structure, op. cit.*; E. Benbassa-A Rodrigue, *Storia degli Ebrei sefarditi, op. cit.*; Y. Kerem, *The Multicultural Background, op. cit.*

Yet, no matter how multinational or international they became, Italy and the Leghorn Jewish community did not disappear from their personal and professional horizon. Jews from Tunisia, Egypt and Libia volunteered in first World War[49]; some established scholarships for poor students born in Leghorn, both Jews and Catholic. In this way they kept alive that special attention to the needs of the whole city which had been a distinctive feature of the history of the Jewish community of Leghorn. As late as 1939 the *Fondazione Dr. Gustavo Valensin Pascià*, a rich physician from Egypt, awarded fellowships to young Livornese[50]. In the same year the Racial Laws obliged the community to found a special school for young Jews in Leghorn[51]. The school was attended also by many children from Smirne, Saloniki, Rhodes, Sofia, Trieste, Istanbul, whose conditions of poverty and general distress were carefully noted by their Leghorn teachers in the *Registri della Scuola Elementare Ebraica* from 1939 to 1943, which are still available[52]. Unfortunately those children were not spared the fate of their own communities, erased in second World War; most were in fact deported with their own families from Italy[53]. After 1945, though the community had become very small, the century-long renown of charities and benevolence of the Leghorn community attracted refugees from Egypt in 1956, from Tunis in 1967 and from Libia in 1971[54].

---

[49] A. Milano, G. Bedarida, "Ebrei d'Italia", in *Convegno gli ebrei nelle forze armate a Livorno*, 2003; S. Minerbi, "L'azione diplomatica italiana nei confronti degli ebrei sefarditi durante e dopo la Ia guerra mondiale", *RMI*, XIL, 1981, pp. 86-119.

[50] ComuneLi, *Comune Post Unitario, Bilanci Preventivi*, 241-242, (1926), *Municipio*, 55, 11 novembre 1939-xviii, *Dr. Gustavo Valensin Pascià*, ("5 posti di studio").

[51] See Regio-Decreto-Legge 5 settembre 1938-XVI, No. 1390: *Provvedimenti per la difesa della razza nella scuola fascista*; *1938 – La Scuola ebraica di Livorno. Un'alternativa alle leggi razziali*, Museo Ebraico, Yeshivà Marini, Comunità Ebraica di Livorno, 1997.

[52] ACELi, *Giornali di classe delle Scuole Israelitiche*, classi I, II, III, IV, V, a. s. 1939-40, 1940-41, 1941-42 etc. See E. Fintz Menasce, "Gli Ebrei a Rodi. Storia di una comunità che viveva "in perfetta armonia con le altre nazionii", in *Ebraismo e rapporti con le culture del Mediterraneo, op. cit.*, pp. 27-78; M. Sakiroglu, "Presenza ebraica in Turchia dalla Prima Guerra Mondiale alla creazione dello Stato d'Israele", *ivi*, pp. 107-116; H. Asseo, "Du miel aux cendres. Où sont passés soixante-dix mille Juifs de Salonique ?", *Les Temps Modernes*, 1979, p. 400, pp. 828-845.

[53] See *Il Libro della Memoria. Gli ebrei toscani deportati nei campi di sterminio*, Regione Toscana, Giunta Regionale, Firenze, 2003.

[54] ASLi, *Sussidi straordinari dati ai profughi, Sussidi ordinari ai profughi, Prefettura* 222, 224, [1971; to refugees from Egypt, Libya, Tunis, Tripoli, Rhodes, Izmir]. Most among them still retained Italian citizenship and were reckoned as "connazionali rimpatriati dall'Egitto". See L. Picciotto, *Gli ebrei in Libia, op. cit.*, pp. 79-106. See also S. Varsano, "Ebrei di Salonicco immigrati a Napoli 1917-1940, una testimonianza", *Storia Contemporanea*, XXIII, 1992, pp. 119-135.

I would like to conclude these brief notes on the migrations and travels of the Jews from Leghorn with a Mediterranean note taken from the *Romancero Sephardi*, the large collection of popular songs typical of the Sephardi heritage and transmitted by women throughout generations. "Mi padre era de Francia/ Mi Madre de Aragòn/ Yo ero regalada [only child]/ De chica me cazò [I was married as a young girl]/ Me cazò con un Franco/ Venido de Estambol/ El duerme en la cama/ En la 'sterica yo" [he sleeps in his bed, I sleep on the floor][55].

It can be considered as a rigmarole. It can be read it as an indication of gender roles. Alternatively, it can also be seen as a testimonial, however small, to the exceptional mobility of Jewish families across the Ottoman Empire, that continent that British Foreign Officers, tinged with Oxonian Orientalism, used to call "the changeless East".

---

[55] *Romancero Sephardi. Chants judéo-espagnols recueillis et notés par Isaac Levy*, World Sephardi Federation, London, s.d., p. 4. See also *Repertorio tradicional infantil sefardì*, Madrid, Compañia literaria S. L. Padilla, 2001; S. G. Armistead & J. H. Silverman, "The traditional balladry of the Sephardic Jews; a collaborative research project", *RMI*, XLIX, 1983, *op. cit.*, pp. 641-667 ; N. Wachtel, *La foi du souvenir. Labyrinthes marranes*, Paris, Seuil, 2001, p. 107.

Entre Orient et Occident

Les loges maçonniques du Grand Orient d'Italie en Méditerranée entre les XIXe et XXe siècles

Fulvio CONTI

Université de Florence

1. Les premières loges maçonniques furent fondées en Italie vers 1730 et elles se diffusèrent rapidement dans les principales villes de la péninsule. Durement combattues par l'Église catholique, qui dès fin 1738 menaça d'excommunier quiconque y appartenait, elles devinrent un instrument important de diffusion des idéaux des Lumières, de liberté et de tolérance[1]. Après les difficultés de la fin du XVIIIe siècle, lorsque les souverains des anciens États italiens virent en elles le lieu d'incubation des principes révolutionnaires et en décrétèrent la dissolution, les loges connurent alors une phase de grand essor durant l'époque napoléonienne. Suite aux processus d'unification politique et administrative auxquels on assistait en Italie en cette période, en 1805 naquit même une première organisation maçonnique au niveau national qui prit le nom de Grand Orient d'Italie[2]. De nouveau mise au ban au moment de la Restauration, car identifiée comme une instigation à la subversion et une menace contre l'ordre politique existant, la franc-maçonnerie ne réapparut que vers fin 1859, après la conclusion victorieuse de la seconde

---

[1] Sur les origines de la franc-maçonnerie en Italie, l'ouvrage de C. Francovich demeure fondamental, *Storia della Massoneria in Italia. Dalle origini alla Rivoluzione francese*, Florence, La Nuova Italia, 1974. De façon plus générale sur la franc-maçonnerie du dix-septième siècle, *cf.* G. Giarrizzo, *Massoneria e illuminismo nell'Europa del Settecento*, Venise, Marsilio, 1994 ; et M. C. Jacob, *Massoneria illuminata. Politica e cultura nell'Europa del Settecento*, Turin, Einaudi, 1995.

[2] Sur la présence franc-maçonne à l'époque napoléonienne, les chapitres dédiés à l'Italie sont à voir dans F. Collaveri, *La Franc-maçonnerie des Bonaparte*, Paris, Pajot, 1982 ; et E. Stopler, « Contributo alla storia della massoneria italiana nell'era napoleonica », *Rivista massonica*, 1977, n° 3, pp. 153-160, et n° 4, pp. 215-237, 1979, n° 6, pp. 269-297. Voir aussi A. A. Mola (ed.), *Libertà e modernizzazione. Massoni in Italia nell'età napoleonica*, Foggia, Bastogi, 1996.

guerre d'indépendance, coïncidant de façon significative avec la naissance du Règne d'Italie.

Dans l'Italie unie, à la différence de ce qu'il advint dans les pays anglo-saxons et par analogie en revanche au cas français et à celui espagnol, la franc-maçonnerie eut une vocation politique prononcée et un rôle important dans la vie publique du pays[3]. Politiquement orientée dans un sens démocratique et progressiste, elle s'engagea directement dans les batailles pour la défense de l'État laïc contre le légitimisme clérical, pour l'élargissement des droits de citoyenneté (le suffrage universel, l'émancipation de la femme, le divorce, l'abolition de la peine de mort), pour l'amélioration des conditions sociales et politiques des classes populaires, surtout à travers l'instruction et l'associationnisme. De nombreuses et illustres personnalités politiques appartinrent à la franc-maçonnerie – outre la principale icône du *Risorgimento* national, Giuseppe Garibaldi –, parmi lesquelles plusieurs présidents du Conseil (Depretis, Crispi, Zanardelli, Fortis), ministres et parlementaires. Certainement pas comparable à un véritable parti, comme le soutint Antonio Gramsci en 1925, elle recueillit des affiliés dans une vaste aire politique qui allait des libéraux aux socialistes en passant par les radicaux et les républicains. L'adhésion au front interventionniste en 1914 et, par la suite, la défense de la guerre et des valeurs patriotiques en 1919-1920 rapprochèrent la franc-maçonnerie même au mouvement fasciste, qui, toutefois dès 1923, se détacha d'elle. En 1925, au moment où Mussolini commençait la construction de l'État totalitaire, il la déclara hors-la-loi. Pour le Grand Orient d'Italie et pour les autres institutions maçonniques de la péninsule commença alors une nouvelle période de difficultés, durant laquelle de nombreux francs-maçons furent condamnés à la prison, assignés à résidence surveillée ou bien obligés à l'exil. Et c'est seulement à l'étranger (d'abord à Londres, puis à Paris), durant l'entre-deux-guerres, qu'un Grand Orient d'Italie put se reconstituer, cherchant à maintenir vive la tradition maçonnique.

2. Durant l'âge d'or de la franc-maçonnerie – celui de l'Italie libérale, entre 1860 et 1922 –, la principale organisation, c'est-à-dire le Grand Orient d'Italie, eut un nombre de loges qui oscillait entre 100 et 150 les premières années de l'Unité et entre 400 et 450 durant les deux premières décennies du XXe siècle. Des cinq à six mille inscrits de la phase originaire, elle dépassa les vingt mille en 1914. Ainsi, une contribution consistante aux capacités d'organisation de cette institution, que

---

[3] Sur la franc-maçonnerie dans l'Italie unie, je ne signale que A. A. Mola, *Storia della Massoneria italiana dalle origini ai nostri giorni*, Milan, Bompiani, 1992 ; et F. Conti, *Storia della massoneria italiana. Dal Risorgimento al fascismo*, Bologna, Il Mulino, 2003.

ce soit en termes de loges que d'inscrits, vint des structures constituées hors des frontières nationales et, en particulier, par celles situées dans les pays de la Méditerranée et de l'Amérique latine. Sur environ soixante dix mille noms affiliés au Grand Orient entre la fin du XIXe siècle et 1923, près de neuf mille appartenaient à des loges fondées à l'étranger[4].

Ce rayonnement de la franc-maçonnerie italienne dans le bassin méditerranéen commença tout de suite après l'Unité, s'il est vrai que déjà lors de la première assemblée constituante du Grand Orient d'Italie, qui eut lieu à Turin en décembre 1861, participèrent trois loges égyptiennes (la *Iside* et la *Pompeia* d'Alexandrie et la *Eliopolis* du Caire) et une de Tunis dénommée *Figli scelti di Cartagine e Utica*[5]. À l'époque de l'assemblée maçonnique de Florence en août 1863, le nombre des loges étrangères s'avérait plus élevé[6] : à Alexandrie avait été créée une troisième loge, la *Cajo Gracco*, et une seconde au Caire, la *Alleanza de' popoli*. Fut en outre constituée la loge *Italia* à Constantinople, avant-garde d'une présence maçonnique en Turquie, destinée à jouer un rôle public particulièrement important, alors qu'une seconde loge était née aussi à Tunis, la *Attilio Regolo*, et une autre, la *Figli di Leonida*, avait vu le jour à Syra, en Grèce (même dans ce cas, il s'agissait du premier élément d'un foyer de loges helléniques, qui quelques années plus tard abandonnaient le Grand Orient d'Italie pour donner vie à une obédience franc-maçonne grecque autonome)[7].

La constituante maçonnique, qui eut lieu à Florence en 1864 et vit l'élection de Giuseppe Garibaldi au poste de grand maître, enregistra une expansion ultérieure, pour la plupart localisée en Turquie[8]. Outre la loge *Panellenico* d'Athènes, on eut cette année-là la constitution des loges *Macedonia* de Salonique et *Stella Jonia* de Smyrne, qui préparèrent le terrain pour une prolifération des organisations francs-

---

[4] Pour un développement plus détaillé de l'organisation de la franc-maçonnerie italienne et de la répartition géographique des loges en Italie et à l'étranger, *cf.* F. Conti, *Storia della massoneria italiana, op. cit.*

[5] *Cf. Lux. Sunto del protocollo dei lavori della prima costituente massonica italiana,* Valle di Torino, 5861, [Torino, 1862].

[6] *Cf. Protocollo dei lavori della terza assemblea costituente massonica italiana tenuta in Firenze il 1, 2, 3, 4, 5, 6 del 6° mese dell'anno 5863 della Vera Luce,* s.l., Tip. dei Franco Muratori, [1863].

[7] *Cf.* « Creazione del Grande Oriente Ellenico », *Bollettino del Grande Oriente della massoneria in Italia,* Vol. II, 1867, pp. 113-120.

[8] *Cf. Protocollo dei lavori dell'assemblea generale costituente della massoneria italiana tenuta in Firenze nei giorni 21, 22 e 23 del 3° mese dell'anno 5864 della Vera Luce,* s.l., Tip. dei Franco Muratori, [1864].

maçonnes. Entre 1867 et 1873 naquirent en effet huit autres loges[9] : trois à Smyrne, dont la *Fenice* réservée aux Grecs, la *Orkanie* aux Turcs et la *Armenak* aux Arméniens[10] ; trois à Constantinople, dénommées *Fenice*, *Sincerità* et *Speranza*, lesquelles par ailleurs en 1868, à cause du faible nombre d'adhérents, se fondit dans la loge *Tre in Una* ; une autre, la *Luce d'Oriente*, à Büyük Dere, un petit village situé sur la rive européenne du Bosphore, proche de la capitale de l'Empire ; et enfin, une fondée à Magnesia, au nord de Smyrne, et dédiée à Anacleto Cricca, maître vénérable de la *Stella Jonia*, de laquelle cette loge en était directement le fruit[11].

Justement, Anacleto Cricca représente une figure emblématique pour comprendre dans quels milieux sociaux et culturels naquirent ces loges et quelles finalités elles entendaient poursuivre. Médecin et fervent patriote originaire de Bologne, il fuit l'Italie en 1849 après la chute des Républiques de Rome et Venise et, avec Daniele Manin et Niccolò Tommaseo, se réfugia à Corfou. De là, il se rendit à Smyrne où, toujours en 1849, il fonda un Comité d'émigration, dans lequel confluèrent de nombreux exilés politiques impliqués dans les mouvements révolutionnaires et persécutés par les polices des gouvernements restaurés[12]. Les villes de l'Empire ottoman – de l'Asie mineure jusqu'en Égypte – représentèrent en effet une des destinations préférées de l'émigration politique du *Risorgimento*, qui allait ainsi gonfler les rangs de la communauté italienne jusque-là composée tout au plus de commerçants et d'expéditionnaires de tous bords, d'artisans, de professions libérales, d'artistes et d'une poignée de bureaucrates et de fonctionnaires gouvernementaux. Ce fut au sein de ces groupes sociaux que la franc-maçonnerie puisa ses propres affiliés, auxquels elle offrit tout d'abord un lieu de rencontre et de sociabilité, et donc différentes formes d'aide et de protection, mais aussi un instrument pour conserver un lien idéal avec la mère patrie et cultiver un sentiment d'appartenance à la lointaine communauté nationale.

L'idéal et les typologies de l'engagement des loges méditerranéennes ne furent pas bien différents de ceux des consœurs italiennes. Outre à

---

[9] *Cf.* « Elenco generale delle logge e corpi massonici appartenenti alla comunione nazionale italiana », *Rivista della massoneria italiana*, 15 mars 1873.

[10] *Cf.* « Smirne », *Rivista della massoneria italiana*, 15 juillet 1872.

[11] *Cf.* « Le logge italiane in Oriente », *Bollettino del Grande Oriente della massoneria in Italia*, Vol. II (1867), pp. 184-188.

[12] À ce propos, voir le chapitre de Ersilio Michel dans *Dizionario del Risorgimento nazionale*, (M. Rosi, ed.), Milano, Vallardi, 1933, Vol. II, p. 777 ; et du même, « Esuli italiani nelle isole ionie (1849) », *Rassegna storica del Risorgimento*, XXXVII, 1950, fasc. 1-4, pp. 323-352.

pratiquer une régulière activité à caractère philanthropique, elles se mobilisèrent à l'occasion d'épidémies ou de calamités naturelles pour secourir les populations locales. Elles promurent en outre la création de structures mutualistes, éducatives et d'assistance, dont les bénéfices s'élargissaient même aux profanes. Ainsi, par exemple, en 1863, la loge *Alleanza dei popoli* du Caire réussit par ses propres moyens à aménager un petit « hôpital franc-maçon » avec dix lits et lança le projet d'un « Collège international ». Son vénérable, le docteur E. Rossi, était un notable de la ville et, décoré du titre de « bey », était devenu le médecin personnel du prince[13]. En 1864, la loge *Italia* de Constantinople institua en revanche une école élémentaire pour les enfants pauvres, sans distinction de nationalité, qui dès la première année fut fréquentée par 42 élèves. Ces derniers demeuraient à l'école de neuf heures à quatre heures de l'après-midi et, en plus de l'instruction, ils recevaient trois fois par semaine du pain et de la soupe de légumes. Pour en financer l'activité, elle organisa des foires et des spectacles de bienfaisance, où lors d'une de ces occasions, en janvier 1865, on vit même la participation de la compagnie théâtrale de la célèbre actrice Adélaïde Ristori[14].

Un autre outil auquel les loges eurent recours pour recueillir des fonds destinés aux diverses activités philanthropiques furent les banquets, forme typique de sociabilité informelle du XIXe siècle[15]. Ils représentèrent aussi le moyen de consolider les rapports avec la communauté locale et d'établir un réseau de relations, pouvant être utilisé par la suite par les « frères », les membres de la loge, dans les domaines les plus divers : économiques, sociaux et politiques. Anacleto Cricca décrit ainsi un banquet organisé à Smyrne par la loge *Stella Jonia* :

> À cette table étaient assis fraternellement des hommes de toutes races et de toutes religions, italiens et allemands, français et anglais, européens et turcs,

---

[13] *Cf. Bollettino officiale del Grande Oriente Italiano*, Vol. I, 1863, pp. 152-153 ; et « Loggia Alleanza dei popoli », *ibid.*, pp. 232-233. Sur la présence de la franc-maçonnerie italienne en Égypte, voir A. A. Mola, « Le logge "italiane" in Egitto dall'Unità al fascismo », in R. H. Rainero et L. Serra (dir.), *L'Italia e l'Egitto dalla rivolta di Arabì Pascià all'avvento del fascismo (1882-1922)*, Milano, Marzorati, 1991, pp. 187-205.

[14] *Cf.* « Una protesta », *Bollettino del Grande Oriente della massoneria in Italia*, Vol. I, 1865, pp. 210-211 ; et « Le Scuole laiche italiane a Costantinopoli e la R.L. Italia risorta », *Rivista della massoneria italiana*, 1890, n° 11-12, pp. 181 ss. Pour une plus ample confrontation, voir A. Iacovella, « La massoneria italiana in Turchia : la loggia "Italia risorta" di Costantinopoli (1867-1923) », *Studi emigrazione/Études Migrations*, XXIII, 1996, n° 123, pp. 393-416.

[15] Pour certaines références, voir R. Romanelli, « Depretis a Stradella. Il successo politico misurato a tavola », *Storia e Dossier*, II, 1987, n° 11, pp. 11-14 ; et R. Balzani, « Il banchetto patriottico : una "tradizione" risorgimentale forlivese », in F. Tarozzi et A. Varni (dir.), *Il tempo libero nell'Italia unita*, Bologna, Clueb, 1992, pp. 21-33.

il y avait les représentants de chaque grande église chrétienne, auprès des fils de la Synagogue étaient assis des disciples de Mahomet[16].

Cette ouverture vers l'extérieur, vers les différents groupes ethniques et religieux de la ville, constitua un élément caractéristique de la présence maçonnique italienne dans les régions bordant la Méditerranée. En effet, les loges n'accueillaient pas que des citoyens italiens. Au contraire, dès le début, elles ouvrirent leurs portes aux diverses composantes des populations locales et elles se distinguèrent donc par une connotation cosmopolite marquée, typique par ailleurs de la franc-maçonnerie des origines, celle élitaire du XVIIIe siècle, mais qui s'était perdue progressivement au cours du siècle suivant, quand les organisations maçonniques – en Italie mais pas seulement – avaient pris une physionomie toujours plus provinciale et localiste[17]. Le vénérable de la loge *Alleanza dei popoli* du Caire, dans une lettre du mois d'avril 1863, illustrait ainsi la ligne suivie jusque-là dans l'œuvre de prosélytisme :

> Dans notre propagande, nous avons cherché à convertir des indigènes. C'est la même chose que de se dire que notre action choisit les meilleurs de ceux-ci. Ils seront pour nous un moyen puissant pour vulgariser les principes francs-maçons chez les Égyptiens et, si d'un côté, il était un devoir sacro-saint que de restituer aux Égyptiens ces mêmes lumières qu'ils nous transmirent, de l'autre, il s'agissait de se servir d'une arme de bonne trempe pour abattre l'ignorance et le fanatisme qui oppriment ce peuple depuis tant de siècles[18].

Cricca, dans un rapport adressé au grand maître Giuseppe Mazzoni en 1872, déclarait que dans les loges de Smyrne étaient représentées toutes les nationalités et qu'on y comptait à peine neuf citoyens italiens[19]. En parcourant la liste des affiliés à la loge *Italia risorta* de Constantinople, fondée en 1867 et active jusqu'en 1923, on découvre que les Italiens en cette longue période représentèrent moins de dix pour cent, alors qu'était beaucoup plus important le groupe des Turcs, des Arabes, des Grecs, des Arméniens, avec également une présence signifi-

---

[16] « Banchetto a Smirne », *Bollettino del Grande Oriente della massoneria in Italia*, Vol. I, 1865, p. 209.

[17] Souligné par J.-P. Viallet, « Anatomie d'une obédience maçonnique : le Grand-Orient d'Italie (1870-1890 circa) », in *Mélanges de l'École française de Rome, Moyen Âge – Temps modernes*, t. 90, 1978, n° 1, pp. 171-237.

[18] *Bollettino officiale del Grande Oriente Italiano*, Vol. I, 1863, p. 153.

[19] *Cf.* « Smirne », *Rivista della massoneria italiana*, 15 juillet 1872. Sur la communauté italienne à Smyrne, *cf.* L. Missir di Lusignano, « La collettività italiana di Smirne », *Storia contemporanea*, XXII, 1990, n° 1, pp. 147-172 ; et M.-C. Smyrnelis, « Gli italiani a Smirne nei secoli XVIII e XIX », *Altreitalie*, VI, 1994, n° 12, pp. 39-59.

cative des Allemands, des Russes, des Polonais et des Slaves[20]. Les loges reflétaient donc le caractère cosmopolite des villes de l'Afrique septentrionale et de l'Asie mineure, et constituaient un lieu de rencontre précieux, où le traditionnel esprit de tolérance et l'agnosticisme en matière religieuse de la franc-maçonnerie créaient les conditions idéales pour lier de fécondes relations parmi les affiliés.

Quant au lien avec l'Italie et à la décision d'adhérer à ce Grand Orient plutôt qu'à celui de France ou bien à la Grande Loge d'Angleterre, qui avaient déjà de solides bases dans la région, on peut affirmer qu'un rôle important en ce sens a été joué par les communautés italiennes de religion juive[21]. Parmi les inscrits aux loges tunisiennes, égyptiennes et ottomanes, le nombre des Juifs séfarades était très élevé, et ils conservaient traditionnellement d'étroits rapports avec les familles et les groupes italiens dont ils étaient issus[22]. Rien que dans la capitale ottomane, par exemple, le recensement de 1871 signalait 4 733 citoyens italiens, dont 709 étaient Juifs ; tandis qu'à Salonique, sur 1 336 habitants de nationalité italienne, les Hébreux étaient au nombre de 472[23], alors qu'en Égypte en 1897, ils représentaient de loin le groupe le plus nombreux (17,8 %) derrière celui de religion catholique[24].

Les liens avec l'Italie trouvaient par la suite leur confirmation dans la pleine syntonie des idées, qui régnait parmi les loges d'outre-mer et le Grand Orient sur certains des grands principes, autours desquels tournait l'engagement maçonnique dans la vie publique : avant tout la pleine adhésion à la cause de l'indépendance nationale, vue comme le préliminaire indispensable pour réaliser une véritable fraternité des peuples libres et, ensuite, un laïcisme qui très souvent débordait en un rigide anticléricalisme. Ces sentiments étaient bien résumés dans un discours prononcé au printemps 1863 par Sansone Terni, membre de la loge

---

[20] *Cf.* A. Iacovella, « La massoneria italiana in Turchia », *op. cit.*, pp. 408 ss.

[21] Sur les rapports entre franc-maçonnerie et Juifs, je me limite à signaler J. Katz, *Jews and Freemasons in Europe, 1723-1939*, Cambridge (Mass.), Harward UP, 1970 ; et L. Nefontaine, J.-P. Schreiber, *Judaïsme et franc-maçonnerie. Histoire d'une fraternité*, Paris, Albin Michel, 2000.

[22] Sur la période initiale du XXe siècle, on peut trouver quelques informations dans E. Enriquez del Arbol, « Masoneria y diaspora Sefardi en el siglo XX : el origen de las logias otomanas (1907-1909) », in *Masoneria Española y America*, V Symposyum Internacional de Historia de la Masoneria Española, Caceres, 16-20 juin 1991, Zaragoza, Cehme, 1993, pp. 551-590.

[23] A. Milano, *Storia degli ebrei italiani nel Levante*, Firenze, Casa editrice Israel, 1949, pp. 187 ss.

[24] D. Amicucci, « La comunità italiana in Egitto attraverso i censimenti dal 1882 al 1947 », in P. Branca (dir.), *Tradizione e modernizzazione in Egitto, 1798-1998*, Milano, Angeli, 2000, p. 84.

Pompeja d'Alexandrie, dans lequel il célébrait l'aboutissement de l'unification nationale, la destruction du pouvoir temporel et la « continuité du progrès social ». Même le langage qu'il utilise – avec ses artifices rhétoriques et l'appel à un patriotisme œcuménique pour soutenir la jeune monarchie de la maison de Savoie – mérite une juste considération :

> Faisons, frères, un vœu pour notre grande mère l'Italie, pour cette très fameuse femme aux douleurs et aux gloires. Que ses enfants puissent revendiquer en liberté d'être toujours tempérés et concordes ; que ses ministres soient honnêtes et sages, son roi loyal et fort – tous véritablement italiens –, puissent ses enfants, qui gémissent encore sous la tyrannie étrangère, se soulever comme un seul homme, quand aura sonné l'heure de l'ultime rescousse et, unis à leurs frères, renouveler les miracles de Pontida et de Legnano ! Que la Rome des papes, cette éhontée prostituée de tous les despotes, lave les séculaires souillures et retourne briller de ses sept collines, pure, lumineuse et belle, devenue le centre et le cœur de la grande famille italienne libre[25].

À en juger de l'attention avec laquelle même les loges étrangères suivaient le débat interne à la franc-maçonnerie italienne, Sansone Terni envoya peu après un bulletin officiel du Grand Orient pour défendre le choix du rite symbolique, articulé en seulement trois degrés, contre la proposition d'un autre membre de la loge, qui visait en revanche à introduire le rite écossais antique et accepté, divisé en trente-trois degrés. Il jugeait les degrés supérieurs « tous plus ou moins farcis de mysticisme » et voyait en cette complexe et « byzantine » structure rituelle « la main des prêtres, l'astucieuse fraude sacerdotale, laquelle ne réussissant pas à combattre la franc-maçonnerie à visage découvert a cherché à l'égarer en la faisant dégénérer ». Dans son article, le dignitaire de la loge égyptienne invitait à maintenir ferme la foi dans les principes fondamentaux de la franc-maçonnerie universelle, parmi lesquels figurait « le dogme de l'existence de Dieu, non brouillé par des nébulosités métaphysiques, ni par des antinomies allemandes, ni par des équivoques panthéistiques »[26] : ce grand Architecte de l'Univers, en somme, dans le culte duquel pouvaient se reconnaître et se rassembler même des hommes qui professaient les diverses religions monothéistes

---

[25]   *Bollettino officiale del Grande Oriente Italiano*, Vol. I, 1863, pp. 123-125.

[26]   « Discorso letto dal fratello Sansone Terni alla Loggia Pompeia, Oriente di Alessandria d'Egitto », *Bollettino officiale del Grande Oriente Italiano*, Vol. I, 1863, pp. 165-167.

– chrétienne, hébraïque, islamique – qui avaient toutes eu comme origine ce même morceau de terre entre Orient et Occident[27].

3. Durant les décennies suivantes, la présence maçonnique italienne sur les rives de la Méditerranée connut des hauts et des bas, qui furent influencés par les vicissitudes internes de chaque pays et par les attitudes changeantes des gouvernements respectifs. Relativement stable et constant fut le nombre de loges actives en Égypte, atteignant dix en 1885, descendant à six en 1897 et remontant à onze en 1914, dont six avaient leur siège à Alexandrie, trois au Caire, une à Suez et une à Port Saïd. Ces mêmes loges étaient encore actives en 1920[28]. À la fin du XIXe siècle disparurent en revanche les loges tunisiennes, comme conséquence probablement des rapports tendus entre la France et l'Italie après le coup de Tunis de 1881. Elles furent de nouveau présentes dans la région au début du XXe siècle et, en 1914, au moment de l'expansion maximale du Grand Orient d'Italie, on en comptait cinq, trois à Tunis, une à Sousse et une Sfax. À cette date, une implantation maçonnique relativement consistante existait en Libye, depuis peu colonie italienne : deux loges étaient situées à Tripoli, une à Benghazi et une à Derna[29].

En ces mêmes régions, une autre obédience maçonnique connut aussi un fort enracinement. Elle vit le jour en 1908 d'une scission avec le Grand Orient d'Italie et prit le nom de Grande Loge d'Italie, autrement dite *Piazza del Gesù*, du lieu où elle installa son propre siège, à Rome[30]. En 1922, elle comptait cinq loges à Tripoli et une à Bengazi, Homs et Saganeiti. En outre, elle en avait au moins quatorze en Égypte (dont sept à Alexandrie, six au Caire et une à Khartoum), six en Tunisie (quatre à Tunis, une à Bizerte et une à La Goulette), une au Maroc (à Casablanca) et une seulement en Turquie (à Constantinople)[31].

D'autre part, justement la Turquie, et plus en général l'Empire ottoman, fut la région où les loges italophones jouèrent le rôle le plus significatif dans la vie publique locale, mêlant leurs affaires avec certains

---

[27] Sur le culte maçonnique du grand Architecte de l'Univers, *cf.* C. Porset, « Grand Architecte de l'Univers », in E. Saunier (dir.), *Encyclopédie de la Franc-Maçonnerie*, Paris, Librairie Générale Française, 2000, pp. 345-347.

[28] *Cf.* A. A. Mola, « Le logge italiane », in *Egitto, op. cit.*

[29] *Annuario massonico del Grande Oriente d'Italia. XX settembre 1914*, Roma, Tip. Bodoni di G. Bolognese, 1914 ; « I centri massonici regolari secondo l'Annuario universale per il 1914 », *Acacia*, février 1914.

[30] Sur la scission de 1908, *cf.* F. Cordova, *Massoneria e politica in Italia, 1892-1908*, Roma-Bari, Laterza, 1985 ; et F. Conti, *Storia della massoneria italiana, op. cit.*, pp. 180 ss.

[31] *Cf.* Gran Loggia Nazionale, *Elenco delle Logge. 1° gennaio 1922*, S.n.t. (Archivio storico del Grande Oriente d'Italia, Rome).

groupes d'orientation libérale qui furent parmi les plus actifs dans la lutte pour la démocratisation et la modernisation du pays. Les loges d'obédience du Grand Orient d'Italie rejoignirent ici la plus grande diffusion au début des années 1870, quand on en compta alors une douzaine. Après 1876, avec la montée sur le trône du sultan Abdulhamîd II, on assista cependant à un changement important. À la différence de son prédécesseur Mourad V, qui avait même été initié dans une loge du Grand Orient de France et ne régna que trois mois[32], il inaugura en effet une politique d'aversion rigide à l'égard de la franc-maçonnerie, qui subit ainsi une violente diminution. En 1885, les loges italophones encore actives s'étaient réduites au nombre de deux et, plus tard, il n'en resta plus qu'une, la loge *Italia risorta* de Constantinople.

La présence maçonnique dans l'Empire ottoman fut à nouveau plus consistante au début du XXe siècle, lorsque la loge de Salonique, la *Macedonia risorta*, prit une certaine importance et devint le lieu de rassemblement et une sorte de paravent de coordination du mouvement des Jeunes Turcs[33]. Avocat séfarade d'origine italienne, Emanuele Carasso fut l'artisan de la renaissance de la loge et partisan du rapprochement avec le groupe de nationalistes et de constitutionnalistes de l'Association ottomane de la liberté. Affilié à la *Macedonia risorta* entre fin 1902 et début 1903, il en devint par la suite le maître vénérable et permit l'inscription de nombreuses personnalités, qui occupèrent par la suite des charges de premier rang autant dans le Comité Union et Pro-

---

[32] *Cf.* C. Svolopoulos, « L'initiation de Mourad V à la franc-maçonnerie par C. Scalieri : aux origines du mouvement libéral en Turquie », *Balkan Studies*, V, 1980, n° 21, pp. 441-447. Sur la présence de la franc-maçonnerie dans l'Empire ottoman, *cf.* P. Dumont, « La Turquie dans les archives du Grand Orient de France : les loges maçonniques d'obédience française à Istanbul du milieu du XIXe siècle à la veille de la Première Guerre mondiale », *Économies et société dans l'Empire ottoman*, Actes du second congrès international d'histoire économique et social de la Turquie, Paris, 1983, pp. 171-201 ; *id.*, « La franc-maçonnerie ottomane et les "idées françaises" à l'époque des Tanzimat », *Revue de la Méditerranée et du monde méditerranéen*, LII-LIII, 1989, n° 2-3, pp. 151-159 ; *id.*, « Une délégation jeune-turque à Paris », in E. Eldem (dir.), *Première rencontre internationale sur l'Empire ottoman et la Turquie moderne (Varia Turcica XIII)*, Istanbul-Paris, 1991, pp. 305-331 ; *id.*, « La franc-maçonnerie dans l'Empire ottoman : la loge grecque Prométhée à Jannina », *Revue de la Méditerranée et du monde méditerranéen*, LVI, 1992, n° 4, pp. 105-112.

[33] Sur le rôle joué par la franc-maçonnerie dans la révolution des Jeunes Turcs, voir S. Hanioglu, « Notes on the Young Turks and the Freemasons (1875-1908) », *Middle Eastern Studies*, XXV, 1989, n° 2, pp. 186-197 ; A. Iacovella, « Ettore Ferrari e i Giovani Turchi », in A. M. Isastia (dir.), *Il progetto liberal-democratico di Ettore Ferrari. Un percorso tra politica e arte*, Milano, Angeli, 1997, pp. 90-113 ; *id.*, *Il triangolo e la mezzaluna. I Giovani Turchi e la Massoneria italiana*, s.l., Institut Italien de Culture d'Istanbul, 1997.

grès, que dans le gouvernement qui se constitua en 1909 après la déposition du sultan Abdulhamîd II. Parmi les noms les plus connus figuraient ceux de Mehmet Talat, futur vice-président de la Chambre, Rahmi ben Riza, qui comme Carasso fut député au parlement ottoman pour le collège de Salonique, Midhat Sükrü, secrétaire du Comité Union et Progrès, Ismail Hakki Canbulat et Refik Bey, ce dernier, ministre de la Justice, disparut en 1909. À la loge *Macedonia risorta* adhéra en outre un grand nombre de hauts officiers du commandement militaire de Salonique, y compris le commandant d'état-major Ismail Hakki. Ce corps d'armée, comme on le sait, eut un rôle décisif dans la répression de la tentative de contre-révolution réalisée par Abdulhamîd II en mars 1909. D'autre part, même en Italie en ces années-là, la franc-maçonnerie recueillit de nombreux affiliés dans les rangs des militaires, et ceci contribua remarquablement à attirer sur elle le soupçon d'être d'un côté un instrument occulte pour favoriser des promotions faciles et des carrières rapides, et de l'autre d'être désormais une organisation qui visait à un contrôle progressif et dangereux des organes vitaux de l'État[34].

Après l'arrivée au pouvoir de Mehmet V, le Grand Orient d'Italie revendiqua ouvertement le rôle joué par la franc-maçonnerie dans la révolution des Jeunes Turcs[35]. Mais au déclenchement de la guerre de Libye, en 1911, ceci eut de lourdes conséquences pour l'institution maçonnique, accusée d'antipatriotisme et l'objet d'une contestation virulente de la part du mouvement nationaliste. En Turquie, là aussi, la présence de Juifs et de maçons, parmi les membres du Comité Union et Progrès, fut plus tard instrumentalisée par les opposants aux Jeunes Turcs pour faire circuler l'idée d'un complot judaïco-maçonnique, qui aurait été tramé pour nuire à l'Empire ottoman et à l'Islam[36]. Ces deux thèses n'avaient que peu de fondements mais, dans les années qui suivirent, elles eurent une vaste diffusion et contribuèrent à discréditer l'image de la franc-maçonnerie en Italie et dans le monde arabe.

---

[34] F. Cordova, *Agli ordini del serpente verde. La massoneria nella crisi del sistema giolittiano*, Roma, Bulzoni, 1990, pp. 16 ss.

[35] « Alla giovine Turchia », *Rivista della massoneria italiana*, 31 mai 1909 ; « Onoranze ai fratelli turchi », *ibidem*, juin-juillet 1910 ; « La massoneria e la rivoluzione turca », *Acacia*, octobre 1910.

[36] *Cf.* E. Kedourie, « Young Turks, Freemasons and Jews », *Middle Eastern Review*, 1971, n° 1, pp. 89-104 ; et E. Benbassa, « Les Jeunes Turcs et les Juifs (1908-1914) », *Mélanges offerts à Louis Bazin par ses disciples, collègues et amis*, Paris, 1992, pp. 311-321.

Authoritarian Legacies
and Good Democracy

Southern Europe

Leonardo MORLINO

Università di Firenze

This paper tries to understand the complex forces that influence the quality of democracy in countries such as those of Southern Europe that experienced authoritarian regimes. In the first part of the paper, I shall define what is a "good" democracy, discuss salient authoritarian legacies, and suggest links between such legacies and authoritarian hindrances to good democracy. In the second part, I propose a comparative analysis among the cases signaling the most important legacies, the differences and similarities among the cases, and the possible processes in which authoritarian legacies fade away.

I. What Is Democracy?

The analysis of the quality of democracy – that is, an empirical scrutiny of what 'good' democracy is about – requires not only that we have a definition of democracy, but also that we establish a clear notion of the quality. The minimal definition of democracy (Dahl, 1971) suggests that such a regime has at least universal, adult suffrage; recurring, free, competitive and fair elections; more than one political party; and more than one source of information. In addition, democratic institutions, existing rights and also the decision making process should not be constrained by non-elected elites or external powers (Schmitter and Karl, 1993, 45-6). Among the countries that meet these minimal criteria, further empirical analysis is still necessary to detect the degree to which they have achieved the two main objectives of an ideal democracy – freedom and equality.

Thus, the analysis of a 'good democracy' should theoretically set aside those regimes that are to varying degrees deficient in principal democratic features. Amongst them are hybrid regimes (Diamond, 2002), whose failure to ensure free and fair electoral competition and a minimum level of civil rights keeps them below the minimum threshold to be classified as democratic. Likewise, the *defective democracies* (Merkel and Croissant, 2000) should also be left out of the analysis. This category includes 'exclusive' democracies, which offer only limited guaranties for political rights; 'dominated' democracies, in which powerful groups use their influence to condition and limit the autonomy of elected leaders; and 'illiberal' democracies, which offer only partial guarantees of civil rights. In reality, the last three models may also be seen as institutional hybrids, and thus fall short of the minimum threshold specified above.

Deficient democracy is a recurrent expression used to depict East European regimes, but it often bears a different meaning. These are regimes that have just overcome the minimal democratic threshold, but still experience problems of consolidation. By displaying minimal requirements for democracy, they differ from the hybrid regime (see above) and can be included in the analysis here.

Delegative democracy, sometimes referred to as a *populist democracy*, also fits well within the scope of this analysis, having overcome the necessary threshold. These regimes are usually based on a majority system, and host relatively 'clean elections'; parties, parliament, and the press are usually free to express their criticisms, and the courts block unconstitutional policies (O'Donnell, 1994, 55-69). In practice, however, citizens of these democracies, which O'Donnell finds, for example, in Latin America, 'delegate others to make decisions on their behalf', such that they no longer have the opportunity to check and evaluate performance of their officials once they are elected. Other bodies of government, even those meant for this purpose, neglect or fail to carry out their watchdog functions and, consequently, the rule of law is only partially or minimally respected (O'Donnell, 1994, 60-62).

The second step in evaluating 'good' and 'bad' democracies requires a clear definition of 'quality'. The use of the term in the industrial and marketing sectors suggests three different meanings of quality. First, quality is defined by the established procedural aspects associated with each product; a 'quality' product is the result of an exact, controlled process carried out according to precise, recurring methods and timing. Here the emphasis is on *procedure*. Second, quality consists of the structural characteristics of a product, be it the design, materials or functioning of the good, or other details that it features. Here, the emphasis is on *content*. Finally, the quality of a product or service is indirectly derived from the satisfaction expressed by the customer, by their requesting again the same product or service, regardless of either how it is produced or what the actual contents are, or how the consumer goes about acquiring the product or service. The three different notions of quality are thus grounded either in procedure, content, or result. Each has different implications in empirical research. Importantly, even with all the adjustments demanded by the complexity of the 'object' under examination – i.e. democracy – it is still necessary to keep these conceptualizations of quality in mind as we elaborate definitions and models of democratic quality.

II. What Is 'Quality'?

Beginning with the definition above, and from the prevailing notions of quality, a quality or 'good' democracy may be considered to be one presenting a stable institutional structure that realizes the liberty and equality of citizens through the legitimate and correct functioning of its institutions and mechanisms. A good democracy is thus first and foremost a broadly legitimated regime that completely satisfies the citizens ('quality' in terms of 'result'). When institutions have the full backing of civil society, they can pursue the values of the democratic regime. If, in contrast, the institutions must postpone their objectives and expend energy and resources on consolidating and maintaining their legitimacy, crossing over even the minimum threshold for democracy becomes a remarkable feat. Second, a good democracy is one in which the citizens, associations, and communities enjoy liberty and equality ('quality' in terms of 'content'). Third, in a good democracy the citizens themselves have the power to check and evaluate whether the government pursues the objectives of liberty and equality according to the rule of law. They monitor the efficiency of the application of the laws in force, the efficacy of the decisions made by government, and the political responsibility and accountability of elected officials in relation to the demands expressed by civil society ('quality' in terms of 'procedure').

Keeping the above in mind, five possible dimensions can be indicated here, along which good democracies may vary. The first two are procedural dimensions. Although related to the content, these dimensions mainly concern the rules. The first procedural dimension is the rule of law. The second procedural dimension is accountability (Kitschelt, 1999). The third dimension concerns the responsiveness or correspondence of the political decisions to the desires of the citizens and civil society in general. The final two dimensions are substantive in nature. The penultimate one refers to civil rights expanded through the achievement of certain freedoms; and the final one refers to the progressive implementation of greater political, social, and economic equality.

These five dimensions, thus, will be further elaborated in three sections below. Before undertaking this, the following general considerations shall be emphasized.

The analytical framework proposed here partially differs from other studies on the quality of democracy, such as those of Altman and Perez-Linan (2002, 85-100) and Lijphart (1999). Both of these studies develop a quantitative comparative strategy. Here we stress the virtuous combination of qualitative and quantitative measures in the empirical analysis of the phenomenon. The differences also emerge in the definition of a good democracy, the dimensions of variation and related indicators of quality as proposed above. Altman and Perez-Linan draw on Dahl's concept of polyarchy (civil rights, participation and competition) and may fit into the first substantive dimension, indicated above as well as in the procedural dimensions. Conversely, Lijphart's inclusion in the analysis of the quality of democracy of such dimensions as female representation, electoral participation, satisfaction with the democracy and corruption, indicate their close similarity to the five dimensions mentioned.

The institutions and mechanisms of representative democracies are the main objects of the analysis of the quality of a democracy. This is not to ignore direct democracy as the highest expression of democratic quality, but to acknowledge the secular experience of representative democracies and their actual potential for improvement. If the analysis has to be focused on representative democracies, then accountability – a core feature in the experience of representative democracy – becomes a truly central dimension insofar as it grants citizens and civil society in general an effective means of control over political institutions. This feature attenuates the difficulties that exist objectively when there is a shift from direct to representative democracy.

Accountability is implicitly based on two assumptions from the liberal tradition that highlight the interconnected nature of all of the dimensions explained above. The first assumption is that if citizens are genuinely given the opportunity to evaluate the responsibility of government in terms of satisfaction of their own needs and requests, they are in fact capable of doing so, possessing above all a relatively accurate perception of their own needs. The second assumption is that citizens, either alone or as part of a group, are the only possible judges of their own needs; no third party can decide those needs. To leave these assumptions unmentioned is mistaken. They should instead be stated and taken into account from the outset. It is also erroneous to consider each of them as a mere ideological choice. It is instead important to acknowledge that Western democracies have followed a liberal-democratic trajectory and that any concrete analysis of the quality of democracy must take this into account and the shift towards a direction marked by more egalitarian choices. Those assumptions, however, refer only to vertical accountability and will be examined further in the next section.

Freedom and equality, however they are understood, are necessarily linked to accountability and responsiveness. Indeed, a higher implementation of freedom and equality for citizens and civil society lies in the sphere of representative mechanisms. In addition, an effective rule of law is also indispensable for a good democracy. The rule of law is intertwined with freedom with respect for all of those laws that directly or indirectly sanction those rights and their concrete realization. As the next section will explain, freedom, equality and even accountability are actually unobtainable if respect for the law is ineffective or the government and the administration do not grant decisional efficacy. These are fundamental preconditions necessary for deciding and carrying out policies to achieve a better democratic quality.

The main subjects of such a democracy are the citizen-individuals, the territorial communities and the various, formal and informal associations with common values, traditions or aims. In this sense, the possibility for good democracy exists not only in the case of a defined territory with a specific population controlled by state institutions under a democratic government, but also for wider-ranging entities such as the European Union. The main point is that the above named subjects are at the heart of a democracy in which the most important processes are those that work 'bottom up' rather than 'top-down'. In this way, the transfer of analytical dimensions from the national level to the supranational level – though not uncomplicated and without difficulty – is possible. The key is to hold constant the same elements characteristic of each dimension.

The necessity of capturing the empirical complexity of the notion of 'quality' democracy motivates the employment of the five dimensions elaborated above. This elaboration flags two aspects of each dimension: each might vary from the others in terms of form and degree of development. As such, the analysis calls for indicators, certain measures that reveal how and to what degree each dimension is present not only in different countries, but also in various models of good democracy. These empirical data should also enable an eventual tracking of the growth of quality democracies.

Moreover, such a multidimensional analysis is also justified by the possibility of accepting in this way a pluralist notion of quality. That is, the content, the procedure and the result also correspond to three different conceptions of quality, and each conception has its own basis in terms of values and ideals. In other words, if the notion of democratic quality has to come out of the kingdom of utopia and become a legitimate topic of empirical research then the multidimensionality is essential to capture it empirically, as well as the related acknowledgement that different equally possible notions of quality are likewise necessary to proceed in that direction. The different policy implications of such pluralism should not be ignored. Figure 1 summarizes in a few empirical dimensions and questions the dimensions discussed above.

Figure 1: Dimensions and issues of a 'good' democracy

Rule of law
The rule of law: are state and society consistently subject to the law?
Civilian control of the military and police: are the military and police forces under civilian control?
Minimizing corruption: are public officials free from corruption?
Representative and Accountable Government
Is government accountable to the people and their representatives?
Free and fair elections: do elections give the people control over governments and their policies?
Democratic role of political parties: does the party system assist the working of democracy?
Government effectiveness and accountability: is government accountable to the people and their representatives?
Is government accountable to other elected institutions?
The media and open government: do the media operate in a way that sustains democratic values?
Government Responsiveness and Participation
Government responsiveness: is government responsive to the concerns of its citizens?
Political participation: is there full citizen participation in public life?
Citizenship and Rights
Civil and political rights: are civil and political rights equally guaranteed for all?
Economic and social rights: are economic and social rights equally guaranteed for all?
Democracy Beyond the State
International dimensions of democracy: are the country's external relations conducted in accordance with democratic norms?

Adapted from David Beetham, (1994), pp. 25-43.

III. What Are Legacies?

We define authoritarian legacies as all behavioral patterns, rules, relationships, social and political situations, but also norms, procedures and institutions either introduced or strongly and patently strengthened by the immediately preceding authoritarian regime. Authoritarian legacies influence a broad range of political, economic, and social institutions (see Hite and Cesarini, 2004). Authoritarian legacies are often most visible in the workings and behavior of the security forces (see Hite and Cesarini, 2004). They also include patterns of social domination, as well as highly unequal access to legal and political institutions. Authoritarian legacies may take the form of repressive memories that are latent but activated and manipulated by social and political actors at particular moments. They may be supported by specific actors, interests or identities.

Several aspects of legacies must be signaled. First, an authoritarian legacy carries three key internal dimensions that are strongly related, but may be present only in part in the new democratic arrangement. They are: a. a set of beliefs, values and attitudes; b. one or more public institutions, agencies or simple organizations; and c. the subsequent behaviors emanating from the relationships between the first two dimensions. In processes of political change, these dimensions internal to legacies produce several scenarios: beliefs, values and attitudes can fade away or disappear under the democratic establishment, but the institutions or organizations with their vested interests persist; beliefs may persist in spite of the change of regime, while the institutions disappear; or behavior may persist because of inertia when either beliefs, institutions or both have disappeared. Of course, the higher the number of dimensions that persist, the stronger the legacies and the slower and more difficult the fading away.

Second, as suggested by the above definition, there are two fundamental kinds of legacies: a. those that refer to values, institutions and behavior introduced by the authoritarian regime; and b. those that reinforce, strengthen or entrench previous values and existing institutions by setting up new institutions, agencies or organizations and creating or reproducing subsequent behavioral habits. The second kind of legacy is well-embedded in political culture and is usually stronger and more persistent. As authoritarian regimes are often the institutional transposition of conservative coalitions (Linz, 1964), this second kind of legacy is a more recurrent one. There are also more innovative regimes in terms of institutions, and they are usually regimes with totalitarian features, such as Italian fascism. From an empirical perspective, in order to be considered an authoritarian legacy, the second, more historically embedded kind of legacy has to have been clearly supported by the decisions and policies of the immediately preceding authoritarian regime.

Third, a legacy always implies continuity with a previously existing phenomenon. In broader terms, a legacy could also be considered a reaction to that previous phenomenon. For example, state-crafters of the democratizing regime clearly perceive the need to differentiate the new regime from the previous one, and this specific reaction, while discontinuous, is also a form of legacy. A good example can be found in the Italian Constitutional Charter. As suggested by the debates in the committee that drafted it, several of the proposals and decisions represented attempts to shape governmental institutions as an extreme counter to the fascist regime. One key outcome in this regard was the enormous role of parliament *vis-à-vis* the cabinet, resulting in decisional inefficacy once the strongly dominant role of the Christian Democratic party ended in the mid-1950s. As suggested by Bermeo (1992) and more recently by Pridham (2000), such a reaction may be more appropriately labeled "political learning". For the sake of clarity, we tend toward the narrower meaning of the term of legacy. This means that legacies chiefly involve continuities from the past, though it is difficult to disentangle analytically political learning processes from legacies. We argue that authoritarian legacies are located in both formal and legal institutions and, perhaps just as importantly for our cases, in those interstices linking civil society's engagement with political society and the state, including cultural practices and "lived" experiences (Dirks *et al.*, 1996). Thus, in addition to discussing authoritarian enclaves that continue to pervade formal political institutions, we will examine the influence of authoritarian legacies on both organized and unorganized interests or identities in political and civil society. We will encourage the exploration of authoritarian legacies in what Anthony Giddens terms the "structuration" or routinization of everyday life, as reflected through political consciousness, discourse and practice (1984).

We emphasize this latter exploration of authoritarian legacies and structuration because it may be here where authoritarian legacies are the deepest and most enduring, at the level of personal autonomy as a civil and political right and as a fundamental condition for democratic citizenship and the rule of law (O'Donnell, 1998, Held, 1997, Giddens, 1984).

Remnants and memories of these regimes present an interesting set of paradoxes. On the one hand, memories of repressive patterns and action continue to inhibit political discourse, political participation and individual notions of political efficacy, associability and trust. On the other hand, in the cases of Portugal and Spain, memories of the military regimes also evoke associations with a desire for order, efficiency and predictability, often in the economic as well as political arenas. In the three Southern European cases, partially positive attitudes toward authoritarian pasts still fluctuate above 40%.

To varying degrees, authoritarian regimes have overseen the restructuring of labor-state or capital-labor-state relationships, as well as the restructuring of the political representation of labor. In Italy and Portugal, authoritarian regimes created corporatist arrangements.

Authoritarian legacies as "silencers" are difficult to put into operation, yet they are harbors of structural violence that weighs heavily (though unequally) on polity and society (Habermas, 1986). Preferences for stability and order over debate and dissent reflect a lingering fear of polarization under previous democratic regimes and of brutal state response to conflict. Moreover, as Maravall (1981) has suggested in the Spanish case, it is quite rational for citizens to turn away from politics in the wake of political abuses.

IV.   Possible Links and Determining Factors

We cannot assume that every authoritarian legacy limits democratic expression. On the contrary, there are legacies such as that of efficiency or the building of an effective civil service that are positively related to a "good" democracy. Not every legacy impedes a good democracy. Thus, our key question is: When do authoritarian legacies constrain or impede the best expressions of democracy?

We will argue that the influence of authoritarian legacies on the quality of democracy depends upon three basic dimensions, or sites, for strategic action: 1) the durability of the previous authoritarian regime; 2) the innovation of that regime; and 3) the mode of transition from authoritarianism.

By *innovation* under authoritarianism, we mean both the degree of transformation and institutionalization of authoritarian rules, patterns, relationships and norms, often symbolized by a new constitution (Aguero, 1998), by the setting up of new institutions, but also by the degree of strengthening or weakening of particular organized interests or identities (Hagopian, 1995). In this paper, we will explore the range of authoritarian "exacerbations" and "breaks" with the past in terms of the relationships among the state, political parties and other organized political and social interests and civil society.

By *mode of transition*, we mean the ways in which the transition from authoritarian rule privileged particular incumbents and/or challengers, altered (or left in place) authoritarian institutional rules and procedures, influenced the appeals of the political elite to their constituencies (Munck and Leff, 1997; Linz and Stepan, 1996; Karl and Schmitter, 1991) and/or were characterized by some degree of violence that made discontinuity more probable. Here we will highlight prerogatives for the military and other authoritarian incumbents, pact making, rules governing elections and political parties, and the roles and positioning of organized and unorganized civil society interests in the transition process. We argue that continuous or discontinuous modes of transition mediate whether and how authoritarian legacies endure.

By *durability*, we mean the span of time of the authoritarian regime. If a regime is innovative, then the span of time is less relevant. If, on the other hand, the regime is not innovative, then the regime must be in power for at least fifteen to twenty years, that is, for at least a generation, to be a salient dimension. While we do not examine this here, we are conscious of the importance of exploring transformations in the sites of traditional political socialization under authoritarian regimes, including family, church and educational institutions, which become the primary referents for political socialization in the absence of a public sphere. We argue that the intensity of authoritarian legacies in the posttransition period depends in good part on the enduring shock and penetration of authoritarian rules, norms and practices in the private as well as the public sphere.

There are also important connections between innovation and the mode of transition. If the transition is discontinuous, institutional innovation may be less salient as the new political elite transforms authoritarian institutions. If the transition is continuous, then authoritarian regime innovation is much more relevant, as path dependency is essentially established.

Our task now is to relate key variables of regime innovation, duration and mode of transition to the quality of democracy in the posttransition period. We focus on how such legacies have affected the new democratic institutions as well as the modes of political incorporation. That is, we chiefly examine and analyze political parties, including internal party organization and the relationships between parties and interests (see Morlino, 1998). We will also explore a range of indicators regarding citizens' assessments of their democracy and specific political institutions, as well as their sense of efficacy and investment in their government's decision-making processes regarding the economy and other key issues. Moreover, we will explore the state and reach of political discourse and discursive practices as indicators of the parameters and constraints on a democratic public sphere (Arendt, 1958). When possible, we will examine the links between contemporary political organization and action and authoritarian legacies, including strategies for ameliorating or working with the constraints particular authoritarian legacies have represented.

One difficulty stems from including the exacerbation of historical patterns of egregious social domination as authoritarian legacies, for while we can recognize such patterns as far from democratic, this may be more appropriately framed as a classic question of social inequality and its relationship to political institutions and practices. It raises a basic question regarding the relationship between "irreconciliation" of authoritarian legacies, on the one hand, and structural inequality, on the other.

This suggests that we should focus on the ways in which the most notorious legacies for each case are present in post-authoritarian regime politics. Such legacies may include but are not limited to historical patterns of social domination. We argue that authoritarian ideologies or mentalities (Linz, 1964) and leaders' decisions mark the beginning of the creation of norms or formal rules and institutions that may continue in post-authoritarian settings and, therefore, that reconciling authoritarian legacies rests with the managing and manipulation of legacies between elite and citizenry.

**Figure 2: Authoritarian Legacies as Constraints
to a 'Good' Democracy**

Dimension	Legacy
Regime institutions and norms	Authoritarian legal rules Poor or no rule of law Barely independent judiciary Large public sector of economy (not in Southern Cone)
Elite actors	High military prerogatives Poor or no efficiency of police Radical rightist groups No elite party accountability
Social groups/institutions	Gleichschaltung*
Culture and mass level	Statism (not in the Southern Cone) Passivity/conformism/cynicism Fear/alienation from politics Non democratic attitudes Rightist radical party/ies

*This term is intended to refer to the extreme leveling of cultural/social differences, a policy carried out by the Nazi regime.

Figure 2 is an attempt to list some of the main legacies that authoritarian regimes may transmit to democracies, focusing attention on the quality of the new regimes. We suggest a rough distinction among regime institutions and rules, elite actors, social groups, political culture and the mass level. For each domain, we suggest legacies that constrain the achievement of a "good" democracy. Thus, for example, a statist authoritarian tradition is largely present in the new democracies of Southern Europe (Morlino, 1998), resulting in low political interest and participation. Poor or no rule of law may have already existed in the countries' pasts. In Giolittian Italy at the beginning of this century, there was a saying: "For friends what they want, for enemies the law". Yet the Italian authoritarian regime strengthened such uncertainty regarding due process, and it thus persists as a key legacy that makes the guarantee of equal political and civil rights for all citizens far more difficult.

To flesh out our conceptualization of authoritarian legacies and their influence on the quality of democracy in post-authoritarian regimes, we will examine and compare the Southern Europe an cases: Italy, Spain, Portugal. We excluded Greece, for the Greek authoritarian experience between 1967 and 1973 is neither long enough nor institutionally innovative or meaningful enough to be considered here. Political leader Constantinos Karamanlis, who re-established democracy in July 1973, was already a prominent politician during the previous limited democracy, and he immediately moved to hold the military accountable. Trials, condemnation, and convictions were conducted in the months immediately following democratic reestablishment. The symbolic and real impact of the Greek court decisions were very effective. We will thus start with Southern Europe, beginning with Italy, whose experience and long number of years elapsed since the transition provide a meaningful field for research regarding both authoritarian legacies and their fading away.

A Few Comparative Considerations

In this paper, we have attempted to identify authoritarian legacies that are hindrances to the quality of democracy. Before entering into a comparative discussion of such legacies, we will review the contextual dimensions that influence and condition the authoritarian legacies in each country. Figure 3 lays out the presence and the salience of these dimensions. We use a capital X when we judge the stronger salience of the dimension and a small x when it is less salient but nonetheless present. An empty cell indicates the absence of any saliency of the dimension.

Figure 3: Dimensions influencing authoritarian legacies, per country

Countries / Factors	Italy	Spain	Portugal
Durability	X	X	X
Institutional innovation	X	X	X
Continuous transition		X	

The "durability" dimension is particularly relevant for Portugal and Spain, and as anticipated at the beginning of the paper, it is more relevant when it is accompanied by institutional innovation, as is the case in Portugal.

Regarding institutional innovation – the chief aspect of innovation we consider – again, Portugal stands out as highly innovative regimes. Curiously, for this case, there was a recurring reference to Italian fascism, i.e. to the third case where there was strong innovation. Spain was also fairly innovative regimes, though to a lesser extent in comparative terms. In both cases, again, durability works to enhance the strength of the relative innovation.

Finally, for Spain the modes of transition are continuous. And again, as expected, this was an important dimension when we account for the presence of authoritarian legacies. On the whole, based on our dimensions, we expected to have a stronger, more salient set of legacies in Spain, with Portugal and Italy on a second tier. Such expectations are confirmed by our empirical analyses, as we will see below.

**Figure 4: Authoritarian Legacies as Constraints
to a 'Good' Democracy, per country**

Dimensions	Legacy	It	Sp	Pt
Regime institutions and norms	Authoritarian legal rules	X		
	Poor or no rule of law			
	Barely independent judiciary			
	Large public sector of economy	X		X
Elite actors	High military prerogatives			X
	Poor or no efficiency of police			
	Radical rightist groups	X		
	No party elite accountability	X	X	X
Culture and mass level	Statism	X	X	X
	Passivity/conformism/cynicism	X	X	X
	Fear/alienation from politics			
	Non democratic attitudes	X	X	X
	Rightist radical party/ies	X		

Regarding specific, expected authoritarian legacies themselves (see Figure 2 at the outset), we discern legacies both in the formal rules of governance and in dramatic, explicit assertions of power by unequivocal authoritarian actors. But legacies are also less easy to detect – and even more difficult to measure – in the day-to-day political patterns and daily routines that condition democratic representation and participation. In point of fact, authoritarian legacies pervade most societies, and in spite of the difficulties, attempts to identify them have to be pursued: particular authoritarian legacies become serious hindrances to democracies when agents give legacies unchallenged or unchecked expression, visibility, or power. For clarity's sake, Figure 4 is a way of summarizing our analysis.

As can be seen, when we compare Figures 2 and 4, the dimension concerning *gleichschaltung*, or the leveling of cultural/social/economic differences, is not present. This is so because in none of the cases was this kind of phenomenon – a characteristics of totalitarian regimes – empirically evident. For many years the Franco regime attempted to suppress the ethnic, language, and cultural differences in Catalunia and the Basque Countries, particularly. The only real result was to fuel and further radicalize the violent factions within Basque nationalist demands for independence (see also Aguilar, 2001).

However, the key conclusion we can draw from the connection between the analyses summarized in Figure 3 and Figure 4 is in the intertwining between modes of transition, institutional innovation and durability, on the one hand, and the three dimensions of legacies. Italy and Spain present their own different characteristics. In Italy a few important constraints are present in spite of the discontinuity of transition. The main reason is that in many ways the Fascist institutional innovation was very persistent and prominent as it partially regarded the very building of a more modern state. In Spain the strength of the three influencing dimensions is attenuated by the moment of transition and the immediate insertion of the Spanish democracy within the European democratic area. The case where there is a discontinous transition is Portugal, and such a discontinuity partially soften the strong authoritarian innovation and the longest duration of all authoritarianisms.

Regarding more specifically regime institutions and norms, Italy is the country where authoritarian legal rules remain present in the post-authoritarian period. We also find the legacy of a large public sector of the economy in Italy and Portugal. During Portugal's 1974-82 transition there was massive nationalization of the economy, later transformed radically by Cavaco Silva in the late 1980s. Italy possessed resilient, large public sectors that have been shrunk in part only recently. Undoubtedly, the lack of full civilian control of the army over a sustained period is one of the most important legacies. This is the case of Portugal for virtually a decade after the establishment of a different regime.

The poor efficiency of police, so relevant for the guarantee of civil rights, also emerges as an important legacy (see Pereira and Ungar, 2003). While poor efficiency of the police has been a constant throughout modern Latin America, it is clear that the military regimes exacerbated this legacy. The rightist radical groups are strongly relevant and influential in the Italian political arena.

If we simply consider elite accountability in terms of the possibility of alternation and incumbency, then in different ways, Italy, Spain, and Portugal showed no or low accountability. In Italy, there was no real possibility of alternation until the breakdown of Christian Democracy in the early 1990s. In Spain, there was a long period of socialist dominance given a not fully "clean" right, stigmatized by the Franco regime. And in Portugal, there was an even longer period of no alternation until the mid-1990s.

The third set of legacies concern cultural levels. These legacies are deeper and more pervasive and refer to the basic problems of the modes of incorporation, or the ways citizens have been involved and socialized into politics. By statism, we refer to the constant, continuous reference to public institutions, as well as to people's expectations that the state will initiate and be responsible for every aspect of their lives. Statism has been highly related to the lengthy authoritarian experiences of Southern Europe. Passivity, conformism, and cynicism represent the single set of attitudes toward politics that is most widespread throughout the seven countries under analysis. These two aspects together – statism on the one hand, and passivity, on the other – make accountability much more difficult to achieve. Accountability assumes the existence of an active civil society.

Of course, these two aspects were also well-embedded in the pre-authoritarian regime political cultures of all these countries. Nevertheless, the authoritarian experiences exacerbated these dimensions.

In survey studies, we find widespread non-democratic attitudes across the three Southern European countries. This is so in different ways and to a different extent in each of the cases. In Italy, for example, such attitudes have been present for years, including well into the 1990s. Italian radical right parties were present until the late 1980s-early 1990s (Morlino, 1996). All five aspects converge to represent political cultures less than conducive to civic democracy (see also Hite and Cesarini, 2004). On the whole, this analysis confirms that both the contextual dimensions and the content of legacies show how numerous the constraints were and still partially are to a good democracy in Italy for a lengthy period. Our main conclusion must be that there is no necessary consistency between contextual dimensions and legacies themselves.

Throughout our analysis, we faced analytical challenges that were very difficult to disentangle. We wish to emphasize at least two of them. First, as we have pointed out, authoritarian legacies are often related to pre-authoritarian experiences. It is impossible, for example, to analyze the beliefs, attitudes and behavior at the mass level in Spain that developed under authoritarianism without considering the Second Spanish

Republic and the Spanish Civil War. This may also account for positive assessments of the authoritarian past during the present democratic regimes.

Second, on several occasions, for all seven countries, it was very difficult to analytically separate the influence of authoritarian legacies from the influence of political learning on democratization processes. Such was the case of Italy in the first year after the war, but this is also relevant in the case of Spain, given the contexts of severe repression under authoritarianism.

The problem of the fading away of legacies is largely open. First, the fading away itself cannot be taken for granted. The kinds of attitudes and beliefs at the mass level that we raise in Figure 4 may continue, even when the elapsed time would suggest their disappearance. Such attitudes and beliefs continue not because of fascism, Salazarism, Francoism and various military experiences, but rather because of new features of modernity. Passivity, conformism, cynicism and alienation are features that are both shared and reproduced in contemporary democracies as well as authoritarian regimes. In Italy, this same passivity, indifference and negative feelings toward politics are perpetuated because they are part of specific cultural traditions and are reproduced by the anti-politics of the new millennium. Similar mechanisms can be envisaged in other countries, including Spain. On the other hand, the statism that was characteristic of some authoritarian regimes and that is not reproduced by dominant contemporary cultural and economic paradigms tends, then, to disappear.

Ultimately, we cannot be sure that the fading away of the legacies discussed above is always positive. It cannot be taken for granted that the moderation and low radicalism that have been fundamental components of Spanish democratic consolidation are not inextricably related to the indifference and passivity that have been ever-present tendencies within these complex political cultures. The fading away of the latter may imply the disappearance of the former. However, it is well known that those who have no memories of the past lose their identities and are condemned to make the same mistakes (see, among others, Bendix, 1984). Thus, when we emphasize that some legacies, although hindrances to a "better" democracy, were helpful or very helpful for democratic consolidation, one could conclude that it is wiser to maintain those legacies or – even better – maintain strong memories of them.

Bibliographical references

Aguilar, Paloma (2001), "Justicia, política, y memoria: Los legados del Franquismo en la transición española", *Estudio/Working Paper 163*, Instituto Juan March de Estudios e Investigaciones.

David Altman and Anibal Perez-Linan (2002), "Assessing the Quality of Democracy: Freedom, Competitiveness, and Participation in 18 Latin American Countries", *Democratization*, Vol. 9, No. 2, 85-100.

Arendt, Hannah (1958), *The Human Condition*, Chicago, University of Chicago Press.

Beetham, David (1994), "Key Principles and Indices for a Democratic Audit", in Beetham (ed.), *Defining and Measuring Democracy*, New York, Sage Publications, 25-43.

Bendix, Reinhard (1984), *Force, Fate and Freedom: an Historical Sociology*, Berkeley, Univ. of California.

Bermeo, Nancy (1992), "Democracy and the Lessons of Dictatorship", in *Comparative Politics*, 24 (3): 273-291.

Dahl, R. A. (1971), *Poliarchy. Participation and Opposition*, New Haven, Yale University Press.

Diamond, L. (2002), "Thinking About Hybrid Regimes", *Journal of Democracy*, Vol. 13, No. 2, 21-35.

Dirks, Nicholas, Geoff Eley and Sherry Ortner, (eds.) (1996), *Culture/Power/History: A Reader in Contemporary Social Theory*, Princeton, Princeton University Press.

Giddens, Anthony (1984), *The Constitution of Society*, Berkeley, University of California Press.

Habermas, Jürgen (1986), "Hannah Arendt's Communications Concept of Power", in Steven Lukes (ed.), *Power*, New York, New York University Press, 75-93.

Hagopian, Frances (1995), "After Regime Change: Authoritarian Legacies, Political Representation, and the Democratic Future of South America", *World Politics* 45 (April): 464-500.

Held, David (1997), *Models of Democracy*, Stanford, Stanford University Press.

Hite, Katherine and Paola Cesarini (2004), *Authoritarian Legacies and Democracy in Latin America and Southern Europe*, Notre Dame, University of Notre Dame Press.

Karl, Terry Lynn and Philippe Schmitter (1991), "Modes of Transition in Latin America, Southern Europe and Eastern Europe", *International Social Science Journal* 128 (May): 269-284.

Kitschelt, H. *et al.* (1999), *Post-Communist Party Systems: Competition, Representation and Inter-party Cooperation*, Cambridge, Cambridge University Press.

Lijphart, A. (1999), *Patterns of Democracy. Government Forms and Performance in Thirty-Six Countries*, New Haven, Yale University Press.

Linz, Juan J. (1964), "An Authoritarian Regime: The Case of Spain", in E. Allardt and Y. Littunen (eds.), *Cleavages, Ideologies and Party System*, Helsinki, Westermarck Society: 291-342.

Linz, Juan and Alfred C. Stepan (1996), *Problems of Democratic Transition and Consolidation*, Baltimore, Johns Hopkins University Press.

Maravall, José Maria (1981), *La politica de la transiciòn*, Madrid, Taurus.

Merkl, Peter H. and Aurel Croissant (2000), "Formal Institutions and Informal Rules of Defective Democracies", *Central European Political Science Review*, Vol. 1, No. 2, 31-47.

Morlino, Leonardo (1996), "Crisis of Parties and Change of Party System in Italy", *Party Politics* 2 (1): 5-30.

Morlino, Leonardo (1998), *Democracy between Consolidation and Crisis. Parties, Groups and Citizens in Southern Europe*, Oxford, Oxford University Press.

Munck, Gerardo and Carol Skalnik Leff (1997), "Modes of Transition and Democratization: South America and Eastern Europe in Comparative Perspective", *Comparative Politics* (April): 343-362.

O'Donnell, Guillermo (1994), "Delegative Democracy" in *Journal of Democracy* 5 (1): 55-69.

O'Donnell, Guillermo (1998), "Polyarchies and the (Un)rule of Law in Latin America: A Partial Conclusion", in Méndez *et al.*, *The (Un)Rule of Law*, 303-337.

O'Donnell, Guillermo (1999), *Counterpoint: Selected Essays on Authoritarianism and Democratization*, Notre Dame, Ind., University of Notre Dame Press.

Pridham, Geoffrey (2000), "Confining Conditions and Breaking with the Past: Historical Legacies and Political Learning in Transitions to Democracy" *Democratization* 9: 36-64.

Schmitter, Philippe and Terry Karl (1993), "What Democracy is... and is Not", in Larry Diamond and Marc Plattner (eds.), *The Global Resurgence of Democracy*, Baltimore, Johns Hopkins University Press, 45-6.

Mediterranean Fertility

Similarities and Differences between the Two Shores of the Mediterranean

Letizia MENCARINI
Silvana SALVINI and Daniele VIGNOLI [*]

I. Introduction: Muslim prolificacy and demographic transition

Current fertility in the Islamic Mediterranean countries is approximately half of what it was in the 1970s. The changes, revealed by survey data and estimates of varying degrees of reliability, are such that each year the United Nations lowers both its fertility estimates (generally speaking, now moderate and probably destined to decline rapidly) and the consequent population forecasts (Fargues, 2000)[1]. The representation of the patriarchal family, which is characterized by a dual hierarcy – one vertical (the elderly over the young) and one horizontal (men over women) –, inevitably includes the notion of high fertility, which is highly "rational" in such a context. Yet although the representation seems to persist, recent surveys reveal that fertility has plunged, to the extent that it is now similar to that of non-Islamic countries of the same socio-economic level.

---

[*] Department of Statistics "G. Parenti", University of Florence, viale Morgagni 59, I-50134 Florence, Italy. E-mails: letizia.mencarini@unito.it, salvini@ds.unifi.it, vignoli@ds.unifi.it.

[1] Libya is an example of this. Until 1998 included among the high fertility countries (in 1998 the TFR was estimated as 5.92), the following year, because of the results of the 1996 Survey, the first since the 1973 Census, it was included among moderate fertility countries, with a TFR of 3.5. Another example is Morocco. Forecasts made in 1982 estimated the population would be about 59 million in 2025, but the projections were corrected after the 1994 census to a figure of about 40 million; the latest projections (1998) now estimate the population will be about 38 million in 2025. These corrections are due to the particular rapidity of demographic changes in the South-East shore countries, and also to the persistence, "until proven otherwise", of the stereotype of high Muslim fertility.

The main countries (or perhaps only the forerunners) affected by this demographic revolution are the countries facing onto the Southern (Algeria, Libya, Egypt, Morocco, Tunisia) and Eastern (Turkey) Mediterranean. In these countries the period total fertility rate among women with secondary education is often less than two children per woman; consequently, these recent developments undermine the reputation of this area (apart from Turkey) as a bastion of family conservatism and as having a high fertility rate. But are these groups of educated women forerunners of a broader and more generalized spread of a decline in fertility or only of a plurality of behaviours in the increasing heterogeneity of such societies, which are still very traditional but at the same time are undergoing modernization?

On the northern shores of the Mediterranean, the countries of southern Europe are in turn undergoing a highly singular demographic evolution towards lowest-low fertility rate (Sardon, 2002). Family and social evolution is increasingly distinctive and differs greatly from that of central and northern Europe, due to cultural reasons relating to what seems to be a typically Mediterranean view of family ties and gender balances. Are the southern Mediterranean countries undergoing a demographic transition along the lines of those experienced by countries on the northern shores, with which there have always been close ties and cultural mixing? Can we affirm that a South-North convergence is taking place in Mediterranean fertility?

The aim of our study is to investigate the extent and the value of the recent demographic changes. The question is whether they fit into a particular Mediterranean fertility pattern, with South-East women therefore moving along the path taken by Mediterranean Europe towards an exceptional low fertility rate (a sort of "convergence assumption"), or whether this "developmental" theory might be too simplistic and Eurocentric.

The concept of convergence lies at the heart of the demographic transition theory (Wilson, 2001). Adopting quite a schematic approach, the theory of demographic transition assumes that sooner or later countries must pass through different stages, along a path from high to low levels of mortality and fertility. In fact, apart from some countries in sub-Saharan Africa, a decline in fertility has now begun all over the world, and this process is substantial (albeit with a significant tail of high-fertility). Wilson's (2001) recent review reconfirms that in order to understand this phenomenon it is necessary to look beyond both economic development and special policy inputs. Well aware of the state of pervasive poverty, high levels of illiteracy and gender inequities in many regions, he states: "it is clear that social and demographic change has progressed far more rapidly than economic development". However, in terms of what kinds of social change are relevant for the process, we may only have reached the understanding that "there are many demographic transitions, each driven by a combination of forces that are [...] institutionally, culturally and temporally specific" (Greenhalgh, 1990).

The 2000 World Population Prospects (WPP) demonstrates the current state of the "mobility of countries" down the scale towards low fertility: 21 less developed countries have a fertility at or below replacement level, while the majority of the remaining 122 less developed countries have levels below 5 children per woman but well above replacement level. However, Wilson interprets the trend as one of the growing demographic convergence in the world. He summarizes: "A large majority of the world's population is (or soon will be) demographically modern by any definition".

The WPP prefers to emphasize the opposite, namely growing signs of polarization in the world: "particularly rapid growth is expected to nearly triple between 2000 and 2050 [...]"; 16 countries "exhibit sustained high fertility for which there is either no recent evidence about fertility trends or the available evidence does not indicate the onset of a fertility reduction". With respect to the latter group of countries, the 1998 WPP was too optimistic about incipient fertility declines, and population estimates have been adjusted upwards in the 2000 WPP (Egerö, 2001). Given the extent to which fertility has been declining in almost all countries, Wilson (2001) concluded that the overwhelming trend is for low fertility to become a general feature of poor and rich countries alike and that the distinction between developed and developing countries will therefore be of greatly diminished relevance to fertility. In the convergence theory approach, the timing of the "narrowing process" is very important because, as it influences the achievement of generation replacement, it affects the increase in population and consequently the social development of countries as well (Wilson, 2001).

In this study we will outline current fertility against the broad background of family formation patterns in the Mediterranean countries, attempting to evaluate the "demographic" distance between the two shores. Moving from the macro to the micro level and focusing on education differentials, we will ask whether the characteristics of educated southern Mediterranean women are similar to those that were notably the basis of the determinants bringing about the onset of fertility decline in northern Mediterranean countries[2].

II. Fertility in the Mediterranean context: differences and factors of convergence between the two shores

A. Differences between the two shores and heterogeneity among South-East Mediterranean countries

Changes in fertility patterns are very marked in South-East Mediterranean countries (Figure 1). Fertility levels still appear to be over replacement level in all countries in North Africa and the Near East, but fertility rates have declined sharply in recent decades. The fall in fertility has not been equal across the countries, however, and the current fertility levels of Algeria, Egypt, Libya, Morocco, Tunisia and Turkey range on average from two to three children per woman[3].

Notwithstanding the large decline, comparing current levels of fertility, we can observe that countries facing onto the two Mediterranean shores still show very different behaviors in terms of timing and quantum of fertility. Looking at Figure 2, which shows the paths taken by countries in the post-war period, it can be said on the basis of analysis of current TFRs, that three southern shore countries – Morocco, Tunisia and Turkey, though with different timing – are "following" the same course as the northern shore, with a temporal gap of 20 years compared to Spain and Portugal and 30 years compared to France, Greece and Italy.

In describing the changes in North Africa – though the same holds true for Turkey as well – from 1970 to 2000, Tabutin *at al.* (2001) point out that these recent changes are such that the demographic transition of this part of the world can be qualified as:

a) *late*: fertility decline has occurred at a later date than, for example, Latin America and Eastern Asia;

---

[2]   Here we analyze the most recent survey data (micro data) available for Italy, Spain and France in Mediterranean Europe (and Portugal as well, because of cultural and demographic similarities) and Egypt, Morocco, Tunisia and Turkey on the south Mediterranean shore. At the macro level we also considered Greece, Algeria and Libya.

[3]   The fertility rate remains moderate (greater than three children per woman) in Jordan, Libya and Syria and high (greater than five children per woman) in the WBGS, where demography forms part of the broader political struggle with Israel. Indeed, the total fertility rate in Gaza – an average of more than seven children per woman – is one of the highest in the world.

b) *rapid*: the pace of decline more than compensates for this delay (Rashad, 2000); it has evolved from a classic model of high fertility (with 7/8 children per woman) and precocious and universal nuptiality to a controlled reproduction model (less than 3 children, with a contraceptive prevalence of over 50%, see note 3), with a trend towards late marriage and the emergence of a certain percentage of definitively never married women;

c) *convergent*: the pace of change and the trend may be considered non-homogenous, but the whole region seems to be converging towards a comparable demographic model (with the exception of southern Egypt).

Transition has not been an uninterrupted process (Fargues, 1988). In Morocco, for example, fertility did not decline in a linear way in the period 1962-1972, but actually increased and then declined, while Egypt's first fertility transition between 1965 and 1970 was followed by a bi-decennial stagnation with annual fluctuations. Between 1970 and 1980 fertility increased significantly from 5.30 to 6.15, fell and then rose again to 6.31 in 1987. Even in Tunisia, which is regarded as a text-book case, fertility decline stalled briefly in the early 1990s, suggesting that three children was the basic irreducible minimum (Courbage, 2002), but recently it fell sharply to about two. Given the pre-transitional uniformity, during the process the differences exceed the similarities, whereas recent data suggest that the region is converging towards a comparable fertility model.

The proximate determinants are relatively clear: later marriage and, to a lesser extent, increased access to family planning services, have given women a greater degree of control over their fertility (Salvini, 1990). Consequently, a delay in entry into marital union has been the first step towards the process of convergence of the Islamic Mediterranean shore countries towards the Catholic ones.

The transition in Morocco offers a good illustration of how the two factors (delayed marriage and increased use of contraceptives) have gone hand in hand, except at the beginning. Between 1960 and 1971, the singulate mean age at marriage of only 17.3 years increased, but there was no decline in the general fertility rate. Between 1971 and 1982, the rising singulate mean age at marriage caused a fall in the total fertility rate from over 7 children to 5.5. Of the average annual reduction of 2.40%, nuptiality accounted for 1.45% and contraception for 0.95%. From 1982 to 1987, the fertility decline accelerated and most of the decline was attributed to the rising age at marriage. Finally, in the years 1987-1994, the role of contraception increased (Courbage, 2002).

Union patterns can explain the heterogeneity in fertility between Egypt and Morocco as well; among the older generations the difference used to be negligible (age at marriage was around 17 years); today, Egyptian women born in 1965-70 marry, on average, at the age of 20, while Moroccan women marry at 23.8 years.

The major differences in the process of transition between the southern – and northern shore countries (apart from the persistent imbalance) can be summed up as follows:

Firstly *the spectacular nature of the process*: in just thirty years the southern shore countries have experienced a transition in fertility that often took the European countries about a century (Vallin and Locoh, 2001); they also started with a much higher pre-transitional levels of fertility (6/7 children per woman).

Secondly, *the role of modern contraception*: while the transition in the North took place without safe contraceptive methods, in almost all the southern shore countries there have been programs explicitly aimed at limiting births[4]. However, it is worth underlining that various different approaches have been adopted by family planning services in the region. In Tunisia, for instance, the state took the initiative in family planning in the 1960s, reinforcing its efforts with policies aimed at improving women's status and explicitly recognizing the links between declining population growth and socio-economic development; Morocco only started giving strong support to family planning in the 1970s. After the 1994 ICPD, emphasis was given to services only for health reasons and for social benefits (UNICEF, 2001).

Finally *women's role in society*: in Muslim societies women's empowerment is still a burning issue. The concept is a multidimensional one that encompasses areas such as the practice of arranged marriages, the gender gap in educational enrolment, the low proportion of working women (in particular in the tertiary sector) and the incompatibility in these countries between working and fulfilling the role of wife (more than that of being a mother, as is usually the case). However, significant changes are also taking place in the Arab world with regard to views of male and female identity, family roles, relations between the sexes and the position that women occupy in public life (Lapidus, 1995). There are also marked differences between countries because gender roles are an

---

[4] Data derived from surveys carried out in the 1990s show the following level of contraceptive prevalence among women between 15 and 49: 51% in Algeria, 48% in Egypt, 45% in Libya, 50% in Morocco, 60% in Tunisia, 64% in Turkey. Source: World Bank, World Development Indicators, 1998.

ideological and political issue that are closely linked with religious considerations (Obermeyer, 1992).

However, in the area considered, the drop in arranged marriages, the increase in the level of education, the increase in age at marriage and the fall in the age difference between spouses can all favor the trend towards the weakening of female inequality in the family, a cardinal factor in women's *empowerment* in society[5].

The gender gap in education enrolment is narrowing, but the rates of female labor are still low and have grown little since the 1980s[6]. Work activity varies in inverse proportion to fertility, but with strong differentials between married and single women, more so than between women with or without children (Fargues, 2000). In fact, women tend to abandon work when they marry, effectively making it a prerogative of single people. In southern Europe, although the percentage of working women is much lower than in northern Europe, the "competition" is between the role of worker and that of mother.

The Muslim countries have also seen the emergence of a not insignificant proportion of economically independent women who do not marry (in countries where until recently non-married women were socially almost ignored and had no status of their own whatsoever); there are also a certain number of working mothers, a figure that has grown to the extent that various means of support, including the setting up of nurseries and the provision of small-scale loans, are beginning to be a subject for political debate (Rashad, 2000).

---

[5] See the positive relations that emerge from DHS surveys between dialogue between spouses and the characteristics of female "autonomy", generically correlated with the use of instruments of family planning and a lower number of desired children (for example, see El-Zanaty *et al.*, 1996).

[6] Participation of women in the labor force in 1980 and 1996 were respectively the following: 21% and 25% in Algeria, 26% and 29% in Egypt, 19% and 21% in Libya, 34% and 35% in Morocco, 29% and 31% in Tunisia, 35% and 36% in Turkey. Source: World Bank, 1998.

Figure 1: Fertility trends in South-Est Mediterranea Countries

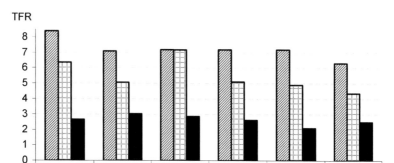

Figure 2 : Fertility trends in the Mediterranea Area: a comparison between Northern and Southern shores TFR$_S$

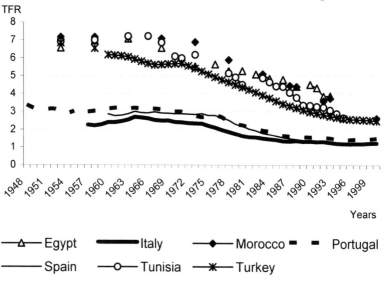

B. Historically strong family ties and marriage in the Mediterranean area: some similarities between the two shores

Possible convergence factors between the northern and southern shores should be sought in cultural and social similarities. There are considerable, historically deep-rooted similarities in family structure among the Mediterranean countries. Demographic and family behaviors in southern Mediterranean Europe, in terms of couple formation, fertility and living in the parental household, are currently quite different from those of central and northern Europe. The explanation of these behaviors (whether it is a delayed second demographic transition or whether they are completely different models) may also lie in the socio-cultural specificity of Mediterranean Europe. The "familism" of southern Europe, where the family in fact takes on many roles that are largely foreign to its tasks in northern countries, contrasts with a "civic culture" where the organization of solidarity for the needy and vulnerable in society is largely accomplished through public and private institutions (Reher, 1998).

Family ties may represent the keystone of socio-demographic evolution. The patterns of family relationships (between spouses, between parents and children, between older and younger generations) that largely characterized, at least until a few years ago, southern European families may be considered quite close to the intra-household relationships in North Africa. The concept of "Asabiyyah" (i.e. "esprit du corps", group solidarity based upon blood ties and reciprocal aid) has the extended meaning of an "alliance among kin" and resembles the concept of the close-knit network of the Mediterranean area (Micheli, 2000).

According to Reher (1998), we can observe strong family ties in the whole Mediterranean region. In other words, the role of family in southern Europe and on the southern Mediterranean shore is undoubtedly important in determining social networks that, in turn, condition some socio-demographic behaviors.

The evolution of marriage patterns also reveal some similarities in the two contexts: during the eighteenth century, female age at marriage continued to be noticeably earlier in much of southern Europe than in the northern part of the continent. It is also noteworthy that in the southern parts of Spain, Italy and Portugal, age at marriage throughout the pre-industrial period was always lower than in northern parts of the same countries. Moreover, even if age at marriage was never as low as in North Africa, in general southern European women married younger than in northern Europe.

Given that fertility takes place essentially within marriage in all the Mediterranean countries (unlike in central and northern Europe), age at marriage (Figure 3) greatly conditions mean age at first birth (in turn a key factor determining trends in higher order births).

Recent changes in the marriage pattern in Muslim countries are also considerable, and regard both the quantum (that is the proportion of the cohort members that finally marry) and the timing (that is the distribution of marriages by age). In many countries, between 7 and 21 per cent of women remain never married in the age group 30-39. While the proportion never married at age 40-49 is currently quite small, the situation of the cohorts now aged 30-39 suggests that it may increase. It is expected that Muslim societies with near universal marriage will soon become the exception rather than the norm (Rashad, 2000). If we look at the data in Figure 4, we can see that a profound modification has also occurred in the timing of marriage. Almost all the countries examined reveal significant changes (Algeria, Libya, Morocco, Tunisia) and the singulate mean age at marriage (SMAM) in some cases is similar to that of women living on the northern shore of the Mediterranean (who nowadays marry much later than some decades ago, probably due to the completion of education at a later age and greater participation in the labor market).

The Arab family is thus evolving towards that of Mediterranean Europe as a result of women's later age at marriage, but also due to a reduction in polygamy and the stabilization of the family unit caused by a drop in repudiation, the institution that for a long time substituted divorce in northern Africa (despite the persistence of a not negligible proportion of arranged marriages; Fargues, 2000).

Figure 3: Trend in the mean age at marriage for North Mediterranean countries

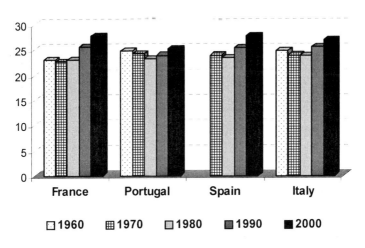

□ 1960   ▦ 1970   □ 1980   ▨ 1990   ■ 2000

Figure 4: Singulate Mean Age at Marriage (1990s data) of South Mediterranean countries

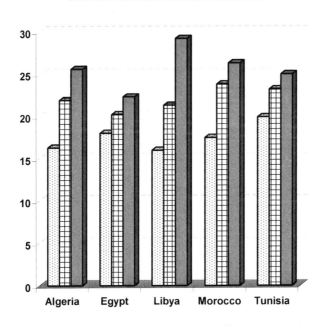

□ Women aged 45-49   □ Women aged 25-29   ■ Most recent data

III. The Relationship between Education and Fertility: Evidence in the Mediterranean Countries

If the drop in fertility is now significant throughout the Islamic world (Courbage, 2002), it has certainly been much faster to arrive in the North African countries than in those of the Middle East, probably due in part to the formers' greater exposure to Western models[7]. The control of fertility in the French-speaking Maghreb countries seems to have been closely related not only to a growth in living standards but also in education, which is increasingly egalitarian between the sexes.

In the countries considered, both in the North and in the South-East, the effect of education on fertility is always inversely proportional (Figure 5 and 6)[8], but there is in any case a very strong variability in the elasticity of fertility in relation to education level (Courbage, 2002). In Portugal and Greece (Symeonidou, 2002), for example, women aged 45-49 with a higher level of education have a slightly higher average number of children than women with an average level of education (Figure 6).

In the South-East Mediterranean countries, the impact of girls' greater access to education and the increasing availability of educational opportunities (although still greater in urban areas) is significant. Girls who reach secondary school are more likely to delay marriage and childbearing, their children tend to be healthier and their participation in the labor force relatively greater. Female education appears to be a determinant factor in the course of fertility whatever the socio-economic level (see, among others, UN 1995; Castro Martin, 1995). Education seems to remove the differences in fertility between the different countries; such differences continue to be high only for illiterate women, are still perceptible for women with a low to medium level of education, and are negligible for the more well-educated. From the first half of the 1990s, the average fertility of women with a high school certificate

---

[7]   See Courbage (2002) for a discussion of the influence of the French language mass media on the educated urban minorities of the Maghreb countries and of the *diaspora* towards Europe. We can assume that a key role in westernization is played by migration and in particular by returning migrants.

[8]   Note that the comparisons have been made on different quantities: on one side, on the southern shore, we have period TFRs, aggregating experiences of contemporary women cohorts, while on the northern shore, we have the cumulation of children ever born for women aged 45-49, a cohort of women who lived through the most intensive period of fertility on average 15-20 years before. This bizarre comparison is due both to the different nature of the data and to the aim of highlighting the temporal lag that divides the two shores in terms of the evolution of fertility.

settled in all the Arab countries at generational replacement levels. Even in Libya, for example, the average number of children of women with a high level of education is 2.1, while illiterate women have on average almost 6 children (Fargues, 2000).

However, some specific cases among Islamic countries suggest that education is not by itself sufficient to explain the different "transitions". For example, the birth rate began to decline in Morocco before it did in Jordan, despite the fact that the former is more rural and has a higher rate of illiteracy.

Another contradictory aspect is the link between education and female employment, and between female employment and the drop in fertility. Countries like Tunisia and Morocco, where the percentages of working women are still low (although they have increased), are those where a decline in fertility took place first (Fargues, 2000).

However, one might readily hypothesize that the process of convergence in fertility behavior in the South-East shore countries towards a Western-type "model", in particular towards the typicity of the countries facing onto the northern shore of the Mediterranean, is led by precursory groups of women who have a higher level of education (or in any case that educational level, in the absence of other variables regarding income or socio-economic status, is a proxy for them).

The relation between fertility and education may change in time and in the course of transition[9]. Caution must therefore be exercised in making comparisons in time and space. It is nevertheless interesting to focus on older women in northern shore countries and to see the differences by educational level, where fertility levels are approximately equal. The comparison is between current differential levels for the southern shore and the differential fertility of the northern shore some years ago, when the reproductive levels and models were, so to speak, less "regulated" and total fertility levels were similar. The process of convergence realized by the countries of the southern shore and the characteristics of the "forerunners" can be better evaluated if we look at fertility differences according to the level of education that existed some years ago, for example in European Mediterranean countries (see Figure 6, where we show data for older women).

---

[9] At a macro level, in comparing countries and placing side by side data relating to education levels and those of fertility, one notes in general a reversed U-effect of education. The effect is weak in poor societies, constituted mainly by illiterate people, pronounced in societies in transition, and weak again as soon as fertility transition is accomplished (Courbage, 2002).

Was the distance between the fertility of educated and non-educated women more accentuated in the past transition of the northern shore countries? Have active family planning policies in the South reduced these "normal" differences?

For the time being we limit the comparison to Italy. Women born in the years 1897-1901 and 1912-1916 show very large differences in the number of children ever born (Figure 7); women without education born at the turn of the century showed a fertility more than double that of women with a diploma or university degree (very few, in those years). Southern Italian regions had higher fertility and larger differences corresponding to education level (the TFR of illiterate women is more than double that of the more educated). The similarity with what is happening now in Tunisia or Morocco, with a temporal lag of some decades, is highly pronounced.

The previous points can guide us in subsequent research. It is reasonable to suppose that in the future there will be both a continuing spread of education and a narrowing of the gender gap, and the acceptance and adoption on the part of less privileged groups of family planning behaviors that have characterized the recent behaviors of more well-educated (and modern) women. One might quite well assume that the analysis of current data will confirm that amongst all the age classes there are "pioneer" subgroups with low fertility, for instance among more educated women.

However, precisely because the group of more educated urbanized women may not be numerically very substantial, the aggregate effect may not be particularly visible. It is thus important to change the focus of the study, and consequently the level of analysis of the data, and to shift from a macro analysis to an analysis of individual data[10]. In the next section of this work, the comparison between the fertility of the South-East and the North Mediterranean is carried out using survival models from one parity to another for groups of women rendered homogenous according to age and educational level. More specifically, due to sample number problems, the level of education is simply dichotomized into the categories of "illiterate or low level education" and "with average or high education"; women are grouped by cohort (born since 1970, from 1960 to 1969, from 1950 to 1959 and before 1950).

---

[10] The "optimum" level of analysis concerning the convergence in demographic behaviors is still subject to debate. Following a so-called classic process and basing our study on the available data, it seemed natural to us to shift from a descriptive study of the differences between states carried out with average measures to one based on individual data, in the search for differential "propensities", understood in a probabilistic sense (Billari and Wilson, 2001).

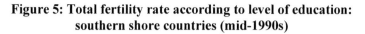

**Figure 5: Total fertility rate according to level of education:
southern shore countries (mid-1990s)**

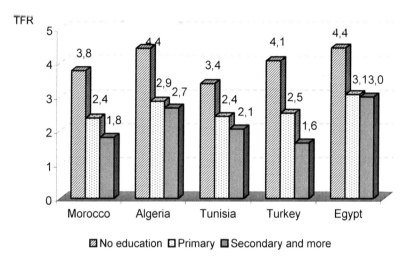

**Figure 6: Children ever born (CEB) to women 45-49 according
to level of education: northern shore countries (mid-90s)**

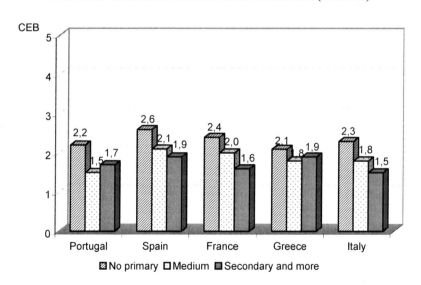

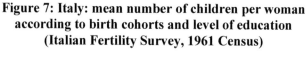

**Figure 7: Italy: mean number of children per woman
according to birth cohorts and level of education
(Italian Fertility Survey, 1961 Census)**

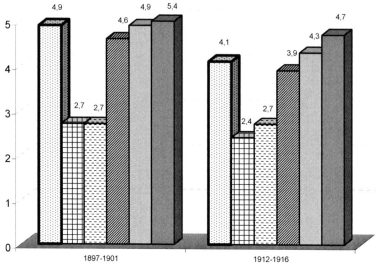

■ Total □ Diploma, degree ▤ Primary school ▨ Elementary school ▦ Read and write ▨ Cannot read and write

Source: ISTAT (1974).

IV. An Analysis of Childbearing Patterns Using Individual Data

The analysis is based on the most recent retrospective survey data available for Egypt, France, Italy, Morocco, Portugal, Spain, Tunisia and Turkey derived from Fertility and Family Surveys (Carrilho and Magalhaes, 2000; Delgado and Castro Martin, 1999; De Sandre *et al.*, 2000; Toulemon and de Guibert-Lantoine, 1998), Demographic and Health Surveys and Arab Maternal and Child Health Surveys carried out in the 1990s[11]. The surveys used detailed birth-history data and information on the demographic and socio-economic background of the respon-

---

[11] Ideally, to better highlight the similarities or differences in fertility patterns and timing during different phases of demographic transition between South-East Mediterranean countries and northern ones, we should have compared individual data of current southern women to those of northern women, when the aggregate level of fertility was similar. The non-availability of individual data is of course the main obstacle to such a comparison.

dent women. The survey designs are quite similar but the southern shore data are collected only for ever married women; so, in order to compare findings, in the North we took into consideration only ever cohabiting women. As we will see later, this represents a limit for our analysis of age at marriage and fertility of younger generations.

In order to understand the contribution of the socio-economic independent variable (covariates), we carried out comparative analyses applying hazard models. We built two models: the first one including only the main effects – a proportional hazard Cox model; the second one including the interactions of the first order between time (duration of the intervals) and the covariates – in this case, it is no longer a proportional hazard model, but simply a hazard model.

In some cases, which we will highlight during the discussion of the results, it has not been possible to consider all the covariates or the same modalities for the variables[12]. The covariates, chosen according to the availability of information and following the results of previous analyses and literature on this issue[13], can be divided into "control variables" (birth cohort, previous birth interval, age at first union, age at previous birth) and "explanatory variables" (place of residence, level of education, professional status of the woman and of the partner).

The dependent variable of the model is represented by the length of interval (measured in months) between union and first birth, between first and second birth and between second and third birth. With this approach, the family-building process is disaggregated into a series of stages beginning with marriage, followed by the first, second, and successive births. An advantage of this approach is that it provides greater insight into the mechanism underlying fertility differentials (Eltigani, 2001).

The results of the first model with the main effects are shown in Figure 8.

The duration of intervals between births currently seems to be significantly influenced by education and by female working status both in the southern European countries, and in the Islamic ones. More educated women show longer intervals, and a lower hazard, than less or not-educated women, in the transition from one parity to the next. But the

---

[12] With regard to women's jobs, only data for countries belonging to the northern shore countries distinguish current working women from those who are retired or students or housewives. In the case of the Morocco data, it has not been possible to include the variable regarding the husband's job, whereas for the Tunisian data we have only information on agricultural and non-agricultural workers.

[13] See among others, Ongaro's study (1990) on the first Italian fertility survey data.

effects are generally different in different contexts. In Spain and Portugal, the risk of passing from one parity to the next is lower by about 20% for educated women compared with the reference category, while in Morocco, Tunisia and Turkey this risk is halved. An exception is represented by Italy, where the differences between more educated and reference groups of women are larger and quite similar to the developing countries.

Among the South-East countries, an important effect of education emerges in particular in the higher intervals (especially in Tunisia, where the hazards are much lower for more educated women). For the first interval, education effects are less evident, probably because all women who marry have at least one child (with the exception of those with fecundity problems).

In the second model, we also considered also interaction terms[15]. Interaction terms relative to education, often significant, are generally positive (with the exception of Tunisia for the third and fourth parities and Egypt for the first interval). This might mean that the greater the duration of the intervals, the more the negative effect, measured by the main effect coefficient, is reduced.

In the northern shore countries working status also generally tends to reduce the hazard for all parities. The high values of coefficients seem to confirm the negative relationships between work and fertility in contexts where the organization of society, work arrangements and gender roles are not "mother-friendly".

In the southern shore countries the results are less evident. Only Turkey shows a pattern similar to the European countries that are also at low parities, while the other countries sometimes have significant negative coefficients only for the higher birth orders.

Residence, as it was reasonable to assume, generally does not have a significant impact on timing of fertility in the lowest-low fertility countries, while the effect is often significant in South-East countries. Living in an urban context decreases the hazard of passing from one parity to the next, apart from in Tunisia, where the coefficients are not significant.

The duration of the previous interval and often the age at the beginning of the interval considered are the most significant of what we call the "control variables". In particular, in the northern shore countries only age at union (marriage or cohabitation) shows an important effect – the higher the age at union, the longer the first interval. With regard to this, it is important to emphasize that the results concerning the interval

---

[15] Results are not reported, but are available on request.

marriage-first birth for the southern Mediterranean countries are difficult to interpret. One possible explanation may lie in the composition of the group of respondents in the first years of marriage, when first births occur. These groups include women who married very young and who are therefore selected from many points of view. The variables taken into account in our study may not entirely explain this complex situation.

Figure 8 : A comparison of the "main effects" for the transition from the 1st and 2nd child

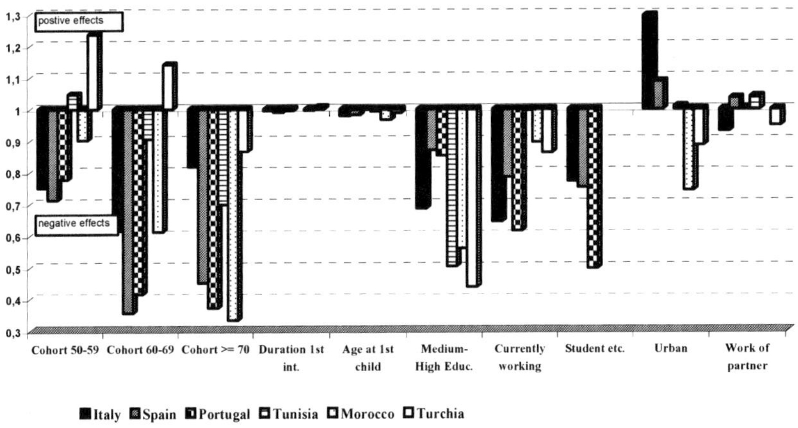

■Italy ▨Spain ▨Portugal ▢Tunisia ▨Morocco ▢Turchia

(results of the hazard models)

V.   Discussion and open issues

The fertility transition is now underway in almost all the countries of the South-East Mediterranean, and the prospect of convergence in the long run with the demographic course of the northern shore countries is no longer improbable.

Widely available education (particularly female) and urbanization have influenced reproductive behavior. Despite the limited presence of women in the labor market, the irreversible drop in fertility seems to prefigure considerable social transformations – erosion of patriarchy and modification of the status of women in society – (Fargues, 2000).

Trends in period fertility are the net result of modifications in timing – that is the distribution of births in the course of the cohorts' life – and in intensity – that is the number of children ever born –. For South-East Mediterranean countries, contemporary TFR is depressed by the rise in the mean age at childbearing.

The question is how will this postponement effect continue in the future? We believe that the trend will continue, if only as a result of the ongoing trend towards greater education amongst women. Education is related to a later entry into both married life and fertility life. What the level of fertility will be when the rise in age at marriage and age at childbearing by order ends in the long run and that particular fertility-depressing effect stops, is of course impossible to say.

In the short run, the trend of convergence of period TFRs between the two Mediterranean shores (although fertility levels are still quite different) should also continue not only because of the postponement of fertility in the South, but also because of the current mechanism in the North. In fact, since 1999 there has been a small increase in the level of period TFRs in France, Spain, Greece, Italy and Portugal, although it is unlikely that South Mediterranean fertility will rebound to replacement level (Bongaarts, 2001); this is partly due to a recuperation effect by the cohorts, and also to the contribution of immigrant women with a higher fertility.

In South-East countries the role of women may represent one of the key factors in the process. Even if at the present moment women have a low participation in the labor market, we can hypothesize that in the future, with the increasing enrolment in higher levels of education, this commitment will increase. Courbage (2002), for example, states that only university and professional education ensure active participation in the labor market, and that fertility seems more sensitive in the transition from inactive to active women (even if they belong to the blue-collar sector) than between uneducated women and primary school educated ones.

On the other hand, Reher (2001) observes, from empirical studies, that once fertility has decreased dramatically, the opportunity cost of children for working females increases but the reproductive process occupies a shorter period of women's active lives, thereby allowing them to increase their labor force participation. Whether this is the description of the future of the Islamic countries that we have considered in this study we cannot say, also because the evolution may be influenced both by underemployment and unemployment, which is very high and increasing in the southern Mediterranean region, and by the unpredictable relationship between women's role and Islamic traditional culture.

References

Billari, F., Wilson, C. (2001), "Convergence towards Diversity? Cohort Dynamics in the Transition to Adulthood in Contemporary Western Europe", Rostock, *MPIDR Working Paper* WP-2001-039.

Bongaarts, J. (2001), "The End of the Fertility Transition in the Developed World", www. popcouncil.org./publications/WP/PRD/rdwplist.htlm.

Carrilho, M. J., Magalhaes, G. (2000), Fertility and Family Surveys in Countries of the ECE Region, Standard Country Report, "Portugal", *Economic Studies*, No. 10 p., UNECE, UNPF.

Castro Martin, T. (1995), "Women's Education and Fertility: Results from 26 Demographic and Health Surveys", in *Studies in Family Planning*, 4.

Courbage, Y. (2002), *New Demographic Scenarios in the Mediterranean Region*, Paris, INED.

De Sandre, P., Ongaro, F., Rettaroli, R., Salvini, S. (2000), Fertility and Family Surveys in Countries of the ECE Region, Standard Country Report, "Italy", *Economic Studies*, No. 10, UNECE, UNPF.

Delgado, M., Castro Martin, T. (1999), Fertility and Family Surveys in Countries of the ECE Region, Standard Country Report, "Spain", *Economic Studies*, No. 10, UNECE, UNPF.

Egerö, B. (2001), "Global Disorder: An Important Agenda for 21st Century Population Studies", paper presented at the IUSSP Conference 2001, Salvador de Bahia Session S35: Demography and Politics (website: http://www.iussp.org/ Brazil2001/s30/S35_P03_Egero.pdf).

Eltigani, E. E. (2001), "Childbearing in Five Arab Countries", *Studies in Family Planning*, Vol. 32, No. 1, pp. 17-24.

El-Zanaty, F., Hussein, E., Shawky, G., Way, A. and Kishor, S. (1996), *Egypt Demographic and Health Survey 1995*, National Population Council, Cairo, Egypt and Macro Int. Inc., Calverton Maryland, USA.

Fargues, P. (1988), "La baisse de la fecondité arabe", *Population*, 43, 6, pp. 975-1004.

Fargues, P. (2000), *Générations arabes. L'alchimie du nombre*, Paris, Fayard.

Fargues, P. (2003), "La femme dans les pays arabes: vers une remise en cause du système patriarchal? ", *Population et Sociétés*, n. 387, pp. 1-4.

Greenhalgh, S. (1990), "Toward a Political Economy of Fertility: Anthropological Contributions", *Population and Development Review* 16, 1, March, pp. 85-101.

Irc-Unicef (2001), *Towards a New Agenda for Children in the Southern Mediterranean Countries: a Rights-based Analysis*, mimeo.

Istat (1974), *Indagine sulla fecondità della donna*, Note e Relazioni No. 50.

Lapidus, I. (1995), *Storia delle società islamiche*, Vol. III, *I popoli musulmani secoli XIX-XX*, Torino, Giulio Einaudi Editore.

Kalbfleisch, J., Prentice, R., 1980, *The Statistical Analysis of Failure Time Data*, New York, Wiley.

Mencarini, L., Salvini, S. (2004), "Mediterranean Fertility: towards a South-North Convergence?", *Popolazione e Storia*, 2.

Micheli, G. A. (2000), "Kinship, Family and Social Network: The Anthropological Embedment of Fertility Change in Southern Europe", *Demographic Research*, 3(13).

Obermeyer, C. M. (1992), "Islam, Women and Politics", *Population and Development Review*, 18, 1, pp. 33-57.

Ongaro, F. (1990), "Demographic and Socio-economic Determinants of Birth Interval Length in Italy; a Hazard Model Analysis", *Working Papers 1990.3*, Dipartimento di Scienze Statistiche, Università degli Studi di Padova.

Rashad, H. (2000), "Demographic Transition in Arab Countries: a New Perspective", *Journal of Population Research*, Vol. 17, N.1, pp. 83-101.

Reher, D. (1998), "Family Ties in Western Europe: Persistent Contrasts", *Population and Development Review*, 24 (2), pp. 203-234.

Reher, D. (2001), "The Demographic Transition Revisited", paper presented at IUSSP Conference *The History of World Population in the Second Millennium*, Florence, Italy, June 2001.

Salvini, S. (1990), "La demografia delle Rive Sud e Est", in M. Livi Bacci and F. Martuzzi Veronesi (ed.), *Le risorse umane del Mediterraneo*, Bologna, Il Mulino, pp. 125-153.

Sardon, J. P. (2002), "Evolution démographiques récente des pays développés" *Population*, 57, No. 1, pp. 123-170.

Symeonidou, H. (2002), Fertility and Family Surveys in Countries of the ECE Region, Standard Country Report, "Greece", *Economic Studies* No. 10w, UNECE, UNPF.

Tabutin, D., Vilquin, E., Biraben, J. N., 2001, "L'Afrique du Nord", paper presented at the IUSSP Conference *The History of World Population in the Second Millennium*, Florence, Italy, June 2001.

Toulemon, L., de Guibert-Lantoine, C. (1998), Fertility and Family Surveys in Countries of the ECE Region, Standard Country Report, "France", *Economic Studies* No. 10e, UNECE, UNPF.

United Nations (1995), *Women's Education and Fertility Behaviour: Recent Evidence from Demographic and Health Surveys*, New York, United Nations.

Vallin, J., Locoh, T. (2001), *Population et développement en Tunisie. La métamorphose*, Tunis, CERES Editions.

Wilson, C. (2001), "On the Scale of Global Demographic Convergence 1950-2000", *Population and Development Review*, 27 (1), pp. 155-171.

World Bank (1988), World Development Indicators 1998.

Not Only Olives and Citrus Fruits
The Language of Agriculture[1]

Luigi Omodei ZORINI[2]

Università di Firenze

I. Agriculture: A "Peculiar" Productive Sector

In the central theoretical scheme of economics (theory of value and/or prices) agriculture is naturally perceived, in a first approximation, as a mere section of the social productive process[3]. The most distinguishing feature is the prevalence of decreasing returns, while elsewhere production is characterized by increasing returns. Like every other productive sector, it produces commodities for the general market. In a monetary economy, supply and demand of agricultural products, like all other products, are mediated by the system of prices. It is assumed that the price provides the producers and consumers of agricultural products, as well as the other producers and consumers, with all the information needed to make their choices.

The technical peculiarities of agricultural production are introduced in a second approximation: its identification with biological processes, the substantial role of solar energy and natural resources, which deter-

---

[1] This paper represents a slightly modified version of a previous one that was written by the Author jointly with Prof. Giacomo Becattini, from the same University, and was presented at the Vth Symposium of the European Group of IFSA (International Farming Systems Association) held in Firenze in April 2002. The two authors agreed upon the use of the paper here.

[2] Dipartimento di Economia Agraria e delle Risorse Territoriali, Università degli Studi di Firenze.

[3] Historically the story to be told is quite different: the physiocratic school of economic thought, shaping its theory on contemporary (18th century) reality, attributed to agriculture a central role in the explanation of economic phenomena. But with the English classical school of political economy, agriculture was reduced to a sector, similar, in principle, to all the others.

mine the seasonality of productive cycles, the diversity of technical conditions, as well as different levels of fertility, and the diversification of productive potentials, with the consequent territorial specialization of agricultural activities and their spatial scattering ("in the open"). The peculiarities of agricultural productions determine, all in all, a prevailing tendency to decreasing returns to scale.

Finally, we can consider a third approximation, rather on the borderline between agrarian economics, rural sociology and cultural anthropology, which relates agricultural activities to their historic-cultural background. This last tendency has found expression and has been discussed mainly by some sectors of European agricultural economists[4], significantly some Italians (Serpieri, Rossi Doria and Bandini in Italy or Malassis in France), but it is largely considered as trespassing on the frontier of proper economic studies.

The representation of the countryside as the site of a mere productive sector, appears now very reductive; since the country is nowadays assuming, or re-assuming, an increasingly multifunctional role, especially in the most developed economies. This reconfirms its crucial role in the general functioning of the socio-economic system.

Indeed, new functions have been added to the traditional function of direct producer of foodstuff. These are: a) a supplier of many raw materials for an increasingly complex and roundabout agro-food industry, b) an important market outlet for products of manufacturers with some means of production, c) an occupational buffer to the employment-unemployment cycle of an industrial origin (e.g., multi-activity families), d) an autonomous, diffuse, directly productive activity aimed at self-consumption, e) an essential contribution to the protection and conservation of the territory; f) a therapeutic function (Senni S., 2001) for social categories undergoing urban *stress* (e.g. urban population), or finding themselves vulnerable or at risk (disabled, drug-addicted).

---

[4] In general, according to the flow of economic-agrarian studies that has developed in Europe, the farm or the agricultural entrepreneur are no longer at the center of the matter, but territory is instead the core issue, in its wider meaning as a system of natural, social and institutional resources, as proved by the thriving of studies on "farming systems" (AFSRE-IFSA, conference proceedings). One of the reasons that led to the discovery, or the rediscovery, of the territorial dimension, following the "fashion" – I'm using this term only as a provocation, aware that this was probably a necessary phase of the process, (De Benedictis, Fabiani and Jacoponi) – of quantitative analysis of a neoclassical and marginalist type, was the realization of the survival and the resilience of the myriad of small farms, even in industrialized countries (in Italy "professional" farms account for no more than 15% of the total).

A. From Simple Needs to Clusters of Needs

Agriculture and animal husbandry are mainly devoted to the production of human foodstuff, albeit with some important exceptions (e.g., the production of wood or textile fibers)[5]. The traditional theory of individual consumption choices does not provide us with any insight on the evolution of human needs, because it takes as a given datum (determined elsewhere) the variables of the choice function (Georgescu Roegen, 1966). This inability of the mainstream choice theory to provide us with useful forecasting on the development of demand over time – which is what we need to plan a suitable policy – suggests resorting to alternative theories of consumption more in tune with modern times. We refer here to the Lancasterian virtual decomposition of goods in their characteristics (K. Lancaster, 1966), meaning by these the proprieties of the goods that are taken, or should be taken, into account by the consumer in order to rationally allocate his buying power. Thus, we no longer say that what a person demands is, for instance, a car, but a certain cluster of characteristics (e.g., transport service, maximum speed, autonomy, comfort, social distinction, etc.). This means that through that commodity the consumer satisfies a certain cluster of explicitly perceived or implicit needs.

There are some basic needs (e.g., certain vitamins, liquid foods, etc.), essential for survival, that are often, but not always, satisfied by single-use goods (e.g. water); the consumption of which ceases when the satiation level is reached and the act of consumption is repeated only when the subject perceives the lack as painful. Since they must all be satisfied, at least to a certain minimum degree, it is not possible to rank them. In contrast, a sort of variable hierarchy of needs does play an important role for all needs that are more strictly related to social life (e.g., need of distinction, of reliability) (Witt, 1998).

A good is defined as "complex" when it jointly satisfies several needs (as the car previously mentioned, or a TV set, for instance, that satisfies the needs of information, entertainment, social distinction, and so on) and as "simple" (but this tends to become an exception) if complexity is attributed the value of one. According to this approach, it may be useful to reverse the usual interpretative scheme of the system of exchanges: in principle, each product satisfies a cluster of needs which overlaps only partially with that of another product. Two products never exactly cover the same cluster of needs. That is, each producer is viewed

---

[5]   Only with the rather late advent of the concept of "primary sector" (which includes agriculture) have mineral raw materials been added to strictly agricultural products.

as a conditional monopolist of a product satisfying a certain cluster of needs.

In a rich and diversified economy, agricultural products, like all others, jointly satisfy several needs (vintage wine serves to quench one's thirst, enjoy special tastes and aromas, increase pleasantness of food, demonstrate one's social position and/or enological expertise, etc.). When a food product enters, so to speak, into the category of complex goods, the saturation level of its demand tends to shift, according to: a) changes in the cluster of satisfied needs, b) competition with other goods – sometimes technologically very distant (e.g., caviar and champagne, furs and jewels) – to satisfy some of those needs[6].

The growth in demand for complex goods increases small-scale production, well modulated on special sets of needs. The production of such kind of goods (food specialties) is not, in fact, easily referable to standardized and mass production. As a consequence shifting towards more and more complex goods: a) increases employment of manpower more than an equivalent increase in standardized goods; b) increases reproduction and development of productive know-how, which can only be learnt by observing the producer in action (contextual knowledge) (Becattini e Rullani, 1993).

B. Role and Destiny of Agriculture in a Capitalistic Society

According to a widespread interpretation of the productive role of agriculture in a capitalistic society, this sector is essentially viewed as: a) a direct or indirect supplier of food products; b) a reservoir of workforce for the development of industrial and service sectors. This means that its importance, in terms of share of GNP, can only decrease. In other words, when the average income of the families of a country increases, the share of their expenditure devoted to food should decline (Engels' laws). The statistics appear to confirm this deduction (Fuà, 1974).

At the same time, the world's vision that is implicit in a great part of political economics tends to reduce countryside to a rearguard, and a backlog, of socio-economic progress. For instance, scientific-technological progress – the *deus agitans*, together with the entrepreneurship, of capitalistic progress – originates exclusively, according to a widely

---

[6] Already in 1947, Serpieri, an acute observer of human behavior, was aware of the evolution in consumption: "Now: in widely industrialized European countries physiological needs and taste in consumption are mainly devoted towards quality products. This consumption is more a nerve consumption than a muscle consumption: the possibility of an increase in the demand for such products is very high, as their cost and prices diminish and the level of wealth in the country increases; while the demand for mass products remains rather rigid" (Serpieri, 1947).

spread opinion, in the urban environment, which is rich in intellectual stimuli, unlike the rural environment, which is static and culturally "empty". The motor of progress, therefore, is inside the city, while the country follows reluctantly at a distance and slows down progress[7].

Therefore, the "natural" tendency of the general economist is to reduce agriculture to a productive sector, in principle, similar to the others, and the countryside to the mere place where agriculture is practiced, delegating all problems of the historical-social roots of agricultural practices to rural sociology, that is to something external to proper agricultural economic studies.

In this view of capitalistic development, the destiny of the countryside is the progressive divarication into areas of "industrialized" agriculture, increasingly similar, *mutatis mutandis*, to industrial areas and recreational sites (golf courses, etc.).

II. From the Agricultural "Sector" to the Rural "Local System"

A. Agriculture and Rurality

Capitalistic economic development has led to a relative enrichment of the upper-middle classes, as a distributive trait dominant in "advanced countries". The strong and continuous increase of *pro-capita* income of these classes has led to a substantial saturation of their basic needs[8] and to the emergence of different types of needs, more differentiated, diversified, personalized. In our terminology, agricultural products have become more and more complex and the overlapping among the different clusters of needs has spread a great deal. However, once the market distributive mechanism of income is taken for granted, this passage to an increasing multiplicity of needs, and to a continuous breakdown and recomposition of clusters of needs, is the basic condition for a continuous expansion of the trade area, which is, in turn, essential to a greater division of labour and to its increased productivity.

Correspondingly to this continuous widening of the set of needs perceived by a substantial proportion of consumers – the middle-upper class – there has been an articulation of the rural world between two limit types of territorial organization, mass production and "integrated specialties", which will be later defined. With the former we intend that

---

[7]   A relevant exception is represented by Carlo Cattaneo.

[8]   Despite the fact that the concept of basic needs always contains an historical element, that causes variation in its composition and level according to the context.

part of processing activity requiring particularly high doses of the factor *land*, the latter refers to processing activities that also require a *very peculiar* input, *local rural society*, for which land, albeit essential, is only the material basis. The former is dominated by competition among producers as a means to satisfy a given, well specified, need (e.g., competition among producers of sunflower or maize) or a given cluster of needs (e.g., competition between different varieties of table or frying oil); the latter involves competition among producers to satisfy/modify contiguous clusters of needs, which overlap and merge with one another (e.g., need of drinks, of distinction, etc.).

This approach does not simply put competition of *quality* against the traditional competition of price, but also extends the concept of a traded commodity from a uni-dimensional object to a multi-dimensional object. In other words, what is produced and sold, in the very last analysis, is a whole complex series of utilities (characteristics), incorporated in an object or a service, which satisfies, in various ways, clusters of needs perceived by the inhabitants of each place (e.g., traditional foods, their process of production being known), and are offered to foreign buyers and visitors together with the *image* of a place (for example Brunello wine and the area of Montalcino). Therefore, we speak of *food specialties* (e.g., "delicacies") and also of *integrated specialties*[9].

In industrial agriculture, no differently from what occurs in every other industrial sector, there is competition among well-identified groups of producers, satisfying a common cluster of needs with a well-specified commodity. The varieties of such product can be graduated according to the content in terms of a main element (e.g., sugar content of sugar cane and sugar beet). In this case the price plays its regulatory role both on the side of consumers and producers.

In the case of production of our *specialties*, and even more so in the case of production of *integrated specialties*, the cost of production, which determines the average competitiveness of the farm representative of a certain place, is, properly speaking, no longer a single farm cost, although we can ascribe it to a virtual single *representative farm*, if the logical conditions apply (e.g., normal unimodal distribution). The cost of production represents, instead, the monetary equivalent of all the efforts and sacrifices (actions and omissions) necessary, on average, for the *normal production*[10] of that complex of goods and services with

---

[9] The concept is not entirely new to economists. In economic works closer to the topic of marketing, the idea that the services of the seller supplement the traded goods is fairly common.

[10] By normal production, we mean that production which is able to guarantee the reproduction of the process without impoverishing the productive background.

normal profits. In other words, a sort of stable solidarity, affecting production costs, is established between the agricultural producers and the embedding community.

B. The Four Agricultures

Against the evolution of needs of a consistent part of consumers, stand different types of agriculture that, in one way, evolved according to patterns of technological innovation and structure of costs similar to industrial ones, mainly located in irrigated plains and low hills, devoted to mass productions. In other ways, instead, it was unable to reach sufficient levels of competitiveness, not only and not so much because of lack of entrepreneurial capacity or availability of capital, but because of the harsher environmental factors. The specificity of agricultural production lies in the close interdependence between productive processes and environment that significantly condition competitiveness.

It is mainly in conditions of non-competitiveness, in terms of techniques and company's costs, that a special development potential can move in, linked to the capacity of agriculture to respond to the above mentioned clusters of needs and that we could call "territorial agriculture". We can therefore distinguish four main types of correspondences between the organization of agricultural production and the local society in which this is embedded.

A first type of agriculture relates to mass-production, with a prevalence of medium and large farms, a strong vertical integration within the agri-food industry, and without a particular identity, related either to the product or the territory. The development of the agricultural sector is here strongly related to exogenous technical-scientific progress and to agricultural entrepreneurship, as well as to positive or negative local externalities. It is governed by the law of company's costs (even if it is subject to the influence of economies external to the business), by the productive returns and the market price (for example cereal and industrial crops areas, etc.). This is actually the case of the companies that are most sensitive and open towards the policy component of the European Union Common Agricultural Policy.

A second type of agriculture is also oriented towards standardized productions, but on a smaller scale, and aimed mainly at self-consumption. Normally included in a local industrial or service system, it plays only a marginal role in the development of it, sometimes entering in conflict with the other sectors of the system for the use of resources. Its main function is residential not bearing any particular connotation of territorial identity and *contextual knowledge* of economic operators is mainly of an urban-industrial type (for example agriculture in the District of Prato) (Cianferoni, 1990 and C. Cecchi, 1988).

A third type of agriculture (specialties) is related to agricultural products historically linked to a certain area, because of some specific characteristics of the territory (e.g. composition of soil, climate, etc.) and/or of a peculiar, well-known and certifiable production process and human know-how. We refer to a typical product linked to the specific characteristics of a productive process strongly rooted in the territory of origin, both due to environmental characteristics and to the slowly developed know-how of the operators (e.g. *know-how* of Parmigiano-Reggiano or Roquefort cheeses or Parma and San Daniele hams).

A fourth type of agriculture – to which we will devote more attention – is typical of territories, which we may call *rural local systems*, with high environmental (e.g., historical remains and literary associations) and landscape value (e.g., position, climate, etc.) and is suitable for quality production (e.g., wine of recognized quality). This is the case in which we talk about *integrated specialties*.

Here, the buyer is offered a full basket of agricultural products, local crafts, sightseeing and cultural services. These situations are deeply rooted in the public's imagination and lead to the identification of products not only with the natural context, but also with the social and cultural context where they take form. Their development is linked to the capacity of creating a system among agricultural and extra-agricultural enterprises, institutions and local population, united by a specific local knowledge, or contextual knowledge, which is not only technical-sectorial, but also cultural and related to territorial resources. The demand for these products comes from outside (mainly from city dwellers) and often takes the form of the agritourism.

III.   The Kaleidoscope of Local Systems

If we move on to consider the social and economic aspects of the problem of local systems development, we must put forth two consider-ations: a) the identification of culturally homogenous areas (a homoge-neity which obviously must be taken with a "grain of salt"), and b) the identification of self-contained areas of exchanges and commuting for personal and employment reasons (a self-containment also to be taken with a "grain of salt").

Cultural homogeneity imparts significance, albeit always a relative one, to the scale of values and major objectives of a given population. Conversely, lack of cultural homogeneity, which corresponds to the random co-existence of different and incompatible scales of values and shared needs, prevents us, strictly speaking, from deciding whether a given change occurring in a certain area should be regarded, for those who live there, as an improvement or a worsening of their conditions of life. Hence the opportunity of adopting at least an indicative delimitation of areas in our countries that are roughly homogenous in cultural terms. There are plenty of statistical indicators available for this task that could be supplemented, if needed, by appropriate surveys and enquiries.

Naturally, this does not mean that in every culturally homogenous area (always in a very relative sense as we saw earlier), there are no disparities and conflicts of interest and aspirations, but rather that such disparities are to be found mainly within a network of some basic common values shared by the vast majority of the permanent residents of the area. Values that differ, in their systemic patterns, from those which are found in other areas of the country. Neither does it mean the rejection of cultural hybridizations, often positive and inevitable regardless, in a fast changing world.

Within areas of fairly large cultural homogeneity (e.g., a whole nation state or a well-defined region of it), we can identify areas of intense and continuous interaction between the conditions of daily life (the places and conditions of work, living, studying, worshipping and so forth) and the specific 'philosophy of life' (i.e. the system of behaviours, values and conscious aspirations) prevailing among the inhabitants. Geographers have approached this concept in terms of "daily urban systems" (Tinacci Mossello, 2000). Another conceptual benchmark may be represented by the 'local labour markets' (ISTAT, 1997).

If within a large area of approximate cultural homogeneity – say a region like Tuscany – sub-areas can be found where a great majority of the population both lives and works, each of these will display, in general terms, a differing intensity of some characteristics rather than others: a sort of local variant of that specific culture.

The actual measurement of the basic social and economic units that roughly correspond to these local variants is a very complex operation that may not, and normally will not, give unambiguous results. Regardless, this involves the use of a large set of statistical indicators, the carrying out of a wide range of targeted surveys, in order to clarify points that there was no other way to ascertain. This means that identifying local systems requires sensitivity, discernment and a clear sense of the interdependence of cultural, social and economic phenomena.

In this sense, we could try to tackle the problem of the various levels of local systems. To which territorial extent can the frequently mentioned strong link among natural environment, history and culture be referred? Whole blocks of administrative regions? Whole regions such as Tuscany, for example? Or smaller entities, such as a consortium of local authorities? For example, a consortium of mountain authorities or a district. If it is a matter of letting coagulate a sufficiently strong sense of belonging, identification and, therefore, responsibility. However, we believe the basic unit has to be relatively small. Something between a small-medium size municipality and present provinces. Now, if we want to create a clear bond between the powers and the tasks of local communities, and obtain a genuine support (not rhetorical nor formal nor superficial) of the citizens, a sense of belonging and identification is certainly necessary. This obviously interferes with the concept of bioregion, built up on quite different parameters: "it has to be sufficiently large to maintain vital ecosystems and biological communities, including the nutrients cycle and the waste cycle, and sufficiently small for the residents to consider it as their own home"[11]. With its relative "vegetable garden". This implies a plurality of levels (local, regional, national and European) among which the various functions, responsibilities and powers are divided. The problems to be solved are many and difficult, but for us the issue remains as the search for a self-reproductive local level, in economic, cultural and naturalistic terms (Omodei Zorini, 2000).

Local identities can be considered as blocks of population that: a) suggest a close interdependence between their economic life and their ecology (apart from intrinsically national or supranational factors); b) bring together individuals who, because of the place where they live, the life that they lead and the work that they mainly do, perpetuate and develop the distinctive characteristics of a common socio-cultural heritage, reacting actively, of course, to the overall world evolution; c) do not dissipate but, on the contrary, jealously guard the conditions of production and reproduction of tacit knowledge linked to productive processes located in their areas, but also well positioned in the world division of labour.

IV. Globalization and Territorial Division of Labour

Finally, let us express our viewpoint on the theme of this paper: the relationship between local identities – i.e. phenomena of local stable development – and globalization.

The fact that a local system can survive and develop in a capitalistic world only if it appropriately preserves its place in the general cultural

---

[11] "The bioregion has to have a cultural identity, on the basis of which the local community has a prior right to choose its destiny: prior right doesn't mean absolute right, but it means that local values, needs and interests represent the starting point for decision making in local sustainable development" (Jacoponi, 2001).

and economic panorama means that no place can be considered separately from what happens to the rest of the world. Our analysis leads to two conclusions, which are only part of a more general discourse not yet fully mature in our mind.

The first conclusion relates to the places producing *specialties*. We have already seen that for their survival and development such types of local systems need to keep the pace of the incessant evolution of needs and technological innovations that occur in the global market, safeguarding at the same time their naturalistic and cultural identity.

We can metaphorically think of a child flying a kite. The child, who is able to cope with running with the wind, represents the answering capacity of the local system, while changes in the direction of the wind represent the continuous evolution, or revolution, of the clusters of needs. For the kite to fly steadily and not to be lost, the legs and the hands of the boy have to be used at their best, while he holds back the kite and lets it go according to the winds.

Similarly, the future of local systems centered on "specialties" depends to a large extent on their capacity to use their productive know-how to respond to the challenges of the worldwide cultural and economic dynamics.

The problem of the local systems producing "integrated specialties" is different and somehow more complicated. Here, what is to be preserved is an image not of a cluster of goods, but of a cluster of goods and, in the background, a whole style of living, i.e. an interrelated complex of goods, activities, values and institutions. This is strongly related to an overall, let us say national, culture. And normally, but not necessarily, dependent on distance and facilities of communication. The general significance of the proliferation of this kind of local systems is an intensification of the network of relationships between cities and countryside[12]. In other words, a restoration, through new forms, of an intimate relationship between city and country, destroyed by the *capitalistic invasion* of the territory.

What assimilates the two cases just considered – places producing specialties and places producing integrated specialties – apparently wide apart, is the fact that both express the ultimate essence of the exchanges of goods, even of the most commercial ones, as services provided by a group of people to other groups. This is the philosophic meaning of the

---

[12] Even agricultural economists are experimenting with new methodologies for the interpretation of rural development as a "web" relationship system as those based on neural nets (Esposti, Sotte, 2001) or on the theory of fuzzy sets (Angeli, Franco, Senni, 1999).

division of labour. In one case this service is given in the form of material goods (specialties), in the other it is given throughout a direct sharing of living experiences (integrated specialties). Both cases show the inescapable human need of human relationships – even if in the form of commercial exchanges – between groups of people.

It is paradoxical – and should make us think – that such a reaction to the culturally de-structuring effects of a capitalistic development is produced precisely by the social stratum, the middle-upper class, that is the main beneficiary of the accumulation and concentration of capital.

A similar paradox occurs at a worldwide level in the relationships between industrialized and wealthy countries and the third world, ever more concerned with the fight against poverty and hunger and for which the evolutionary route generally intended involves mass production, with transfer of technological progress, according to an idea of development that is actually functional for the economies producing the technologies. Even at this level, the question recurs if the consumption of complex products, that incorporate material characteristics (including health characteristics such as in organic products) and non-material characteristics, typical of the territories and local communities here examined, represents an anticipation of future developments able to involve a wider strata of the population.

But what future can there be for those territories that are not competitive from the point of view of profits/costs or specialties, for which it is difficult to imagine the realisation of that net of relations we have spoken of? How can the dramatic lack of communication and social infrastructures that we have seen as the basis for overcoming the isolation of our territories once marginal and now oriented towards integration with the rest of the world be eliminated? How can the conditions for the creation of a "system" among institutions, producers and consumers that are at the base of the development of our local systems be created? Do wild globalisation and the consequent upheaval of a subsistence economy perhaps worsen the insufficiency of basic consumptions in these territories?

The massive movements protesting against the supremacy of wild competitiveness represent the most interesting socio-political novelty of these years. Is it possible to imagine – and this is the question that many are asking – a globalisation bearing a "human face", safeguarding civil, moral and cultural identities of the various territories and people? We have no answers to these questions, but we can hope that the growing strength of the protest will prompt an increasing number of social scientists to dedicate themselves to the problem and a growing number of lealers to take care of it.

Employment and Unemployment in a Multilevel Regional Perspective

Marcello SIGNORELLI

Department of Economics, University of Perugia

Introduction

The aim of this paper is to compare the employment performance at different levels of "regional" (dis)aggregation and to analyse the effectiveness of the European Employment Strategy in favouring net job creation and employment performance convergence.

In the first part, the (quantitative) differences in "regional" labour market performances are highlighted and briefly discussed. In particular, using the main employment indicators, we compare the United States and the European Union, Mediterranean and non-Mediterranean EU countries, "old" and "new" EU members, the Italian macro-Regions, Regions, Provinces and, finally, some local labour systems.

In the second part, the characteristics (method, instruments and final goals) and effectiveness of the European Employment Strategy (a complex "open method of co-ordination" of employment policies) are briefly analysed.

I. Comparison of the Employment Performance at Different Levels of "Regional" (Dis)Aggregation

The difficulties of defining a "regional" perspective are briefly discussed before presenting the empirical analysis at different levels of (dis)aggregation.

The comparative analysis of the labour market performance was conducted using the three quantitative objectives of the European Employment Strategy defined at the Councils of Lisbon (2000) and Stockholm (2001) as statistical indicators: (1) total employment rate (= total employment x 100 / working age population[1]); (2) female employment rate (= female employment x 100 / female working age population); and (3) older worker employment rate (= employed persons from 55 to 64 years old x 100 / population between 55 and 64 years old).

The use of the employment indicators in the comparative analysis is preferable with respect to unemployment indicators[2] for many reasons: (i) difficulties and differences in defining an unemployed condition; (ii) dependence of the unemployment rate on the rate of participation and of the latter on the employment rate. In particular, the compared evidence shows that similar unemployment rates are compatible with significant differences in employment rates[3].

II.A. Difficulties Defining a "Regional" Perspective

A "regional" dimension is characterised by extreme variations in the levels of possible (dis)aggregations and is generally used for comparative analysis between the considered areas.

In order to highlight the potential importance of the level(s) of (dis)aggregation, we have designated five possible levels: A (the highest aggregation), B, C, D and E (the lowest aggregation). Then, with reference to one or more performance variable(s) and considering the possibility that a certain set of units ("regions") has a "high" (H) or a "low" (L) differentiation[4], we discuss a few particular cases (Table 1), arising from the empirical analysis (ex-post) and unknown ex-ante. In case 1, the degree of "regional" differentiation is not significant at any of the levels of aggregation; in case 2 the degree of "regional" differentiation is only significant at one level (level A); in case 3 the degree of "regional" differentiation is significant at more levels (levels B, C, D and E); and in case 4 the degree of "regional" differentiation is significant at every level of (dis)aggregation (A, B, C, D and E).

---

[1] The working age population is considered as the population between 15 and 64 years old.

[2] The unemployment rate is calculated as follows: n° unemployed x 100 / labour force; with labour force = employment + unemployment.

[3] Besides, considering the importance of the fiscal wedge on labour (social contributions and labour income tax), the total employment rates are also relevant indicators of the sustainability of the national welfare systems.

[4] Obviously, the distinction in two possible situations (high or low) is for simplify the theoretical analysis.

Table 1: Some particular cases of multilevel regional differentiation

	Level A NUTS 0 (EU coun- tries)	Level B NUTS I (Macro- regions)	Level C NUTS II (Regions)	Level D NUTS III (Provin- ces)	Level E NUTS IV (Local labour systems)
Case 1	L	L	L	L	L
Case 2	H	L	L	L	L
Case 3	L	H	H	H	H
Case 4	H	H	H	H	H
………	…..	…..	…..	…..	…..

Notes: H = high differences; L = low differences.

The levels of aggregation that can be levels of government are highlighted in bold.

Nuts 0, I, II and III are the statistical regions defined by the European Union and largely corresponding to institutional (government) levels.

Obviously, with one or more "regional" levels that differ signifi- cantly there are important methodological implications and the empirical results depend strongly on the level of analysis chosen. For example, in case 2, we find a "regional" differentiation only if the empirical analysis was carried out at the level of (dis)aggregation A; as for the other levels of (dis)aggregation, the results show that there are no "regional" differ- ences. In case 3, if the empirical analysis was conducted at level A, we do not find significant "regional" differences, but performance differ- ences exist at the other levels of (dis)aggregation. Finally, in case 4 it is useful to consider all the different levels of (dis)aggregation for a com- parative analysis that takes into account the complex multilevel regional differentiation. So, the results and the policy implications (governance) of a comparative ("regional") analysis strongly depend on the level(s) of (dis)aggregation considered. Besides, there is a potential risk in choos- ing just one level of (dis)aggregation and the need for a multi-level comparative investigation arises. A large part of the existing literature that compares the labour market performance only considers one (*ad hoc*) "regional" level of analysis. In this paper, we compare the em- ployment performance at different levels of "regional" (dis)aggregation (groups of countries, national, regional, provincial and local levels), as highlighted in Table 2.

Table 2: Different levels of comparative empirical analysis

Level of (dis)aggregation (increasing order)	
International macro-areas	the European Union (EU) *versus* the United States
	Mediterranean EU members *versus* non-Mediterranean EU members
National level	"old" and "new" EU countries
	Mediterranean EU members
Italian sub-national levels	Italian macro-Regions
	Italian Regions
	Italian Provinces
	Local labour systems in the Umbria Region

II.B. International Macro-areas

Many empirical analyses compare the labour market performance of large international macro-areas. Here we briefly compare the European Union versus the United States and Mediterranean versus non-Mediterranean EU countries.

As is well known, the empirical evidence highlights the existence of significant gaps between the United States and the European Union[5] with respect to employment performance. A part of the empirical and theoretical literature has used the term "eurosclerosis" to describe the lower level of employment and net job creation in the European Union[6].

Table 3: Employment rates in the European Union and the United States (2000)

	Total Employment rate	Female Employment rate	55-64 Employment rate
European Union (15)	64	54	39
United States	74	68	58
coefficient of variation	0.10	0.16	0.28

Source: OECD – Employment Outlook (2002).

Notes: Total Employment rate = employment x 100 / working age population 15-64.

Female Employment rate = female employment x 100 / female working age population.

Older worker Employment rate = 55-64 employment x 100 / 55-64 population.

---

[5] A compared view of employment performance in the US and EU is proposed, for example, in Sapir (2004).

[6] The existence of labour market rigidities is considered one of the main causes of inadequate employment performance in the European Union.

Notice that, at this level of aggregation, Europe is considered as one "region", without the possibility of considering (eventual) differences between (and within) countries.

Some authors[7] have distinguished the European countries into Mediterranean and non-Mediterranean countries, in order to investigate the existence of a particular Mediterranean labour market model (structure and performance). The main employment data are presented in Table 4, using the usual three indicators and distinguishing between "old" and "new" (non-)Mediterranean EU countries[8].

**Table 4: Employment rates in Mediterranean
and non-Mediterranean EU members (2003)**

	Total Employment rate	Female Employment rate	55-64 Employment rate
Mediterranean "old" EU countries: (Italy, France, Spain, Portugal and Greece)	60.7 coeff. of var.= 0.07	50.0 coeff. of var.= 0.16	40.3 coeff. of var.= 0.19
non-Mediterranean "old" EU countries: (Denmark, The Netherlands, Sweden, United Kingdom, Finland, Austria, Germany, Ireland, Luxemburg and Belgium)	68.3 coeff. of var.= 0.07	61.9 coeff. of var.= 0.12	45.5 coeff. of var.= 0.30
Mediterranean "new" EU countries: (Cyprus, Malta and Slovenia)	62.1 coeff. of var.= 0.12	50.5 coeff. of var.= 0.29	34.7 coeff. of var.= 0.40
non-Mediterranean "new" EU countries: (Estonia, Latvia, Lithuania, Poland, Czech Republic, Slovak Republic and Hungary)	59.5 coeff. of var.= 0.08	54.4 coeff. of var.= 0.09	37.7 coeff. of var.= 0.29

Source: elaboration on Eurostat data (2004).

Notice that the well-known negative employment gap of the Mediterranean EU countries versus non-Mediterranean EU members is not true

---

[7]   See, for example, Bettio - Villa (1995).

[8]   Ten new countries entered the European Union in May 2004 (Estonia, Latvia, Lithuania, Poland, the Czech Republic, the Slovak Republic, Hungary, Slovenia, Cyprus and Malta).

considering the total employment rate of the new EU members. Obviously, the above arbitrary aggregations[9] can mask marked employment differences at the national level of analysis.

II.C. National Level of Comparison

The national level of analysis was conducted distinguishing between the "old" and "new" EU members[10], with particular attention directed toward the Mediterranean EU countries.

Considering the main "Lisbon objective", only four countries of the EU-15 have reached a total employment rate higher than 70% (Denmark, The Netherlands, Sweden and the United Kingdom); while eight countries (four of the EU-15 and four "new" EU members) have an employment rate (ER) lower than 60% (Spain, Belgium, Greece, the Slovak Republic, Hungary, Italy, Malta and Poland). The remaining countries (seven of the EU-15 and seven "new" members) show an ER between 60 and 70%. As regards the second "Lisbon objective", eight countries of the EU-15 plus Cyprus have a female employment rate higher than 60% (Sweden, Denmark, The Netherlands, Finland, the United Kingdom, Austria, Portugal and Cyprus), while five countries (three of the EU-15 and two "new" EU members) show a female ER lower than 50% (Spain, Poland, Greece, Italy and Malta). The remaining countries have a female ER between 50 and 60%. Considering the third European goal, defined at the Stockholm Council, only six countries (four of the EU-15 and two "new" EU members) have an employment rate for older workers (55-64) higher than 50% (Sweden, Denmark, the United Kingdom, Estonia, Portugal and Cyprus), while six countries (two of the EU-15 and four "new" EU members) show a 55-64 ER lower than 30% (Luxembourg, Hungary, Belgium, Poland, the Slovak Republic and Slovenia). Five countries have a 55-64 ER between 30 and 40%, while the remaining has an older worker ER between 40 and 50%.

A fourth European objective, not defined in precise quantitative terms, regards the reduction of irregular employment in the shadow economy. In the "old" EU members, the size of the shadow economy (as % of GNP) is the lowest in Austria (9.8%) and the highest in Greece (28.7%) and Italy (27.1%), with an EU-15 mean of 18.6. In the "new" EU members the shadow economy is generally higher than in the "old" EU countries, with an average of 26.9%. In particular, the Slovak and

---

[9] In particular, we decided to include Portugal and Slovenia among the Mediterranean EU countries.

[10] Notice that the EU co-ordination on employment policies is an important part of the Community *aquis*.

Czech Republics have the lowest incidence (18.9% and 19.1%), while the shadow economy is much more relevant in Latvia (39.9%) and Lithuania (30.3%).

It should be noted (Graph 1) that a significant negative correlation exists between the total (regular) employment rate and the size of the shadow economy. So, the countries with the worst employment performances are characterised by a higher incidence of "irregular employment"[11].

Table 5: Employment rates in the EU-25 (rankings 2003)

Total Employment rate		Female Employment rate		55-64 Employment rate	
Denmark	75.1	Sweden	71.5	Sweden	68.6
Netherlands	73.5	Denmark	70.5	Denmark	60.2
Sweden	72.9	Netherlands	65.8	United Kingdom	55.5
United Kingdom	71.8	Finland	65.7	Estonia	52.3
Austria	69.2	United Kingdom	65.3	Portugal	51.1
Cyprus	69.2	Austria	62.8	Cyprus	50.4
Finland	67.7	Portugal	60.6	Finland	49.6
Portugal	67.2	Cyprus	60.4	Ireland	49.0
Ireland	65.4	Estonia	59.0	Netherlands	44.8
Germany	64.8	Germany	58.8	Lithuania	44.7
Czech Republic	64.7	Lithuania	58.4	Latvia	44.1
Luxemburg	63.1	Latvia	57.9	Greece	42.3
Estonia	62.9	Slovenia	57.6	Czech Republic	42.3
France	62.8	France	56.7	Spain	40.8
Slovenia	62.6	Czech Republic	56.3	Germany	39.3
Latvia	61.8	Ireland	55.8	France	36.8
Lithuania	61.1	Slovak Republic	52.2	Austria	30.4
Spain	59.7	Belgium	51.8	Italy	30.3
Belgium	59.6	Hungary	50.9	Malta	30.3
Greece	57.9	Luxembourg	50.8	Luxemburg	29.5
Slovak Republic	57.7	Spain	46.0	Hungary	28.9
Hungary	57.0	Poland	46.0	Belgium	28.1
Italy	56.1	Greece	43.9	Poland	26.9
Malta	54.5	Italy	42.7	Slovak Republic	24.5
Poland	51.2	Malta	33.6	Slovenia	23.5
Mean EU-25	62.9		55.0		40.2
Coeff. of variation	0.10		0.16		0.29

Source: Eurostat 2004. The Mediterranean EU members are indicated in bold.

---

[11] Employment in illegal activities is excluded from the definition of "irregular employment".

Table 6: The size (% of GDP) of the shadow economy in the European Union (1999-2000)

"old" EU members		"new" EU members	
Austria	9.8	Slovak Republic	18.9
United Kingdom	12.7	Czech Republic	19.1
Netherlands	13.1	Hungary	25.1
France	15.2	Slovenia	27.1
Ireland	15.9	Poland	27.6
Germany	16.0	Lithuania	30.3
Denmark	18.0	Latvia	39.9
Finland	18.1	Estonia	n.a.
Sweden	19.2	Cyprus	n.a.
Belgium	22.2	Malta	n.a.
Spain	22.7		
Portugal	22.7		
Italy	27.1		
Greece	28.7		
Luxembourg	n.a.		
mean	18.6		26.9
coefficient of variation	0.29		0.27
mean (all countries) 21.4 coefficient of variation (all countries) 0.33			

Source: Schneider (2003) calculations based on "currency demand approach" (EU-15) and Schneider (2003) calculations based on World Bank data, Washington D.C., 2002 ("new" EU members).
Note: n.a. = not available.

Graph 1: Relationship between the total employment rate and the size of the shadow economy

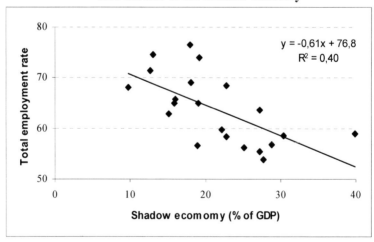

Source: elaboration based on Eurostat (2004) and Schneider (2003) data.

Considering the national level of the Mediterranean EU countries, significant differences arise, especially in female employment rates and "older worker" employment rates. Cyprus and Portugal are at the top of the ranking in all three indicators, with female ER and "older worker" employment rates that are higher than the European objectives. In contrast, Malta and Italy have extremely low employment rates.

Table 7: Employment rates in the Mediterranean EU members (rankings 2003)

Total Employment rate		Female Employment rate		55-64 Employment rate	
Cyprus	69.2	Portugal	60.6	Portugal	51.1
Portugal	67.2	Cyprus	60.4	Cyprus	50.4
France	62.8	Slovenia	57.6	Greece	42.3
Slovenia	62.6	France	56.7	Spain	40.8
Spain	59.7	Spain	46.0	France	36.8
Greece	57.9	Greece	43.9	Italy	30.3
Italy	56.1	Italy	42.7	Malta	30.3
Malta	54.5	Malta	33.6	Slovenia	23.5
Mean	61.3		50.2		38.2
coefficient of variation	0.08		0.20		0.26

Source: Eurostat, Employment in Europe 2004.

Note: The "old" Mediterranean EU members are indicated in bold.

It is of interest to briefly consider the employment rates (for the most numerous nationality groups) of non-EU nationals living in the European Union (15). Notice the significant differences, with the US and Croatia at the top of the ranking and Algeria and Marocco at the bottom (especially considering the female employment rates).

Table 8: Employment rates of third country nationals (rankings 2002)

Total Employment rates		Female Employment rates	
US	71	Croatia	65
Croatia	68	US	59
Albania	64	Bosnia Herzegovina	57
Bosnia Herzegovina	62	Poland	49
Poland	58	Albania	47
Turkey	47	Russia Federation	39
Russia Federation	43	Turkey	32
Marocco	40	Algeria	22
Algeria	39	Morocco	21
EU nationals	66		59

Source: Eurostat, LFS (2003).

In conclusion, it should be noted that empirical evidence highlights the existence of huge differences in national employment performances in the European Union. So, the EU cannot be properly considered as just one (homogeneous) "region" (for example, to be compared to the US).

II.D. Italian Sub-National Levels

The national averages can mask remarkable sub-national differences. In this part we briefly consider the Italian sub-national levels of (dis)aggregation: macro-Regions, Regions, Provinces and, briefly, the local labour systems in the Region of Umbria.

A first level of (dis)aggregation distinguishes the country in four macro-regions ("Northwest", "Northeast", "Centre" and "South and Islands"). The employment performance differences are notable, especially in the female ER.

Table 9: Employment rates (ER) in the Italian macro-regions (2003)

	Total ER	Female ER	55-64 ER
North-east	65.4	55.1	29.0
North-west	63.2	52.3	26.0
Centre	59.1	46.9	33.4
South and Islands	44.1	27.1	32.8
Coefficient of variation	0.17	0.28	0.11

Source: Istat, Labour Force Survey (2004).

However, the macro-regional level can hide significant differences that arise only with a higher (dis)aggregation. Therefore, we analysed the main employment indicators for the 20 Italian Regions and the 103 Provinces.

As for the main "Lisbon objective", in 2002 all the Regions had an employment rate lower than 70%. In particular, nine Regions (Emilia Romagna, Trentino Alto Adige, Valle d'Aosta, Lombardy, Veneto, The Marches, Piedmont, Friuli Venezia Giulia and Tuscany) had an employment rate (ER) in the upper part of the ranking (60-70), five regions had an ER between 50 and 60% and, finally, six regions (Sicily, Campania, Calabria, Puglia, Basilicata and Sardinia) had an ER lower than 50%. Considering the second "Lisbon objective", all the Regions had a female employment rate lower than 60%, ranging from a maximum of 59.1% to a minimum of 24.3%). In particular, nine Regions had a female employment rate (FER) in the upper part of the ranking (50-60), four Regions had an ER between 40 and 50%, two Regions had a female

ER between 30 and 40% and, finally, five Regions (Campania, Sicily, Calabria, Puglia and Basilicata) had a female ER lower than 30%.

Table 10: Total employment rates in Italian Regions (2002)

ER 40-50%	Sicily (42.2), Campania (42.2), Calabria (42.3), Puglia (45.5), Basilicata (46.3) and Sardinia (47.0).
ER 50-60%	Molise (52.1), Lazio (55.2), Abruzzo (55.8), Liguria (58.5) and Umbria (59.2).
ER 60-70%	Tuscany (61.8), Friuli Venezia Giulia (62.2), Piedmont (62.2), The Marches (63.0), Veneto (63.4), Lombardy (63.4), Valle d'Aosta (66.4), Trentino Alto Adige (66.6) and Emilia Romagna (67.8).
	Coefficient of variation = 0.16

Source: Istat, 2003.

Table 11: Female employment rates in Italian Regions (2002)

ER < 30%	Campania (24.3), Sicily (24.5), Calabria (26.6), Puglia (27.7) and Basilicata (29.7).
ER 30-40%	Sardinia (31.5) and Molise (37.1).
ER 40-50%	Abruzzo (41.3), Lazio (41.4), Liguria (47.1) and Umbria (48.1).
ER 50-60%	Veneto (50.9), Tuscany (50.9), Piedmont (51.8), Friuli Venezia Giulia (51.9), Lombardy (52.0), The Marches (53.0), Trentino Alto Adige (55.0), Valle d'Aosta (56.5) and Emilia Romagna (59.1).
	Coefficient of variation = 0.27

Source: Istat, 2003.

As for the older workers (55-64), it should be noted that the lowest ER was in the Northern Regions (Table 12).

Table 12: Older worker (55-64) employment rates in Italian Regions (2003)

ER <25%	Friuli Venezia Giulia (24.2).
ER 25-30%	Lombardy (25.7), Piedmont (26.2), Liguria (27.0), Sardinia (27.3), Veneto (27.8), Valle d'Aosta (29.2) and Umbria (29.5).
ER 30-35%	The Marches (30.1), Trentino Alto Adige (30.6), Basilicata (31.5), Tuscany (31.6), Emilia Romagna (31.6), Sicily (31.7), Puglia (31.8) and Campania (34.4).
IER >35%	Molise (37.2), Lazio (36.3), Calabria (36.1) and Abruzzo (35.8)
	Coefficient of variation = 0.12

Source: Istat (2004).

Finally, the Regions with lower (regular) employment rates are generally characterised by higher incidence of irregular employment[12] (Table 13).

Table 13: Irregular employment rates in Italian Regions (2000)

IER 10-15%	Emilia Romagna (10.1), Lombardy (10.5), Veneto (11.2), Piedmont (11.2), Trentino Alto Adige (13.0), Tuscany (13.2), Friuli Venezia Giulia (13.2), Liguria (13.3), The Marches (13.8) and Abruzzo (14.1).
IER 15-20%	Valle d'Aosta (15.9), Umbria (16.6), Lazio (17.4), Molise (18.1) and Sardinia (18.3).
IER 20-25%	Puglia (20.0), Basilicata (22.0), Sicily (23.6) and Campania (24.7).
IER more than 25%	Calabria (29.2).
	coefficient of variation = 0.32

Source: Istat, National Account (2002).

Note: Irregular labour units as % of total labour units.

The empirical evidence at the Regional level can also hide differences arising at a Provincial level of aggregation (Tables A1 and A2 in the Appendix). In particular, three Provinces (Bolzano, Ravenna and Reggio Emilia) have reached the main "Lisbon objective" (70%), 16 Provinces (Modena, Forlì, Bologna, Belluno, Siena, Mantova, Aosta, Biella, Cuneo, Novara, Treviso, Parma, Vicenza, Prato, Pordenone and Ferrara) have a total employment rate near the European objective (from 65% to 70%), 36 Provinces have an ER in the 60-65% class and 48 Provinces have an ER lower than 60%. Notice that 20 Provinces have an ER between 50 and 60%; 22 Provinces have an ER in the class 40-50% and, finally, six Provinces have an extremely low ER (lower than 40%).

As illustrated in Figure 1, the Provincial level presents a much more articulated differentiation with respect to the well-known "North-South" dualism.

---

[12] In Table 13, irregular employment is measured in labour units corresponding to full time employment (for example, two part-time irregular jobs are computed as one irregular labour unit). So, the number of workers involved in "irregular jobs" is much higher than the number of labour units.

Figure 1: Groups of Provinces according to the total employment rate (2002)

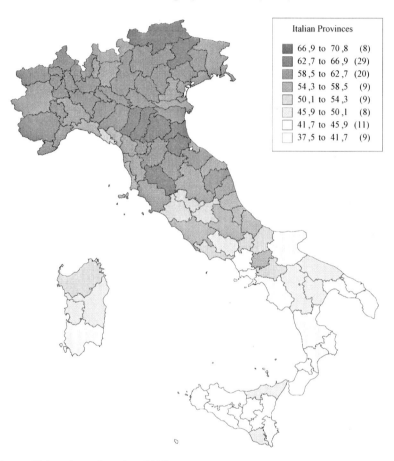

Italian Provinces	
66,9 to 70,8	(8)
62,7 to 66,9	(29)
58,5 to 62,7	(20)
54,3 to 58,5	(9)
50,1 to 54,3	(9)
45,9 to 50,1	(8)
41,7 to 45,9	(11)
37,5 to 41,7	(9)

Source: Elaboration on Istat data (2003).

The provincial differences in the female ER (Table A2 in the Appendix) are huge, with a maximum of 62.5% (Ravenna) and a minimum of 16.7% (Caltanisetta). In 2002 only six Provinces (Siena, Forlì, Bologna, Modena, Reggio Emilia and Ravenna) had reached the second "Lisbon objective" (more than 60%). Eight other Provinces followed in the 55-60% class and 31 Provinces were in the 50-55% class. It should be noted that 57 Provinces report a female employment rate lower than 50% and, in particular, 22 Provinces have a female ER that is lower than half (30%) of the European objective.

Notice that, the Provincial level of empirical analysis can also be inadequate if significant differences exist at the local level. Introducing the concept of the local labour system that belongs to the more general category of the "travel-to-work areas" allows the issue of a functional repartition of the Italian territory into local socio-economic systems to be addressed (Istat, 1997). Some studies have highlighted the existence of significant differences in employment performance between the 784 Italian local labour systems, also within the same Province (or Region)[13]. Notice that even considering a small Italian Region, like Umbria[14], it is possible to find significant differences in employment performance among the 16 local labour systems (Table A3 in Appendix). Obviously, the employment performance differences, at the local labour system level, in the larger and southern Regions (and Provinces) are much higher than in the Region of Umbria.

In conclusion, since all the possible levels of "regional" (dis)aggregation show a significant degree of differentiation, the comparative empirical analysis must consider all the levels of (dis)aggregation, in order to derive articulated suggestions for an effective co-ordinated mix of (European, national, regional and local) policy interventions.

II. E. A Synthetic View of the Degrees of Multilevel Regional Differentiation

Here the differences in employment performances are briefly compared considering the variability (range and coefficient of variation) at the various levels of (dis)aggregation previously considered. The ranges (max-min) of employment rates are remarkable at various levels of (dis)aggregation, especially for the female ER (Graph 3), but they are particularly high at the Italian sub-national levels.

---

[13] See, for example, Perugini-Signorelli (2004). Notice that the distances in the stock indicator (employment rate) can be the result of huge differences in the flow indicators.

[14] The Umbria Region is composed of two Provinces, Perugia (divided into 13 local labour systems) and Terni (divided into three local labour systems).

Graph 2: Range (max-min) of total employment rates

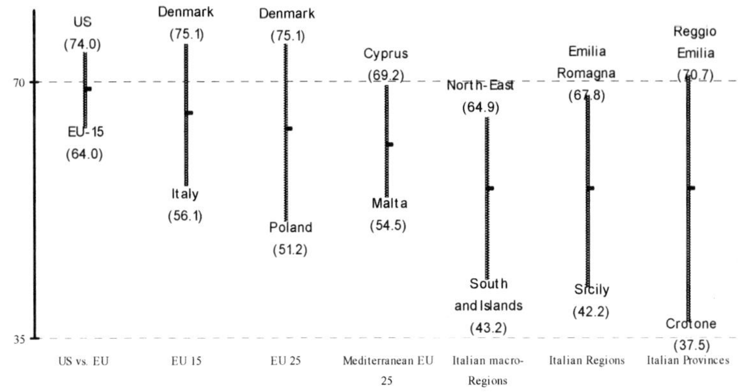

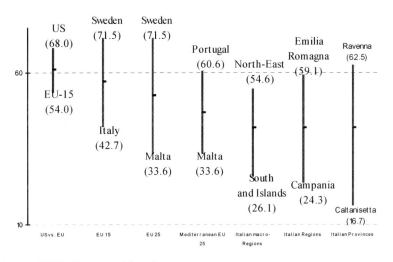

Source: OECD, Eurostat and Istat data.

Note: 2000 for US vs. EU; 2003 for EU-15, EU-25 and Mediterranean EU-25; 2002 for Italian sub-national levels.

Graph 3: Range (max-min) of female employment rates

Source: OECD, Eurostat and Istat data.

Note: 2000 for US vs. EU; 2003 for EU-15, EU-25 and Mediterranean EU-25; 2002 for Italian sub-national levels.

The "regional" variability at different levels of (dis)aggregation has been briefly analysed using the coefficient of variation (c.v.)[15]. In general, this index is much higher for female employment rates than for total employment rates (Graph 4), highlighting a lower variability in the male employment rates. Notice that, the c.v. for the female employment rate in the Mediterranean EU countries is higher than that reported for the EU-15 and EU-25; the opposite is true for the total employment rates. Finally, the coefficients of variation are particularly high at the Italian sub-national levels, with the exception of the macro-Regional level for the total employment rate.

Graph 4: Coefficient of variation of the total and female employment rates

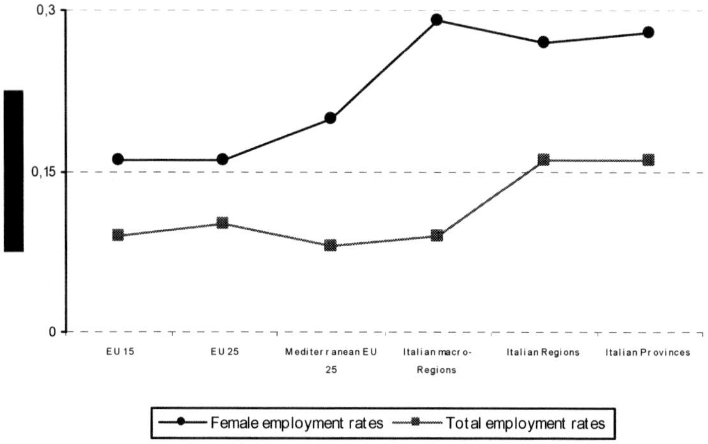

Source: elaboration on OECD, Eurostat and Istat data.
Note: 2003 for EU-15, EU-25 and Mediterranean EU-25; 2002 for Italian sub-national levels.

III.   The European Employment Strategy: an Effective Open Method of Co-ordination?

The Luxembourg Job Summit (1997) launched the European Employment Strategy (EES) based on the new provisions in the Employment title of the Amsterdam Treaty. At the Lisbon Council (2000), the European Union set a new strategic goal for the next decade: "*to become the most competitive and dynamic knowledge-based economy in the world, capable of sustainable economic growth with more and better*

---

[15]   The coefficient of variation is a "pure number" and is obtained by dividing the standard deviation by the mean.

jobs and greater social cohesion". The strategy was designed to enable the Union to regain the conditions for full employment[16]. The EES is designed to be the main tool for giving direction to and ensuring the co-ordination of the employment policies of the Member States. In particular, the EES initiated a new working method (the so called "open method of co-ordination") based on five key principles: (i) subsidiarity, (ii) convergence, (iii) management by objectives, (iv) country surveillance and (v) integrated approach. The co-ordination of the employment policies at the EU level consists of: (i) *Employment Guidelines* of the European Council, following a Commission proposal; (ii) *National Action Plan* (and Regional Action Plan) which describes how the Guidelines are put into practice at the national (and regional) levels; (iii) a *Joint Employment Report* presented by the Commission and the Council examining each National Action Plan; (iv) *Recommendations* decided by a qualified majority of the Council, in response to a proposal by the Commission, and addressed to all members (general recommendations) and to each country (country-specific recommendations).

The Employment Guidelines are a set of objectives that, until 2003, consisted of four "pillars": (i) employability, (ii) entrepreneurship, (iii) adaptability and (iv) equal opportunities. The 2003 revision of the EES highlighted three "new" general objectives [(i) full employment, as defined in Lisbon and Stockholm; (ii) quality and productivity at work (employment growth must be accompanied by productivity changes in order to permit real wage increases); and (iii) a cohesive and inclusive labour market (employment is a crucial means to social inclusion)] and ten specific guidelines [(i) active and preventive measures for the unemployed and inactive (for example: job search assistance and personalised action plans); (ii) job creation and entrepreneurship; (iii) address change and promotion of adaptability and mobility in the labour market (for example: introduce diversity of contractual and working arrangements; favour a better balance between work and private life and between flexibility and security; increase the transparency of employment and training opportunities); (iv) promote development of human capital and lifelong learning; (v) increase labour supply and promote active ageing (for example: make work pay and reform early retirement schemes); (vi) gender equality (for example reconciling work and private life); (vii) promote integration and combat discrimination against disadvan-

---

[16] The Lisbon Council confirmed the EES and defined two employment goals to be obtained by 2010: (i) an overall EU employment rate of 70% and (ii) a female employment rate higher than 60%. The Stockholm European Council (2001) added a third goal: (iii) an employment rate higher than 50% (by 2010) for older (55-64) workers.

taged people in the labour market; (viii) make work pay through incentives to enhance work attractiveness (for example, reducing the high marginal effective tax rate, especially for low-wage workers); and (ix) transform undeclared work into regular employment; (x) address regional employment disparities. The European Social Fund is the main financial support for the European Employment Strategy. Notice that the EES, and the Employment Guidelines in particular, have increasingly incorporated the local dimension, by inviting member States to involve the regional and local levels. Obviously the governance of the EES also depends on the political and constitutional structure of each Member State. However, the implementation of the Strategy calls for the involvement of all relevant actors (Member States, Regions, social partners, civil society), in accordance with the wide diversity in national institutional structures and social dialogue practices.

The evaluation of the results of the EES is extremely difficult, but there is some striking evidence for the period 1997-2003: (i) employment (especially permanent employment) significantly increased in the European Union, even in recent years with the extremely low GDP growth rates (employment/GDP elasticity increased remarkably); (ii) unemployment declined, especially long-term unemployment (the decline of unemployment was lower than the increase of employment due to higher participation in the labour market); (iii) the process information exchange between Member States permitted a better evaluation of the transferability of good practices; (iv) since 2000, a better definition of the objectives (total employment rate, female employment rate and older worker employment rate), with a greater emphasis on net employment creation, rather than unemployment reductions, has favoured some labour market reforms, and better use of many instruments (public and private employment services, life-long learning, wage moderation, etc.).

As for the quantitative employment changes in the period 1997-2002, the significant positive change in each EU member State should be noted, with a 3.6 total ER increase in the European Union (Table 15). Notice that the net employment creation was more than 12 million in five years, with around 10 million new permanent jobs.

Table 15: Employment changes (period 1997-2002)

	Changes in total employment rate ER 2002 – ER 1997	Changes in total employment (in thousands)	Changes in permanent employment employees (in thousands)	Changes in temporary employment employees (in thousands)
Spain	+9.1	+3031	+2346	+699
Ireland	+7.8	+349	+287	-30
Netherlands	+5.9	+908	+568	+303
Finland	+4.8	+304	+251	+55
Italy	+4.2	+1451	+1069	+381
Sweden	+4.1	+412	+251	+185
Luxembourg	+3.8	+20	+16	+4
France	+3.5	+2203	+1658	+521
Belgium	+3.0	+249	+188	+61
Portugal	+2.6	+496	+144	+422
United Kingdom	+1.7	+1710	+1972	-182
Germany	+1.7	+763	+746	+194
Greece	+1.6	+266	+228	+38
Austria	+1.5	+119	+122	-4
Denmark	+1.0	+66	+109	-49
European Union 15	+3.6	+12346	+9957	+2598

Source: Employment in Europe, European Commission (2003).

The employment growth during the period 1997-2002 included a 79% increase in permanent contracts (+44% female and +35% male) and 21% increase in temporary jobs (+13% female and +8% male). In addition, the employment creation is divided into +69% full-time contracts (+36% male and +33% female) and + 31% part-time jobs (+24% female and +7% male).

Graph 5 (A and B): Employment growth composition (period 1997-2002)

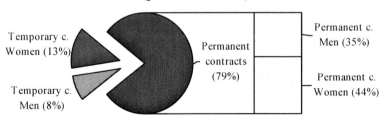

Source: elaboration on Eurostat data (2003).

It should be noted that a negative relationship exists between the total employment rates in 1997 and the net job creation[17] in the period 1997-2002. The countries with lower employment rates in 1997 had better performances in the period 1997-2002, causing a convergence process of national employment performances. Thus, the period 1997-2002 was extremely positive in terms of both net job creation (in all the EU-15 countries) and employment performance convergence.

Graph 6: Relationship between the Initial (1997) Total Employment Rates and the Net Job Creation (period 1997-2002)

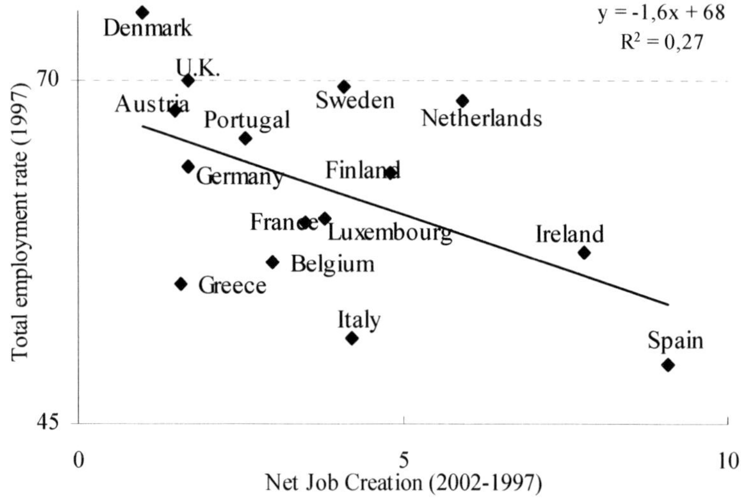

Source: elaboration based on Eurostat (2004) and Schneider (2003) data.

Considering the NUTS II level[18] of (dis)aggregation in the EU-15, we estimate the following regression for 201 Regions in the period 1999-2003[19].

---

[17] The net job creation in the period 1997-2002 is measured by the difference between the total employment rate (ER) in 2002 and the total ER in 1997.

[18] As for Italy, this level corresponds to the 20 Regions.

[19] In the period 1999-2003 the regional (NUTS II level) data are comparable.

**Table 16: Convergence of Regional Employment Rates
in EU-15 (period 1999-2003): Estimates**

Dependent variable: ER growth 1999-2003	Coefficient	P-values
ER_{1999}	-0.173	(0.000)
Constant	0.746	(0.000)
Number of Observations: 209 Adjusted R-squared: 0.330 Prob F: 0.0000		

Source: elaboration on Eurostat Regions Database (2004).

The regression exhibits an estimated value of the coefficient which is negative and significant, implying a convergence dynamic in total employment rate in the 201 European Regions. Thus, the EU-15 Regions with the lower total employment rate in 1999 performed better in the period 1999-2003.

We argue that the European Employment Strategy, which favours a multilevel governance that is aware of the extreme differences at the different levels of "regional" (dis)aggregations, has contributed positively to net job creation and employment performance convergence in EU countries and (NUTS II) Regions.

IV. Some Policy Implications

The existence of more than one "regional" level of significant differentiation has important methodological consequences. In particular, the empirical results (and policy implications) are very dependent on the level(s) of analysis chosen.

A comparative multilevel "regional" analysis provides crucial information for defining an effective governance of employment policies. In particular, because the differences in employment performance are significant at many levels of (dis)aggregation, as highlighted for EU members and, especially, at the Italian sub-national levels, the policy implications clearly favour a governance based on multilevel "regional" employment policies, co-ordinated at the highest level of aggregation (European level) and implemented at the lower levels (national, regional and local), according to the subsidiarity principle[20].

The European Employment Strategy (EES), adopting an "open method of co-ordination"[21], takes into account the significant differences

---

[20] It is important to take in to account the possible (negative and positive) spatial spillovers (e.g. Bollino-Signorelli, 2003).

[21] The EES is based on both vertical and horizontal subsidiarity principles.

in employment performance at the various "regional" levels of (dis)aggregation. We argue that the notable net job creation and employment performance convergence in the EU countries and Regions were partly due to the positive role played by the EES in favouring the creation and implementation of co-ordinated multilevel "regional" employment policies.

Further employment growth in the worst-performing EU countries (and Regions) can be obtained favouring the emersion of irregular labour and the diffusion of part-time contracts. Obviously, improvement and changes in the composition of the European[22] and national/regional budgets will help accelerate the process towards "*more and better jobs*" (European Council, Lisbon, 2000)[23].

References

Baddely M., Martin R., Tyler P. (1998), "European Regional Unemployment Disparities: Convergence or Persistence?" in *European Urban and Regional Studies*, 5(3), pp. 195-215.

Bettio F., Villa P. (1995), "A Mediterranean Perspective on the Break-down of the Relationship between Participation and Fertility", *Discussion Papers*, University of Trento.

Blanchard O. J., Katz L. F. (1992), "Regional Evolutions", *Brookings Papers of Economic Activity, 1,* 1-61.

Boldrin M., Canova F., (2001), "Europe's Regions – Income Disparities and Regional Policies", in *Economic Policy*, April, pp. 207-245.

Bollino C. A., Signorelli M. (2001), "Structural Factors and Labour Demand in Italian Macro-Regions", (with C. A. Bollino), *Economia & Lavoro*, No. 3.

Bollino C. A., Signorelli M. (2003), "Evolution of Production Structure in the Italian Regions", (con C. A. Bollino), in *The Italian Economy at the Dawn of the XXI Century*, M. Di Matteo and P. Piacentini (eds.), Ashgate, Aldershot.

Calzoni G., Perugini C., Polinori P., Signorelli M. (2004), "Regional Economic Convergence and Employment Performance: Poland vs. Italy", in *Proces Globalizacjii Gospodarki*, M. Klamut (ed.), Akademia Ekonomiczna, Wroclaw, Poland.

Caroleo F. E., De Stefanis S. (2004), "Regions, Europe and the Labour Market: Recent Problems and Developments", Physica Verlag, Heidelberg.

---

[22] For example, a reduction in European resources devoted to the agricultural sector (characterised by a low and decreasing sectoral employment rate) would be accompanied by an increase in the European Social Fund supporting the European Employment Strategy.

[23] In this paper the analysis is limited to the main quantitative indicators of labour market performance, without considering the quality of the jobs (e.g. the diffusion of the "working poor") and the changes in productivity and real wages.

Croci Angelici E., Farina F. (2000), "Convergenza fra Nazioni e Divergenza fra Regioni nell'Unione Europea", *Quaderno DIEF*, No. 8, Università di Macerata.

Decressin J., Fatas A. (1995), "Regional Labor Market Dynamics in Europe", *European Economic Review*, 39.

European Commission (2000), "Sixth Periodic Report on the Social and Economic Situation and Development of Regions in the European Regions", Bruxelles.

EU (2003), "Employment in Europe 2003", European Commission, Luxembourg.

EU (2004), "Delivering Lisbon. Reforms form the Enlarged Union", *Report from the Commission to the Spring European Council*, Bruxelles, 2004.

EU (2004), "Employment in Europe 2004", European Commission, Luxembourg.

Farina F., Tamborini R. (eds.) (2002), "Da Nazioni a Regioni. Mutamenti istituzionali e strutturali dopo l'Unione Monetaria Europea", Il Mulino, Bologna.

Genda Y., Pazienza M. G., Signorelli M. (2001), "Labour Market Performance and Job Creation", in *Comparing Economic Systems: Italy and Japan*, A. Boltho, A. Vercelli e H. Yoshikawa (eds.), Palgrave (Macmillan), London and New York.

Istat (1997), "I sistemi locali del lavoro", Sforzi F. (ed.), *Serie Argomenti*, No. 10, Roma.

Marelli E. (2004), "Evolution of Employment Structure and Regional Specialisation in EU", *Economic Systems*, 28-1.

Martin R., Tyler P. (2000), "Regional Employment Evolutions in the European Union: a Preliminary Analysis", *Regional Studies*, 34.

Pieroni L., Signorelli M. (2002), "Labour Market Institutions and Employment Performance", *Quaderni del Dipartimento di Economia Politica*, Università di Siena, No. 364.

Perugini C., Signorelli M. (2004), "Labour Market Performance in Central European Countries", *Quaderni del Dipartimento di Economia*, Università di Perugia, No. 11, giugno.

Perugini C., Signorelli M. (2004), "Labour Market Structure in the Italian Provinces: a Cluster Analysis", *Quaderni del Dipartimento di Economia*, Università di Perugia, No. 12, luglio.

Perugini C., Signorelli M. (2004), "I flussi in entrata nei mercati del lavoro umbri: un'analisi di Cluster", *Quaderni del Dipartimento di Economia*, Università di Perugia, No. 13, luglio.

Ranieri A., Scarpetta S. (1994), "La segmentazione del mercato del lavoro in Italia: analisi dei differenziali di disoccupazione tra mercati locali", in F. Pasquini, T. Pompili, P. Secondini (eds.), *Modelli d'analisi e d'intervento per un nuovo regionalismo*, Franco Angeli, Milano.

Reyneri E. (1997), *Occupati e disoccupati in Italia*, Il Mulino, Bologna.

Sapir A. (2004), "An Agenda for a Growing Europe. The Sapir Report", Oxford, OUP.

Svejnar J. (1999), "Labor Markets in the Transitional and Central Eastern European Economies", in *Handbook of Labor Economics*, Vol. 3, in Ashenfelter O. and Card D. (eds.), Elsevier Science.

Schneider F., Enste D. (2000), "Shadow Economies: Size, Causes and Consequences", *The Journal of Economic Literature*, 38/1, pp. 77-114.

Schneider F. (2003), "Shadow Economy around the World: Size, Causes and Consequences", paper presented at the *AIEL annual conference* held in Messina (Italy), September 2003.

Signorelli M. (1997), "Uncertainty, Flexibility Gap and Labour Demand in the Italian Economy", *Labour*, 1, 1997, pp. 141-175.

Signorelli M. (2000), "Relazioni Industriali e occupazione in Italia in una prospettiva comparata", *Stato e Mercato*, No. 3.

Signorelli M., Tiraboschi M. (eds.) (2004), "Mercato del lavoro, norme e contrattazione", ESI, Napoli.

Signorelli M., Vercelli A. (1994), "Structural Changes in the Post-War Italian Economy" in *Economic Performance: a Look at Austria and Italy*, B. Boehm e L. F. Punzo (a cura di), Physica-Verlag, Heidelberg, Berlin and Vienna.

Tronti L. (2003), "Fruitful or Fashionable? Can Benchmarking Improve the Employment Performance of National Labour Markets?", mimeo.

Appendix

Table A1: Total employment rates in Italian Provinces (2002)

ER < 40% (6 Provinces)	Crotone (37.5), Agrigento (38.1), Caltanisetta (38.1), Palermo (39.1), Caserta (39.3) and Naples (39.8).
ER 40-45% (8 Provinces)	Enna (40.9), Reggio Calabria (41.3), Catania (41.6), Cosenza (42.4), Foggia (42.6), Vibo Valentia (42.7), Taranto (43.3) and Salerno (44.5).
ER 45-50% (14 Provinces)	Cagliari (45.1), Catanzaro (45.2), Lecce (45.2), Siracusa (45.5), Brindisi (45.7), Trapani (45.7), Matera (46.0), Potenza (46.6), Nuoro (46.7), Messina (46.7), Bari (47.8), Oristano (47.8), Ragusa (48.2) and Frosinone (49.9).
ER 50-55% (11 Provinces)	Sassari (50.2), Rieti (50.7), Latina (50.8), Avellino (51.4), Campobasso (51.5), Viterbo (51.8), Terni (53.6), Isernia (53.9), La Spezia (54.3), Benevento (54.4) and Chieti (54.6).
ER 55-60% (9 Provinces)	Massa (55.0), Teramo (55.6), Livorno (56.3), Pescara (56.4), L'Aquila (56.9), Rome (57.0), Genova (57.6), Trieste (59.0) and Lucca (59.2).
ER 60-65% (36 Provinces)	Turin (60.2), Padua (60.4), Alessandria (60.4), Grosseto (60.5), Venezia (60.9), Pisa (61.0), Bergamo (61.1), Ascoli Piceno (61.2), Perugia (61.3), Gorizia (61.6), Sondrio (61.7), Savona (62.1), Udine (62.2), Imperia (62.4), Ancona (62.4), Rovigo (62.5), Rimini (62.6), Lecco (62.6), Trento (62.8), Brescia (62.9), Verona (63.1), Florence (63.2), Verbania (63.6), Milan (63.6), Asti (63.6), Pistoia (63.8), Como (63.8), Pesaro-Urbino (63.9), Lodi (64.0), Arezzo (64.0), Pavia (64.0), Cremona (64.2), Piacenza (64.2), Vercelli (64.3), Varese (64.3) and Macerata (64.9).
ER 65-70% (16 Provinces)	Ferrara (65.0), Pordenone (65.0), Prato (65.0), Vicenza (65.6), Parma (65.8), Treviso (65.9), Novara (66.2), Cuneo (66.2), Biella (66.2), Aosta (66.4), Mantova (66.5), Siena (67.6), Belluno (67.7), Bologna (67.9), Forlì (69.1) and Modena (69.8).
ER > 70% (3 Provinces)	Bolzano (70.5), Ravenna (70.5) and Reggio Emilia (70.7).
	Coefficient of variation = 0.16

Source: Istat, 2003.

Table A2: Female employment rates in Italian Provinces (2002)

ER < 25% (9 Provinces)	Caltanisetta (16.7), Crotone (20.5), Agrigento (20.6), Naples (20.8), Enna (21.1), Caserta (21.8), Palermo (22.4), Foggia (22.7), Siracusa (23.8).
ER 25-30% (13 Provinces)	Catania (25.1), Trapani (25.4), Cosenza (25.4), Taranto (25.9), Vibo Valentia (26.5), Ragusa (27.1), Salerno (27.8), Matera (27.9), Reggio Calabria (28.1), Bari (28.9), Nuoro (29.0), Lecce (29.6) and Catanzaro (29.9).
ER 30-35% (8 Provinces)	Cagliari (30.3), Brindisi (30.6), Potenza (30.6), Latina (32.3), Frosinone (32.5), Oristano (32.9), Messina (33.2) and Sassari (34.6).
ER 35-40% (5 Provinces)	Avellino (35.8), Campobasso (36.2), Viterbo (37.0), Rieti (37.0) and Isernia (39.5).
ER 40-45% (10 Provinces)	Benevento (40.4), La Spezia (40.6), Chieti (40.7), Pescara (40.8), L'Aquila (41.2), Terni (41.5), Teramo (42.5), Livorno (43.0), Massa (43.8) and Rome (44.4).
ER 45-50% (12 Provinces)	Bergamo (45.6), Lucca (45.8), Genova (46.3), Padua (46.6), Venice (47.3), Grosseto (47.6), Alessandria (48.1), Lecco (48.6), Imperia (49.2), Verona (49.2), Brescia (49.6) and Sondrio (49.9).
ER 50-55% (31 Provinces)	Pisa (50.1), Turin (50.2), Trento (50.4), Perugia (50.5), Gorizia (50.8), Rovigo (51.2), Rimini (51.3), Cremona (51.3), Udine (51.4), Ascoli Piceno (51.5), Asti (51.5), Trieste (52.1), Como (52.3), Lodi (52.3), Prato (52.4), Piacenza (52.5), Ferrara (52.6), Pistoia (52.8), Verbania (52.9), Pesaro-Urbino (53.0), Treviso (53.1), Pordenone (53.3), Milan (53.5), Ancona (53.6), Savona (53.7), Florence (53.7), Pavia (53.8), Macerata (53.9), Vercelli (54.1), Arezzo (54.3), Cuneo (54.9) and Mantova (54.9).
ER 55-60% (8 Provinces)	Varese (55.1), Vicenza (55.6), Aosta (56.5), Novara (56.9), Parma (57.5), Biella (58.4), Belluno (58.8) and Bolzano (59.7).
ER > 60% (6 Provinces)	Siena (60.3), Forlì (60.3), Bologna (61.1), Modena (62.2), Reggio Emilia (62.3) and Ravenna (62.5).
	Coefficient of variation = 0.28

Source: Istat, 2003.

Table A3: Total employment rates in the 16 local labour systems of the Region of Umbria

ER 60-63% (9 Local labour systems)	Perugia (62.6), Assisi (62.5), Umbertine (62.0), Castiglion del Lago (60.7), Gualdo Tadino (60.6), Norcia (60.5), Cascia (60.3), Città di Castello (60.1), *Fabro (60.0)*.
ER 56-60% (7 Local labour systems)	Marsciano (59.9), Gubbio (59.8), Todi (59.6), *Orvieto (59.4)*, Foligno (58.6), Spoleto (58.6), *Terni (56.3)*.
	coefficient of variation = 0.026

Source: Elaboration on ISTAT data.
Note: The local labour systems in the Province of Terni are indicated in *italics*.

TROISIÈME PARTIE
IDENTITÉ DANS L'EUROPE MÉDITERRANÉENNE

PART III
IDENTITY IN MEDITERRANEAN EUROPE

Regions, Ethnic Identities, and States in Mediterranean Europe

An Attempt at a Comparative View

Xosé-Manoel NÚÑEZ

Universidade de Santiago de Compostela

The aim of this session is to develop a kind of trans-state approach to the topic of ethnic and national identity, going beyond the limits of the established states and attempting to look at regions, ethnic minorities, stateless nations and "small states" that developed in the old continent's Mediterranean area. I shall focus mainly on Europe's Western Mediterranean, with a few references to the Eastern Mediterranean area. Of course, the comparison that I'm proposing here could include a higher number of cases and therefore expand indefinitely the number of exceptional cases, nuances and details. As historians, we know well that each case is unique. As social scientists, however, we are forced to outline a certain number of common features that may allow us to establish typologies. As modern historians, our objective is to combine both perspectives and to attempt to outline some kind of diachronic typology, while seeking to understand what has been most important in the process of identity formation in Mediterranean Europe.

It is nothing novel to insist upon the fact that identity-formation is a construction process, built principally upon a diversity of cultural materials and social aspects, and which over time define the fundamental elements that constitute a collective identity. The extent to which this discourse and representation is shared by a given population in a given territory may serve as an indication of how strong a collective, territorially-bound identity is. Identities tend to look like concentric spheres: they can be local, regional/subnational, national, continental, etc. They are constantly subject to change, to new influences and the incorporation of different elements that were not present at their shaping moment. In other words, identities are the result of a constant interaction and not one given, unchangeable factor[1]. In my view, four variables have to be considered when studying ethnic and collective identity, particularly from the point of view that is implicit in this session[2]. They are:

1. How old, efficient, and therefore "nationalising" the nation-states established in the Mediterranean basin have been since the end of the eighteenth century.

2. How resilient and resistant "popular" cultures and ethnic identities have been, as evidenced by the survival of traditional legal codes or of a social consciousness of collective identity, and the existence of cultural and social elites interested in preserving a form of cultural, political or institutional distinctiveness, along with a minority language. These languages exist mostly at a pre-standardised and illiterate level. With the exception of Catalan (in Catalonia, not in the Balearic Islands or in Valencia) and perhaps Occitan, almost none of the linguistic variants spoken in the western Mediterranean have a significantly high literature, and the institutional framework and basis for their survival has been and is quite weak.

However, a peculiarity of the western Mediterranean must be noted: in contrast with other areas of Europe, almost all the Mediterranean territories have experienced during their existence a rich and complex history of migrations, population transfers, trade and cultural exchanges. Therefore, each of these substate regions can be defined as a "land of passage" marked by a multiplicity of influences, which can be greater (Sicily) or lesser (Balearic Islands). This can be seen in the abundant traces of Arabic influence on the Catalan dialect of the Balearic Islands, in the English influence on the Catalan dialect of Menorca after several decades of British occupation in the 18th century, or in the linguistic diversity that characterises the island and language of Sardinia, with its many peculiar linguistic variants. This defines one of the distinctive features of the Mediterranean substate identities: the identity-builders' "foundation myth" tends to build upon a "melting pot" of different influences and does not usually involve being "the first and sole people

---

[1] See Anthony Smith, *National Identity*, London, Penguin, 1991.

[2] For a further development of this model, see X. M. Núñez, *Movimientos nacionalistas en Europa. Siglo XX*, Madrid, Síntesis, 1998, pp. 9-26. This paper is based on much of the books' content, so we opted for reducing the footnotes to a minimum. See also M. Hroch, "From National Movement to Fully-Fledged Nation", *New Left Review*, 198 (1993), pp. 3-19, and *id.*, *On the National Interest*, Prague, Charles University, 2000; see also J. Coakley, "Introduction: The Challenge", in *id.* (ed.), *The Territorial Management of Ethnic Conflict*, London/Portland, Frank Cass, 2003, [2nd ed.], pp. 1-22.

to have inhabited that territory". In contrast, many border regions and overlapping areas throughout East-Central Europe manifest the usual dispute over: who came first, which results in frequent historiographic and cultural quarrels, or other more serious disputes. Obviously, which identity and which element of the past is emphasised as dominant depends on how far back one wants to go. But if there is a common feature of all Mediterranean identity discourse, it is the emphasis on the plurality of ingredients that shaped a peculiar melting pot after centuries of trade, exchanges and empires around a common sea.

3. How conflictive the relationship has been between the "nationalising states" (borrowing Brubaker's definition)[3] and the "substate collective identities", or to what extent the homogenising objectives of the nation-states clashed with the political, social and cultural efforts of survival and resistance adopted by the substate *ethnies* (in Anthony Smith's terms). In addition, we need to examine how these relations led to elite settlements or social conflicts, and resulted in negotiations between the states and local elites, particularly in the context of social and economic modernisation in these regions, which gradually converted them into peripheries of the new or old-established nation-states.

4. How powerful and socially influential the different forms of ethnonationalism, regionalism, or any other form of territorially-based social and political mobilisation have been throughout the "long twentieth century".

According to these paradigms, one can establish the following hypotheses in a preliminary way

Point one: France has generally been considered a leading example of state efficiency in pushing forward the process of ethnocultural and national homogenisation, along with Greece. Spain, in contrast, may be seen as a case of belated and unfulfilled nation-building. Italy can perhaps be considered a case to be located somewhere in the middle – it experienced a strong push towards unity in the 19th century, followed by structural weakness in its nationalising state structure until the rise of Fascism. In contrast, the Balkans and the regions that emerged from the ruins of the Ottoman Empire after 1870 are cases of just the opposite: they constituted a mosaic of extremely weak consolidated nation-states coexisting with a multiplicity of multiethnic and multinational polities

---

[3]   R. Brubaker, *Nationalism reframed. Nationhood and the National Question in the New Europe*, Cambridge, CUP, 1996.

that failed in their attempts at consolidating themselves as nation-states, perhaps with the relative exception of Albania[4].

The Western Mediterranean area is characterised by the relatively early consolidation of "historic" nation-states such as France and Spain, while the emergence of the Italian nation state was somewhat later; these nations have pursued nationalising policies since the end of the 18th century, which have been more or less effectiv[5]. Therefore, the predominant model of nation-building in that area has been different from that which prevailed in Eastern Europe or that which was typical of the eastern Mediterranean area. The main difference lies in that there is no significant overlap in the western Mediterranean between ethnic and social structures. The ethnic and cultural borders in this area have historically been quite fluid, and citizenship as a criterion for belonging to the nation-state and ascribing to an identity made its appearance at least seventy five years earlier than in the eastern Mediterranean area (with the exception of Greece). In the western Mediterranean, instead of multinational empires, there were ethnically diverse nation-states that since the mid-nineteenth century, have systematically attempted to erode subnational cultures and local identities.

Point two: The importance of "little folk cultures" and languages has been, of course, more important in the Balkans than in the Western Mediterranean, perhaps with the exception of the Greek area – one simply has to note the contrast between the rapid (and forcible) assimilation of Macedonians in Greece and the persistence of Macedonian identity in the former Ottoman Empire and later in Yugoslavia as well as in southern Bulgaria. A further differentiation can be established in "Western Mediterranean Europe", which may be divided into three groups or ideal types. They are characterised by the following features:

(A) Existence of a weak ethnicity (as expressed in language, culture, social networks of differences) in the context of a strong national(ising) state. This would be the case for Occitany, Provence, French Catalonia, and Italy's Occitan-speaking regions. In all these examples a weak consciousness of political identity has remained through the second half of the twentieth century, and beyond[6]. One can easily conclude that the

---

[4]   See F. Veiga, *La trampa balcánica*, Barcelona, Grijalbo, 1995.

[5]   H.-J. Puhle, "Nation States, Nations and Nationalisms in Western and Southern Europe", in J. G. Beramendi, R. Máiz & X. M. Núñez (eds.), *Nationalism in Europe. Past and Present*, Santiago de Compostela, USC, 1994, Vol. 2, pp. 13-38. Also see the early comparative attempts by E. Allardt, "Le minoranze etniche nell'Europa occidentale. Una ricerca comparata", *Rivista Italiana di Scienza Politica*, 1 (1981), pp. 91-136.

[6]   See, for a joint view, S. Gras and Ch. Livet (eds.), *Régions et régionalisme en*

strength, the legitimacy and the modernising agency of the nation-state, which ran parallel to a process of social modernisation, transformed these peripheries into fully integrated parts of their nation-states, and in some cases played a leading role in that process (i.e. Piedmont).

(B) Existence of a strong ethnicity or, if one prefers, "ethnic distinct iveness", which is characterised by the survival of ethnic languages and popular cultures, but lacking social elites interested in "breaking away" from a central state that has had a weak nationalising process. This situation tends to result in the presence of a strong cultural sentiment of being a region, but more or less stable and peaceful integration within the nation-state through a mechanism of construction of regional identities that are seen as complementary to national identities: this would be the case in the Balearic Islands, the Valencian region and Sardinia[7].

Of course, the interpretations of the process of peripheral nation-building and of region-building since the 19th century are both based on a constructivist paradigm. This means that, in our view, different elements of regional history, traditional and material culture, linguistic peculiarities and local variants have been consciously selected by local elites, movements and institutions, in order to define the main markers of a standardised "regional/national culture", which in turn become a frame of meaning for the actors involved in collective action. One can recall the clashes over the definition of a Catalan linguistic standard at the beginning of the 20th century, the much more recent disputes concerning the "Valencian" identity, or the problems in establishing what was to be the linguistic norm of the Sardinian, Corsican and Occitan languages. Conversely, one may also ask the opposite question: why was Sardinian not standardised earlier despite the presence of a rather significant regionalist party in the 1920s, and why did the strongly differentiated Sicilian dialects not constitute the basis for the establishment of their own *language*? Obviously, the answer is very simple: there were no elites interested in backing such an endeavour, particularly when the integration of Sicily into the united kingdom of Italy was so tardy, and Sardinia was already integrated within a part of the peninsula (Piedmont) in the 18th century. However, as Petrosino demonstrates nicely in his contribution to this volume, the Sicilian dialects have shown greater strength and persistence than Sardinian, which seems to be in a situation of inexorable decline.

---

[7] *France. Du XVIIIe siècle à nos jours*, Paris, PUF, 1977.
 Concerning the case of Valencia, see F. Archilés and M. Martí, "Ethnicity, Region and Nation: Valencian Identity and the Spanish Nation-State", *Ethnic and Racial Studies*, 24: 5 (2001), pp. 779-97.

(C) Presence of a strong or reasonably strong ethnicity, along with the survival of languages, dialects, a popular culture and a socially widespread historical consciousness of a "glorious" past, while at the political level some kind of permanent bargaining exists between local or regional elites and the central state, all of which may eventually lead to the resurgence of strong ethnonationalist sentiments. We can distinguish here four different levels: (a) a predominance of clientelistic links and social relations (i.e. Sicily, or Corsica until the 1960s), which have been adapted to the process of social modernisation and regional consolidation within the institutional structure of the nation-state; (b) enduring clientelistic bargaining and coexistence with the emergence of minority nationalism, unable to gain a social majority status but able to determine the rhythm and evolution of the political agenda (Corsica)[8]; (c) a prevalence of political elite accommodation and strong national consciousness, though not aimed at a full separation from the state (Catalonia); and, finally, (d) a strong national consciousness, strong ethnonationalism, the presence of a high degree of violence, while seeking statehood, particularly in a context of regime change and break up of existing nation-states and multinational empires (Macedonia).

Point three: Regional elites have manifested varying degrees of integration and influence in the central governments of the nation-states to which they belonged. Above all, one must note the prevalence of clientelism in many Western Mediterranean areas. However, clientelism is an all-embracing concept, a catch-all label that serves to depict a very diverse collection of different situations. The fact that local politicians from a given region may become ministers, influential state officers and even heads of state, and that a myriad of family links may exist between the regional elites and the different levels of civil servants of the state (e.g. in Sicily, Sardinia, Corsica, and the Balearic Islands), does not change the fact that these policy-makers and patrons are meant to represent territorial interests. This does not mean that territorial identity becomes an outstanding issue on the political agenda. The fact that Sardinians or Corsicans have historically been overrepresented among the administrative and political elites of the Italian and French nation-states does not necessarily mean that Sardinia or Corsica is represented. Instead, it reflects a "brain-drain" situation arising from the limited opportunities in the skilled labour markets of their regions of origin.

In all these cases, the "regional question" has not been a significant matter on the political agenda until very recently. However, this may well indicate how far regional elites wish to go when deciding whether

---

[8] D. Gerdes, *Regionalismus als soziale Bewegung: der Fall Korsika*, Frankfurt a. M, Campus, 1985.

to put territorial interests on the negotiating table and fight for them, or the extent to which they choose to promote regional mobilisation instead of resorting to traditional political bargaining in the corridors of ministries and state parliaments. The Catalan example may be good proof of this: in this rich periphery the elites only decided to promote a minority nationalist movement in order to put pressure on the state once they realised that no other means of influence were open to them after 1898. At the same time, these elites always kept in mind the aim of extending their influence over all of Spain[9]. Obviously, Catalanism had a strong cultural and historical tradition, and relied on a collective memory of territorial governance that lasted until 1714. A few Catalan nationalist groups had the opportunity to access power and influence in 1898-1901 thanks to the strategic support of economic and social cultural elites, while Sardinians, Valencians and Corsicans still have not had that chance.

Point four: There is an evident lack of symmetry between Catalonia, where since the first quarter of the 20th century the regionalist/nationalist movement has experienced fast-paced growth towards achieving a social majority, and the rest of the regions and sub-state *ethnies* of the Western Mediterranean. Regionalist and nationalist parties have obtained very diverse results, and their evolution can show quite differentiated *tempos*. While Catalonia took the lead from the start of the 20th century on, only a few regionalist groupings have emerged in the Valencian region and the Balearic Islands. The higher level of industrialisation and greater social changes experienced in Catalonia had much to do with this. Conversely, though the Balearic Islands were (and still are) considered to be a "deposit" of Catalan ethnic identity, preserved until the 1960s thanks to isolation and backwardness, they have not experienced a social context that would enable territorial mobilisation to follow the same path it followed in Catalonia. The overwhelming power of clientelistic elites, which have mediated between the Balearic population and the central state, have had a lot to do with this[10].

Similarly, the Occitan, French-Catalan, Corsican, Sardinian and Sicilian movements had hardly developed before World War I, with the exception of a few intellectuals, public figures and journals devoted to the defence of the region, along with a certain amount of cultural agitation that was not always of a strictly ethnocultural nature, but may have also been political. Social mobilisation reached Sardinia in the aftermath

---

[9]   See E. Ucelay-Da Cal, *El imperialismo catalán. Prat de la Riba, Cambó, D'Ors y la conquista moral de España*, Barcelona, Edhasa, 2003.

[10]   A. Cucó, *El valencianisme polític, 1874-1939*, Catarrosa, Afers, 1999 [2nd edition]; A. Marimón, "El nacionalisme polític a Mallorca", *El Mirall*, 72 (1995), pp. 11-21.

of World War I, but to a great extent this was induced from the outside. Veterans of war whose group identity was reinforced by the common experience of the trenches became the leading social group of the powerful Sardinian regionalist movement of the 1920s[11]. Corsica and Sicily also witnessed a certain degree of political and cultural agitation that had regionalist/nationalist overtones. The shadow of fascism extended over these movements and fiercely repressed them, although the Sardinian autonomist movement managed to re-emerge after World War II, while the Sicilian movement experienced a temporary and short-term radicalisation due to the renewed desire of some Sicilian elites to play the independence card with potential support from the Allies, in order to oppose a potential "red" Italian republic. Similarly, the Corsican movement suffered from a profound loss of support as a result of its close proximity to Italian fascism and its collaboration with the Italian troops that invaded the island after 1940[12]. Consequently, the Corsican movement experienced a process of decline that was similar to that of other regionalist/nationalist movements within France (such as the Alsatians or the Bretons)[13]. In fact, the Sicilian independence movement faded away by the end of the 1940s, once the Sicilian elites managed to get regional autonomy and, particularly, to have their local interests granted by the new Italian republic[14].

It was not until the 1960s that a new generation of "ethnic activists" took the lead in the territorial movements of the western Mediterranean. In this geographical area, with the exception of Catalonia, ethnonationalism was refounded and re-framed as a left-wing doctrine due to the impact of the theory of "internal colonialism", originally introduced by the Occitan thinker Robert Lafont, and the influence of "Third-Worldism", particularly present and due to the weight of the Algerian example. During that decade a more radical "wave" of ethnonationalist groups came to the forefront in Sardinia, Occitany, Corsica, Valencia and the Balearic Islands. While some of them managed to consolidate themselves as minority parties within the different national/subnational party systems, others influenced the preexisting regionalist party and achieved its ideological and strategic radicalisation in the mid-term (as,

---

[11] S. Sechi, *Dopoguerra e fascismo in Sardegna. Il movimento autonomistico nella crisi dello stato liberale*, Torino, Einaudi, 1969.

[12] See H. Yvia-Croce, *Vingt années de corsisme (1920-1939). Chronique corse de l'entre-deux-guerres*, Ajaccio, Ed. Myrnos et Méditerranée, 1979.

[13] See F. Arzalier, *Les perdants. La dérive fasciste des mouvements autonomistes et indépendantistes au Xe siècle*, Paris, La Découverte, 1990, and Istituto Storico della Resistenza in Valle d'Aosta (ed.), *Les minorités ethniques vis-à-vis du nazisme et du fascisme*, Aosta, Musumeci, 1985.

[14] See G. C. Marino, *Storia del separatismo siciliano*, Roma, Editori Riuniti, 1979.

for example, in Sardinia). In the Corsican case, ethnonationalism managed to win a prominent place on the political agenda of the island, despite the fact that the nationalist vote has never been above 25 percent of the average regional vote. However, this prominence is related to the persistent violence associated with this issue, though it has displayed so far quite a low level of intensity (at least compared to the Basque or Northern Irish cases). This case is perhaps the exception within the ethnonational/regionalist mobilisations in the western Mediterranean context, partly due to the interaction between a very unique social structure, the repressive politics of the French state, and the presence of immigrants from former French Algeria[15].

Regionalism and ethnonationalism have constituted throughout the 20th century and still constitute a steady though socially reduced expression of most culturally distinct Mediterranean 'ethnies'. During the 1990s ethnonationalism typically received around 10 percent of the average regional vote in Sardinia, and even less in Sicily, Occitany or French Catalonia (under 3-5 percent) and the Valencian region (around 5 percent), while it received a bit more support in the Balearic Islands (around 15 percent). In Catalonia the nationalist vote regularly tallies around 50 percent of the total, and regional identity claims are generally accepted by the vast majority of social and political actors present in the public sphere, so it is the exception rather than the norm.

In spite of this, the politics of regional and cultural identity have increasingly become a part of the agenda in almost every region of the western Mediterranean. This has to do with the institutional implementation of decentralised governmental structures. Sicily and Sardinia became "special statute regions" after 1948-49; the three Spanish-Catalan regions became "autonomous communities" after the beginning of the 1980s; while a more tepid process of regionalisation is also taking place in France, though its evolution is subject to permanent debate and, particularly in the Corsican case, is far from being settled. There has also been a demonstration effect influencing some peripheries due to the ethnic reawakening or the "separatist challenge" in other parts of the same nation-state. This has opened up the way for a discussion of further reforms of the state structure in Spain and Italy, while in France this discussion is present due to the Corsican conflict. This has also

---

[15] See among other comparative studies, D. Petrosino, "La costruzione dell'identità etnica. I movimenti etnici in Sardegna ed in Veneto", Ph. Thesis, Università degli Studi di Catania, 1987; P. Elton Mayo, *The Roots of Identity: Three National Movements in Contemporary European Politics*, London, Allen Lane, 1974; W. Beer, *The unexpected rebellion: Ethnic Activism in Contemporary France*, New York, New York UP, 1980. A contemporary and passionate perspective can be found in S. Salvi, *Le nazioni proibite*, Firenze, Vallecchi, 1973.

contributed to transform identity discourses into a highly instrumental tool used as electoral material by almost all regional branches of the political parties. However, the extent to which this corresponds to the real importance ascribed to these discourses by the electorate involved is a matter of debate[16].

Something similar may be said when testing the survival of subnational cultures, languages and dialects in the Western Mediterranean. For example, some sectors of the Balearic Islands' nationalist movement, but also of the local population, are increasingly concerned that a "new national minority" will consolidate its presence among the islanders due to the growing presence of German-speaking residents on the island of Mallorca, along with the possibility that they may stand for local elections thanks to the emergence of a German Party [*Partido Alemán*] in Mallorca. This may become in a near future a typical East European or Balkan-like situation, while the predominant feature of Western-Mediterranean "ethnies" has been their fluid and plural identities, whether in Catalonia, Sicily, or Corsica. The very fact that they were "lands of passage" for peoples and cultures of different origins has shaped a quite unique relationship between the diverse cultural materials that forged the present structure of all these lands. Good proof of this may be found even in the case of Malta, described in Frendo's paper, where the English colonial heritage coexists with a peculiar and autochthonous language, which in turn derives from a mixture of southern Italic and Arab influence. Statehood has not diminished plurality even in conflictive cases such as Cyprus, as is demonstrated by Sia Anagnostopoulou's paper.

Another relevant question is how important the consciousness of "Mediterranean identity" is among the inhabitants and cultural elites of the regions concerned. One can say that the Mediterranean dimension of identity, far from being concrete, is fading and nebulous. The Nation-State identity and the overall European identity appear as stronger components of the different spheres of ascriptive identities that individuals share, beyond defining themselves as Catalans, Corsicans or Sicilians. Cross-cultural and political models may have played an am-

---

16 See D. Petrosino, "Is it Possible to Invent Ethnic Identity? Some Reflections on Ethnic and Territorial Politics in Italy", in Beramendi, Máiz and Núñez (eds.), *Nationalism in Europe*, Vol. 2, pp. 609-44; C. Levy (ed.), *Italian Regionalism: History, Identity and Politics*, Oxford, Berg, 1996; Y. Mény, *Centralisation et Décentralisation dans le débat politique français (1945-1969)*, Paris, Pichon/Duran-Auzias, 1974; X. M. Núñez, "Regions, Nations and Nationalities. On the Process of Territorial Identity-Building During Spain's Democratic Transition and Consolidation", in C. H. Waisman and R. Rein (eds.), *Spanish and Latin American Transitions to Democracy*, Brighton, Sussex Academic Press, 2005, pp. 55-79.

biguous role, sometimes stimulated by the influence of mass return-migration (e.g., from North America to Sicily, from Marseille to Corsica) as well as by mass immigration (of Castilians and Andalusians into Catalonia and, to some extent, into Valencia and the Balearic Islands, or of "retired" elderly Northern Europeans now moving into these regions, or of permanent mass tourism in the Balearic Islands, or of the *pied noirs* in western Corsica). On the one hand, they have contributed to strengthen a sense of belonging to the broad nation-state and to reduce the social spheres of vernacular languages, as well as to create transatlantic or transnational links which may have forged new spheres of identification – between New York and some areas of Sicily, or between the Boedo district of the city of Buenos Aires and some areas of heavy migration in the Balearic Islands. On the other hand, these processes also contributed to set the preconditions for the emergence of cultural and political reactions that sought to proclaim the defence of "threatened" cultures and ways of life. This was developed through the framing of mobilising discourses, which included the vindication of a glorious past, the elaboration of new cultural codes that aimed at representing the real "tradition" of the regions concerned, and the new value ascribed to symbols, languages and mores which had been virtually neglected as a relic of a pre-modern past by local social and political elites. The reaction against the so-called "invasions" of, let's say, Algerian pied-noirs or Castilian-speaking immigrants played an important role in the mobilisation of certain elites in both Corsica and Catalonia, particularly in a context of the delegitimisation of the nation-state, which occurred in Spain during the 1898 crisis and again during Francoism, while in France it had to do with decolonisation and the aftermath of the Algerian crisis, along with the "ethnic revival" of the 1960s.

Finally, we shall conclude this article with a reference to the Mediterranean identity. "Mediterranean-ism" as a cultural construct may have played a certain subsidiary role in shaping a sort of transnational pattern of reference for ethnonationalist movements in the western Mediterranean. Thus, the artistic and musical revival that took place in the "Catalan-speaking" countries since the late 1960s often referred to Greek, Sicilian or Corsican music as a model to be imitated, and sought to find similarities that would make Catalan culture closer to a global Mediterranean culture rather than to Castilian or Andalusian culture (much in the way the Galicians, in the opposite corner of the Iberian Peninsula, claimed to be a part of the "Celtic world" of Atlantic descent). However, it can also be argued that "Mediterranean-ism" has been more of a cultural image than a politically influential model among Western

Mediterranean ethnonationalisms[17]. Thus, both Ireland and to some extent Catalonia played a certain discursive role as models for the emerging Sardinian regionalist movement in the 1920s. For Catalan nationalists, the models to be emulated were variable throughout the twentieth century, ranging from the Hungarian nationalists and the "*Ausgleich* model" to the Irish nationalists in the 1920s and the Quebecois in the 1980s and 1990s. Finally, the most developed regionalist/nationalist movements have consistently had a certain "demonstration effect" for other movements in the Western Mediterranean, as for example the impact of the model offered by the *Partito Sardo d'Azione* on the Corsican ethnonationalists during the 1920s, or the permanent influence of the more developed Catalan nationalist movement on the more delayed but related movements of Valencia and the Balearic Islands.

---

[17] See X. M. Núñez, "Pan-Atlanticism and Pan-Mediterraneanism. The Seas and the Articulation of Transnational Identities among European Ethnonationalist Movements, 1870-1939", in A. Varsori & M. Petricioli (eds.), *The Seas as Europe's External Borders and Their Role in Shaping a European Identity*, London, Lothian Press, 1999, pp. 1-22.

Pressures on Assumed Identity at the Border

Malta in Europe, Empire and Mediterranean

Henry FRENDO

University of Malta[1]

This paper attempts to look critically at an earlier chapter contributed by the same author to a book he himself co-edited, entitled *Malta: Culture and Identity*, just a decade ago. In the light of major changes that have been taking place at a strikingly rapid pace, the approach here shifts somewhat from one of attribute to process, underlying some tensions and contradictions within this complex dynamic[2]. Rather than limiting itself to a standard empirical manifestation and perception of seemingly overt characteristics, it tries, in addition, to point at three forces which can be seen and felt penetrating and changing the traditional mould of a long vaunted national self-identity, to the extent that such a notion existed as a *donnée* in the first place, and was not partly a myth. The first of these forces or movements, which it calls the pan-

---

[1] Senior professor of history at Malta, Henry Frendo has taught in European, Australian and American universities. His most recent books are *The Origins of Maltese Statehood: A Case Study of Decolonization in the Mediterranean*, Valletta, 1999, 2nd ed., 2000; *Censu Tabone: The Man and His Century*, Valletta, 2000, 2nd ed. 2001, *Zmien l-Inglizi: Is-Seklu Dsatax*, Vol. I, in the series *Storja ta' Malta*, Vol. 3, Klabb Kotba Maltin, 2004, and *The Press and the Media in Malta*, European Network on Trans-Integration Research, Erich-Brost Institute for Journalism in Europe, Dortmund Univ., 2004. On 3rd August 2004 his keynote address to the International Society for the Study of European Ideas conference at the University of Navarra, Pamplona, was entitled "Co-existence in Modernity: A Euromed Perspective" see *The European Legacy*, Oxford, 2005, No. 3.

[2] See however the author's paper 'The National and the European in Maltese Identity', in *The Limits of Europe: From National Identity to European Unity?*, Berlin, 2004. See also H. Frendo, 'Life during the "British" period: strains of Maltese Europeanity', K. Gambin (ed.), *Malta: Roots of a Nation*, Valletta, Heritage Malta, 2004, pp. 101-118.

European factor, is mainly political and civil. The second, which it defines as the globalist phantom, is mainly economic and technological. The third, arguably the most potent and seminal for small 'frontier' peoples of the European Mediterranean, is labelled the clandestine mass migratory phenomenon. The paper first sketches out a traditional or classical typology of Maltese ethnic-cultural identity, as it evolved over the past few centuries, generally as a historical-geographical mould of Europe, Empire and Mediterranean; and then questions it, mainly on the strength of contemporary perspectives bearing on the three novel forces or factors at play in what (for want of a better terminology) may be called post-colonial times. The author asks how far, how quickly, and with what effect, could assumed identities at the border over-lap and change, possibly beyond recognition, within living memory, and how would one then identify a non-crystallized 'cultural' identity or identities, in time and space.

The increasingly topical discourse on identity – self, national, regional, or indeed global, or anything else – raises questions with have engaged the attention of scholars from Descartes, Hume and Kant to Durkheim, Mead and Freud, giving rise to schools of thought or method, such as structuralism, and now a deconstructing post-modernism. Closer to home, it has been central to our understanding of individuality, uniqueness, nationality and nationalism, extending from Vico to Michelet and well beyond them. When Herder used the expression "the fetter has worn through" he meant that an indigenous language-culture would have been suppressed, assimilated and vanquished: "to have lost entirely the national language is death"[3]. In searching for identifiable characteristics of nationality and nationhood, however elusive, the historian has to fish for facts, be these fossils or documents, structures or memories, be they static or mobile, in being or becoming. The same approach would have to be adopted in seeking out shared qualities or interests in regionality, as several writers from Strabo to Burkhardt, and from Camus to Braudel, among others, have sought to do, in one way or another, for the Mediterranean. Anthony Smith has noted with chagrin that just as the nation itself may be regarded as an 'imagined community', the construct of rulers and intelligentsia,

> so a global culture that is a pastiche of the past underpinned by science and telecommunications is humanity's most daring, all-embracing act of the imagination. Yet the texts of which such cosmopolitanism is necessarily composed, the satirized components of this patchwork, are just those myths, memories, values, symbols and traditions that form the cultures and dis-

---

[3] See H. Frendo, *Party Politics in a Fortress Colony: The Maltese Experience*, Valletta, 1979, 2nd ed 1991, p. 11.

courses of each and every nation and ethnic community. It is these nations and ethnies that set historical limits to our discourses[4].

The small island, more easily discernable and manageable, has frequently served researchers in the past as a test case for observing ritual and deciphering meaning. Islands can also be microcosms, and paradigms, depending on their proximity to or remoteness from so-called mainstream events. In the case of the Maltese Islands, insularity would suggest distance, but location lent a centrality, the more so because of prized natural harbours. History became altogether disproportionate to size, and a buffer to redress its limitations. Slowly *heimat* became *patria*: "patria mea dulcissima", as a Maltese geographer described it already in 1590.

Whether it can be proved that the account of St Paul's shipwreck in the Acts of the Apostles refers definitely to Malta and not possibly to anywhere else, for centuries this occurrence has been held and propagated in Malta as undeniably true, leading to an ingrained popular cult of reverence, festive and symbolic, richly manifested in art, architecture, robes and precious stones. Hard evidence of Christian practice emerges three centuries later, but there is nothing to show that at least some Maltese had not converted to Christianity already in the first century. In islands on the frontier between continents, such a Christian legacy became a matrix of identity, of Europeanity, by the Middle Ages, when Christian religious orders began to arrive and install themselves. By the 16th century it was a dominant motif, judging by the hundreds of churches and chapels in town and country alike. In the meantime, there had been an Arab interlude, with considerable Islamisation, until from the Norman period in the 11th century onwards the continuum of belonging to and with Christian European powers remained uninterrupted and was consolidated.

For the inhabitants of the Maltese Islands to be a people endowed with a separate identity, Christianity was doubly important, not only to exorcise the Muslim Arab spell through re-conversion, but to counterbalance the prevalence of a spoken tongue that retained its Semitic roots. Whether by accident or design, when Maltese first started being written very sporadically in the 15th century, it was in the Roman script; and there is no evidence to suggest that it was ever written otherwise. This is understandable, because – as the notarial and other archives show – the literary languages were Latin and subsequently Sicilian-Norman, until Italian eventually became the language of town and gown, church and cloister. This recourse to Italian continued during the time of the

---

[4]   A. D. Smith, *National Identity*, London, Penguin, 1991, p. 159.

knights, from the 16th to the 18th century, although most knights were actually French. If one could speak of a "national language" at all, it was and continued to be Italian, for all official purposes, until the first decades of the 20th century; but the sub-stratum of Maltese, closer to the soil, was always present, and more widespread, as a vernacular. To the idealistic German historical school, the "national language", however, would have been Maltese, not Italian.

Not so, however, at least not initially, to the emerging political class, composed mainly of *professionisti*, especially lawyers, who had been moulded in Italian from elementary school to university, and who pleaded in it at the bar. Nor, equally, to the numerous priesthood and religious confraternity, although Maltese was a better means of reaching the ordinary faithful through the confessional and otherwise. Rome, in other words, became a cultural as well as a spiritual capital, in islands that, notwithstanding Charles V's cession of them as a fief to the Order of St John in 1530, *stricti juris* continued to belong to the *Regno delle Due Sicilie*. This sense of belonging, of affinity, assumed a different role in the wake of first a French invasion in 1798, which in Malta, as elsewhere, quickly led to an armed popular insurrection; and subsequently a British military occupation, in time for the *Risorgimento*, which in Malta was experienced at close quarters through the hundreds of Italian exiles and agitators who sought refuge, transit or an operational base there – from Gabriele Rossetti to Nicola Fabrizi, Ruggero Settimo, Adriano Lemmi, Francesco Crispi and the Bandiera brothers[5].

Typically, the sense of a national awakening accompanied the flouted but still influential revolutionary ideals, and gradually the clash of culture between Nordic, Anglo-Saxon and Protestant, on one hand, and Catholic, Latin and Mediterranean, on the other. The prototype of a Maltese aspiration in 19th century 'Nationalist' discourse was the latter, to the point that, verging on the separatist edge, a young Nationalist leader, Enrico Mizzi, a graduate of Urbino and Rome, in 1912 boldly proposed a *pactum foederis* with Italy, while allowing Britain full use of Malta's harbours. Such a posture, of which Mizzi's proposition was an extreme, unrepresentative example, was portrayed and has come down in historiography as Maltese nationalism, even irredentism, which is how the colonizers labelled it[6]. But was it?

---

[5]   For a general history of Malta during the 19th century, including a chapter on Malta and the *Risorgimento*, see H. Frendo, *Zmien l-Inglizi*, Vol. 1, in the series *Storja ta' Malta*, Vol. 3, Valletta, Klabb Kotba Maltin, 2004, *passim*.

[6]   On this see especially H. Frendo, *Party Politics in a Fortress Colony, op. cit.*, *passim*.

The year 1957 was a great time to hold a 'post-nationalist' European Round Table, convened by the Council of Europe in Rome, to discuss Europe and the Europeans – almost as great a time as now, when the Dutch presidency is initiating a comparable initiative on European values in The Hague, not only for the benefit of the ten new member states of the European Union[7]. In those Rome encounters, Arnold Toynbee had incapsulated Europe within the boundaries of a religious geography, "those inhabitants of the north-western peninsula of the Old World, and of the adjacent islands", although he was prepared to include, in his definition, "other inhabitants of adjacent parts of the Old World who, in modern times, have adopted the secular civilization of Western Europe without having adopted West European religion." But, as Max Beloff observed, this merely adds to the confusion "since the only reason under this criterion for omitting the inhabitants of North America and Australia would be precisely the geographical convention that Professor Toynbee himself discards as artificial." European culture if it existed, he added, must be "capable of definition at once by contrast and by content"[8]. He then went on to explore that, with chapters on historical foundations, economics and politics, the cultural heritage, and various tasks ahead, since partially fulfilled, even as the scenarios have changed.

In taking Italian, rather than Maltese, as the standard bearer of Malta's self-government credentials, this Nationalist Party was hardly adopting a purist linguistic-nationalist stance but one which, today, might be dismissed, albeit superficially, as an elitist or liberal one. On the contrary, it was arguing on grounds of educational tradition, geographical proximity, religious commonality, even commercial custom. In reality this was a survivalist policy: it needed to bolster its anti-colonial stance by positing one recognized mainland European culture, to which it was closely linked, against another, seen as less European and more alien, which was politically and economically dominant, increasingly more assertive and assimilationist. Even its compromise solution of teaching English and Italian *pari passu* fell foul of the imperialist lobby because, in the words of Gerald Strickland, the Maltese had to become English in their speech, in their thoughts as well as in fact. For this, while suppressing Welsh in Wales and Gaelic in Ireland, the British in Malta, while anglicizing as in India on the Macaulay principle,

---

[7] This European intellectual summit lasting from October to December 2004, meeting in various capital cities, had as its main agenda "the politics of European values", and indeed "Europeanity" as such.

[8] Max Beloff, *Europe and the Europeans. An International Discussion*, with an introduction by Denis de Rougemont, London, 1957, pp. 7-8.

became great supporters of the Maltese vernacular, some conveniently identifying it with Arabic, and as a means whereby anglicization could prosper further. Ironically, but understandably, the 'pro-Italian' Nationalist Party saw this stratagem as a Trojan horse to eliminate *italianita'* and *latinita'* in preference for, allegedly, an uncultivated vernacular, reminiscent of the Saracen conquest. But, protested the *Partito Nazionale*'s founding-father, in eloquent Italian, in 1902:

> How can we, in the central Mediterranean, surrounded by Latin peoples, how can we, us 160,000 souls, adopt as our language the Anglo-Saxon tongue? How would we, through it, express our sentiments? How on earth could we, caressed by this sun, we who are a poetic and music loving people, adopt the language of a people who inhabit the Nordic snows? How can we adapt our way of thinking and of feeling to the way of thinking and of feeling of the English people? And if we cannot strip away the soul from the word, that is the thought, how can we ever dress this thought in any other form but that which suits our sentiments, that is the Italian form?[9]

Although this discourse obviously is as replete with aspects of social class, racial and religious feeling, as it is with the right to cultural heritage and self-determination, it is probably in the history of language that the three spurs to the Maltese dilemma – Europe, Empire and Mediterranean – most come together eclectically. Neither English nor Italian, Spanish or Sicilian, not Arab or Muslim, but somehow containing strains of all of these stitched together, Malta's race as mixed as its language, but one which in the fullness of time more or less homogenized as one of the smallest and still surviving ethno-linguistic communities in the world, eventually transforming into a unitary nation-state. Half-way between Gibraltar and Cyprus, Malta is a cross between them – the former, at the tip of Spain from whom it was wrested, more British than the British; the latter, just to the south of Turkey, with *enosis* as its main platform for decades. This is not simply a discourse on identity; it is a language of smallness and separation, of insecurity and peripherality. It is a cry of anguish and of fear, the groping for a brand name to wear, sell and see oneself in, a mirror of inventive resistance to one allegiance or dependence rather than another, a process of self-reckoning, of self-rendering, which changes, with difficulty, through continued inter-action, and as the times move on. So long as foreign occupation prevailed, the patriotic front would not lower its guard, although to the extent that once it had been consensual this became dented, even split, by economic, financial, class, sectoral and political interests, reflected in positions such as integration, as proposed by

---

[9] H. Frendo, *Party Politics in a Fortress Colony, op. cit.*, p. 114.

Mintoff's Labour Party in 1956 – not with Italy but with Britain[10]. The battle for language was ultimately won by Maltese, helped along not only by the likes of Joseph Chamberlain or Gerald Strickland, as well as devotees and promoters of the language's authentic and deserving literary development, but also, in the end, by the likes of Benito Mussolini who took Italy to war in 1940, commencing with an unprecedented aerial bombardment of Valletta.

Malta's post-colonial times may be seen in three stages. First, independence from Britain in 1964, with defence and finance treaties, followed by an artistic and economic flourishing not uncontaminated by a degree of neocolonialism. Second, the long Mintoff period from 1971 to 1987, nationalistic, socialistic, protectionist, neutralist, often impulsive, increasingly erratic and repressive, until a return to relative normality and civility through the polls, including a greater internalization of the alternating transfer of power as a norm. Third, membership of the European Union in 2004, hard fought for by the onetime 'pro-Italian' Nationalist Party but almost as strongly opposed by the onetime 'pro-British', and then 'anti-British', Labour Party. This state of affairs is now accepted and seen more or less as a relief, hopefully guaranteeing an equitable place and share for a part in the whole.

The disappearance of the colonial cocoon no longer required a patriotic front, nor any juggling with cultural superiority and inferiority between countries which were equally represented in international fora, and now equally members of the same union. In this sense, Malta came of age, and moreover, which is more significant, unlike many other ex-colonies, it managed to retain a working parliamentary democracy; no military coups, no ethnic-religious splits, no clinging, or not much of it anyway. As concerns changed, so did the sense of identity or identities, and the lifestyle. Aspects of such changes may be broadly and briefly categorized under three headings.

Membership of the EU introduces a pan-European factor not only into island politics but, well beyond insular mentalities, a creation of precious space, an opening up of opportunity, which historically could be seen as a more natural fall-back position than an emigration to the far-flung corners of the British empire or elsewhere. This has a special resonance for the younger generations, who feel less hemmed in or constrained by island confines, even if such confines may reside to some extent in the mind.

Secondly, Malta certainly has not been immune to the globalist phantom, which, though it may seem invisible, is nonetheless prevalent. But

---

[10] See D. Austin, *Malta and the End of Empire*, London, Frank Cass, 1971.

not altogether. The removal of the protectionist, state-monopoly, bulk-buying, student-worker mentalities which had characterized the Mintoff period were removed as a result of political change: computers and colour TV sets were no longer prohibited or restricted, nor were consumer choices with regard to chocolate or toothpaste, and so on. The post-1987 'normalisation' period saw a revamping of the infrastructure in its essentials: water supply, energy, communications, education. Money was a problem, but on the whole it was rather well spent. Foreign policy changed to a more pro-European one; while relations with Gaddafi's Libya were toned down, so that the colonel no longer came to Malta with armed body guards to address mass meetings, as in the more neutral, non-aligned 1970s. Generally, there was a democratic stabilisation. After 1991, broadcasting was liberalised, ending the government control over national radio and TV, so much in evidence since 1975. This meant that, increasingly, dozens of channels from all over the world on cable or satellite or even local ones, became like instant coffee, not without the caffeine. Even *Playboy* magazine was allowed in by the censors, although by now hardly anyone bought it, or even looked at it. Computers became widely available, even in schools, and of late e-government has become a government priority. Central power was also devolved, to some extent, by the creation of so-called local councils, of which there are now 68. In spite of all this, or perhaps because of it, creative artistic talent increasingly came to the fore, and ventured beyond Maltese shores, while popular social traditions, such as the *festa* – not only San Pawl – with its colourful, convivial bands, processions, petards, fireworks and revelry, show no signs of abating. Forty years ago, one Dutch anthropologist had prophesied that *festas* would decline, but they haven't really, although younger people of a certain set may care less about them[11]. Tourism – Malta gets 1.3 million visitors annually – is an added market incentive, although it is false to assume that such in-group conviviality is acted out for the benefit of tourist voyeurs.

Thirdly, by coincidence since Malta's EU membership appeared on the cards, illegal immigrants, mostly from sub-Saharan Africa, started flooding into the Maltese islands like never before. In 2002, nearly 2,000 arrived within a few months. This may seem like a small number, but with a population of 400,000 on 246 square kilometers, Malta is the European Union's smallest and most densely populated country. The 2002 figure of nearly 2,000 boat-load arrivals in a few months amounted very nearly to 50% of the native birth-rate. If such numbers were to be worked out in proportion to, say, Italy, which is far larger and richer,

---

[11]   See in particular Jeremy Boissevain, *Saints and Fireworks: Religion and Politics in Rural Malta*, London, 1965.

with a population of some 55 million, they would have to be multiplied more than 100 fold, coming to a quarter-of-a-million or so. Just in July and August 2004, over 500 have landed or have been rescued, i.e., by that same yardstick, well over 50,000; and so on. Since 2001 Malta stopped using UNHCR as a conduit for asylum-seekers and enacted its own Refugee Act, as well as waived its objection to the 1967 protocol, thus assuming responsibility for asylum-seekers from anywhere, in accordance with EU principles. Within a week, a newly-built reception centre, planned on the usual trickles of such arrivals, was over-run, and makeshift emergency placements arranged to shelter and feed several hundred uninvited guests from markedly different ethnic, linguistic, religious and social backgrounds. Malta's Refugee Commission has been taking a very kind, correct approach, respecting UNHCR's advice to grant temporary humanitarian status to anyone from Somalia, Eritrea, Iraq, and elsewhere, so that it is now granting protection of one kind or another to as many as 53% of its applicants, which compares with 3% in Cyprus and not much more than that in European countries such as Belgium, Switzerland, or even Britain, which may be more liberal[12]. This is a special and pressing problem for frontier states, especially but not only smaller ones, the more so for as long as the so-called Dublin Convention rules continue without drastic modification, thus implementing the solidarity principle, which is not solely or simply a financial one. According to this rule, it is the country of first asylum that is obliged to assume responsibility for processing an applicant. If she or he moves to another member state she or he should or could be sent back to the former one. That first contact country, in practice, is likely to be a frontier one facing Africa, the Near East, the Balkans or the East. This means that, for example, in 2004 Italy returned to Malta scores of illegal immigrants/asylum-seekers, mostly from the African continent, who had made their way there after first arriving in Maltese waters, or having stepped ashore in Malta.

It is too soon to fathom what consequences such an influx could have on identity formation and the sense of national or even regional belonging. Many leave, somehow or other; but others stay. In the recent past, several immigrants from the former Yugoslavia integrated, even inter-

---

[12] In November 2004, the Court of Appeal in Valletta ruled that the Refugee Appeals Board was not obliged to hold an open hearing for every appellant, on the ground that a request for asylum was not equivalent to a civil right. In the meantime, however, on UNHCR's advice, all Eritrean illegal immigrants/asylum-seekers, including those appealing against their rejection at all stages of the adjudication process, had been granted temporary humanitarian status in the Maltese Islands, however manifestly unfounded their claims may have been. In other words, they should not be returned to Eritrea unless and until the political situation there improved.

married, without problems, but they would have fitted, at least partly, into Toynbee's definition, whereas most of these others certainly don't. If, in spite of the best multicultural intentions, social cohesion were seen to be put at risk, xenophobic reactions could arise, and to some extent they already have, increasingly so. Clearly, the national homogeneity, of which prime minister Borg Olivier had boasted at the time of independence, is ending. Hopefully, this new turn can make for an integration and a mutual acceptance in a more varied and colourful but still liberal-democratic, socio-religious mix within the body politic. Arab immigrants, who are mostly Muslim, learn Maltese fairly quickly, as the patriotic *latinità*-inclined Mizzis turn in their graves. However Somalis, who are reputed to be more fundamentalist, don't.

Taken together with a declining respect for traditional values, such as the family and religious practice, among the Maltese, especially younger people, it is not clear what, if anything, can fill the ensuing void, if such it is. Catholic religious practice is still high, at some 80%, and any Catholic charity fund-raiser, not least for the asylum-seekers themselves, is likely to be over-subscribed. So far there is only one functioning Libya-built mosque, with a growing retinue, while the tiny Maltese Jewish community, which largely keeps to itself, is much older and fully integrated. Anti-semitism is practically unknown in contemporary times. Fear of difference could conceivably lead to a reassertion of some traditional core values – although Malta still has no divorce or abortion laws, even as gender equality slowly takes root. But if European trends are anything to go by, the tendency is likely to be in an opposite direction – more lay and secular – a marked departure from the colonial nation shrouded in symbolic wishful thinking to justify control and aspiration.

All this is not as new as it seems. Maltese shores, like other shores on all sides of the Mediterranean littoral, have seen many a mix and match and turn-around, since time immemorial. It may be a compliment to Europe's success, or is it her failure, that so many non-Europeans want to leave home and travel here. What seems strikingly different, however, is the suddenness, the disproportion, the persistence, and the mobility, through a well-organized inter-continental human traffic, operating from and across lands well beyond the historic Mediterranean itself. There is nothing Braudelian about it, except a possibly illusory economic pull; these newcomers are not normally even the Christians or Moors or old. In a 'globalized' age, and an increasingly 'unionized' continent, this is where the real problem for any identity or identities at the border, any border, may now lie. How far, how quickly, and with what effect, could assumed identities on the frontier over-lap and change, possibly beyond recognition, and how would one then identify a non-crystallized 'cultural' identity or identities, in time and space.

Without a distillation and fermentation, integration and ghettoization cannot really co-exist simply because they are mutually contradictory. On the other hand, the changing demographic and economic needs for Europe's survival are no les real.

There has been some suggestion that one should stop talking about identity, or at any rate about national identity. During the Berlin encounter in the course of the Dutch presidency's 'European intellectual summit' (23rd-24th October 2004) a Dutch EU commissioner, who has written about "the limits of Europe", noted that to continue talking about a European cultural identity if Turkey joined the EU, would be "a waste of breath". Europeanity, in other words, would become a misnomer, except in so far as it related mainly to economic, political and juridical integration. Then it would be the turn of the EEC's founding fathers, together with the de Rougemonts no less than the Mizzis, to turn in their graves. As the lines get blurred, perhaps we could conceive instead of one big *minestrone*, which could be fine, even delicious, if only all its ingredients were chopped up vegetables, simmering in a pot[13].

But in fact, given so many long-standing European traits, literary, artistic and philosophical, how likely is such a scenario in the foreseeable future? Dialogue and dialectic, synthesis and eclecticism, admixture and overlap, have been a profoundly creative, distinctive European inheritance, starting in and around the Mediterranean's shores in Judaeo-Christian and Graeco-Roman times. Moreover, islands have tended to have special protective in-group survivalist mechanisms, which, with rare exceptions, as in Malta's case, they so far have rather employed to good advantage over the centuries, if and when their existence was threatened.

---

[13] See for example the last few chapters in *L'Europe à la recherche de son identité*, edited by Christiane Villain-Gandossi, Paris, 2000.

Identity and Hybridism
in Sardinia and Sicily

Daniele PETROSINO

Università di Bari[1]

Introduction

Whoever lands on the largest of the Italian Mediterranean islands (Sicily and Sardinia) will certainly appreciate their natural beauty and geographical differences in comparison to the continent. When our traveler then walks within these islands, he/she will soon begin to discover the internal differences (accents, languages, food) between mountain and sea, city and country, south and north, east and west. If our traveler then decides to sail towards the other islands of the Mediterranean Sea, he/she will come across languages that are alike (the Corsican language will remind him/her of Gallurese, the Sicilian language of Maltese, the Catalan of Genoese) and ways of behavior that are similar, but will find that each island still maintains its own identity. This is due to the fact that the larger Mediterranean islands are part of a state (and this is not only a political or administrative issue), a continent and a sea in which the various peoples, cultures and histories from the east and west meet and clash. All of these factors have made each one distinct from the others, creating great internal differences.

Therefore, tracing a picture of their identity is extremely complex, firstly because identity should point out both the common and distinctive elements, secondly because from these elements borders can be drawn. Identity, then, is built on subjective dimensions and on shared recognitions and, perhaps, on some objective dimensions.

Under the subjective profile, each island has a strongly developed sense of identity, but an identity that is not necessarily exclusive and

---

[1] Address: Dipartimento di Scienze Storiche e Sociali, Palazzo Ateneo, Università degli Studi, 70121 Bari, Italy.

opposed to others. You can be Sicilian and Sardinian and to a large extent still identify with being Italian and European. The Mediterranean affiliation, however, is vaguer, only recently surfacing as a classification among the different references. Currently, this affiliation appears to be a link between ancient history and projection into the future. Certainly, the attention given this ancient and, yet, new form of identification is quickly developing and, it should be said, is being enhanced by the processes of globalization.

Globalization puts identities in danger of disappearing, causing homogenization of cultures, but at the same time, it stresses awareness of differences. This, however, is not a new process. Sicily and Sardinia have lived through a history of globalization, that is of interlacements and intercourses with the outside, which has incorporated the islands, little by little, into something larger than they are. Perhaps, we can outline the theme of identity of these two territories beginning from this history.

Insularity has never really isolated these islands. Due to their centrality in the Mediterranean area, they were constantly the focus of the powers that during different moments of history have dominated these islands. These islands certainly have many differences that reflect their different geographical positions and their different inland conformation. Now, they return on the Mediterranean scene as possible frontiers among the continents and the countries that surround this sea: those from developed Europe and those from the developing south shores. The dramatic events that involve the channel and the Sicilian islands almost daily underline how much this frontier is real, is quite physical. Borders, however, are not just closed doors; they are also places of passage and meeting, of the infiltration and blending of different worlds. Sicily has always been this and its identity carries the signs of these passages. Sardinia has instead been much more isolated. The differences between the two islands mark their different relationships with the Italian state, which represents a decisive point of transition in their history and identity. The Sicilian and Sardinian identities, if and in the form in which they exist, could not be set aside from the relationship held with the nation-state that, apart from judging them, has contributed to shaping them, either through antagonistic or homogenizing relationships. The reconstruction of the identity myth, the same search for signs of identity and their defense, takes place because they can be observed with the distance and the reflection of one who is by now within a plurality of cultural references. Of course, this does not mean that the identities tied to these territories are an invention, but simply that two aspects must be considered. The first is that any collective identity requires a selective process and is the result of a construction. As one speaks about an

Italian identity, one must account for the differences that converge within and are a part of it; a regional identity is also the product of differences as well as an historical process of formation of identity. The second is that participation with the national Italian state occurred in a crucial moment in the history of those islands (and of Italy, too), which is the moment of transition to what we now call modernity. Therefore, different processes interlace: the disappearance of traditional society and the entry as peripheries in one nation-state. In many other cases the center–periphery relationship was conclusive to constitute a specific, antagonist and conflictive identity of peripheral areas (see Rokkan & Urwin, 1982), certainly starting from pre-existent elements, which are reinterpreted in the new conditions. Sicily and Sardinia are not off from this model and they show, at the same time, a long duration and an unusual weakness for the territorial claim/protest. We are in front of two cases – quite different from each other – in which a reasonably strong identity element is present, and this has given birth to a relationship of continuous conflict with the nation-state, but not the radicalism that, in other cases, has been and is present. What are the reasons for this? At this point, it is possible to outline a few hypotheses. The two islands, especially their ruling class, notwithstanding the persisting economic and social difficulties that have tormented them, were part of the construction process of the nation-state, the general modernization of the country, particularly during the Republican stage, and redistribution of national resources, which caused their radical transformation and homologation to Italian society. At the same time, the institutional solutions adopted – notwithstanding their weakness or improper uses – have given a sufficient answer to the request of space by the local ruling class, by thus decreasing the possible potential voice. Thus, on one hand, there is a reaction of defense against the homogenization process, which is translated into the revitalization of some elements that are specific to the traditional culture, especially its language. On the other, it is possible to accommodate this revival in an institutional framework. All this now takes place at a moment in which identity becomes a resource within the wide, generalized processes of communication and exchange.

I. Traces of identity

A. Sicily and Sardinia in the Mediterranean Sea

The history of the two largest Italian islands can be read only in the context of the relationship system in which they are placed, that is in the Mediterranean region. While the Mediterranean Sea had a central role in world history (at least in the western hemisphere), the two islands were the focus of the powers of the time, although in a very different position. Sicily (Aymard, 1987) was more exposed than Sardinia (Mattone, 1998), which was in a marginal position. As soon as the Mediterranean Sea lost its central position, the two islands became both marginal, and were considered interesting only as points of support or military bases, but outside the greater routes of interchange. The colonial development that affected the south shore of the Mediterranean Sea tormented these islands as well. Of course, it is necessary to make some distinctions. The European colonialism in North Africa and in the Near East has specific features and it cannot be compared to the processes of state unification that has interested the islands. Notwithstanding, a post-colonial interpretation could offer interesting suggestions. The history of the islands was a subordinate history.

Sardinia appeared poorly populated by self-sufficient communities, with reduced mutual communications and, fundamentally, far from the sea. A boundary between the external cities populated by the conquerors of the island and the inland villages, between the mountains and the lowlands, has always been present in Sardinian history. The Sardinian sea was the pirates' hunting ground up to the 18th century, making the activity of fishing unsafe and no states with interests in Sardinia was willing to risk a fleet to protect the island. This meant cutting Sardinia off to outside communication because of the various dangers and difficulties of transport, but also the isolation of the inland dividing sea and mountain, city and countryside. A Sardinian dictum says, "The devil comes from the sea". This dictum should be interpreted both as a refusal of what comes from the "outside" and that whatever it was it brought only suffering to the island, as fear and something extraneousness from the sea. This does not mean, however, that the sea is not central in Sardinian history and identity, but it is tied, above all, to the conquerors that have occupied the island.

Sicily is much wider and more densely populated than Sardinia, and sea and inland have been constantly interlaced. Of the two islands, Sicily has had more exposure to the influences of people coming from outside. In Sicily, there is no dictum similar to the Sardinian one; on the contrary, a Sicilian proverb (*Cu' nesci, arrinesci*) invites flight from one's birthplace. Among others, it was a target of the Saracen and Arab raids, although the time of occupation was limited. Nevertheless, whoever arrived in Sicily and remained, became "Sicilian." Greeks became naturalized, Arabs became naturalized, Normans became naturalized and Spaniards merged with the local nobility on the island. We could say that the island did not reject anyone (MackSmith, 2003; Renda, 2003).

Sicily was thus crossed by migratory currents coming from the sea and the peninsula, which caused from the beginning an amalgam of people and different identities each, leaving its mark as it mixed with the others. We know that the foundation identity myths claim purity and authenticity of origin. In the case of Sicily, this purity is absent. Who are the Sicilians? Whose children are they? They are the children of Siculis, Greeks, Romans, Saracens and then Spaniards, the French and many others. If a distinctive trait must be looked for, we might find it in this aboriginal mixture that accompanies Sicilian history. It is a mixture that is not hidden, but exhibited, and therefore an essential component of identity. Like each process of hybridization/creolization, the dominant-dominated relationship is infused with suffering and resistance, but its path never leads in just one direction only. Sicily too is suffused with all those who have dominated it (Renda, 2003).

The two islands reach the thresholds of modernity carrying with them a history that is at the same time similar yet different, made up of invasions and invaders. Since the advent of Christianity, Sicily has maintained statuality, even if within the larger entity – the Kingdom of Sicily disappeared only at the beginning of the 19th century – and it absorbed the invaders, amalgamating them into the island population. For a long time, Sardinia was internally divided among the different political entities (*Giudicati*) and it rejected/isolated those peoples that invaded it. The Tabarchina and Catalan enclaves are examples of this.

With regard to the peninsula, the two islands were considered, at least partially, outsiders. Indeed, they were subject to being exchanged on the international chessboard based on indirectly offering political advantage to the different governing dynasties. Peaking in the 20th century with the falling out between borders, this is reflected in the Mediterranean Sea's loss of relevance since the discovery of America. Perhaps, as Renda (2000) affirms, it is from the beginning of the end of bipolarism, with a renewal of human movement in the Mediterranean Sea, that this area returns to its central position for those countries that traverse it (and, perhaps, not only for those), and the islands within it become the fulcrum of exchanges within this area, once again.

B. Language and Literature as Signs of Identity

Sardinian language, after several trials and struggles, finds its first official recognition with law 26/97 by which the Sardinia Region recognized its linguistic status, defined the norms of standardization and has promoted the institution of courses of Sardinian language inside the school curricula. What happened to the Sardinian language is quite significant (Paulis, 1998). Its scientific discovery was due to the work of a German researcher at the beginning of the 20th century, but it is a language with limited cultural and literary references and, above all, it presents great variations among the different areas of the island, thus not allowing the development of one spoken uniform language (a koiné). The process of standardization and definition of the linguistic norms will take place only at the end of the 20th century. However, many linguistic scientists disagree on the SLU (Sardinian Unified Language), considering the preservation of the different dialectal varieties of Limba necessary (see Argiolas & Serra, 2001; Bolognesi & Helsloot, 1999; Marras, 2000). Meanwhile, the infiltration of the Italian language, even within the internal zones, and the process of literacy (with all the linguistic forcing that this has involved) make the use of Limba more and more restricted, both in functional or geographical areas and in generational cohorts, thus making fear of its disappearance a reality.

At the beginning of the seventies, a mobilization to defend "sa limba", led mostly by intellectuals, spread, involving vaster and vaster segments of the political world and population. This is a possible sign that the language is disappearing, as it indicated an extreme attempt to defend a sign of identity. What followed, in the final decades of the recent century was a political mobilization, using linguistic rights to revive and renew the mobilization of an ethno–national type. The dynamics were similar to that of many other situations in and outside Europe. The ethno-national revival crossed Sardinia and language became one of the central themes. Nevertheless, the process of decline does not seem to be stopping and the Sardinian language can hardly oppose the vehicular languages that dominate communication (English and Italian). A survey carried out in 1995 underlines how the Sardinian language is less and less spoken among young people. This happens not only in public and formal contexts, but also in daily interactions. The report concludes:

> This would appear to be yet another minority language group under threat. The agencies of production and reproduction are not serving the role they did to generation needle. The education system plays no role whatsoever in supporting the language and its production and reproduction. The language has no prestige and is used in work only as to natural as opposed to systematic process. It seems to be to language relegated to highly localized function of interaction between friends and relatives]. Its institutional basic is extremely weak and declining. Yet there is concern among its speakers who have an emotional link to the language and its relationship Sardinian to identity. (Source: "Sardinian language use survey" 12-01-1995 [http]://www.uoc.es/euromosaic/web/document/sard/an/e1/e1.html)

The literature itself shows the difficulty of this operation. The literary Sardinia includes important writers who have written in the Italian language and whose writings contain regionalisms, but the Sardinian language is not an integral part of the writing. There is also a vast and rich production of Sardinian poetry, but only a limited production of fiction and non–fiction (this is also due to objective reasons – the potential public is extremely small) (Lavinio, 1991; Pirodda, 1989, 1998)

As of yet, we cannot know if approval of the regional law 26/97 has modified or will modify this situation. Experience from other situations induces a certain pessimism. But the current point, however, is not how many people speak the Sardinian language, but the fact that the large public campaign on this issue has brought it to the forefront and has shown it to be one of the fundamentals of Sardinian identity. Even if the Sardinian language does not become the language most spoken by the Sardinian population, no one will be ashamed of using it, that is it will re-enter the group of approved and recognized linguistic culture options. Under this profile, it symbolically helps the process of Sardinian identity differentiation, which otherwise shows signs of a growing homologation.

The Sicilian situation is quite different. The Sicilian language is not included among the languages protected by the 482/ 99 law. It does not enjoy a regional law, but it is highly diffused and is considered a true language of linguistic and literary importance and with a well known history (Alfieri, 1992; Contarino, 1989; Lo Piparo 1987; Mattesini, 1994; Sipala, 1987; Trovato, 2002; Varvaro, 1981). In fact, infiltration of the Sicilian language in Italian literature, as well as the Sicilian literary production, is anything but negligible. The UNESCO report (Tab. 1) on languages in danger of extinction does not consider the Sicilian language to be one of these, while this danger is present for the Sardinian language.

Table 1: Endangered languages of Italy

Endangered languages	Potentially endangered languages	Not endangered languages
Algherese Catalan	Francoprovençal	German
Ladin	Piemontese	Venetian
Friulian	Ligurian	(Tuscan & Central) Italian
Gallurese Sardinian	Lombard	Southern Italian (incl. Neapolitan)
Logudorese Sardinian	Emilian	Sicilian
Campidanese Sardinian		
Sassarese Sardinian		
Arbëreshë Albanian		

Source: adaptation from Tapani Salminen, *Unesco Red Book on Endangered Languages: Europe*, Helsinki, 1993

The ISTAT survey (Tab. 2) on the use of the dialect also shows us how such use is more diffused in Sicily than in Sardinia (although the Sardinian people have not accepted the ISTAT definition of "dialect" for their own language and prefer the definition of "other language").

Table 2: Considering people of 6 years and older according to the language habitually used in different relational contexts for region and autonomous province. Year 2000 (values in percentages)

	WITH FAMILY				WITH FRIENDS				WITH OTHERS			
	Only or prevalence of Italian	Only or prevalence of dialect	Both Italian and dialect	Other languages	Only or prevalence of Italian	Only or prevalence of dialect	Both Italian and dialect	Other languages	Only or prevalence of Italian	Only or prevalence of dialect	Both Italian and dialect	Other languages
Region												
Piedmont	58.6	11.4	27.3	2.2	64.7	76	25.6	1.6	858	2.2	11.3	0.3
Valle d'Aosta	55.5	12.6	24.4	7.1	61.3	4.8	28.5	4.9	84.1	1.1	9.8	4.5
Lombardy	58.3	10.7	27.9	2.0	62.8	10.0	24.4	1.6	86.7	2.3	8.8	0.7
Trentino-Alto Adige	24.3	23.1	15.3	36.4	25.5	21.3	16.8	35.7	42.8	6.3	17.4	32.6
Bolzano-Bozen	21.1	1.8	5.7	70.0	22.1	0.7	5.8	70.0	24.7	0.6	6.9	66.4
Trento	27.4	43.6	24.6	4.1	28.7	41.1	27.4	2.5	60.3	11.8	27.6	0.1
Veneto	22.6	42.6	29.8	3.9	23.7	38.2	34.4	2.7	52.4	14.2	32.0	0.2
Friuli-Venezia Giulia	34.3	16.6	24.5	24.0	333	13.5	34.8	18.0	63.1	5.9	29.8	0.5
Liguria	67.5	124	17.9	1.4	70.9	7.1	20.3	0.9	87.6	1.7	9.4	0.4
Emilia-Romagna	56.6	14.2	26.7	1.8	60.9	11.2	26.3	1.1	84.8	3.0	11.6	0.3
Tuscany	83.0	4.1	10.1	2.2	84.7	3.6	9.4	1.5	89.1	2.6	6.6	0.8
Umbria	50.8	13.0	34.9	0.8	52.7	11.9	34.2	0.6	67.9	8.6	22.7	0.1
Marche	37.7	18.1	42.2	1.0	412	16.0	41.7	0.2	67.5	9.3	22.4	0.0
Lazio	58.9	8.1	29.8	1.8	61.8	6.9	28.4	1.1	81.1	2.6	14.1	0.3
Abruzzo	29.4	22.9	45.7	1.3	35.3	19.0	44.2	0.7	71.3	7.8	19.9	0.1
Molise	29.0	27.3	36.0	7.4	32.4	21.2	39.3	6.7	75.8	8.9	14.6	0.4
Campania	21.5	30.5	467	0.5	26.5	26.2	46.0	0.3	53.6	15.4	30.1	0.0
Puglia	31.6	17.7	49.8	0.4	36.9	13.6	48.6	0.4	71.0	5.6	22.3	0.2
Basilicata	28.8	25.9	42.1	2.5	33.4	23.5	40.1	2.2	68.3	8.7	22.1	0.1
Calabria	17.8	40.4	39.4	0.9	22.4	30.8	44.4	0.8	60.7	13.1	24.4	0.1
Sicily	23.8	32.8	42.5	0.2	28.4	26.6	44.2	0.2	57.1	12.7	29.4	0.0
Sardinia	464	0.9	38.1	13.9	49.0	0.7	37.6	11.7	75.8	3.2	19.6	0.2
Italy	44.1	19.1	32.9	3.0	48.0	16.0	32.7	2.4	72.7	6.8	18.6	0.8

Source: ISTAT, *Lingua italiana e dialetti in Italia*, tab. 3, Roma, 12 marzo 2002.

As we know, the distinction between language and dialect is very fluid and substantially tied more to public recognition than to objectively verifiable real differences (Cortellazzo, 1994; Pacagnella, 1983, 1994). What emerges is that the linguistic claim becomes central in relationship to the weakness of the language/dialect. The Sicilian language seems then more consolidated and stronger in the regional reality than the Sardinian language (Dettori, 1994, 1998, 2002; Lo Piparo, 1987; Mattesini, 1994).

The linguistic vicissitudes of the two regions are, however, interesting also under a historical profile, since they present some differences that could offer insight on the characteristics of the identity of the two regions. The Sicilian language originated and changed through the influence of multiple languages: Greek, Latin, Spanish, French, and it competed, at least in the beginning, with Tuscan as the literary and administrative language. For a long period, it also held an important place in official acts (Mattesini, 1994; Trovato, 2002; Varvaro, 1981). The Sardinian language, in its different variations, developed in a more isolated way, although this isolation could not keep linguistic contamination at bay, due to the different populations that landed on the island. It is not by chance that Wagner studies the language among the villages of Barbagia, where isolation has allowed the dialect to thrive. The Sicilian language has mixed with the other Mediterranean Sea languages and with the languages of its colonizers. The appropriation of these languages guarantees its own vitality, while Sardinian seems to have withdrawn from contact, safeguarding a presumed purity, as regards other neo-Latin languages. Such different linguistic attitudes, can be found in Italian literature written by Sicilian writers, full of references and uses of dialect", even in its most sophisticated expression (compare for example Pirandello and Grazia Deledda).

The Mediterranean Sea was and is a sea of continuous contacts and linguistic blending. In Sardinia, this assumed the aspect of the presence of linguistic enclaves, such as Tabarchina, Catalan in Alghero, dialects similar to Italian and Corsican in Sassarese and Gallura, while in Sicily, where important Arberesch and Galloitaliche enclaves also existed, words and expressions from other languages have translated into an enrichment of the local language.

II. Identity and Homologation

A. *The Population*

Identity consists in a totality of objective and subjective factors of self–representation and recognition. The way in which a population reproduces itself, its demography, its familiar structures, constitutes a fundamental part of this identity. In the two cases we are analyzing, we are dealing with quite contradictory phenomena. On one hand, we find the characteristics of peripheral and colonial experiences – migrations that assume a diaspora-like character, for example – on the other hand, we find a clear transition towards models typical of metropolitan areas, i.e. reduction in the rate of population growth, reduction in the number of family members, (partial) substitution of the emigration processes with immigration processes. Thus, the islands seem to highlight a borderline feature.

Table 3: Resident population for year of census– Census 2001

REGION	Census years			
	1971	1981	1991	2001
Sicily	4,680,715 (8.65%)	4,906,878 (8.68%)	4,966,386 (8.75%)	4,968,991 (8.72%)
Sardinia	1,473,800 (2.72%)	1,594,175 (2.82%)	1,648,248 (2.90%)	1,631,880 (2.86%)
Italy	54,136,551	56,556,911	56,778,031	56,995,744

Source: ISTAT Census.

B. Demographic Transition

From a historical point of view, the demographic dynamics of the two islands are rather different. Sicily shows an expansive demographic profile: the population grows, it moves in and out of the island, maintaining, however, a fairly elevated density (198 in./km^2). The island has similar dynamics to that of the other southern regions. It has a higher population growth than the rest of Italy, composed of a greater birthrate – although in decline-, inferior mortality, the dynamics of returning emigrants and growth of foreign immigration, particularly from Northern Africa. However, the overall local demographic trend indicates that Sicily, with the characteristics appropriate to any peripheral area (particularly in the South), is moving along with the European demographic trend (Longhitano, 1987) and not in a radically dissimilar way from the rest of the peninsula and the continent. This seems to contradict, according to Longhitano, the arguments of those who saw a demographic frontier between developed and underdeveloped countries crossing Italy, associating the South and Sicily to the demographic dynamics of the Mediterranean area (particularly the countries of the southern and eastern shores). The historical trend clearly shows how in action it is a process of demographic homologation with regard to Italy.

Certainly, an essential component of these dynamics, particularly in the 20th century, has been emigration, which has relieved demographic pressure, and reproductive behaviors have evidently changed.

Sardinian demographic dynamics were never similar to the South, although for reasons tied to the typical features of the island (isolation of the communities, endogamy, high rate of mortality, etc.); it presents fairly different characteristics from the Sicilian demographics. The most evident of these characteristics is the low density of the population (68 / km^2), even in the period of maximum peopling. The island has always been poorly populated and this has greatly influenced its history. Up to the 18th century, Sardinia had a population of about 300,000, and only beginning from 1861 has it experienced notable growth, tripling its own population; however, without surpassing the Italian average density. This growth was due to the decrease in mortality (thanks to resolution of the malaria problem) and, above all, to increased fertility in the mid-20th century, which, in the last decades has aligned itself with the peninsula, completing the demographic transition towards a society of low fertility (Gatti-Puggioni, 1998). Despite the low density and long duration of demographic dynamics that are inferior to the Italian average, Sardinia has seen important migratory flows, while continuing to be the center of little migratory flow of both returning and foreign emigrants.

The patterns of family structure (member number, relationship type, generational bonds) are an essential component of the identity of a population. Under this profile, structures and family behaviors are extremely meaningful. In Sardinia, the average number of children per woman and members of the familial nucleus is close to the Italian average, diverging from the South, which is instead close to Sicily. Sicily, in fact, shows indicators that are slightly more elevated than the Italian numbers and oscillates around the average of the other southern regions.

Table 4: Demographic Indicators by Region – Year 2002

REGION	Demographic Indicators					Indicators of the population structure (on January 1)					
						percentage			index		
	Average number of children per woman	Life expectancy at birth		Total marriage rate (by 1000)		0-14 years	15-64 years	65 years and more	Elderly	Structural dependency	Elderly dependency	Average age
		Male	Female	Male	Female							
Sicily	1.40	76.6	81.9	747	767	17.4	65.9	16.7	96.4	51.8	25.4	39.4
Sardinia	1.06	76.4	83.0	560	590	13.9	70.0	16.1	115.8	42.9	23.0	40.6
ITALY	1.26	76.8	82.9	618	675	14.3	67.1	18.6	130.3	49.1	27.8	41.9
South	1.34	76.7	82.3	694	715	17.0	66.8	16.2	95.5	49.7	24.2	39.3

Source: Sistema di nowcast per indicatori demografici (E); Popolazione residente comunale per sesso, anno di nascita e stato civile (R). (a) Estimatiom

In general terms, Sicily and Sardinia have different family structures, but both present similar features. The number of families with five or more children is higher than the Italian average, but less than the southern one (showing different values between the two islands), the reconstituted families and the single–parent units show a similar trend.

Table 5: Families and persons by typology regions, geographical repartition – Average

		2001 – 2002									
	Single Families (a)	Single, 60 years and older			5 Components and more families (a)	Families with more units (a) (c)	Familiar units			Unmarried children 18-30 years old (e)	Average number of familiar components
		Male (b)	Female (b)	Total (b)			Couples with children (d)	Couple without children (d)	Single-parents (d)		
REGIONS											
Sicily	21.5	36.5	79.6	65.3	9.9	3.7	65.5	23.6	10.9	70.1	2.8
Sardinia	23.4	35.6	72.0	56.4	8.6	4.3	65.5	21.0	13.4	79.3	2.7
Italy	24.8	37.1	74.4	60.5	6.9	5.2	59.8	28.2	11.9	73.3	2.6
Souther Italy	20.5	42.9	80.3	67.5	12.0	5.6	67.1	21.3	11.6	75.5	2.9

(a) Every 100 families of the same zone.
(b) Every 100 singles of the same zone.
(c) Families composed of two or more units or by a unit with other aggregate people.
(d) Every 100 units of the same zone.
(e) Every 100 young persons 18-30 years old of the same zone

Source: Istat, Indagine multiscopo sulle famiglie

Table 6: Rates of reconstituted family units – Census 2001

Sicily	3.64
Sardinia	3.65
Southern Italy	3.18
Italy	5.1

Source: Istat, Census 2001

Therefore, all these indicators highlight what was previously affirmed: a difference between the two islands, which is progressively decreasing, and a growing proximity of Sardinia, in all studied areas, to the continental datum.

A benchmark of the social traditional structure of peripheries, that is the family, seems therefore oriented toward a homologation to the models of the metropolitan areas. In spite of the delays and deficiencies of economic development in terms of occupation rate and per capita/GNP, the family structures tend to homogenize to those of the other regions of the peninsula.

Table 7: Per capita GNP (% in Italy)

	1995	1996	1997	1998	1999	2000
Sicily	65.05	65.00	65.67	65.76	65.54	65.54
Sardinia	74.61	73.72	75.29	74.87	76.14	74.94
South	66.42	66.27	66.87	67.08	67.66	67.51
ITALY	100.00	100.00	100.00	100.00	100.00	100.00

Source: Istat, Conti economici regionali, 2002

III. A. The Diaspora

An important component of the process of identity construction of the peripheral populations is the presence of the diaspora phenomena, or the spreading of a very substantial part of the same population to many foreign countries. The diaspora phenomena have a double and ambivalent effect. On one hand, they maintain an almost mythical memory of one's own origin in a segment of the population. On the other hand, however, they cause blending and hybridization, thus deeply transforming the identities of those people that are directly or indirectly involved.

Sardinia and Sicily share a sad supremacy: they are among the Italian regions that have mostly fed the migratory flows towards the Italian peninsula, Europe and the other continents. Hundreds of thousands of Sardinians and Sicilians migrated and lived outside the islands, preserving and feeding a mythical identity – as always happens in the migratory phenomena. If the loss of population has, on one hand, relieved the condition of depression on the islands through revenues and decreasing the unemployed work force, on the other, it has deprived the islands of great working and intellectual energies (the intellectual work force also emigrated). For instance, in the case of Sicily, this latter has fed the Italian state bureaucracy.

Sicilian emigration, with destinations toward other continents, especially North America and Europe, began in the 19th century, primarily during the postwar period of the Second World War. Between 1861 and 1971, emigration absorbed half of the demographic natural balance (Aymard, 1987).

Sardinian emigration, however, presents different characteristics compared to the southern regions: it took place later (after the Second World War) and it was mainly towards the peninsula and other European countries (Germany, Belgium, The Netherlands – where there already was a concentration of Sardinian emigrants) (Zurru, 2002; Pinelli, 1982).

III. B.   Immigration

We have already remarked the demographic novelty of the last decade: immigration. Also here, Sardinia and Sicily show slightly different dynamics, but both are similar to the South. The resident foreigners in relation to the resident population are well under the Italian percentage. Requests for regularization, although a notable percentage in relation to the resident foreigners, are inferior to the Italian percentage as well. Notwithstanding, the migratory dynamics are very interesting since Sicilians tends to be specialized in any productive activity, and the island holds an evident territorial relationship with the countries of the Mediterranean Sea southern shore (Caritas Dossier 2001, 2003; on Sardinia Zurru 2002). Sicily, more than Sardinia, is a point of passage, a frontier of Europe, but also a place for finding work and taking up residence.

Table 8: Foreign resident population – Italy – Census 2001

	Foreign resident population	% in Italy	% of pop/res. pop.
Sicily	49,399	3.70	0.99
Sardinia	10,755	0.81	0.66
Italy	**1,334,889**	**100.00**	**2.34**

Source: Istat, Census 2001

If the diaspora character of the islands' migrations is a sign of the increasingly peripheral and subordinate condition of the two islands – according to a typical post-colonial model – immigration is, on the contrary, a sign of integration in the strongest areas of the Mediterranean Sea, and thus the destination of other migrations.

III. C. Economic Life

Participation of the two islands in the Unitarian state was marked by deep changes in their economies. These changes were tied to the general processes of "modernization" and were certainly influenced by national politics.

Changes in the material structures of the two regions are an essential component of their process of homologation as identity is rooted in the various forms of material production of the human existence. The disappearance of traditional work and traditional forms of production is part of a vast process and it marks definitively the passage to another epoch (Angioni, 1998).

Sardinia and Sicily show, historically, two different models, although both rural: Sicily was founded in agriculture – particularly on the large landed estates, and Sardinia in breeding, primarily, sheep (Aymard, 1987). The latter was self–sufficient and independent, the first open to the international trade. Both were victims of forms of despoliation by the dominant metropolises and erroneous plans of industrial development; both were open to the development of a tourist economy that is still only partly constructed.

Distribution of the active population among the different economic activities shows that the islands are currently far from their ancient rural supremacy. Sicily and Sardinia – as all the South – have passed from a rural economy (which is still important in terms of product, as Sicily is one of the first producers of citrus fruit and Sardinia leads in sheep) to a tertiary one without having passed through the industrial phase . Yet, both have suffered the many consequences of erroneous industrialization plans, a common dynamic in areas that enter modernity in a later phase (Ruju, 1998; Giarrizzo, 1987). Sicily and Sardinia were the targets of the industrial initiatives of the state during the second postwar period, with wrong choices – above all, the petrochemical industries – that were incapable of generating a self-propelling development, causing environmental and social damage that has been very difficult to heal. However, the economic mentality of the period privileged central planning and basic industry in general, not only in Sardinia and in Sicily. In addition to these errors, the incapability of the regional ruling classes to be an active part of this process, if not by deleterious forms of bargaining, contributed to the ruin of these same autonomistic choices.

The result of this is clearly evident if we consider the serious employment problem that interests the two islands, as does the rest of the South. The prevalence of facilities (primarily traditional facilities), the high rates of unemployment and inactivity, the scarcity of a female work force are all clear indicators of marginal economies, peripheral, but within metropolitan areas.

Table 9: Resident population by professional condition, economic activity of employees and sex (% in Italy)

| | Labor force | | | | | | No labor force | |
| | Employed | | | | People looking for work | | | |
	Agri-culture	Indus-try	Ser-vices	Total	% of labor force	% of popula-tion	No labor force/labor force	No labor force/pop-ulation
Sicily	9.3	20.4	70.3	100.0	20.1	35.0	186.1	65.0
Sardinia	8.7	23.5	67.8	100.0	18.5	40.8	145.1	59.2
Italy	5.0	31.8	63.2	100.0	9.0	41.7	139.5	58.3
North-Centre	3.5	34.7	61.8	100.0	4.7	44.7	123.9	55.3
South	8.7	24.4	66.9	100.0	18.3	36.6	173.3	63.4

Table 9: continued: Females

| | Labor force | | | | | | | | No labor force |
| | Employed | | | | People looking for work | | | | Total |
	Agri-cul-ture	Indus-try	Ser-vices	Total	N.	% of labor force	N.	% of population	
Sicily	16.4	8.6	37.2	29.4	46.4	28.4	32.8	22.3	61.5
Sardinia	16.1	10.0	43.6	33.3	52.8	26.4	36.9	29.6	60.4
Italy	31.9	23.9	45.2	37.7	53.0	12.2	39.1	31.8	60.2
North-Centre	31.5	26.8	48.7	40.5	59.6	6.8	41.4	35.9	59.6
South	32.4	13.5	36.9	30.8	49.4	26.4	34.2	24.4	61.1

Source: Istat, Rilevazione trimestrale sulle forze di lavoro, anno 2002 media.

Tourism is the resource on which both islands are trying to revive their own economy; however, in the face of hardened competitors, particularly in the Mediterranean area. The development of a tourist economy is of particular interest (Fadda, 2001, 2002), since it thrives on the process of construction/maintenance of a specific cultural identity. Both islands, from this point of view are experiencing a phase of reflection due to their development of tourism. They have both been tourist destination for a long time, primarily for their numerous natural resources. The discovery of identity as a resource to sell on the tourist market has occurred over the last years and is directly proportional to integration in the global market. According to Hannerz (1992) and

Cassano (1996), identity can be played with on a purely instrumental/commercial level. It can then develop into a type of prostitute (the invention of folklore follows this model), and vice versa it can refuse contact and isolate itself (this is the fundamentalism of some identity movements — for instance, the Corsican), but it can also try to valorize the elements of identity/differences that are part of a common culture. The latter seems to be the approach selected by Sardinia, at least as indicated by the last regional elections (see Soru's program).

The model of tourist development also shows the ambivalent character of the two islands as a frontier: from a peripheral form, subordinate and purely founded on the intensive and uncontrolled exploitation of natural resources, they are passing, along with internal conflicts, to more careful forms of a tourist economy. This is not only in the sense of paying attention to sustainability and thus preservation of non-reproducible resources, such as the natural ones, but also in the sense of better exploitation of human and cultural resources.

IV. Politics and Identity

A. Sicily, Sardinia and National State

As in many other parts of Europe, an autonomous state capable of both unifying the territory and dealing with foreign powers was not constructed in Sicily and Sardinia. There are many reasons for this: the weakness of the ruling class, their internal divisions, the scarcity of available resources for any unifying plan, although the history of both islands is punctuated by revolts and unsuccessful attempts to create a politically independent entity. In the Sardinian case, this rebellious attitude was defined the "costante resistenziale sarda", while Sicily mythically remembers the Sicilian Vesper. Yet, movements of resistance and independence have never had the strength to develop into a national and state building process. This is a good point from which to begin interpretation of the problematic relationship with the Italian state: the institutional and economic claim on one hand, and integration and negotiation on the other.

Sardinia and Sicily enter the Italian state from two different doors: the Kingdom of Sardinia – name taken from the Savoy kingdom, which disguises its subordinate relationship with Piedmont, and the Kingdom of the Two Sicilies.

Sardinia (Sotgiu, 1984), after a long period of Spanish domination punctuated by revolts, entered the orbit of Piedmontese politics and attached itself to the Savoy kingdom at the beginning of the 18th century. While, in the first phase, the Savoy monarchy did not modify but maintained the established Spanish institutions, by the second half of the century, a process of Italianization had begun: Spanish was abolished and the teaching of Italian was embarked upon. This deep transformation really only interested the ruling class, since the population continued to speak the local languages. At the end of the 18th century, Sardinia, as all of Europe, was shaken up by movements of revolt, after which a rigid restoration and a process of Piedmontesization of the island's society followed.

Abolition of the feudal regime finally set the premise for the loss of the prerogatives of autonomy, which still persisted in Sardinia due to its inclusion in the Savoy kingdom. With perfect fusion, complete entrance of Sardinia in the kingdom as a province passed through the process of disownment and decline of Sardinian differences. Sardinia abdicated, through its ruling class, the prerogatives of autonomy that were guaranteed as being part of the kingdom, hoping for involvement through the reforms that were taking place on the peninsula:

> Sardinia abdicated after five centuries to the formal autonomy that had characterized the juridical condition in the aragonese period and in the years of the Savoy domination. It was the end of the *Regnum Sardiniae* and the beginning of the contemporary history of Sardinia as a region of Italy. (Melis, 1982: 115)

However, with the unification the position of marginality worsened, first in the Savoy kingdom and then in the Italian state. The hypothesis that Sardinia could be given to other powers in the course of the process of Italian unification testifies the disengagement and the abandonment of Sardinia (Sotgiu, 1986). The model of the relationship that was realized is the colonial type: resources were drained from Sardinia, without promoting, if not in a limited and an insufficient measure, development and structural unification with the Italian state. A Sardinian issue, which is part of a more general southern issue, can be recognized already in the second half of the 19th century. Even the circumstances of World War I and what followed did not change the relationship of the island with the continent that was substantially far and extraneous. Only in the second postwar period, with the beginning of the autonomist phase and plans for development (although badly conceived) were the ties between the island and Italy renewed.

Sicily instead maintained its autonomy during the various dominations, finding then, in the Bourbon kingdom, state recognition (Benigno & Giarrizzo, 2003; Mack Smith, 2003; Renda, 2003). In 1718, the exchange that brought Sardinia into the Savoy dynasty and Sicily to Charles VI of Austria, along with the kingdom of Naples, was achieved, lasting just a few years up until when the kingdom of Naples and Sicily, under Bourbon leadership, was proclaimed. The brief rule of both the Piedmontese and Bourbon kingdoms recognized Sicily as an autonomous entity. Under the Bourbon kingdom, the institutions of the two members of the kingdom were acknowledged and maintained separated.

In the 19th century, following the Napoleonic uprisings and the restoration that followed, the relationship between the kingdoms of Naples and Sicily changed (they now became the Kingdom of the two Sicilies), making Sicily a province and no longer a kingdom in its own right.

The Kingdom of the two Sicilies born through deliberation at the Congress of Vienna, the diplomacy of the Bourbons and King Ferdinand's intrigues destroyed the kingdoms of Naples and Sicily, which were among the most ancient Italian and Sicilian states. This, above all frustrated the relationship of a federal type union that favored political stability and economic, social, political and cultural development. The 19th century South, separated into two autonomous but united kingdoms under the same monarch, represented the most important Italian event of the century. A large part of the Italian peninsula explicitly organized into an independent Italian monarchy. (Renda, 2003 [vol. II] p. 839)

The Italian unity, founded in the event-myth in the landing of "The Thousand" in Sicily, placed Sicily into a position tightly subordinate to the political center due to the defeat of the federalist options. Until the approval of the statute of autonomy, Sicily lost all institutional autonomy. This does not mean that its ruling class did not influence national decisions. The presence of Sicilian prime ministers during the period between Unification and Fascism was considerable. However, bias toward the national Italian state seemed to prevail among the ruling classes.

Intensified by the allied invasion, upheaval over independence particularly surfaced at the end of World War II, which was considered a good moment to separate from the peninsula. The *Movimento Indipendentista* was carried out quickly and Sicily gained the power of self-government to a certain extent, at least formally (Marino, 1979). The institutional configuration of the island did not change the power structure and the social inequalities present on the island up until the Republican Age. The wielders of power were large and noble landowners, who experienced the changes in rulers without injury. As the Prince of Salina, the famous character in Tomasi of Lampedusa's *Gattopardo* says, "To such power is subdued a population which throughout the histories of the island, in those sympathetic and in those hostile, was depicted in conditions of poverty and of abandonment". Furthermore, all are in agreement in criticizing the forms through which the power was administered. For example, Caracciolo, sent to the island as viceroy, recalls the difficulties he constantly faced in his program of reforms.

Thus, the two islands arrived at unification with the Italian state in a different manner. Sardinia as a province of the conquering kingdom, or at least of the kingdom leading the process of unification, Sicily as a province of the conquered kingdom. Both, however, in a state of deep impoverishment and substantial backwardness, and with social interaction still based in feudalism. Both islands, however, together with their local ruling class and intellectuals, were part of the construction of the Unitarian state, as were the ruling classes of many other Italian regions, although in a subordinate position.

It could be inferred from this that Sardinia and Sicily lived the Italian unification in a passive way, feeling it rather as an occupation. Really, many regions, or rather the populations of these regions, suffered at the hands of Unification in the sense that they had not chosen it, had not actively participated in it, despite the fact or perhaps because they were plebiscites. However, the ruling class participated, and unity of the country was achieved first by the ruling class. A part of the nationalistic literature affirms, on the contrary, the colonialist hypothesis. However, this interpretation seems to be wrong. Sardinia and Sicily took part in the construction of the Italian state, and they put their hopes into it, largely disappointed, as an improvement of their conditions. The Unification of the Italian state was not a simple conquest like the others the two island had suffered in the past, but instead a political project that involved all political entities.

The Italian Unification, the construction of the national state, was something very different from what had occurred in previous centuries. Previous occupations had two different scenarios in terms of contact between the different cultures. The first was that of the ruling class, who used a plurality of communicative tools and cultural codes, maintaining the different codes and functionally using them. So on the islands, mixtures of Spanish and Sardinian, Italian and Sardinian, French and Sicilian, Spanish and Sicilian, and so on were spoken. The second was that of the illiterate population, who maintained its own code along with widespread infiltration of the dominant codes. No one really set forth to "change" the cultural traditions, the system of values or the expressive forms of the population. Interest for the entire society was limited to the administration of justice and the collection of taxes. The Italian Unification, because of its centralistic form and the interlaced modernization process, changed these dynamics substantially. There was not only an imposition of a juridical and fiscal regime (with serious consequences

for the two islands), but the building of a nation-state and its industrialization required cultural homogenization.

Regional unification was a by-product of the process of national unification. Probably both Sicily and Sardinia – Sicily above all – were
already greatly aware of themselves, but both islands suffered from
internal differences and difficulties of communication. The nation-state
first put of all the populations of such regions in communication with
each other, allowing each to discover their common elements with and
differences to other Italians. The case of the Sassari Brigade was emblematic. The eradication of illiteracy, the infrastructures, the military
draft all caused a process of unification that was absent before, primarily
at the regional level.

B. The Politics of Identity

Particularly beginning from the 1970s and the 1980s, the identity revival took on a political form. Throughout Europe, political movements
based on identity claims either rose or revitalized, promoting mobiliza-
tions, and sometimes obtaining significant results under the electoral
profile. Identity as a tool of political struggle has bi-directional dynamics. On one hand, it could constitute the basis on which to develop
political mobilization, on the other, the political mobilization selects,
reveals and strengthens the signs of identity. Putting aside the electoral
results, the discourse on identity has continued, and we could say that it
now permeates the entire political field.

From an institutional point of view, the two islands are similar, but
have very different political dynamics. Sicily and Sardinia both enjoy
the status of autonomous regions with a special statute, a status, which,
in the Italian institutional organization, provides some privileges. The
autonomous regions are borderland and/or insular regions with specific
features falling under the identity profile. The Italian institutional organization has, at least partially, and only gradually recognized such
uniqueness (Nevola, 2003).

Sicily achieved its own autonomy by approving the regional statute
and, in this way, the separatist movements, which had risen on the island
under the liberation, were defeated. The Sicilian statute guaranteed some
important privileges of autonomy to the island, recognizing a condition
unique within the context of the southern regions. However, the autonomy quickly became an empty simulacrum: with formal attributions, but
very little substantial possibility of action, primarily because of the
ruling class who favored subaltern relationships of bargaining with the
government and the political center (Violante, 2003).

If, under the institutional profile, Sicily clearly obtained a special position, under the political profile the forces that more openly evoked the independence hypothesis resulted in being a temporary success. Finocchiaro Aprile's MIS, which obtained significant results in the first republican elections, melted like snow in the sun because of the instrumentality of its leader's actions and the inclusive action of the national political forces (Marino, 1971, 1979). Such force will opportunistically disposses itself of appropriate autonomist discourse. In the last years as well, independence has been proposed by some movements, which show, however, little ability to attract consensus. Sicilian political autonomy had an important impact as a negotiating factor, but, contrary to what happened immediately after Unification, no Sicilian politician has raised the ladder of the institutional and parties' politics. There are no Sicilians at the head of the principal parties, there are no Sicilian prime ministers (excluding the brief Scelba government), there are no Sicilian Presidents of the Republic. There are Sicilians in important offices, such as ministers and deputy ministers. Certainly, it could be asserted that other regions have also not had their own people in top positions, and that such positions do not necessarily have territorial significance. The fact is, however, that this absence could mean a certain tendency to remain on the island and negotiate from this position with the aim of maintaining consent and power within the island. In Sicilian political discourse, a specific identity claim does not seem to appear (the myriad of independence movements that run in the elections are not able to obtain consensus). This, however, does not mean that a Sicilian identity is not acknowledged, but it has declined mostly in terms of the autonomist claim, rather than a sudden waking of identity. The identity discourse becomes more an object of marketing than of true identity politics.

Sardinian political dynamics is quite different. It approved the statute of autonomy with a delay compared to Sicily because of dissent and conflict within the Sardinian political forces, but it has a very strong autonomist/independence movement (Accardo, 2003). The Sardinian Party of Action (PSD'Az) had already had a long history when the Italian Republic began. It came into existence after the first world war by the initiatives of Emilio Lussu, who later contributed to the foundation of the Party of Action, and immediately developed a campaign in favor of the autonomy of Sardinia, which obtained wide consensus in the immediate first post-war period. The second post-war period instead witnessed the party's gradual loss of strength due to inside conflicts and errors in political strategy, and also because achievement of the regional autonomy statute and the possibility of getting resources from the central government moved the consensus towards political government forces (DC) that were locally interested in feeding an autonomist discourse. Unlike Sicily, although less notable under the electoral profile and the party's internal profile, Sardinia has provided Italy with Presidents of the Republic, Prime Ministers and Secretaries of the most important Italian parties.

The ruling classes of these two islands have in common an incomplete and inefficient use of the autonomistic tool.

Above all, in Sardinia, the difficulties and the failures of the autonomist process and of the rebirth promises have once again strengthened the independence initiatives (Melis, 1979; Petrosino, 1988, 1992; Sechi, 1985). One of the protagonists of the independence revival is the PSD'Az, although more radical nationalist movements look out on the political scene, too. Unlike the MIS, the PSD'Az did not disappear from the political scene, but it survived for some decades until the end of the seventies when it had a blaze of resumption, canalizing both the protest against the missing promises of development and the identity revival. Although the party was not able to capitalize on the consensus, the general framework of Sardinian politics turned strongly toward an autonomist direction and all the political forces appropriate to it, that share the identity claim, an example of which was approval of the law regarding the Sardinian language. The growing focus on internal themes took place in a moment when Sardinia had lost its importance in national politics. There were no more significant politicians who could adequately represent the island. Sardinian politics seems then to have taken the road of the politics of identity without, however, sharing the separatist declination, although in Sardist circles the hegemony of the PSD'Az is under discussion by new, more radical groups that tend to receive the consensus, albeit extremely limited (Roux, 2003). The identity revival, also when it assumes the character of the separatist claim with ethnic characteristics, has never, had the isolationist aspect or, worse, the racist aspect, as in other identity movements. The identity claim goes together with recognition and the opening to plurality.

In both cases, new contexts of reference, especially in European and Mediterranean politics are cultivating the seeds of defining the regional dimension in a wider context than the national state itself.

B. Plural Identities

It is undeniable that Sardinia and Sicily are now closer and similar to the continent than they have ever been. They have contributed in building the Italian identity and this too has become part of their identity. Unlike other situations, however, in these regions a dual type identity exists in which the various identities do not meld together, but instead coexist. This result, perhaps considered a failure from the point of view of national identity, is on the contrary a privilege. According to Bhabha (1994), who like the people of the peripheries had already experienced the problems of relations among different cultural worlds that must co-habitate without canceling each other out, they can now face the challenges of cultural pluralism with more experience than those from the metropolitan areas.

The history that we have recounted could have a variety of different endings not yet written. The Italian state has set up a federalist process, the result of which is not known at the moment, but that, if it continues, will certainly meaningfully modify the institutional context in which the two regions move, giving deeper content to decentralization, in absence, however, of that compensatory effort that took place in the second postwar period. Europe has widened its own frontiers and this balances the equilibrium of the union more to the East than before, and Euromediterranean politics show a certain impasse. The same Mediterranean politics of the two islands seem to have a more formal than substantial content (many conferences, many signatures of declarations). Yet the need to compete in a hardened market pushes all, including our two regions, to underline the theme of their own specificity, sometimes promotionally evoking an authentic traditional society that no longer exists. The ability to sell its own identity as a brand on various products is certainly a component of the actual processes of globalization, but if it is an empty simulacrum, it loses its own competitive potentiality, as well. Close to this there is, however, the reinterpretation of identity. Sardinia and Sicily, at least the literary ones, are betting on a new declination of identities that include the past, but are the product of lived experiences and thus could not be anything other than plural identities greeting the infiltration of new cultures that are derived from the relationships in which they have been and are emerged.

References

Accardo, A. (2003), "Sardegna: le inquietudini di una regione autonoma", in Nevola, G. (ed.), *Altre Italie*, Roma, Carocci, pp. 107-132.

Alfieri, G. (1992), "La Sicilia", in Bruni, F., *L'italiano nelle regioni*, Vol. I, Torino, UTET, pp. 791-842, Vol. II 798-860.

Angioni, G. (1998), "Sardegna 1900: lo sguardo antropologico", in Berlinguer-Mattone (ed.), *La Sardegna*, Torino, Einaudi, pp. 1123-1152.

Argiolas, M., Serra, R. (eds.) (2001), *Limba Lingua Language. Lingue locali, standardizzazione e identità in Sardegna nell'era della globalizzazione*, Cagliari, CUEC.

Avolio, F. (1994), "I dialettismi dell'italiano", in Asor Rosa, A., *Storia della lingua italiana* (vol. III.), *Altre Lingue*, Torino, Einaudi, pp. 561-595.

Aymard, M. (1987), "Economia e società: uno sguardo d'insieme", in Giarrizzo-Aymard (ed.), *La Sicilia*, Torino, Einaudi, pp. 5-37.

Aymard, M., Giarrizzo, G. (ed.) (1987), *La Sicilia*, Torino, Einaudi.

Benigno, F., Giarrizzo, G. (eds.) (2003), *Storia della Sicilia. 2. Dal seicento a oggi*, Roma-Bari, Laterza.

Benigno, F., Giarrizzo, G. (eds.) (2003), *Storia della Sicilia. 1. Dalle origini al seicento*, Roma-Bari, Laterza.

Berlinguer, L., Mattone, A. (eds.) (1998), *La Sardegna*, Torino, Einaudi.

Bhabha, H. K. (2001), *The Location of Culture*, Londra, Routledge; trad. it., *I luoghi nella cultura*, Roma, Meltemi.

Bolognesi, R., Helsloot, K. (eds.) (1999), *La lingua sarda. L'identità sociocultural della Sardegna nel prossimo millennio*, Cagliari, Condaghes.

Brigaglia, M. (ed.) (1982), *La Sardegna. Enciclopedia.* Vol. I, Cagliari, Edizioni della torre.

Brigaglia, M. (ed.) (1982), *La Sardegna. Enciclopedia.* Vol. II, Cagliari, Edizioni della torre.

Cassano, F. (1996), *Il pensiero meridiano*, Roma-Bari, Laterza.

Contarino, R. (1989), "Il Mezzogiorno e la Sicilia", in Asor Rosa, A., *Letteratura italiana. Storia e Geografia* (vol. III), Torino, Einaudi, pp. 711-789.

Cortellazzo, M. (1994), "I dialetti dal cinquecento ad oggi", in Asor Rosa, A., *Storia della lingua italiana* (vol. III.) *Altre Lingue*, Torino, Einaudi, pp. 541-559.

Dettori, A. (1994), "Sardegna, Torino, Einaudi", in Asor Rosa, A., *Storia della lingua italiana* (vol. III.) *Altre Lingue*, pp. 432-489.

Dettori, A. (1998), "Italiano e sardo dal Settecento al Novecento", in Berlinguer-Mattone (ed.), *La Sardegna*, Torino, Einaudi, pp. 1153-1197.

Dettori, A. (2002), "La Sardegna", UTET, Torino, in AA.VV., *I dialetti italiani: storia struttura uso*, pp. 898-958.

Fadda, A. (2002), *Isole allo specchio*, Roma, Carocci.

Fadda, A. (ed.) (2001), *Sardegna: un mare di turismo*, Roma, Carocci.

Gatti, A. M., Puggioni, G. (1998), "Storia della popolazione dal 1847 a oggi", in Berlinguer-Mattone (ed.), *La Sardegna*, Torino, Einaudi, pp. 1037-1079.

Giarrizzo, G. (1987), "Sicilia oggi (1950-86)", in Giarrizzo-Aymard (ed.), *La Sicilia*, Torino, Einaudi, pp. 600-696.

Hannerz, U. (1992), *Cultural Complexity. Studies in the Social Organization of Meaning*, New York, Columbia University Press; trad. it., *La complessità culturale*, Bologna, Il Mulino, 1998.

Lavinio, C. (1991), *Narrare un'isola. Lingua e stile di scrittori sardi*, Roma, Bulzoni.

Lo Piparo, F. (1987), "Sicilia linguistica", in Giarrizzo-Aymard (ed.), *La Sicilia*, Torino, Einaudi, pp. 733-807.

Longhitano, G. (1987), "La dinamica demografica", in Giarrizzo-Aymard (ed.), *La Sicilia*, Torino, Einaudi, pp. 983-1020.

Mack Smith, D. (2003), *Storia della Sicilia medievale e moderna* (7[a] ed.), Roma-Bari, Laterza.

Marino, G. C. (1971), *L'ideologia sicilianista*, Palermo, Flaccovio.

Marino, G. C., 1979, *Storia del separatismo siciliano*, Roma, Editori Riuniti.

Marras, G. C. (ed.) (2000), *Lingue, segni, identità nella Sardegna moderna*, Roma, Carocci.

Mattesini, E. (1994), "Sicilia", in Asor Rosa, A., *Storia della lingua italiana (vol. III.) Altre Lingue*, Torino, Einaudi, pp. 406-432.

Mattone, A. (1998), "Le origini della questione sarda. Le strutture, le permanenze, le eredità", in Berlinguer-Mattone (ed.), *La Sardegna*, Torino, Einaudi, pp. 3-129.

Melis, G. (1982), "La Sardegna contemporanea", in Brigagli M. (ed.), *La Sardegna*, Enciclopedia, Vol. I, La Storia, Edizioni della Torre, Cagliari, pp. 115-141.

Melis, G. (1979), "Dal sardismo al neosardismo", *Il Mulino*, p. 263.

Nevola, G. (ed.), 2003, *Altre Italie. Identità nazionale e regioni a statuto speciale*, Roma, Carocci.

Pacagnella, I. (1994), "Uso letterario dei dialetti", in Asor Rosa, A., *Storia della lingua italiana* (vol. III.) *Altre Lingue*, Torino, Einaudi, pp. 495-539.

Pacagnella, I. (1983), "Plurilinguismo letterario: lingue, dialetti, linguaggi", in Asor Rosa, A., *Letteratura italiana* (vol. II) *Produzione e consumo*, Torino, Einaudi, pp. 103-167.

Paulis, G. (1998), "La lingua sarda e l'identità ritrovata", in Berlinguer-Mattone (ed.), *La Sardegna*, Torino, Einaudi, pp. 1199-1221.

Petrosino, D., 1992, "Regional and National Movements in Italy: The Case of Sardinia", in J. Coakley (ed.), *The Social Bases of Nationalist Movements*, London, Sage, pp. 124-146.

Petrosino, D. (1988), "La costruzione dell'identità etnica: il caso della Sardegna e del Veneto", *Studi di Sociologia*, n. 1, pp. 75-86.

Pinelli, A. (1982), "L'emigrazione", in Brigaglia, M. (ed.), *La Sardegna*, Cagliari, Edizioni della Torre, pp. 165-175 (La geografia).

Pirodda, G. (1989), "La Sardegna", in Asor Rosa, A., *Letteratura italiana. Storia e Geografia* (vol. III), Torino, Einaudi, pp. 919-966.

Pirodda, G. (1998), "L'attività letteraria tra otto e novecento", in Berlinguer-Mattone (ed.), *La Sardegna,* Torino, Einaudi, pp. 1081-1122.

Renda, F. (2003), *Storia della Sicilia dalle origini ai giorni nostri*, Palermo, Sellerio.

Renda, F. (2000), *Sicilia e Mediterraneo. La nuova geopolitica*, Palermo, Sellerio.

Rokkan, S., Urwin, D. (1982), "Introduction: Centres and Peripheries in Western Europe", in Rokkan & Urwin, *The Politics of Territorial Identity*, London, Sage, pp. 1-17.

Roux, C. (2003), *I partiti regionalisti nel mezzogiorno: il caso della Sardegna*, Realazione al congresso annuale della Società Italiana di Scienza Politica, Trento, 14-16 settembre.

Ruju, S. (1998), "Società, economia, politica dal secondo dopoguerra ad oggi (1944-98)", in Berlinguer-Mattone (ed.), *La Sardegna*, Torino, Einaudi, pp. 775-992.

Sechi, S. (1985), "Autonomia fallita e subnazionalismo in Sardegna", *Italia contemporanea*, p. 161.

Sipala, P. M. (1987), "Ideologia e letteratura nella Sicilia del primo novecento", in Giarrizzo-Aymard (ed.), *La Sicilia*, Torino, Einaudi, pp. 813-860.

Sotgiu, G. (1981), *Storia della Sardegna Sabauda*, Roma-Bari, Laterza.

Sotgiu, G. (1986), *Storia della Sardegna dopo l'Unità*, Roma-Bari, Laterza.

Trovato, S. C. (2002), "La Sicilia", in AA.VV., *I dialetti italiani: storia struttura usi*, Torino, UTET, pp. 834-897.

Varvaro, A. (1981), *Lingua e storia in Sicilia*, Palermo, Sellerio.

Violante, P. (2003), "Sicilia (in) Felix. Sicilianismo e autonomismo", in Nevola, G. (ed.), *Altre Italie*, Roma, Carocci, pp. 53-106.

Zurru, M. (2002), "Chi viene e chi va: immigrati e lavoro in Sardegna", in Zurru, M. (ed.), *Chi viene e chi va*, Angeli, Milano, pp. 17-84.

Zurru, M. (ed.) (2002), *Chi viene e chi va. Immigrati in Sardegna*, Milano, Franco Angeli.

The Problem of Identities in the Second Half of the 20th Century

Conflict or Conversion? The Case of Cyprus

Sia ANAGNOSTOPOULOU

University of Cyprus

Cyprus, despite its small size, constitutes an important historical paradigm, especially as far as the problem of the construction of identities is concerned. We can observe, in the case of Cyprus, some of the great historical problems of the broader eastern Mediterranean area. Apart from this, the perpetuation of the Cyprus issue, even today, when Cyprus is a member of the European Union, is an unquestionable testimony to a complex and complicated history.

The second half of the 20th century, on which I shall be focusing, signifies, for Cyprus as well as for almost the whole of the eastern Mediterranean, the end of colonialism. It also signifies, for the entire European space – and not only Europe –, the beginnings of the Cold War. It is exactly in this framework, i.e. the transition from colonialism to the reality of the Cold War, that I will be trying to present some of the aspects of the problem of the construction of identities in the area of the eastern Mediterranean. More specifically, I will try to expose some of the reasons why this transition process in Cyprus evolves through the revival and modernization of certain mechanisms of a vague past.

I. The Cypriot Identity as a Result of Multiple Consensus

In 1960, the independence of Cyprus is based on the recognition and consent of two politically equal communities: the Greek Cypriot and the Turkish Cypriot[1]. Therefore, it is based on the elimination of the colo-

---

[1] "The State of Cyprus is an independent [...] Republic, of presidential system. The President is Greek and the Vice President Turk, elected reciprocally from the Greek

nial reality, a reality in which the two communities – especially in the 1950's – were in conflict[2]. The basis of the Cypriot State, the 1960 constitution, becomes the bearer of the political institutional organization of Cyprus according to the great European principles[3]. The common Cypriot identity functions as a connecting net for Cypriot society, as a convergence point for the identities of the two communities and, last but not least, as a prerequisite for the existence of the state[4]. In short, thanks to the 1960 constitution, the colonial, conflictual reality of the previous decades is terminated; a consensual reality is established within the framework of which the convergence and "cyprization" factors of the two ex-conflictual identities – Greek and Turkish – are brought forth. "Any law or decision of the Communal Boards, [...], cannot have anything against the interest of the security of the Republic or of the constitutional order, [...]"[5].

Thus, the Cypriot State is the product of consent between the two communities – Greek Cypriot and Turkish Cypriot. At the same time, though, it is the product of consent between Greece and Turkey, as well as of the consent of Britain, all three guaranteeing, by their signatures, the independence of the State. Cyprus, then, as an independent state, constitutes the space of neutralization of the past conflict between two states that belong to the western camp – Greece and Turkey. In consequence, Cyprus is the space that ensures balance within the western camp in this area, under the high supervision of Britain.

> The Republic of Cyprus, on the one hand, and Greece, Turkey and the United Kingdom, on the other hand, [...] – I. recognize that the recognition and the maintenance of the independence, of the territorial integrity and of the security of the Republic of Cyprus, [...], is for their common interest. II. They want to collaborate in order to assure the respect of the reality created by the Constitution[6].

---

and Turkish communities of Cyprus, according to the Constitution", I article of the *Constitution of the Republic of Cyprus-1960*, Nicosia, 1972.

[2] For the consequences of this conflict, see D. W. Markides, *Cyprus 1957-1963. From Colonial Conflict to the Constitutional Crisis*, Minesote, 2001, pp. 11-30.

[3] See the 2nd chapter of the Constitution "On the Basic Rights and Liberties", *Constitution of the Republic of Cyprus-1960*, Nicosia, 1972.

[4] 2nd article: "1) The Greek community is formed by the totality of the citizens of the Republic who have Greek katagwgi and mother langue the Greek language [...]. 2) The Turkish community is formed by the totality of the citizens of the Republic who have Turkish katagwgi and mother langue the Turkish language [...]", *Constitution of the Republic of Cyprus-1960*, Nicosia, 1972.

[5] 86th Article §3, *Constitution of the Republic of Cyprus-1960*, Nicosia, 1972.

[6] 181st article of the Quarantie Agreements, in the *Constitution of the Republic of Cyprus-1960*, Nicosia, 1972.

That means that the existence of the Cypriot State signifies, on the one hand, that Greece, having agreed to Cypriot independence, definitively buries all remnants of the Megali [Great] Idea, which, during the colonial period of Cyprus, was constantly reproduced through the Greek Cypriots' demand for union with Greece [Enosis]. Therefore Greece, through the agreements with Turkey, aims to put an end to any revival of a Greek-Turkish war[7]. On the other hand, Turkey, too, definitively buries the remnants of the Ottoman and Pan-Turkist past that was constantly revived in Cyprus under colonial rule, through the demand for partition of the island. Thus, through Cyprus, the modernization and europeanization of these two Mediterranean countries is effected; likewise, the factors constructing the Greek and Turkish identities are also modernized. At the same time, Britain guarantees the definitive end of the colonial era for the area and, thus, assures the annulment of all colonial mechanisms. The term "Cypriot", then, first and foremost comprises the annulment of all mechanisms of colonialism, in the framework of which many a difficult past was being reproduced.

A. The Cypriot Identity as Bearer of the Revival of a Conflictual Past

However, even though the Cypriot State becomes a bearer of modernization for the broader area, it also simultaneously becomes a field of revival for some important inertia of the past. On the one hand, the Greek state, as a guarantor power for the independence of Cyprus, "delegitimizes", by its signature, the existence, in both Greece and Cyprus, of political forces whose ideology would be based on renurturing irredentism as their political message. Nevertheless, the Greek state, as the guarantor of the security of the Greek Cypriot community, recognizes the existence of a part of Hellenism outside the Greek state, for which the Greek state is responsible. The then Greek minister of Foreign Affairs is revealing: "[...] the Greek Government was, along with the Archbishop [Makarios], responsible for the safety of the Cypriot [space]; it was also responsible, by itself, for the safety of the national space, as well as for the interests of the entire Hellenism"[8]. According to this passage, the Greek State shares with Makarios [the leader of the

---

[7] See, "Note of [the Greek minister of Foreign Affairs] E. Averof (22.1.1959), containing the standpoints of the prime minister K. Karamanlis which G. I. Pesmatzoglu presented to [the Turk minister of Foreign Affairs] Zorlu, [...]", in Sp. Papageorgiou, *Τα Κρίσιμα Ντοκουμέντα του Κυπριακού (1959-1967)* [The critical documents of the Cypriot problem], I-III vol., Nicosia, 2000, vol. I, pp. 38-39.

[8] Ev. Averof-Tositsas, *Ιστορία Χαμένων Ευκαιριών. Κυπριακό 1950-1960* [History of Lost Opportunities. The Cypriot problem 1950-1960], I-II vol., Athens, 1982, vol. I, pp. 77-78.

Greek Cypriot community] responsibility for Cyprus; at the same time, though, it is fully responsible for Hellenism in its entirety, including, in consequence, the Greek Cypriots, as part of Hellenism. The Greek Cypriots are Cypriot citizens but also Greeks, part of Hellenism.

Turkey, on the other hand, as a guarantor of Cypriot independence, "de-legitimizes" pan-turkist political forces. However, as a guarantor of the safety of the Turkish Cypriot community, it recognizes the existence of a part of the Turkish nation and territory outside the Turkish State. "You are, today, on that sacred part of the Fatherland. Your sacred duty is to defend the order and the peace in our green island, which had broken away from the Motherland 80 years ago. [...]"[9], the Turkish Cypriot minister of Defense, Osman Orek, points out, addressing the Turkish military detachment, when the latter came to Cyprus, according to the Constitution of the Cypriot State[10]. Cyprus, then, is in a way the point of contact of two circles, those of Hellenism and Turkism. These circles, even though defined in a modernized framework, allow large room for the revival of the past. Britain, in reality, guarantees, by its signature, the functioning of the Cypriot State as a ground of balance between two states of the western camp, two states who ought to, through Cyprus, manage a certain past: a past of conflict. In a Cold War framework this means that, through Cyprus, the Cold War principle *par excellence* is consolidated: a balance of terror, a principle that allows for the surfacing, *in the name of threat*, of local political forces with an autocratic ideology.

The contradictory and complicated function of the Cypriot State is all the more evident in Cyprus itself. As far as the Greek Cypriot community is concerned, its leader, Makarios, who is at the same time the Archbishop, bears the very ambiguous "title" of "Ethnarch". The term "Ethnarch" [Εθνάρχης][11], a term belonging to the Ottoman 19th century, was revived and strengthened in Cyprus during colonial rule. The use of this term is a clear allusion to the existence of Hellenism with national claims. What, then, can be the content of the term "Cypriot" according to the Greek Cypriots, if its bearer is an Ethnarch?

---

9   Newspaper *Halkin Sesi*, 10/10/1062.

10   Annex II of the Constitution of the Cypriot Republic-1960 (181st Article). Agreement of Alliance, 4th article.

11   For the term "Ethnarch", see, S. Anagnostopoulou, *Μικρά Ασία, 19ος-1919* [Asia Minor, 19th century-1919], Athens, 1997, pp. 419-553. See also Anagnostopoulou, "The terms millet, genos, ethnos, ecumenicity, alytrotismos in Greek historiography", in Anagnostopoulou, *The passage from the Ottoman empire to the nation-states*, Istanbul, 2004, pp. 37-55.

Makarios' role is dual and contradictory. As the leader of the Greek Cypriot community he guarantees the Cypriot identity of the Greek Cypriots. But as an Ethnarch and as, at the same time, the elected president of the Cyprus Republic, he guarantees the Greek identity of not only the Greek Cypriots but of the state itself. He guarantees, then, the complete hellenization of the term "Cypriot", but its hellenization according to the principles of the western world. The passage below, taken from a speech by Makarios, is revealing: "Our newly-founded State shall derive, on the one hand, its ideological equipment from the rich source bequeathed to us by the long-standing tradition of our "nation". And, on the other, by the fundamental principles and declarations of the constitutive charter of the United Nations"[12]. On the one hand the heritage of Genos (national heritage, a term of the Ottoman period); on the other, the principles of the United Nations, that is the principles of modernity.

In this framework, Turkish Cypriots do not constitute, for the Greek Cypriots, a politically equal community, as defined by the Constitution, but a minority. But what kind of a minority? The status conferred by the Greek Cypriots to the Turkish Cypriots is not even the status of a minority, at least not that of a minority as defined in a modern framework. It is the status of a community who enjoys certain privileges. The term *privileges*, just like the term *Ethnarch*, is an allusion to the Ottoman era. *Privileges* were conferred by the Ottoman Sultan to his non-Muslim subjects, as long as the latter expressed their submission to the secular and religious leader, the Khalif. It is thus very important to note that, in the second half of the 20th century, a totally anachronistic term is updated within a modern, political institutional framework. Let us see, with the help of a specific passage, the way in which the Greek Cypriot community conceives the status of the Turkish Cypriot community within the Cypriot state.

> As far as the form of government is concerned, the Archbishop has stressed that the beginnings of free political life in Cyprus would be of capital importance. The Greek position would be dominant, regardless of whether *privileges* would be conferred to the Turks. Moreover, these privileges are indispensable for the achievement of free political existence in Cyprus[13].

This statement by Makarios is important for two reasons. First of all, it is the recognition of the fact that the existence of the Cypriot state in the modern era owes its existence to the Turkish Cypriots, too. Secondly, and despite the former, the Turkish Cypriots exist, within the

---

[12]   Parliamentary Proceedings, vol. I, 1961, B' Period, Nicosia, 1990, p. 370.
[13]   Papageorgiou, *op. cit.*, p. 48.

framework of the state, not on the basis of the rights recognized by the constitution, but thanks to the privileges granted to them by the Ethnarch. In this respect, Cypriot identity is defined in relation to the Turkish Cypriots as well, but not on equal terms with them. Cypriot identity is defined as Greek. Turkish Cypriots are Cypriots, as long as they submit to the Greek Cypriots, as long as their being Cypriot is recognized by the Greek Cypriots.

> The Archbishop was very touchy about the national issue. He saw himself as the guardian of the rights of the Cypriot people, as the heir of the Byzantine tradition, as the Ethnarch to whom the national wishes and the desires of the unredeemed nation were confined. His sensitiveness grew more when the privileges given to the Turkish community began to create serious problems and to become dangerous for the nation[14].

In this case, Cypriot identity is defined in terms of submission of a part of the Cypriot population and, thus, potentially in terms of conflict. Cypriot identity does not constitute the product of a synthesis between two community identities, but the product of submission of one communal identity to the other.

Nevertheless, if Makarios recalls, through the state, an anachronistic role, that of the Ethnarch, the leaders of the Turkish Cypriot community, mainly Denktas, also recall an equally anachronistic role: the role of defending the Turkish nation (i.e. the role of Mustafa Kemal) of the early 20th century. The Turkish Cypriot leadership does not claim, through the state, the safeguarding of the "cypriotness" of the Turkish Cypriots in equal terms with the Greek Cypriots; it claims the safeguarding of the turkishness of a part of the state, the safeguarding, through the state, of the existence of Turkism in rivalry with Hellenism. We see, then, a reproduction of the conflictual reality of the early 20th century by means of the state. The passage below is revealing:

> The idea of uniting the two communities within the framework of the state, the "cypr-ization" of the Turks, that is the largest possible increase in contacts with the Greek Cypriots, shall result in the elimination of the national cause from the minds of the Turks of Cyprus, and that shall equal to an elimination of the Turks as a separate community. The agreements were based on the lack of trust and on the animosity that exist between the two communities[15].

---

[14] N. Kranidiotis, *Ανοχύρωτη πολιτεία. Κύπρος 1960-1974* [Open City. Cyprus 1960-1974], Athens, 1985, p. 73.

[15] Extract from a secret Turkish document cited by Gl. Klirides, *Η Κατάθεσή μου* [My Deposition], I-II vol., Nicosia, 1989, vol. I [Annex VII the secret Turkish document. The following is the authentic Turkish text of the secret document found in Dr. Kucuk's coffer, when the special forces burst into his office], p. 500.

Thus, according to the Turkish Cypriot leadership, the Cypriot state was entrusted with the mission of reproducing animosity, so as to legitimize the existence not of two ethnic communities but of two "state" communities. In this respect, Cypriot identity is defined as the product of conflict and animosity between the Turkish and Greek identities. Rauf Denktas himself defines in a most revealing manner the importance of the terms "Cypriot" and "Cypriot identity":

> I am a child of Anatolia. I am Turkish in all that it entails. And my roots are to be found in Central Asia. [...]. I have a state and a Motherland. [...]. [...], they are Greeks, and we are Turks. There is no such thing as Greek Cypriots and Turkish Cypriots, nor Cypriots, of course. Don't you ever ask us if we are Cypriots, because we might take that as an insult. For the only Cypriot in Cyprus are donkeys[16].

For the Turkish Cypriots, Cypriot identity is defined in the terms of the early 20th century – although in a modern framework –, as a means for survival of Turkism, the latter being jeopardized by Greek irredentism.

II. The Cypriot Identity in the Framework of the Cold War

The reproduction of this specific past in Cyprus during the second half of the 20th century constitutes, in my opinion, one of the ways in which this region of the Mediterranean attempts to cope, according to its own realities, with the requirements of an era characterized by the principles of the Cold War. First of all, the reproduction of certain mechanisms of the past in a modern framework draws its tradition in Cyprus from the colonial era, when the colonialists, in order to avoid the formation of a common Cypriot identity that would endanger their own authority, made use of the traditional community separation of the population as a means of imposing their authority. Traditional separation mechanisms were reinforced during the 1940's, when the political activity of AKEL (the Communist Party of Cyprus) was threatening the colonial structure; when AKEL, articulating a common Cypriot discourse, was becoming the carrier needed to form an identity common to both Greek Cypriots and Turkish Cypriots. An identity that was threatening the foundation of colonialism. Indeed, the only political force that tries, at least up to 1963, to create a common and unifying political context for the two communities, is AKEL: "The main duty of the Cypriot people is the struggle for the accomplishment of the Cypriot

---

16 Rauf Denktas' interview to the Turkish newspaper *Ortam*, 13 November 1995, cited by N. Kizilyurek, *Milliyetcilik Kiskacinda Kibris* [Cyprus in the clamp of nationalism], Istanbul, 2002, p. 294.

independence, for democracy, [...]. In order to realize this basic aim the [...] unity, the cooperation and the common struggle of all the patriotic forces of the Cypriot people, i.e. Greeks, Turks, Armenians, [...], are absolutely necessary"[17].

A. The Cypriot Identity as a Communist Threat

It is exactly this colonialist tradition, totally appropriated by the leaderships of the two communities, that is proven to be very effective, in a Cold War context, for the imposing of local autocratic policies. This tradition, through which a past conflict is continuously reproduced, allows forces of the extreme right to limit, in the name of a threatened Hellenism or Turkism, the action of the leftist forces to a strictly community level. AKEL is accused "as of extraneous influences and internationalist, as antinational". "You must be on your guard and you must enlighten people. [...]. We ought to, all of us, realize, believe profoundly that the national future of our country, that the aim [...] in which we believe is in threat [...] and is in danger because of the [...] communists"[18]. So the left is forced to limit its political discourse to a national-community level, instead of an internationalist (Cypriot) one. Thus, community authorities reproduce their extreme-rightist, anti-communist ideology within the framework of the community and state through traditional mechanisms and in the name of a threatened Hellenism or Turkism. In this respect, a Greek Cypriot or a Turkish Cypriot is Cypriot, i.e. Greek or Turkish, because he is not a national traitor, i.e. a leftist. A Cypriot identity common to both (Greek Cypriots and Turkish Cypriots) is the product of a left-wing ideology and, in consequence, constitutes national treason. The struggle for Union [Enosis] with Greece is the cast-iron proof for the patriotism of the Greek Cypriots, as the extreme-rightist, anticommunist organization "Akritas" asserts. "Our Organisation [Akritas], after [...] many sacrifices, finally gained momentum. [...]. It is the shield of protection to any act for our national consummation [Enosis]"[19].

At the same time, the autocratic leadership of each community tries to impose itself on an international level as the only guarantor, in Cyprus, of the security of the western camp's interests and the only carrier

---

17 "Resolution of the 10th Congress of AKEL", *Neos Demokratis*, 9(1962), pp. 84-89, p. 87.

18 Extract from the leaflet of the extreme-rightist and anticommunist, nationalist Greek-cypriot organization "Akritas". "The communists and we", in Papageorgiou, *op. cit.*, 222.

19 "There is only one national organisation – Ours", Papageorgiou, *op. cit.*, p. 225.

of western values. Both of them, then, accuse the other either of sympathy to communism or of violation of western values. In this manner, the common Cypriot identity is, according to the right-wing parties, either pro-communist or anti-western (contrary to western values). However, according to left-wing parties as well, the common Cypriot identity is imperialistic. A part of the Left in Cyprus, but mainly in Greece and Turkey, puts forth an anti-imperialistic discourse, in which, though, many of the traditional national patterns of the Right are assimilated. In the 1960s and 1970s – but also in the 1980s – the anti-imperialist movement also developed in this region of the Mediterranean, based to an extent on the following traditional perception: from 1922 onwards, Hellenism is constantly shrinking because of the Turks, who are an agent of imperialism. In a similar manner, Turkism is under threat because of the Greeks, imperialism's favorite children. According to this scheme, the Ethnarch, as well as Cyprus, is, for Greek Cypriots and Greeks, Hellenism's last bastion against imperialism, Turkism being imperialism's agent in this region. The same goes for the Turkish side, too. It is not a coincidence that Turkey's invasion of Cyprus in 1974 has the complete support of the Turkish Left, since the invasion is thought to be an operation for the salvation of a part of Turkism that is being threatened by Greek imperialism.

Cypriot identity is formed, then, through an intricate itinerary, where the past is brought up to date in the framework of a difficult historical reality. However, during this critical era, some forces that were promoting the concept of a Cypriot – although bicommunal – identity, firstly on a social level, but also on a political level, never ceased to exist, mainly in Cyprus itself. The end of the Cold War signifies for Cyprus – but also for the Greek-Turkish space – the beginnings of the forming of a Cypriot identity, through which the mechanisms for the reproduction of this specific past are starting to be dissolved.

QUATRIÈME PARTIE

RELATIONS EXTÉRIEURES DE L'EUROPE MÉDITERRANÉENNE

PART IV

EXTERNAL RELATIONS OF MEDITERRANEAN EUROPE

Stratégie de développement, option Identitaire

La Turquie et l'Europe occidentale, de l'aide multilatérale à l'association à la CEE

Elena CALANDRI

Università di Firenze

La nébuleuse de pays périphériques qui entouraient la Communauté économique européenne à sa naissance comprenait des États différents, tous singuliers. La Turquie partageait avec certains d'entre eux le retard économique, la prépondérance du secteur agricole et certaines imperfections de la démocratie. Une note interne du Quai d'Orsay la définissait, avec la Grèce, comme un « pays européen en voie de développement, en quête des débouchés pour [ses] produits agricoles et des crédits pour le développement de [son] économie ». Mais deux éléments caractérisaient fortement son profil international : en premier lieu, une identité nationale forte, définie par une volonté idéologique de rejoindre l'Occident, symbole de modernité et de développement. En second lieu, par sa position géographique, elle était un enjeu important dans la guerre froide, un élément clef pour n'importe quelle stratégie militaire anti-soviétique et un segment essentiel du cordon devant prévenir la contagion du monde arabe et de l'Afrique par le communisme, ce qui lui avait valu l'admission à l'OTAN en 1952.

L'accord d'association entre la Turquie et la Communauté économique européenne, signé le 12 septembre 1963, comportait pour une période, dite préparatoire, de dix ans au maximum des engagements très limités. Il renvoyait toutes décisions pour le démarrage d'une union douanière à des négociations à tenir durant ce laps de temps. Par rapport au seul accord d'association précédent, le traité d'Athènes de 1961, le traité d'Ankara marqua un net repli, contrastant presque avec l'esprit, sinon avec la lettre, de l'article 238 du traité de Rome et des élaborations politiques des premières années de vie de la Communauté.

Pour la Turquie, nous ne sommes pas en mesure d'expliquer le sens ultime de ce choix « minimaliste » ; mais nous pouvons tracer les contours politiques et économiques des buts en question, entre la volonté d'appartenance au monde occidental, clef de la « révolution kémaliste », et les difficultés et les avantages d'une association à des États industrialisés. Cet accord était-il le maximum d'engagement possible, vu les conditions économiques de ce pays ? Ou bien les élites turques qui signèrent le traité, n'étant pas celles qui avaient posé la candidature, ne redoutaient-elles pas d'engager politiquement le pays au-delà du degré nécessaire aux buts économiques de leur stratégie de développement ?

Du côté des Six, la documentation nous permet une reconstitution plus complète des enjeux et des positions des protagonistes. Les études sur l'histoire de l'intégration européenne ont beaucoup approfondi les dynamiques internes des institutions de coopération multilatérale nées en Europe occidentale après 1945, les efforts pour gérer de manière non conflictuelle l'interdépendance et de faire survivre et relancer leurs États[1]. Ces thèmes ont quelque peu obscurci les moteurs extérieurs du processus d'intégration, l'intervention maïeutique des Américains et la menace soviétique, qui s'imbriquèrent dans les autres et qu'il faut faire ressortir afin d'avoir une vision complète. La Communauté économique naissait *outward looking*, ouverte à d'autres adhésions et « militante » occidentale dans un système international polarisé. Mais dans le traité de Rome, sa physionomie externe restait floue : exception faite des relations avec les colonies et du cas spécial de l'OECE, le traité se bornait à établir le cadre juridique, forme et procédures, pour des futurs accords avec des tiers. Les premiers actes de politique extérieure du Marché commun, la délimitation de sa sphère d'action extérieure, la distribution des tâches, la formulation des règles internes et finalement les politiques vis-à-vis de l'étranger, ont été cruciaux pour définir son rôle parmi les autres organisations. Les Six ont-ils proposé un équilibre entre intérêts économiques et signification politique, capable de séduire les pays périphériques ? L'attitude d'une élite – comme celle de la Turquie – attentive à la dimension identitaire des choix internationaux est significative de la capacité des Six à toucher des cordes pas seulement économiques. En outre, la genèse de cet accord peut contribuer à définir la place de la CEE dans la diplomatie politique et économique de la guerre froide.

---

[1] Voir le travail pionnier de A. S. Milward (ed.), *The European Rescue of the Nation State*, London, Routledge, 1992.

I. Alliance et assistance à l'ombre de la guerre froide

Pendant la Seconde Guerre mondiale, la Turquie avait gardé une neutralité visant avant tout à décourager les convoitises de l'Union soviétique. À la fin de la guerre, Ismet Inönü, héros de la « guerre d'indépendance » qui avait succédé à Kemal Atatürk à la tête du Parti républicain du Peuple, au pouvoir depuis l'établissement de la république en 1923, avait cherché dans la liaison avec les alliés occidentaux la protection et les moyens financiers pour le développement de son pays. Lors de la crise de l'alliance anti-nazie, la Turquie trouva un bon accueil à Washington, surtout après la conversion de l'administration Truman au *containment*[2]. À l'abri des confins méridionaux de l'URSS, dans la *striking distance* de ses régions industrielles méridionales et contrôlant le canal d'accès de la marine russe à la Méditerranée, la Turquie était déterminante aux yeux des diplomates et des militaires américains pour maintenir la Méditerranée orientale et le Moyen-Orient sous influence occidentale. Elle était un des rares points solides dans une région, le Moyen-Orient, où le secrétaire d'État John Foster Dulles devait admettre que le danger soviétique était un concept abstrait et lointain, eu égard à la blessure ouverte du conflit arabo-israélien. Ankara s'avéra un partenaire fidèle et volontaire dans la politique américaine au Moyen-Orient, que les Européens jugeaient parfois inutilement et dangereusement provocatrice.

L'élite turque chérissait ce rapport intime avec le *leader* de l'Occident, se traduisant dès 1947 par un crédit financier qui plaçait leur pays parmi les plus grands bénéficiaires d'aides[3]. La victoire en 1950 du *Democrat Partisi* ne modifia pas, au contraire renforça, la relation[4]. Ce parti, sorti du RPP dont il gardait les conceptions fondamentales, représentait moins l'*establishment* kemaliste de militaires et fonctionnaires

---

[2]   Sur les relations militaires turco-américaines de la période, voir les travaux de Bruce Kuniholm et surtout O. Sander, *Türk-Amerikan Iliskileri 1947-1964*, Ankara, Ankara Universitesi Siyasal Bilgiler Fakültesi Yayinlari, 1979.

[3]   De 1947 à 1954, la dépense américaine pour les aides militaires à la Turquie se monta à 704,3 millions de dollars, d'avril 1948 à 1954 la contribution en aide économique et en assistance technique fut évaluée à 262 millions de dollars : *FRUS 1955-57*, Vol. XXIV, doc. 320 NSC 5510/1 ; voir aussi C. J. Paca Jr., *Arming the Free World. The origins of the United States Military Assistance Program 1945-1950*, Chapell Hill et Londres, The University of North Carolina Press, 1991, pp. 88-129 ; en 1952, la Turquie fut un des quatre pays bénéficiaires du *Technical Cooperation Act*, la loi qui obviait en partie à la réorientation de l'*European Recovery Program* dans un sens militaire, en autorisant la concession des premières aides au développement.

[4]   Sur cette période, voir K. K. Karpat, *Turkey's Politics: The Transition to a Multiparty System*, Princeton, Princeton University Press, 1959 ; F. Ahmad, *The Turkish Experiment in Democracy 1950-1975*, Boulder CO, Westview Press, 1977.

que les intérêts des propriétaires agricoles et des premiers entrepreneurs industriels et commerciaux. Il entreprit une politique d'investissements publics et d'importations de capitaux. Le « miracle économique » turc des années 1950-1953 – un taux de croissance de 13% – fut alimenté par l'exportation de produits agricoles et de matières premières et par l'augmentation de la consommation intérieure. L'aide extérieure était une partie intégrante du budget et les prêts étrangers à long terme et à bas intérêt étaient les moteurs du développement[5].

Au même moment, Ankara participait à la construction politico-économique d'une Europe occidentale partenaire des États-Unis. Comme pour d'autres pays méditerranéens, tels que l'Italie et la Grèce, Washington avait initialement forcé quelque peu la main aux pays guides du processus, qui hésitaient à admettre dans leurs rangs des pays pauvres, faibles et stratégiquement exposés. Mais, tandis que Rome et Athènes, tout en demeurant très attachées au « patron » d'outre-Atlantique, trouvèrent dans l'Europe naissante un pilier important de leur stratégie internationale, Ankara continua de cultiver surtout ses liens avec Washington, qui s'avéraient capables d'ouvrir beaucoup de portes, comme le démontrait l'admission à l'OTAN en 1952. Il existait donc une relation triangulaire : Washington patronnait la participation de la Turquie aux développements politiques et économiques européens. Être reconnu partie de l'Europe satisfaisait un des buts essentiels du *leadership* turc[6]. Cependant, faute de force réelle, la CEE offrait surtout un ancrage politico-culturel : on peut se demander si les États-Unis n'avaient pas remplacé l'Europe appauvrie et humiliée d'après-guerre comme modèle de référence.

Ces deux axes de la politique extérieure turque – la relation spéciale turco-américaine, moteur d'une stratégie de croissance rapide, l'ascendant américain sur l'intégration européenne – commencèrent à chanceler vers la moitié des années cinquante. À l'intérieur, l'augmentation des prix, le déficit extérieur et la dévaluation de la livre furent le prix à

---

[5] L'historien et politologue Kemal Karpat a écrit : « Au début des années 1950, le gouvernement du *Democrat Partisi* d'Adnan Menderes parut décider que l'Occident avait un intérêt militaire et stratégique dominant en Turquie, et qu'il financerait ses plans de développement, quelque extravagants et mal planifiés qu'ils fussent. En échange, le gouvernement fit tout son possible pour remplir sa part dans l'affaire, en respectant pleinement ses obligations militaires et politiques […] ». K. Karpat (ed.), *Turkey's Foreign Policy in Transition 1950-1974*, Leiden, 1975, p. 6 ; voir aussi I. C. Shick et E. A. Tonak, « The International Dimension: Trade, aid and debt », in *Idem* (eds.), *Turkey in Transition. New Perspectives*, Oxford, Oxford University Press, 1987, pp. 333-340.

[6] Sur ce thème très complexe, voir B. Lewis, *The Emergence of Modern Turkey*, 2e ed., London, 1968 ; R. Davidson, *Turkey. A short History*.

payer par la Turquie à la politique de modernisation rapide. La situation se précipita en 1954 : la croissance tomba à 9,5 % et elle allait se fixer à 4 % dans les années suivantes. Les exigences du budget de l'État, obéré par le passif de l'industrie publique, par des plans d'investissements ambitieux et par des subventions élevées au secteur agricole, la réévaluation de la monnaie et le réarmement firent monter l'inflation. Les réserves d'or et de numéraire s'épuisèrent, au point que même les importations de pétrole se trouvèrent menacées. Au même moment, à Washington, on reconsidérait la logique de l'aide à l'étranger. Le Congrès défiait l'administration républicaine de tenir ses promesses électorales de réduction des dépenses publiques. Le Trésor voulait sortir du cercle vicieux où s'étaient placés les États-Unis en encourageant, dans certains pays alliés, un réarmement disproportionné par rapport aux capacités de leurs économies, et mettre fin aux gaspillages des aides de la part des gouvernements bénéficiaires. Lorsque, en 1954, le gouvernement turc sollicita un prêt important, le Trésor conditionna la concession à des garanties, telles que l'adoption et le maintien de mesures structurelles d'assainissement, et il résista au *crescendo* de plaintes, menaces et promesses orchestré par Ankara et soutenu par le Pentagone. La tentation de jouer entre les deux pôles du système international toucha alors cette élite turque, pourtant liée à l'Occident, anticommuniste et russophobe : à partir de 1955, elle se servit des avances moscovites pour alarmer Washington et l'amener à diminuer ses velléités d'austérité. Après 1957, elle accepta même, dans une mesure limitée, des aides soviétiques.

Tout en demeurant convaincu de l'importance stratégique et politique de la Turquie, Washington entendait donc réviser les termes de la relation, en particulier faire partager aux pays européens la responsabilité de l'assistance aux pays alliés moins développés. La Turquie et la Grèce, membres de l'OTAN et de l'OECE, étaient les candidats les plus naturels. En 1956, l'Allemagne accepta de payer une partie des dépenses du réarmement turc, comme de celui de la Grèce. Mais pour donner une réponse globale à ce « problème financier et économique colossal »[7], il fallait des actions à long terme permettant des réformes structurelles. Cette logique, qui allait inspirer la transformation de l'OECE en OECD, fut appliquée pour la première fois en direction de la Turquie.

Il serait quand même faux de penser que le patronage américain façonnait les relations entre les Six et la Turquie. La solidarité occidentale tenait, les relations économiques fleurissaient. L'Allemagne, l'Italie et

---

[7] Voir E. Calandri, *Le relazioni tra Stati Uniti e Turchia (1954-1960)*, in A. Donno (ed.), *Ombre di guerra fredda. Gli Stati Uniti nel Medio Oriente durante gli anni di Eisenhower (1953-1961)*, Napoli, ESI, 1998.

l'Autriche étaient les principaux fournisseurs de produits industriels, et l'Allemagne le premier importateur de produits agricoles turcs. Cependant, les difficultés augmentèrent en raison de l'endettement turc. En décembre 1955, les crédits des exportateurs des pays de l'Union européenne de paiements étaient estimés à 160 millions de dollars, auxquels s'ajoutaient 30 millions de crédits des compagnies pétrolières britanniques. Selon une note du ministère des Affaires étrangères français, souvent assez sévère, Ankara éludait les obligations de l'UEP et essayait de

> profiter à la fois des avantages du multilatéralisme et de ceux du bilatéralisme. Sur le plan multilatéral, [la Turquie] bénéficie pour ses exportations des mesures de libération des échanges prises par les pays membres en vertu des règles du Code de la Libération des Échanges [...] Sur le plan bilatéral, le Gouvernement turc négocie avec les pays créditeurs d'arriérés et obtient d'eux des conditions favorables à ses exportations par un système de péréquation qui permet de régler les créances des exportateurs européens avec des livraisons de produits turcs[8].

Au total, le montant des dettes arrivant à échéance dans les années 1956-1959 était insurmontable ; mais après avoir admis la nécessité d'un rééchelonnement qui renvoyât les échéances au début des années soixante, le Premier ministre se dérobait aux demandes d'ouverture de négociations. Aucune condamnation formelle ne fut émise par l'OECE. Mais l'idée que les Turcs devaient être forcés de respecter les règles communes et de tenir une conduite financière vertueuse était répandue chez ses partenaires. Bien sûr, les Américains craignaient surtout des répercussions sur l'orientation internationale du pays. Dans une étude évaluant le pour et le contre d'un règlement multilatéral de la dette, Owen T. Jones, conseiller économique à l'ambassade américaine à Ankara, concluait :

> Si le financement était réalisé dans les conditions actuelles, et si le commerce restait à dominante bilatérale, l'aide à l'exportation en Turquie pourrait conduire les différents pays à continuer à acheter les coûteux produits turcs. Plus un tel commerce deviendra multilatéral, moins ces pays auront d'encouragements à acquérir de tels produits. Cela tendra à augmenter les exportations de la Turquie vers le bloc soviétique et les autres pays qui fonc-

---

[8]   ASCE, MAEF, DE-CE OECE 361, Direction des Affaires économiques et financières, Service de coopération économique, *Note pour le Secrétaire d'État*, 20.12.1954 ; certains pays de l'UEP établirent une liaison entre des nouveaux crédits et le paiement des arriérés. L'Italie, l'Autriche et la Suisse réussirent à négocier des accords pour financer de nouvelles exportations. Au contraire, la Grande-Bretagne avait accumulé à la fin des années 1952-1953 des arriérés se montant à 42-43 millions de dollars et, en 1955, elle réussit laborieusement à en obtenir le remboursement en sept ans.

tionnent sur le régime des compensations. Ne fût-ce que pour cette raison, le financement des arriérés devrait être utilisé comme stimulant pour la réalisation d'un programme complet de stabilisation[9].

On comprend donc que des différences sensibles existaient entre les Six. Le pays européen le mieux disposé, le plus intéressé et le plus à même d'aider la Turquie était la République fédérale d'Allemagne. Bonn ne perdait pas l'occasion de souligner la valeur d'avant-poste antisoviétique de la Turquie. Dès le début des années cinquante, l'Allemagne était redevenue le premier partenaire commercial de la Turquie. Elle était donc directement intéressée à la solvabilité du pays. Intérêts politiques collectifs et intérêts économiques nationaux s'additionnaient donc. De plus, Bonn n'avait pas de désaccords politiques avec Ankara. En 1957, elle concéda un crédit de 100 millions « qui – commentait Ludwig Erhard au début de l'année suivante – fut gaspillé sans réforme interne importante »[10]. Début 1958, un prêt important concédé par l'OECE à la France fit naître des espoirs chez le gouvernement turc. En février, Zorlu visita Bonn. Mais cette fois, sa demande de prêt fut rejetée. Soutenus, et même encouragés par les Américains, les Allemands refusèrent un accord bilatéral et renvoyèrent Zorlu aux organisations financières internationales[11].

Ici, les argumentations politiques ne pouvaient grand-chose contre les critères techniques et Ankara avait plus de difficultés à refuser les examens préalables et les contrôles de ses programmes économiques. L'intervention de l'EPU étant empêchée par des règles restrictives et par les objections probables des neutres, l'OECE et le FMI restaient les seuls interlocuteurs possibles. Fin juillet 1958, le gouvernement turc adopta des mesures de redressement, dictées en grande partie par ces deux organisations[12]. Le programme incluait une dévaluation de fait de la monnaie de 2,80 à 9,025 par rapport au dollar, des restrictions de crédit, des mesures de déflation. Une aide occidentale de 334 millions suivit. À travers l'OECE, la France, l'Angleterre et l'Allemagne accordaient un prêt de presque 100 millions de dollars, la moitié par la RFA. C'était la condition posée par les Américains pour accorder leur propre contribution, un total de 234 millions en prêts, subventions, fournitures et renonciations à crédits, plus 25 millions de droits de retrait du FMI.

---

[9]   RG 59, box 4909, 882.10/3-2656, National Archives, Washington, D.C. (NA).

[10]   RG 59, box 4909, 882.10/2-1853 HBS Paris, 18-2-1958, NA.

[11]   *Ibid.*

[12]   La mission de l'OECE, qui travaillait en Turquie pendant l'été pour « évaluer » le plan, avait recommandé de revoir à la baisse et complété d'assignation de responsabilités précises et de pouvoirs de contrôle les investissements publics.

Au début de 1959, on arriva aussi à un accord euro-turc sur le refinancement de la dette commerciale, qui atteignait désormais 400 millions.

Au niveau politique, les relations entre la Turquie et les États de l'Europe occidentale n'étaient pas uniformément positives et elles étaient même teintées de quelque mauvaise humeur. Au moment de la crise de l'influence européenne au Moyen-Orient, une partie de la classe dirigeante turque jouait avec l'idée d'un rôle de bras droit des États-Unis auprès des pays arabes. Après 1954, non seulement les débordements de violence de la crise de Chypre insinuèrent un élément de méfiance réciproque; mais la question de Chypre elle-même conditionnait l'action internationale d'Ankara : elle la menait à rechercher la sympathie des pays du Tiers Monde pour gagner la bataille contre la Grèce aux Nations Unies, et donc à prendre ses distances envers les pays coloniaux. De plus, les Turcs n'oubliaient pas les empiètements des puissances européennes sur l'empire ottoman et les origines de la République, issue de la rébellion contre le partage de l'Anatolie prévu par le traité de Sèvres.

En résumé, les rapports entre la Turquie et les Six transitaient en grande partie par Washington. Aux accords bilatéraux occasionnels, fondés surtout sur une solidarité économique, les Européens commençaient à ajouter dans la deuxième moitié des années cinquante l'intention d'interventions collectives. L'Allemagne était la plus disposée et la plus apte à épauler les États-Unis. Sans entrer dans les détails des intentions américaines, on peut noter que, tout en favorisant l'action multilatérale, Washington encourageait et même exigeait un rôle majeur de l'Allemagne : dans le cas du prêt de juillet 1958, Bonn dut assurer la couverture du montant européen, quelles que soient les contributions de la France et de l'Angleterre. S'il nuançait les rôles nationaux, le caractère de l'OECE permettait d'établir des conditions et des contrôles sur l'emploi des capitaux mis à disposition. Le sauvetage de l'été 1958 était loin de satisfaire les besoins : pour redresser les finances turques, et plus encore pour le développement du pays, il fallait octroyer des capitaux sur une longue période et établir des relations commerciales stables avec l'Europe. Mais, à la requête d'un « flux continu de capitaux à long terme pour financer les investissements nécessaires, tant pour le développement du pays que pour une amélioration durable des conditions de la balance des paiements », la mission de l'OECE avait répondu que l'organisation n'avait ni les ressources financières ni les procédures appropriées[13]. D'autre part, les données de base de la situation turque – la croissance démographique de 3 %, la situation socio-économique mauvaise, le déficit structurel de la balance des paiements, la rareté de

---

[13]   ASCE, MAEF, Papiers Wormser, 290, OECE, CES/8.103, 19-7-1958, *Situation in Turkey*, Note by the Secretary General to the Heads of delegations, confidential.

matières premières et de ressources matérielles – compliquaient toute stratégie de développement. Le gouvernement turc ne paraissait pas être en mesure d'appliquer ses programmes d'assainissement : début 1959, certaines mesures de l'été 1958 étaient déjà assouplies.

II. La Turquie dans les initiatives d'intégration économique européenne

À la fin de la conférence de Venise, à l'été 1956, le gouvernement Menderes avait communiqué son désir de participer à la conférence de Bruxelles, où les Six allaient négocier sur la base du rapport Spaak. La surprise mêlée de satisfaction de l'initiateur de la relance, Paul-Henri Spaak, avait toutefois cédé à la prudence : Ankara était invité à attendre[14]. Ensuite, Menderes n'avait pas renouvelé ses avances : il s'était conformé à l'initiative anglaise de chercher un arrangement entre les Six et les autres à l'intérieur de l'OECE.

L'inscription du Marché commun dans une aire de libre-échange continental des produits industriels posait forcément le problème des relations entre pays riches et pays moins développés. Le rapport présenté en janvier 1957 par le groupe de travail intergouvernemental reconnut qu'il serait nécessaire de prévoir des conditions spéciales pour les économies les plus faibles. Il envisageait deux alternatives : soit retarder l'entrée des pays moins développés jusqu'à ce qu'ils fussent à même de respecter les critères normaux, soit, comme le demandaient les intéressés directs, leur accorder des conditions spéciales pour les faire participer dès le début[15]. À la réunion du Conseil des ministres de l'OECE en février 1957, le *Working Party 23*, sous la présidence de l'ambassadeur Fay[16], fut chargé de la question des *low developed countries* (LDC). La Turquie, avec l'Islande, l'Irlande et la Grèce, demanda à en faire partie.

Dans le rapport soumis afin d'établir le bien-fondé de sa requête de traitement différencié, le gouvernement turc demandait en premier lieu que le pays soit dispensé de toutes les principales obligations durant une période de vingt-cinq ans environ. À la fin de cette période, l'Organisation examinerait de nouveau la situation de la Turquie, afin de déterminer dans quelle mesure le pays serait désormais apte à se conformer aux obligations de la Zone de Libre-Échange. Il réclama donc de pouvoir maintenir ses tarifs et ses restrictions quantitatives, ainsi que ses subventions à l'exportation. De plus, il posa comme condition *sine qua*

---

[14] M. Camps, *Britain and the European Community 1955-1963*, Princeton, Princeton University Press, 1964, p. 66.

[15] *Ibid.*, p. 113.

[16] Délégué permanent de l'Irlande à l'OECE.

non que les produits agricoles reçoivent le même traitement que les produits industriels et sollicita l'institution d'un fonds d'adaptation et d'un fonds d'investissement, pour fournir les capitaux nécessaires respectivement à la formation de la main d'œuvre et à l'aménagement des industries existantes, et à l'élargissement de l'infrastructure industrielle du pays[17]. Par la suite, Ankara assouplit quelque peu ses requêtes : il acceptait que la condition économique du pays fût reconsidérée à la fin de la dixième année, puis tous les cinq ans, et promit quelques autres ouvertures au libre marché[18].

Dans l'ensemble, les demandes des LDC rencontrèrent quelques résistances. À la conférence des 24-25 juillet 1957, les gouvernements acceptèrent l'idée d'une agence pour le développement dans les nouveaux *terms of reference* pour les travaux du WP 23, mais sans s'engager quant à sa création[19]. En vue de la conférence d'automne à Paris, Fay fixait les conditions nécessaires aux LDC pour pouvoir participer à la FTA : augmentation de leurs exportations agricoles, maintien de tarifs protecteurs plus élevés que les autres, moyens financiers pour accélérer le développement[20]. Mais les Six n'arrivèrent pas à s'entendre sur une position commune à ce sujet[21]. Une proposition fut ébauchée en octobre 1958 par la Commission mais sans aucune dimension officielle. Il vaut la peine de rappeler qu'elle acceptait une période d'élimination des tarifs double des États industrialisés, envisageait des examens périodiques de la situation des États privilégiés et établissait des modalités pour l'aide financière. Celle-ci comprenait la même clef de répartition des charges qu'à l'OECE – ce qui signifiait que les pays en cours de développement auraient contribué eux aussi au fonds –, une assistance sous forme d'emprunt, une évaluation du coût des programmes d'ensemble et des projets individuels, de la fixation des conditions de l'emprunt, du contrôle de la réalisation des projets par un comité *ad*

---

[17] « La Zone de Libre-Échange », *Chronique de politique étrangère*, Vol. XII, n° 5-6, septembre-novembre 1959, pp. 663-677. Le groupe demanda des informations complémentaires et, dans son rapport du 19 juillet 1957 au président du Conseil des ministres de l'OECE, il laissa le cas turc en suspens : Paris, OECE, FTC (57)1, 19.7.1957.

[18] Paris, OECE, FTC (57)2, 15.10.1957, *in Chronique de politique étrangère*, Vol. XII, n° 5-6, septembre-novembre 1959, pp. 676-677.

[19] *FRUS* 1958-60, VII, doc. 32, Burgess a Dp State, 28-7-1958.

[20] Paris, OECE, FTC (57)2, 15.10.1957, *Chronique de politique étrangère*, Vol. XII, n° 5-6, septembre-novembre 1959, pp. 673-676. Il proposait des règles de réduction tarifaire, qui prévoyaient une période transitoire double de celle des autres pays et une réduction progressive de 5 % au lieu de 10 %.

[21] ASCE, CM 2 1958, Série Sessions COREPER 106, 25e session, 25.9.1958.

hoc[22]. Plus tard, la Commission elle-même, dans le « premier mémorandum » de février 1959, après la faillite des négociations des Dix-Sept, avançait deux idées importantes : l'aide au développement était l'une des missions primordiales de la Communauté ; pour sa souplesse, l'association pouvait être la réponse la plus facile pour lier à la Communauté des pays qui ne voulaient pas aller jusqu'à l'adhésion[23].

Dans les travaux de la Commission Maudling, les Turcs n'eurent pas une position très visible. Lorsque ces négociations s'arrêtèrent à la fin de 1958, le pays se trouva isolé, du fait de son exclusion du groupe qu'allait fonder l'EFTA. En novembre, la Turquie adressa aux Six une demande de suppression du tarif d'entrée de 30 % *ad valorem* imposé au tabac turc[24] et, en janvier 1959, elle réclama que les abaissements de droits et les augmentations de contingents accordés entre les Six fussent immédiatement étendus aux pays de l'OECE en voie de développement[25]. Un mois plus tard, le conseiller de l'ambassade de France à Ankara s'entendit réclamer l'ouverture de négociations bilatérales, « pour remédier aux inconvénients qui pourraient résulter [...] de l'entrée en vigueur des accords de Rome »[26]. Ankara n'était pas la seule à se préoccuper de ce que le marché unique pénalisait ses exportations ; mais les Six refusaient de se reconnaître obligés d'indemniser quiconque.

L'attitude que l'ambassadeur de France à Ankara définit comme une « prudente réserve »[27] envers la CEE se maintint face aux signes de naissance de l'EFTA et durant presque deux mois après la candidature grecque à l'association à la CEE, début juin 1959. On peut seulement spéculer sur les raisons de ce délai. Une adhésion pleine au Marché commun présentait des difficultés économiques insurmontables, même si, auparavant, Zorlu avait révélé le projet d'entrer dans le Marché commun et de servir de trait d'union entre ce dernier et le reste de l'OECE[28]. Puis, il déclara qu'il avait voulu attendre l'issue des négocia-

---

[22] ASCE, BAC 61/1982, 47, *Projet pour une proposition de la Commission*, 15.10.1958.

[23] Voir le texte du mémorandum dans *Chronique de politique étrangère*, Vol. XII, n° 5-6, septembre-novembre 1959, pp. 750-774 ; voir aussi M. Camps, *Britain and the European Community, op. cit.*, pp. 184-190.

[24] ASCE, CM2, 1958, 827, Mission permanente de la Turquie auprès de l'Office européen des Nations Unies à L. Fricchione, Secrétariat du Conseil des ministres de la CEE, 10.11.1958, n° 550.

[25] ASCE, DE-CE, 696, tél. R. de Margerie à ambassade d'Ankara, 21.1.1959.

[26] ASCE, DE-CE, 696, tél. Spitzmüller (Ankara) à Affaires étrangères, 7.2.1959.

[27] ASCE, DE-CE, 696, H. Spitzmüller (Ankara) à Direction générale des Affaires économiques et financières, 2.2.1959.

[28] ASCE, DE-CE, 696, H. Spitzmüller (Ankara), 2.8.1959.

tions pour l'aire de libre-échange. On peut avancer l'hypothèse qu'Ankara attendit la réponse des Six à la Grèce. En fait, quatre jours après que le Conseil des ministres des Six offrit à Athènes d'ouvrir des conversations exploratoires, le gouvernement turc présenta sa candidature. Dans un aide-mémoire aux six ministres des Affaires étrangères, il expliqua que, européen par sa position géographique, occidental des points de vue politique, économique et militaire, le pays subirait un fort dommage de la marginalisation de ses produits agricoles des marchés des Six, avec lesquels se faisaient 35 % de ses importations et 40 % de ses exportations. Puisque la Turquie n'était pas à même d'assumer les obligations des traités de Rome, elle demandait « une association avec le Marché commun qui lui reconnaîtrait le bénéfice d'une période transitoire de dix ans, […] un traitement spécial […] tel que l'élimination graduelle des droits de douane et des contingents […], une aide économique et technique visant à supprimer l'écart entre son niveau économique et social et celui des pays du Marché commun ». Dans un appendice confidentiel, il demanda, vu la ressemblance des économies grecque et turque, « qu'aucun décalage ne se produise tant dans les négociations que dans l'application touchant l'association de ces deux pays à l'organisation […] L'application du même régime à l'égard de la Turquie et de la Grèce devrait être un impératif certain »[29].

III.   Le poids des contraintes internes

Si la Grèce n'avait pas reçu de réponse favorable, Ankara aurait-elle posé sa candidature ? Sans doute, la requête d'août 1959 était très influencée par la volonté de ne pas être devancé. Les exportations des deux pays, produits agricoles méditerranéens, étaient en concurrence et chaque préférence gagnée par Athènes aurait pénalisé les exportations turques. Au niveau politique, l'affaire de Chypre était la plus importante. Mais il y avait aussi la crainte de la marginalisation, crainte partagée par les Américains : en mars 1958, le Département d'État avait épousé la position des LDC de l'OECE et indiqué parmi les conditions pour l'approbation américaine d'une aire continentale de libre-échange qu'elle « comprendrait des pays tels que la Grèce, la Turquie et d'autres pays de l'OECE moins développés, en prévoyant que ceux-ci assumeraient progressivement les obligations de la pleine participation à la FTA »[30]. Lors de la crise des négociations, fin 1958, Washington craignit qu'un fractionnement du continent ne marginalisât les « cinq ou-

---

[29]   ASCE, DE-CE, 696, Ambassade de Turquie, *Aide-mémoire*, 3.8.1959, et MAEF, Wormser, 290, tél. O. Wormser à Ankara, 3.1959.

[30]   *FRUS 1958-60*, Vol. VII, doc. 12, *Circular Instruction from the Department of State to certain diplomatic Missions*, 20.3.1958.

bliés » : Grèce et Turquie, Irlande, Islande et Portugal. Plus tard, un des rares mérites qu'il attribua à l'EFTA était qu'elle pousserait les pays exclus, Grèce et Turquie, à se rapprocher de la CEE[31]. Les deux candidatures répondaient donc aux préoccupations politiques américaines. C'est autre chose que de dire que Washington supporterait l'association. Après s'être laissé entraîner à soutenir l'association de la Grèce, Washington se refusa pendant longtemps à toute intervention en faveur de la Turquie : il s'opposa à toute démarche qui créerait autour de la CEE une zone de commerce préférentiel.

L'itinéraire de la candidature turque suivit d'abord la même ligne que celle de la Grèce. La réaction favorable de la Commission était motivée par les mêmes arguments que Walter Hallstein présenta à propos de la Grèce au Conseil des ministres le 25 juillet : le cas remplissait les conditions de l'article 238 du traité de Rome, qui envisageait l'établissement d'un lien structurel de la CEE avec des pays n'étant pas en mesure d'assumer la totalité des obligations qu'entraînerait l'adhésion. De plus, le pays était membre de l'OTAN et sa candidature jouait en faveur de la CEE dans la dialectique Six-Sept. Hallstein proposa donc le binôme réponse positive et conversations exploratoires, offert aussi à la Tunisie, pour ne pas engager la Communauté et les gouvernements à l'aveuglette[32].

La candidature ne fut discutée par le Conseil des ministres qu'après l'été[33], pour des raisons techniques aussi bien que politiques ; la majorité était pourtant d'avis de traiter les deux candidatures à la fois[34]. Mais après les premières conversations exploratoires, tenues par le commissaire Jean Rey et l'ambassadeur turc à Bruxelles du 28 au 30 septembre, l'idée de la « synchronisation » fut abandonnée[35]. Les propositions

---

[31] Voir par exemple *FRUS 1958-60*, Vol. VII, doc. 63, *Circular Telegram from the Department of State to certain diplomatic Missions*, 27.6.1959, et doc. 65, Burgess à Department of State.

[32] ASCE, CM2 1959, 11, *Procès-verbal de la réunion restreinte tenue par le Conseil à l'occasion de sa session du 25 juillet 1959. Examen de la demande d'association de la Grèce*, 13.8.1959.

[33] Le 8 septembre — deux jours avant le début des conversations préliminaires avec la Grèce — par le COREPER et le 11 par le Conseil ; les Turcs avaient beaucoup insisté pour que leur cas soit examiné par le Conseil avant l'été, mais Wormser liquida avec une certaine irritation la requête d'un traitement prioritaire : ASCE MAEF, Wormser.

[34] Le gouvernement allemand, opposé au début, déclara ensuite le souhaiter : ASCE, DE-CE, 696, tél. Paris à Bonn, 18.8.1959, et Direction des Affaires économiques et financières, Service de coopération économique, *Note*, 27.8.1959.

[35] L'idée du représentant permanent allemand de faire participer le président du COREPER ne fut pas retenue, pour ne pas engager trop tôt les gouvernements : ASCE, CM 2 1959, 90, R/640/59, COREPER, *Projet de procès-verbal, réunion restreinte, 7-8-septembre 1959*, 16.9.1959.

turques étaient peu élaborées et surtout elles étaient réticentes en matières d'engagements, même lorsqu'elles réclamaient un régime analogue à celui qui serait concédé à la Grèce ; d'où, selon la Commission, l'opportunité de séparer les deux négociations pour ne pas être contraint à réduire la portée de l'accord avec la Grèce. Ce qui ne signifiait nullement que l'accord n'était pas à rechercher[36]. Hallstein le confirmait le 13 octobre devant le Conseil :

> La décision des gouvernements grec et turc [...] résulte d'une évolution longuement mûrie dont l'origine est bien antérieure à la constitution de la petite zone [EFTA], et trouve sa véritable explication dans le besoin effectif d'un soutien politique qu'éprouvent ces deux États. Dans un tel ordre d'idées, une issue favorable des négociations en cours leur conférerait un plus grand sentiment de sécurité et de prestige. La Communauté, de son côté, ne pourrait rester indifférente à la perspective d'augmenter [...] son prestige personnel et son propre pouvoir d'attraction[37].

Les deux candidatures obligeaient pourtant à considérer la question de l'association en général, l'instrument politique de relation extérieure par excellence. À l'ordre du jour du 13 octobre figuraient les thèmes suivants : 1) accord-cadre ou solutions individuelles ? 2) participation des associés aux institutions communautaires ; 3) équilibre général des concessions ; 4) durée de la période transitoire ; 5) conformité aux règles du GATT ; 6) participation des associés à la politique agricole commune ; 7) mécanismes de l'aide financière. Au printemps 1960, le COREPER produisit des rapports de mise au point sur la politique d'association[38]. La position de la Grèce et de la Turquie demeurait peu claire. Parfois, elles paraissaient compter parmi les pays européens et africains du bassin méditerranéen qui, n'étant pas destinés à adhérer à la Communauté, seraient associés à travers une union douanière ou une zone de libre-échange comportant certaines obligations d'harmonisation, notamment en matière tarifaire. À coté des raisons juridiques découlant du GATT, il fallait préférer l'union douanière ou la ZLE pour plusieurs raisons : ne pas défavoriser les PTOM déjà associés ; assurer plus de garanties pour les investissements des Six, un accès privilégié sur le marché des pays associés. Le COREPER déconseillait de faire participer des États associés aux institutions de la Communauté, donc aux déci-

---

[36] Selon le rapport présenté au COREPER, le 1er octobre : ASCE, CM 2 1959, 97, 7.10.1959, R/746/59, Comité des Représentants permanents, *Projet de procès-verbal, réunion restreinte*, 1.10.1959.

[37] ASCE, CM 2 1959, 18, R/792/59, V, *Procès-verbal de la réunion restreinte tenue par le Conseil à l'occasion de la session de 13 et 14 octobre 1959*.

[38] ASCE, BAC 118/1986, 1562, AE/19/60, COREPER, *Considérations sur les principes d'une politique d'association de la Communauté*, 30.4.1960.

sions en matière de tarif extérieur commun et à d'autres domaines de la politique commerciale. Il proposait des institutions bilatérales où l'État associé aurait exercé un droit de consultation. Même s'il refusait le système, préconisé par le WP 23, de prolonger les périodes de réduction des tarifs, le COREPER admettait qu'il serait difficile de réaliser l'équilibre des obligations et des charges dans l'association des pays sous-développés. On touchait alors aux raisons de fond de la politique d'association, « instrument des plus efficaces dans la lutte contre la pénétration communiste ». Son essence était indiquée dans le caractère de permanence de la liaison, et le COREPER se demandait « s'il n'est pas de l'intérêt même des États membres de concentrer l'essentiel de leurs efforts d'aide aux pays en voie de développement sur ceux de ces pays qui auront accepté non seulement de leur accorder des avantages commerciaux certains, mais encore de faire le choix politique qu'implique une coopération permanente avec la Communauté et, à travers celle-ci, avec l'Occident »[39]. Le cœur de l'opération était donc franchement politique ; et pourtant, les enjeux économiques allaient conditionner le résultat. De plus, une contradiction allait se produire : les associations pouvaient servir la cause de l'Occident et également servir de canal pour l'aide au développement des Six ; mais ceci pouvait faire obstacle aux buts de la Communauté, surtout si aux associés étaient offertes des conditions très favorables.

La candidature turque posait tous ces problèmes. En sus des intérêts économiques nationaux étaient en jeu notamment les préoccupations de Couve de Murville et de l'ambassadeur Cattani, déjà apparues le 25 juillet, concernant d'éventuelles difficultés économiques. Pour la France, l'industrie n'avait rien à craindre de l'association des deux pays, qui offriraient de nouveaux débouchés, tandis que quelques problèmes de concurrence pourraient surgir dans le secteur des céréales (vis-à-vis de l'Algérie) et de celui du vin dans le cas de la Grèce. Les finances publiques devraient assumer de nouvelles charges. D'autres questions dérivaient de la structure du commerce extérieur turc : puisque 30 % de celui-ci seulement concernait les Six, Ankara devrait se préoccuper de ne pas léser les intérêts des pays tiers, ce qui pouvait expliquer l'absence de référence à l'adoption du tarif extérieur commun. Puisque près de 20 % de ce commerce se faisait avec les pays d'Europe de l'Est, Moscou put chercher à faire pression sur Ankara ou ce dernier demander des

---

[39] ASCE, BAC 118/1986, 1562, AE/19/60, COREPER, *Considérations sur les principes d'une politique d'association de la Communauté*, 30.4.1960 ; à l'Assemblée parlementaire également, le but de la « lutte contre l'impérialisme communiste » était posé énergiquement par le parlementaire socialiste néerlandais Van der Goes van Naters : Assemblée parlementaire européenne, *Débats 1960*, 15.1.1960, p. 204.

compensations[40]. L'Italie craignait que l'association de pays à économies agricoles et produits méditerranéens se fît au détriment des productions du Mezzogiorno, pour lesquelles Rome attendait des avantages de
l'élaboration de la politique agricole commune[41]. Pour les Six, la requête
la plus difficile à accepter était la participation à titre d'observateur à
toutes les institutions communautaires. Finalement, tout revenait à
l'équilibre des obligations et des charges, puisque « les premières conversations [avaient] montré que ledit pays envisageait une première
période préparatoire pendant laquelle il n'assumerait pratiquement
aucun engagement envers la Communauté, lorsque cette dernière concé-
derait déjà tous les avantages que les États membres se consentent
mutuellement en raison du Traité de Rome »[42].

Les Six et la Commission débattaient aussi sur les questions de procédures et de compétences, au lendemain de la faillite des négociations
pour l'aire de libre-échange. Déjà les conversations exploratoires donnaient l'occasion de reprocher à la Commission de déborder de ses
compétences[43]. Lorsque Rey proposa de référer de la suite des conversations au COREPER et de consulter des experts nationaux sur des questions techniques, on décela l'intention de réserver à la Commission la
conduite exclusive des négociations : le COREPER, surchargé de travail, aurait donné peu d'attention aux associations et des experts de secteur n'auraient pas pu évaluer de façon globale les intérêts nationaux en
jeu. Il fut décidé qu'un comité spécial, « Association Pays Tiers », sui-
vrait les négociations en liaison permanente avec la Commission. Mais
la compétition entre la Commission et les gouvernements se répercuta
sur la négociation.

À la suite du deuxième tour de conversations exploratoires, le Conseil retarda une décision de fond. À la fin mars, le gouvernement turc,
poussé par ses organisations industrielles, réclama l'accélération des
pourparlers[44]. Mais c'est seulement le 11 mai 1960 que le Conseil donna
mandat à la Commission de discuter les contenus possibles d'un accord.
On n'était donc pas encore au début de la négociation lorsque le coup

---

[40] ASCE, DE-CE, 696, Direction des Affaires économiques et financières, Service de
coopération économique, *Note*, 27.8.1959.

[41] Rosemary Galli et Saverio Torcasio, *La partecipazione italiana alla politica agricola
comunitaria*, Bologna, Il Mulino, 1976.

[42] ASCE, CM 2 1959, 18, R/792/59, V, *Procès-verbal de la réunion restreinte tenue
par le Conseil à l'occasion de la session des 13 et 14 octobre 1959.*

[43] Par exemple, la délégation néerlandaise critiqua durement le communiqué, délivré à
la presse après le deuxième tour des conversations exploratoires avec la Grèce, où
l'approbation du Conseil aux aides financières était tenue pour sûre.

[44] ASCE, MAEF, Wormser, 290, O. Wormser à Valery, *Note*, 22.3.1960.

d'État du 27 mai mettait hors jeu les hommes du *Democrat Partisi*. Le Comité d'Union nationale qui prit le pouvoir demanda la suspension des conversations prévues pour le mois de juin. L'interruption ne fut pas longue. Le 8 septembre, le nouveau ministre du Commerce, Mehmet Baydur, sollicita la reprise des contacts. Les conversations débutèrent le 14 octobre.

La transition politique en Turquie se prolongea pendant plus d'un an. Avant de rendre le pouvoir aux autorités civiles, le Comité décida qu'une nouvelle Constitution et une nouvelle loi électorale devaient être adoptées. La Constitution de juillet 1961 donna au peuple turc toutes les libertés civiles et politiques et envisageait des droits sociaux et économiques ; pourtant elle perpétuait, à travers le Conseil de Sécurité nationale, le contrôle des militaires sur les institutions[45]. Pour répondre aux problèmes de l'économie, qui avaient peut-être été la cause principale du coup d'État, la nouvelle Organisation d'État de Planification était chargée en novembre 1960 de sortir le pays du chaos, par la formulation de plans quinquennaux[46].

Cette lente évolution ralentit la mise au point du rapport entre la CEE et la Turquie. Derrière le Comité, certains voyaient déjà l'ombre d'Ismet Inönü[47], qui allait en effet revenir au pouvoir en 1961. La précarité de la démocratie augmentait les difficultés[48], mais elle renforça aussi les raisons en faveur d'un accord. On espéra – à tort, fallut-il le constater – que la reprise des négociations pourrait éviter la peine capitale aux *leaders* du *Democrat Partisi*, jugés pour haute trahison[49]. En général, on se préoccupait des initiatives de l'URSS, qui multipliait ses offres d'amitié et de coopération économique[50]. Mais, tandis que le gouvernement allemand n'éprouvait aucune doute, en France, on se demandait s'il fallait engager la Communauté à long terme[51]. Les négociations

---

[45] De plus, en novembre 1960, les radicaux à l'intérieur du Comité avaient été arrêtés et expulsés ; ce qui créa des remous chez les cadres inférieurs de l'armée, qui furent à l'origine de deux tentatives de renversement du gouvernement en février 1962 et en mai 1963.

[46] F. Ahmad, *The making of Modern Turkey*, London, Routledge, 1993, pp. 121-130.

[47] De l'ambassade de France, Francis Huré mettait en garde contre le risque qu'Inönü adoptât une politique de neutralité intéressée et de marchandage : ASCE, MAEF, Wormser, F. Huré (Ankara), 28.5.1960.

[48] Voir, par exemple, ASCE, DE-CE 696, H. Spitzmüller à Direction des Affaires économiques et financières, 21.9.1960, 743/DE.

[49] Des quinze peines capitales, douze étaient commuées, mais Menderes, le ministre des Finances, Hasan Polatkan et Zorlu étaient pendus en été 1961.

[50] ASCE, MAEF, Wormser, 290, *Note*, sur les colloques franco-allemands de Bonn, 10.10.1960.

[51] ASCE, DE-CE 696, *Note*, 193/CE, 17.10.1960.

piétinaient aussi pour des raisons économiques : d'abord, la récession débutée en Turquie au printemps 1960, produite par l'instabilité politique, par la mauvaise récolte de 1961 et par les mesures anti-inflationnistes adoptées par le gouvernement ; ensuite, la mise au point du plan quinquennal ; enfin, les caractéristiques de ce plan : pour éliminer le problème structurel le plus grave des années cinquante – le passif de la balance des paiements –, les nouveaux dirigeants choisirent de développer une industrie nationale de substitution aux importations et d'imposer une discipline restrictive du commerce extérieur, deux décisions peu conciliables avec les règles et la philosophie du libre marché.

La mise au point d'une relation se fit donc de plus en plus difficile. Jusqu'en août 1961, le gouvernement turc confirma qu'il voulait une union douanière entrant immédiatement en vigueur. Mais le Conseil des ministres, à la fin de 1961, avança l'idée de renoncer à l'union douanière et de signer un accord de pré-association, une convention économique, financière et commerciale, d'une durée de cinq à sept ans, au terme de laquelle la possibilité de l'union douanière serait réexaminée. Début 1962, après que l'Autriche, la Suède, la Suisse et l'Espagne eurent posé leurs candidatures, l'Assemblée parlementaire avança des critiques à l'augmentation « inconsidérée » du nombre des associés[52], peut-être en réaction aux conditions, pourtant déclarées exceptionnelles par la Commission, accordées à la Grèce[53]. L'Allemagne continuait à pousser en faveur de l'accord et d'un haut niveau d'aide financière, mais Paris augmentait la résistance, dont on retrouve quelques raisons dans une note d'Olivier Wormser :

> Le Ministre – écrivait-t-il – est absolument opposé à l'octroi d'une aide à la Turquie. Son raisonnement est le suivant : on donne de l'argent à des pays étrangers pour y créer une influence ou pour la maintenir et la développer. Or, la Turquie est tombée sous l'influence américaine et c'est aux Américains de faire le nécessaire s'ils le jugent utile [...] Le Ministre ne veut donc pas que les Six prennent la Turquie en charge, pas plus que l'OTAN [...][54].

À la réunion de mars 1962, le Conseil chargea le COREPER de définir le régime de pré-association et de préparer le mandat de négociation pour la Commission. Ce travail avança lentement[55] : la situation économique et l'endettement de la Turquie rendaient difficiles toute analyse et tout programme. Le mandat était formulé pour le mois de juin.

---

[52]   Assemblée parlementaire européenne, *Débats 1962*, pp. 54-60.

[53]   Qui lui reconnaissait un droit de consultation dans la politique commerciale.

[54]   ASCE, MAEF, Wormser, 290, 19.1.1962.

[55]   ASCE, MAEF, Wormser, 310, 31.3.1962.

Lors du tour décisif des négociations des 18-22 juin 1962, le gouvernement turc se borna à demander pour l'immédiat des mesures discriminatoires pour dix produits « méditerranéens » ; mais il refusa de renoncer à la perspective de l'union douanière. À la réunion du Conseil du 4 décembre 1962, les éléments clefs étaient finalement arrêtés. Les difficultés majeures venaient de l'Italie, préoccupée par l'agriculture du Mezzogiorno. En vérité, les discriminations en faveur des produits turcs ajoutaient peu à ce qu'avait comporté l'association de la Grèce, qui avait, elle, annulé certains des avantages entrés dans la balance négociée dans le traité de Rome. La tension entre Bonn et Paris sur le montant de l'aide financière se poursuivit jusqu'au printemps 1963, au lendemain du veto français à l'adhésion de la Grande-Bretagne[56]. Wormser proposa alors aux Allemands d'avancer de manière « synchronisée » trois questions d'intérêt français et quelques points du « Programme d'action pour la deuxième phase », formulé par la Commission en octobre 1962, parmi lesquels une aide importante à Ankara[57]. À la réunion suivante, toutefois, l'hypothèse de 500 millions descendait à 125-150 millions. La lettre envoyée le lendemain à Couve de Murville par le ministre allemand Schröder[58] était peut-être responsable de la remontée finale à 175 millions.

IV. Le traité d'Ankara

Au début des négociations, Ankara avait repris en matière de commerce les conditions envisagées par le rapport du WG 23. Concernant l'aide, elle demandait environ le montant de l'aide américaine « ordinaire », 120 millions de dollars par an[59]. Cette correspondance et le fait que, dans la même période, les États-Unis rejetaient de nouvelles requêtes d'assistance avancées par le ministre des Finances Hasan Koraltan et par Menderes nous ramènent au point de l'influence de la politique américaine sur le rôle extérieur de la Communauté européenne. L'administration américaine perfectionnait le projet de transformer l'OECE en bras de l'Occident pour l'aide au développement. En janvier 1960, à Paris, les Européens approuvaient la réforme et autorisaient la création du *Development Assistance Group*, où un délégué de la CEE participait à côté des représentants nationaux à l'élaboration d'un projet d'expan-

---

[56] Voir, par exemple, ASCE, MAEF, Wormser, 290, *Note pour le Ministre*, 29.11.1962, et *Note*, 28-11-1962.

[57] *Akten zur Auswärtigen Politik des Bundesrepublik Deutschland*, 1963/1, doc. 134, 28.3.1963.

[58] *Akten zur Auswärtigen Politik des Bundesrepublik Deutschland*, 1963/1, doc. 139, 3.4.1963.

[59] *FRUS 1958-60*, VII, doc. 83, *Memorandum of Conversation*, 10.12.1959.

sion du flux de capitaux à long terme aux pays en voie de développement. Washington dirigea donc les Turcs vers ces nouveaux organismes et les encouragea à imiter le modèle de « consortium », qui coordonnait désormais l'assistance occidentale à l'Inde. En 1962, un consortium aurait été créé, où les Six auraient assumé une charge de 57 millions de dollars pour l'année 1963. L'association à la CEE apparaissait donc comme un segment d'une opération politique complexe, qui intéressait l'ensemble du monde occidental.

Le cœur de l'accord de septembre 1963 se bornait à établir un calendrier pour le passage de la première phase, « préparatoire », à la deuxième, « transitoire », dont les deux parties pouvaient négocier les conditions dans le Conseil de l'Association à partir de la quatrième année de l'entrée en vigueur du traité. Le but de la Turquie dans la phase préparatoire était, selon l'article 3, de « renforce[r] son économie, avec l'aide de la Communauté, en vue de pouvoir assumer les obligations qui lui incomberont au cours des phases transitoire et définitive ». Les conditions de la phase préparatoire étaient définies dans le Protocole provisoire et dans le Protocole financier annexés à l'accord.

L'accord décevait les Turcs. Sans entrer dans les détails, la position turque visait à une aide financière consistante (on espérait de l'ordre de 250-300 millions), à des mesures discriminatoires pour dix produits[60], à un droit de participation aux institutions communautaires pour faire valoir ses intérêts en matière commerciale. Ankara reçut une aide de 175 millions sur cinq ans et des mesures discriminatoires pour quatre produits, représentant environ 40 % de ses exportations totales, mais pas le droit de participer aux institutions communautaires et d'être consulté sur de futurs accords avec d'autres pays.

L'Italie s'était durement opposée à l'augmentation du nombre des produits et avait surtout protégé ses agrumes, au moment où l'Espagne, elle aussi, demandait l'association, ainsi qu'Israël et l'Afrique du Nord. La Grèce fit valoir également le droit de parole sur la politique commerciale que lui avait reconnu le traité d'Athènes. Pour le tabac et les raisins secs, on décida de protéger la position de ce pays qui avait donné à la Communauté des contreparties, et on octroya à la Turquie des contingents tarifaires équivalant *grosso modo* aux moyennes des importations normales des Six pendant les dernières années. Pour le tabac (12 % des exportations à lui seul), la Turquie obtenait 12 500 tonnes en tout pour la première année, mais la moyenne était calculée sur 1958-1959-1960, et sans tenir compte de l'année 1961 qui avait été exceptionnellement

---

[60] Tabac, raisins secs, figues sèches, noisettes, deux variétés de poissons de mer, lentilles, oranges, citrons, pamplemousses et pêches.

favorable en raison d'une maladie frappant les cultures européennes. Ces dispositions restrictives pouvaient d'autre part être assouplies et les contingents tarifaires augmentés dès la deuxième année, mais avec accord unanime. Les autres pays protégèrent aussi leurs clients : la France défendait les intérêts agricoles de l'Afrique du Nord, le Benelux et l'Allemagne refusaient de défavoriser les États sud-américains. Le traité garantissait donc à la Turquie le maintien des débouchés existants, mais il n'offrait pas un traitement préférentiel aux productions à développer. On oubliait donc l'objectif d'augmenter les exportations turques, même si on le reconnaissait essentiel pour améliorer le déficit chronique de la balance des paiements[61]. L'Italie obtint aussi d'autres mesures commerciales et financières de protection et de compensation. Elle était exonérée d'ouvrir des contingents pour les noisettes et les figues sèches et bénéficia indirectement du système des contingents tarifaires « nationaux » sans possibilité de transferts. Sa production jouissait d'un écoulement préférentiel sur le marché des partenaires : les figues sèches obtenaient une préférence décroissante, les noisettes une préférence fixe de 2,5 %. Sa contribution à l'aide financière était limitée à 18,28 % du montant, par rapport aux 33,42 % à la charge de l'Allemagne et de la France.

En janvier 1963, la Turquie renonçait à obtenir les garanties importantes inspirées de l'accord d'Athènes, un droit de veto sur la politique commerciale en matière de tabac et raisins secs, sur la politique agricole commune pour le tabac et un droit de consultation en cas d'adhésion ou d'association d'autres pays à la Communauté, même si les Six s'accordèrent sur des consultations de fait. Assez décevante était la prévision pour la question de la main d'œuvre : le sujet n'était pas inséré parmi les compétences expressément reconnues au Conseil, mais seulement comme une éventualité.

Avec 175 millions de prêts à long terme, la Turquie obtenait seulement 50 millions de plus que la Grèce, un rapport beaucoup moins satisfaisant que le 30/70 appliqué normalement par les Américains. Le montant était établi, eu égard aux prévisions d'un déficit de la balance des paiements d'environ 250 millions, plus l'amortissement de la dette extérieure. Le fonds était administré par la Banque européenne d'investissements ; France et Allemagne contribuaient pour un tiers et détenaient un poids proportionnel dans le Comité, qui aurait examiné les demandes de prêts soulevant des réserves[62]. En avril 1963, la Turquie vit

---

[61] *Ibid.*, p. 19.
[62] Le Protocole financier et un accord interne entre les Six réglaient la question de l'aide.

aussi rejeter sa requête de donner au Conseil le pouvoir d'établir un programme d'assistance technique, de l'ordre de 15 millions de dollars.

D'autre part, la Turquie était gagnante si l'on considère que toutes les obligations qu'elle assumait se résumaient dans l'affirmation que l'aide « constituait un effort supplémentaire par rapport à celui accompli par l'État turc ». Le traité entra en vigueur le 1er décembre 1964.

Conclusions

La stipulation de l'accord d'association entre la Turquie et la CEE montrait une Communauté renfermée sur elle-même, dont les actions extérieures étaient étouffées par les conflits et quelques fois exploitées pour des preuves de force internes. Pendant les années 1960-1963, l'attention se concentra en effet sur les questions internes, entre les propositions françaises de réforme intergouvernementale, la question de l'adhésion anglaise, etc. Ce n'est pas simplifier qu'imaginer que l'association de la Turquie n'a pas été envisagée comme un problème politique majeur, mais tout au plus comme une question économique mineure, vu la marginalité des produits intéressés, surtout après le renvoi de toutes les décisions sur l'union douanière. La question paraît donc être : pourquoi un accord de portée si limitée a-t-il été tellement difficile à signer ? L'opposition italienne, défenderesse des intérêts agricoles du Mezzogiorno, se fit sentir : mais on se demande si elle n'était pas surtout à usage interne. Les divergences d'opinion franco-allemandes en matière d'aide financière étaient aussi réelles et elles retardèrent la conclusion de l'accord. La détermination des Turcs à chercher des conditions semblables à celles que la Grèce avait obtenues a aussi compliqué la question. La Communauté en tant que telle ne se montra pas très active. La Commission, apparemment déçue par le faible intérêt politique des Turcs, ne paraît pas avoir joué un rôle très dynamique. Le directeur général, allemand, de la Direction des Affaires extérieures, qui signa l'accord, a peut-être épousé les positions favorables de l'Allemagne, seul pays qui tout au long des négociations n'a jamais fléchi. On sait d'autre part que, en général, tous les États préfèrent les canaux bilatéraux d'aide au développement, qui garantissent une correspondance plus directe entre concessions et contreparties. Apparemment, le canal communautaire ne convenait pas aux pays intéressés à développer leur influence externe, comme la France. Attirer dans l'orbite des Six un pays si profondément lié aux États-Unis apparaissait un but impossible.

Pourtant, l'accord a été signé et cela doit également être expliqué. Il est clair d'un coté que l'on ne pouvait pas laisser simplement faillir une négociation entre pays alliés, parties du même système de sécurité

occidental et des mêmes organisations ouest-européennes de coopération économique. On peut pourtant s'interroger sur l'influence des
événements internationaux des années 1962-1963 sur le cours et l'issue
de la négociation : il est difficile d'imaginer que les répercussions de la
crise de Cuba sur la position militaire de la Turquie à l'égard des Américains – en clair, la décision du président Kennedy de retirer les missi-
les *Jupiter* des bases alliées en Turquie même en dehors d'un accord
avec Khrouchtchev – n'ont pas pesé sur les positions du *leadership* turc
et même européen. Encore plus clairement, on perçoit l'influence de ces
véritables moments clefs de l'histoire européenne qu'ont été le refroidis-
sement des relations franco-américaines, le rejet français de la candidature britannique à la CEE et la recherche d'une entente franco-
allemande.

La relation Turquie-CEE ne guérit jamais d'une certaine ambiguïté.
En 1965, une aggravation de la crise de Chypre produisit une fracture
entre la Turquie et les États-Unis, dont les relations ne se rétablirent
jamais entièrement. Le « télégramme de Johnson », où le président refusait l'assistance militaire américaine dans le cas où une action militaire
turque provoquerait une réaction soviétique, s'inscrivit dans la mémoire
collective turque comme une trahison. Un nouveau cours était donc
envisagé par Ankara, qui visait à faire de la Turquie un pont entre
l'Occident, en particulier l'Europe, et les pays moins développés. En
novembre 1970, un protocole additionnel au traité d'Ankara sanctionna
le passage à la phase transitoire. Il entra en vigueur en janvier 1973 ;
mais son application ne fut pas sans problèmes et lorsqu'en 1987 le
gouvernement de Türgüt Ozal posa la candidature de la Turquie à
l'adhésion, la Commission émit deux ans plus tard un avis négatif, pour
des raisons à la fois économiques et politiques, notamment des réserves
sur la situation des droits de l'homme. La fin de la guerre froide et la
montée de la question islamique allaient tout bouleverser.

EU Policies towards Southeast Europe

From Stabilisation towards Integration

Milica UVALIC

University of Perugia

I. Introduction

An important part of Mediterranean Europe is the region covering the Balkan states, or Southeast Europe (SEE). Following the European Union (EU) recent terminology, the SEE countries are today often referred to as the "western Balkans" comprising five states: Albania, Bosnia and Herzegovina, Croatia, Former Yugoslav Republic of Macedonia (FYRoM), and Serbia and Montenegro (until February 2003, the Federal Republic of Yugoslavia). The present paper will mainly focus on this group of countries (or the SEE-5), although occasionally it will also consider the wider SEE region which also includes Bulgaria and Romania (or the SEE-7).

Whereas the other countries in Central and Eastern Europe (CEE) were able to intensify their political and economic relations with the EU fairly quickly after 1989, these processes were substantially delayed for most SEE countries. After a difficult period of political and economic stability throughout the 1990s, all the SEE countries are today also aspiring to join the European Union. In what follows, we will discuss the various phases of relations between the EU and the SEE countries after 1989, the year that marked the beginning of the transition to market economy and multiparty democracy. We will briefly consider EU policies towards SEE in the 1990s (part 2); the key elements of the new EU approach developed after the end of the Kosovo conflict in mid-1999 (part 3); the main achievements and failures of the new EU strategy (part 4); and make some concluding remarks (part 5).

II. EU Policies towards SEE in the 1990s

EU policies towards the SEE countries during the 1990s have been directly influenced by the political events which accompanied the break-up of SFR Yugoslavia into five independent states in 1991. During 1991-2001, we witnessed 5 military conflicts in the SEE region – in Slovenia (1991), Croatia (1991-92), Bosnia and Herzegovina (1992-95), Serbia/Kosovo (1998-99), and FYRoM (2001). During these difficult years, the newly-created states pursued nationalistic objectives and inward-oriented economic strategies, which implied the imposition of trade and other barriers *vis-à-vis* the neighbouring states, whereas FR Yugoslavia has also been under severe international sanctions. These events inevitably had serious economic consequences, resulting in extreme macroeconomic instability throughout most of the decade, and substantial delays in implementing transition-related economic reforms. Political and economic instability in the SEE countries has, in turn, also greatly delayed the process of their integration with the rest of Europe.

Today, there is a general consensus that the EU did not have a clear and long-term strategy towards the SEE countries in the 1990s. Although after 1996 the EU launched its 'Regional Approach' intended to promote regional cooperation among the SEE-5, the initiative failed to bring any substantial results. The EU instruments backing the Regional Approach were vague and inadequate, while the SEE-5 countries were, at that time, still not willing to engage in any meaningful regional cooperation (see Uvalic, 2001). The political conditions in the war-affected SEE countries remained highly unstable and unfavourable. Consequently, EU policies resulted in being more generous towards Albania, Bulgaria and Romania, than towards the other SEE countries. During the 1990s, the EU indeed applied very different policies towards the single SEE countries regarding financial assistance, trade preferences, and contractual relations.

Albania, Bulgaria and Romania benefited from EU support of the transition since the early 1990s. They received financial assistance through the PHARE programme (Bulgaria since 1990, Albania and Romania since 1991). Bulgaria and Romania also signed Association Agreements with the EU in 1993, which enabled duty-free entry of their products into the EU, gradual integration of markets and other forms of cooperation, which later led to the implementation of pre-accession strategies and European partnerships, preparing the ground for their accession to the EU in 2007. Albania signed a Trade and Economic Cooperation Agreement with the EU in 1992, which is less extensive in scope than the Association Agreements, but still allowed preferential access of Albanian products to EU markets. Not surprisingly, the EU became the main trading partner of these SEE countries fairly quickly; in 2003, the export shares going to the EU ranged from 58% for Bulgaria, to 68% for Romania and 93% for Albania (see Uvalic, 2005).

In the meantime, the four SEE countries from former Yugoslavia were included only selectively in some EU programmes, and at a later stage, after 1996. The stabilisation of the general conditions in the SEE region after the signing of the Dayton Peace Agreement in late 1995 led to the extension of some of the main programmes supporting the transition to several SEE countries. Thus PHARE was extended to Bosnia and Herzegovina and FYRoM in 1996, but not to Croatia and FR Yugoslavia. In addition, a specific EU programme for the war-affected SEE countries – the OBNOVA programme – was launched in 1997, which was to help their reconstruction efforts. However, the amount of financial aid envisaged by the OBNOVA programme was very limited, only around € 218 million, and 64% of the total amount went to Kosovo (see Commission, 2002).

Similarly regarding trade concessions, FYRoM was the only country that was able to conclude a Trade and Economic Cooperation Agreement with the EU in 1996, in force since 1998, similar to the one concluded with Albania. As to the other countries, it is only after 1996 that some trade preferences were given to Bosnia and Herzegovina and to Croatia. These trade concessions were also extended to FR Yugoslavia in 1997, but were withdrawn a year later. It should also be recalled that throughout most of the 1990s FR Yugoslavia was under severe economic and political sanctions of the EU (and the wider international community), which effectively prohibited any Foreign Direct Investment and even trade with the outside world. During the 1990s, the EU has assisted the SEE-5 prevalently by offering humanitarian aid and with its military presence, but forms of assistance typically extended to the other transition countries in CEE came with a substantial delay.

The very different types of policies of the EU towards individual SEE countries is fully understandable in view of the highly unfavourable political circumstances which characterised the war-affected Balkan countries in the 1990s. Nevertheless, the initial exclusion from major EU programmes of assistance of all countries of former Yugoslavia has also contributed to the slow pace of economic and political reforms. The *ad hoc* policies of the EU were more frequently based on the use of the "stick" and practically no "carrots", which did not bring the expected results. The problems were accumulating and reached their peak in 1999, with the NATO bombardments of FR Yugoslavia.

III. EU Policies towards SEE after 2000

A fundamental change in EU and international strategies towards the SEE-5 began emerging after the end of the Kosovo conflict in mid-1999. Soon after, positive internal developments in two key countries also contributed to such changes in international strategies. In Croatia, the political climate changed radically after Tudjman's death in January 2000, whereas in Serbia, the September 2000 elections marked the end of the Milosevic regime and enabled a democratic government to come to power soon after. These political changes greatly contributed to the speeding up of both internal transition-related reforms in the SEE countries, and of the process of their integration with the EU.

Since then, a number of EU initiatives have been undertaken to support the SEE countries. Immediately after the end of the conflict NATO-FR Yugoslavia, in June 1999, the *Stability Pact for Southeast Europe* was launched to help the economic reconstruction of countries affected by the Kosovo war (the SEE-7, therefore including Bulgaria and Romania). The main partners of the Stability Pact, in addition to the beneficiaries and the neighbouring states, include the European Commission, the OSCE, NATO, all major international financial organisations, the EU member states, the USA, Japan, Russia, Canada, and a few other countries. Its main mechanism is the Regional Table which coordinates the work of three Working Tables – for Democratisation and Human Rights, for Economic Reconstruction, Development and Co-operation, and for Security. During the past five years, the Stability Pact has been active in various areas in all SEE countries.

Even more importantly, soon after the EU launched its *EU Stabilisation and Association Process* for the SEE-5, offering these countries contractual relations through the possibility of signing a Stabilisation and Association Agreement (SAA), similar to those signed with the CEE countries in the 1990s. Moreover, for the first time since 1989, the SEE-5 were also offered prospects of joining the EU, though without any precise timetable. In order to prepare the ground for signing a SAA, joint EU-SEE Consultative Task Forces were to be created for each country, which were to evaluate the situation in each specific area of reform. As a next step, the EU Commission was to prepare a positive Feasibility Report, confirming that a country is ready to start negotiating a SAA, and the successful completion of negotiations would eventually lead to the signing of a SAA.

In order to enable privileged access of products from SEE countries to EU markets even before the conclusion of SA Agreements, in early 2000 the EU granted autonomous trade preferences to the SEE countries, which were also extended to FR Yugoslavia on 1 November 2000.

These EU trade concessions provide for the elimination of duties and quantitative restrictions for around 95% of goods from the western Balkans entering the EU market, including agricultural and sensitive industrial products, with only a few exceptions[1]. These trade preferences were recently renewed until the end of 2010 (see Commission, 2006, p. 7).

Another important element of the SA Process is a new programme of financial assistance, the CARDS programme, which is providing around € 5 billion in financial aid to the SEE-5 over the 2000-6 period. In order to increase the efficiency in aid delivery, the EU has also established the European Agency for Reconstruction (EAR) in charge of managing the implementation of economic reconstruction in FR Yugoslavia (Serbia, Montenegro, Kosovo) and FYRoM. The EAR was officially inaugurated in Thessaloniki in March 2000 and, soon after, EAR offices were set up in all the countries where it operates.

Further steps for strengthening the SA Process have been taken at the Thessaloniki EU-SEE Summit in June 2003. On that occasion, an important new instrument was introduced for the SEE-5 countries: the European Partnership, similar to the Accession Partnerships designed for the CEE countries, which have identified the main priorities and checklists (see Commission, 2004). The Thessaloniki provisions also enhanced for the opening of various EU programmes which were previously reserved only for candidates, including "twining", TAIEX, ISPA, SAPARD, and FP6. Thus operators from the SEE-5 countries can now participate in tenders conducted under the pre-accession instruments. The Commission has also proposed a new pre-accession financial instrument (IPA) which ought to supersede the existing instruments. Joint Parliamentary Committees were established in 2004 between the EU, Croatia and FYRoM, while regular inter-parliamentary meetings have been held with Albania, Bosnia and Herzegovina, Serbia, Montenegro and Kosovo.

IV.   The New EU Strategy: Achievements and Failures

What have been the overall results of the EU measures undertaken to support the SEE-5 over the last five years? There is no doubt that many important objectives have been carried forward successfully.

Within the Stability Pact for SEE, several major international conferences have been organised by the joint EU-Word Bank office in Brussels with the purpose of determining priority projects in the SEE-7

---

[1]   Some fishery products, baby-beef, and wine, while trade in textile products is covered by bilateral agreements.

countries, verifying the availability of finance, and collecting offers from potential international donors. These efforts have led to the provision of substantial donors aid from the EU Commission, the EU member states, other western countries (USA, Switzerland, Japan), international financial institutions (the World Bank, the European Bank for Reconstruction and Development), and the UN and its specialised agencies (UNDP, UNECE, UNESCO). Over the last five years, international donors assistance provided to the SEE has been used to fund economic, political and security-related projects in all possible areas (see www.stabilitypact.org). Financial assistance to the SEE-7 countries, including western countries bilateral aid, EU programmes and International Financial Institutions loans, has been in the order of €6-7 billion per year during the period 2001-5 (see Table 1). In recent years, however, there has been a sharp reduction of grant assistance to SEE countries, in favour of loans.

Table 1: Financial assistance to South East Europe, 2001-05 (in billion €)

Donor	South East Europe				
	Actual				Estimates
	2001	2002	2003	2004	2005
Bilateral aid + EU Commission	3.9	3.7	3.3	3.3	3.0
International Financial Institutions	2.6	3.0	3.3	2.7	4.3
Total	6.5	6.7	6.6	6.0	7.3

Source: www.seerecon.org

Many Stability Pact projects have been launched on a regional basis, therefore promoting regional cooperation among the SEE countries, with the aim of contributing to reconciliation, increasing political and economic stability, and faster resolution of common problems. One of the most important initiatives within the Working Table II for Economic Reconstruction, has been the project on trade liberalisation. In June 2001, a Memorandum of Understanding on Trade Liberalisation and Facilitation was signed by the Foreign Trade Ministers of the SEE-7 (the initiative was later also extended to Moldova). By early 2006, some 33 bilateral free trade agreements have been signed among the SEE countries providing for the abolition of most tariff barriers among the participating states (see Uvalic, 2005). It is expected that this network of bilateral free trade agreements will be transformed into a Single Free Trade Agreement for the SEE by mid-2006, with entry into force in 2007. Trade liberalisation has contributed to increasing trade among the SEE countries, in this way also facilitating economic recovery.

There has also been a lot of criticism of the Stability Pact, however, for a variety of reasons: initial delays in raising funds and initiating projects, limited donors support for Working Table I (democratisation) and Working Table III (security) projects, unclear division of competencies between the EU and the International Financial Institutions, the general problem of insufficient coordination of donors' aid, problems of limited aid-absorption by the recipient countries. Some initiatives have had a limited impact so far, such as the one against corruption, or on the return of refugees. There has also been a prevalence of donor-driven projects, that have not sufficiently taken into account the priorities of the countries' beneficiaries. Frequent complains have also been heard about there being small amounts of "fresh" money, since a large portion of aid was actually returned to the western donors (e.g., for the repayment of debt, or experts fees).

The measures undertaken within the SA Process can probably be evaluated more positively. In the area of trade, the privileged access to EU markets has had a very positive impact, since SEE-EU trade has generally been increasing, especially in case of those countries like Serbia and Montenegro which previously were not given any trade preferences of this kind. The prospects of EU membership offered to the SEE-5 have also been very positive for ongoing internal reforms, as they have meant the initiation of harmonisation of laws to EU norms in many important areas. EU financial assistance to the SEE-5 has also progressively increased, in comparison to the 1990s. From €1.4 billion of financial aid that the EU extended in 1991-94 to the SEE-5, the overall amount increased to €3.1 billion during 1995-99 and to € 5 billion during 2000-06 (see Uvalic, 2001). Although these amounts are still relatively low if compared to what was given to the ten associated countries from CEE, they have played an important role in supporting ongoing economic, political and legal reforms in the SEE-5.

The SA Agreements are also on their way, although the process of associating the SEE-5 to the EU has taken much longer than initially expected. SA Agreements were concluded relatively quickly with FYRoM (in April 2001) and with Croatia (in October 2001; see Bartlett, 2002). In the meantime, both countries have obtained candidate status, Croatia also started accession negotiations in October 2005, while FYRoM should follow soon. For the remaining three countries, the process has been taking much longer. Albania has been negotiating a SAA since February 2003, but for reasons linked to political instability the negotiations have taken very long and the SA Agreement was signed only in February 2006. For Bosnia and Herzegovina, a positive Feasibility Report was prepared by the Commission in November 2003, but the beginning of negotiations pended on a number of conditions that were fulfilled only recently, enabling the initiation of negotiations on a SAA at the end of 2005.

The greatest delays, however, have taken place in the case of Serbia and Montenegro. The main stumbling block, in addition to the sensitive political issues[2], regards the very complex relations between Serbia and Montenegro. Initially, the EU Commission insisted on the full harmonisation of a number of economic laws that are different in Serbia and in Montenegro, and the process was stalled by the inability to reach a mutually acceptable solution (see Uvalic, 2002). The EU finally, in 2004, decided not to insist any longer on the harmonisation of legislation, but to proceed with the "twin track" approach: deal separately with the two republics on policies which Serbia and Montenegro conduct separately (trade, economic and sectoral policies), while continuing to work with the country as a whole where it is the State Union that is the competent authority (international political obligations, or human rights). The Feasibility Report was re-launched and approved by the Council of Ministers on April 25, 2005. On October 3, 2005, the Council approved the beginning of negotiations on a Stabilisation and Association Agreement, which should be concluded by the end of 2006.

These are the most important achievements of the SA Process so far. However, there are also various elements in the new EU strategy that have been criticised.

One of the most frequent points of criticism regards the low level of *financial assistance*. An important proposal advanced by the Greek Presidency at the EU-SEE Thessaloniki Summit in 2003, that was not endorsed, were specific cohesion policies for SEE to help their economic development. The lack of more concrete cohesion policies for the SEE-5 is today considered one of the weakest points of current EU policies towards this region. It has been stressed that there is a contradiction between the EU proclaimed political objectives – full integration of the Western Balkans into the EU – and the economic means to achieve them – limited financial assistance (Uvalic, 2003c). The financial resources presently offered to the SEE-5 are largely insufficient to bridge the gap in economic development with respect to the EU-25. Most SEE-5 countries are very poor, their present GDP per capita remains at the level of 10-30% of the EU average, while countries like Serbia and Montenegro or Bosnia and Herzegovina are still at the level of 60% of their 1989 GDP.

---

[2] The critical political issues include the unresolved constitutional issues (relationship between Serbia and Montenegro, the future of Kosovo) and collaboration with the Hague Tribunal.

It has also been stressed that the SEE countries are subject to *stricter EU conditionality* in comparison to the conditions that were applied to the CEE transition countries. First, the conditions are more numerous, since in addition to the standard Copenhagen criteria formulated in 1993 for all countries aspiring to join the EU, the SEE-5 are also expected to show progress in implementing regional cooperation, and ought to comply with all international obligations (e.g. collaboration with the Hague Tribunal). Second, the phases envisaged as part of the EU-SEE integration process are more numerous, so the SEE countries have to follow a much longer procedure before they can actually become associated to the EU (as described earlier). The procedure was much simpler in the early 1990s, when the CEE countries signed Association Agreements fairly quickly.

Another point of criticism regards *regional cooperation* in SEE, which has become an important part of EU conditionality *vis-à-vis* the SEE. Despite EU's insistence that it will evaluate each country for its own merit, the SEE countries also need to show concrete progress in implementing regional cooperation. This has frequently been interpreted negatively, as the more advanced SEE countries would not like to be penalised by the slow progress of others in the SEE-5 group.

A related critique regards the *EU border regime* (see Uvalic, 2004). The 2004 EU enlargement has led to the elimination of all remaining visa-free travel regimes between the new member states and the countries in the western Balkans, except for Croatia which enjoys a visa-free status in all Schengen countries, thus creating new dividing lines. In addition, preparations for the next enlargement in 2007 have already imposed the obligation on the two candidate countries, Bulgaria and Romania, to re-introduce visas for the western Balkans, thus closing borders and impeding links with their neighbours well before accession. Regional cooperation among the SEE countries will not take place in conditions of closed borders. The creation of a free trade area among the eight SEE countries will do little to stimulate trade flows, business links, and joint regional projects, if some SEE countries maintain visas for neighbouring countries. The current visa regimes are directly impeding the full realisation of this important objective of the EU.

There have also been complaints on account of the *EU trade measures*. Although the EU has been rather generous in opening up its markets, in practice the trade liberalisation measures have not really led to very significant results. In addition to low competitiveness of SEE products on EU markets as probably the most important reason, remaining EU barriers should also not be neglected. Some of the products exempted from the duty-free regime are precisely those products where the SEE countries are most competitive, and there are still a number of non-tariff barriers which impede greater trade penetration of SEE products to EU markets. Table 2 presents figures on exports of the Western Balkans to the EU during 1999-2002, based on a sample of goods, which are illustrative in this regard.

Table 2: Western Balkan exports to the EU, 1999 and 2002

	Number of products exported		Number of exported products according to tariff level in 2002 and their share in exports (% in parentheses)		
Country	1999	2002	Zero	Same as in 1999	Lower than in 1999
Albania	34	23	7 (8%)	2 (6%)	14 (54%)
B&H	44	40	12 (18%)	26 (48%)	1 (1%)
Croatia	128	126	32 (22%)	83 (37%)	3 (2%)
FYRoM	42	37	5 (10%)	27 (48%)	2 (4%)
S&M	80	70	15 (11%)	0	45 (48%)
SEE-5	Na	na	(16.6%)	(28.3%)	(16.9%)

Source: EU Commission (2004), *SAP Third Annual Report*, March 2004, p. 31.

The figures reveal that *zero tariffs* apply to a very small number of exported products, products that represent a very low percentage of the overall exports of the SEE countries to the EU – ranging from 8% of exports in Albania, 10% in FYRoM, 11% in Serbia and Montenegro, to 18% in Bosnia and Herzegovina and 22% in Croatia. These extremely low percentages of duty-free exports suggest that as much as 80-92% of exported products from the SEE region *are* subject to some EU tariff barriers, which seems to contradict the declared principle of substantial trade liberalisation. In addition, for most countries, there actually were *limited changes in tariffs* for their exports to the EU during 1999-2002. In 2002, there was no change with respect to 1999 in the tariff level for almost half (48%) of the exports to the EU from Bosnia and Herzegovina and FYRoM, and for 37% of exports to the EU from Croatia. The EU trade regime for Serbia and Montenegro has, on the contrary, greatly improved since 1999, as not even for one product exported to the EU has the tariff remained the same. For Albania, tariffs remained the same as in 1999 for only 6% of exported products. These figures clearly suggest that over the period 1999-2002, improved access to EU markets has been secured primarily for Albania and Serbia and Montenegro, much more than for the other countries.

V. Concluding Remarks

Prospects of EU membership have finally been offered to the western Balkan countries in late 2000 and have been reconfirmed at the Thessaloniki Summit in 2003. In the meantime, for all SEE countries

EU membership has become one of the most important foreign policy objectives. But when will these countries actually be able to join the EU? There are clearly a number of uncertainties regarding future integration processes, not only linked to the SEE countries accession, but also more generally. Accession of the SEE countries to the EU will depend only in part on their eventual readiness for membership. Future EU enlargements will very much depend on the readiness of the EU to admit new members. Not incidentally, the fourth Copenhagen criteria – the EU's readiness to absorb new members – is nowadays mentioned more and more frequently. The 2004 EU enlargement has introduced changes in the functioning of EU institutions which cannot be absorbed overnight. The negative outcomes of the referendum in France and in the Netherlands on the EU Constitutional Treaty have also added further concern and scepticism about the future. These are some of the reasons why, almost unavoidably, the EU strategy towards the SEE countries still today remains somewhat vague and unclear, as it is difficult to foresee the dynamics and possible year of entry of single SEE countries into the EU.

Under such conditions of high uncertainty, the EU may need to offer additional incentives to SEE countries not likely to join the EU soon, in order to avoid the risk of backsliding in the reform process. The present very distant perspectives of membership may prove insufficient as an anchor to keep the momentum of accelerated economic, political and legal reforms which are well on the way in all SEE countries. What today has not been worked out is what will happen between the moment when all SEE countries have signed a SAA, have applied for EU membership and have been accepted as candidates, and the actual entry into the EU. If the EU is not ready by then for its southeastern enlargement, for how long can it be postponed?

In conclusion, policies of the EU towards the SEE region today are no longer based on containment, as until a few years ago, but on accession. The EU enlargement towards the CEE countries has also been slow, characterised by continuous changes in policies, declared principles, and time-frame, but the problems related to the EU south-eastern enlargement are even greater, among other reasons because of the complexity of the political problems still prevailing in the region. An important element, however, adds optimism to future EU-SEE integration prospects: the fact that Croatia has recently started negotiating EU membership, in this way tracing the way for the other SEE countries to follow. It is possible that future EU enlargements will be slowed down, but they are unlikely to be stopped.

References

Bartlett, W. (2002), "The EU-Croatia Stabilisation and Association Agreement – A Stepping Stone to Membership or Semi-Permanent Satelisation?", paper prepared for the 7th bi-annual conference of the European Association for Comparative Economic Studies (EACES), Forlì (Italy), June 6-8, 2002.

Bianchini, S., and Uvalic, M. (eds.) (1997), *The Balkans and the Challenge of Economic Integration – Regional and European Perspectives*, Ravenna, Longo Editore.

Daianu, D., and Veremis, T. (eds.) (2001), *Balkan Reconstruction*, London, Frank Cass.

Commission of the European Communities (2002), *CARDS Assistance Programme to the western Balkans – Regional Strategy Paper 2002-2006*, Brussels.

Commission of the European Communities (2004), *Report from the Commission – The Stabilisation and Association Process for South East Europe – Third Annual Report*, Brussels, March 30, COM (2004), 202/2 final.

Commission of the European Communities (2006), Communication from the Commission – The Western Balkans on the road to the EU: consolidating stability and raising prosperity, Brussels, January 27, COM (2006), 27 final.

European Bank for Reconstruction and Development (EBRD) (2005), *Transition Report*, London.

European Communities (2000), "Council regulation (EC) No. 2666/2000 of 5 December 2000 on assistance for Albania, Bosnia and Herzegovina, Croatia, the Federal Republic of Yugoslavia and the Former Yugoslav Republic of Macedonia, repealing Regulation (EC) NO. 1628/96 and amending Regulation (EEC) No. 3906/89 and (EEC) No. 1360/90 and Decisions 97/256/EC and 1999/311/EC", *Official Journal of the European Communities*, L 306/1, 7 December 2000.

Grabbe, H. (2001), "The effects of EU enlargement on the countries left outside", in Economist Intelligence Unit (2001), *Country Forecast – Economies in Transition – Eastern Europe and the former Soviet Union – Regional Overview*, London, pp. 5-13.

Nuti, D. M. (1996), "European Community response to the transition: aid, trade access, enlargement", *Economics of Transition*, 4 (2): 503-511.

Papic, Z. *et al.* (2001), *International Support Policies to South-East European Countries – Lessons (Not) Learned in B-H*, Sarajevo, Muller.

Samardzija, Visnja (2003), "Croatia's preparation for the EU accession", paper presented at the WIIW conference, Vienna, November.

Stability Pact for Southeastern Europe, Cologne, June 1999.

Uvalic, M. (2001) "Regional cooperation in South-Eastern Europe", *Journal of Southeast Europe and Black Sea Studies*, 1 (1), also in Daianu and Veremis (eds.) (2001).

Uvalic, M. (2002), "Economic cooperation between Serbia and Montenegro: Which way towards the European Union?", *Review of International Affairs*, new series, Vol. LIII, No. 1106, April-June 2002, pp. 13-17.

Uvalic, Milica (2003a), "Economic Transition in Southeast Europe", *Southeast European and Black Sea Studies*, Vol. 3, No. 1, pp. 63-80.

Uvalic, M. (2003b), "Southeast European economies: From international assistance towards self-sustainable growth", in Wim van Meurs (ed.) *Prospects and Risks Beyond EU Enlargement. Southeastern Europe: Weak States and Strong International Support*, Bertelsmann Foundation Risk Reporting, Leske + Budrich, Opladen, pp. 99-115.

Uvalic, M. (2003c), "Integrating Southeast European countries into the European Union – Problems and prospects", in Vojmir Franicevic and Hiroshi Kimura (eds.), *Globalisation, Democratization and Development – European and Japanese Views of Change in South East Europe*, Zagreb, Masmedia, 2003, pp. 93-105.

Uvalic, M. (2004), "The impact of the 2004 EU enlargement for Southeast Europe" (in German, "Die Auswirkungen der EU Erweiterung auf Sudosteuropa"), *Ost-West Gegeninformationen*, Wien, No. 1/2004, pp. 16-21.

Uvalic M. (2005), "Trade liberalisation in Southeast Europe – Recent trends and some policy implications", UNECE Spring Seminar 2005, *Financing for Development in the ECE Region: Promoting Growth in Low-income Transition Economies*, Geneva.

World Bank (2000), *The Road to Stability and Prosperity in South Eastern Europe: A Regional Strategy Paper*, Washington, D. C., World Bank.

Western Cultural Policy in the Mediterranean during the 20th century

Lorenzo MEDICI

Università di Perugia

After September 11, the agonizing question in the United States, which is "Why do they hate us so much?", would suggest failure on the part of American cultural diplomacy in the Mediterranean area. After that day, the Americans have become aware of the great hostility of the Arab public opinion toward the American culture. In the United States and in other western countries, there has been extensive reflection on the reasons that caused this hate and on the necessity to adopt a new cultural policy in the Mediterranean, mainly in the Arab and Islamic world, in order to avoid the mistakes of the past. Nevertheless, it is not easy to understand fully what western cultural policy in the region was. Historical analyses, many of them written by former officials, are not numerous and discuss the subject only generally. Only in rare cases are such analyses related to this particular area. In spite of these limits, this study will attempt to review, necessarily briefly, the public and cultural diplomacy promoted by some western countries in the Mediterranean.

In the last century, the US tried to promote friendly cultural relations with the Arab world. Recently, to win over "hearts and minds", the White House established an Office of Global Communications to coordinate US information campaign worldwide, and a new emphasis was given to the Under Secretary of State for Public Diplomacy and Public Affairs. Public diplomacy deals with a direct influence on foreign public attitudes toward a country's foreign policy, through a one-way relationship and with a short-term perspective. This approach contrasts with the educational and cultural relations promoted by the government, properly called cultural diplomacy, which is finalized through a two-way exchange. Cultural diplomacy represents a long-term perspective, to influence the elites, the future leaders and the opinion makers of other countries. The main tools of public diplomacy are radio and television broadcasts, while those of cultural diplomacy are educational and cultural institutions and educational exchange programs[1].

But after September 11, one could argue that American public and cultural diplomacy in the Mediterranean was useless. What are the reasons for this failure?

The United States' reputation in this region has declined mainly because of decades of support given to Israel in the Middle East conflict, with the consequent displacement of hundreds of thousands of Palestinian refugees, and to autocratic and unpopular Arab governments. The policies instituted to guarantee a flow of abundant and cheap oil to the western countries have not strengthened the American image abroad. But also, the characteristics and the purposes of the US cultural policy in the last fifty years contributed to ruin America's image in the Mediterranean.

During the 1930s, the US concentrated its initiatives in Latin America in response to Nazi Germany's cultural offensive; after the Second World War, and at the beginning of the Cold War, America was deeply concerned about Soviet propaganda. The US countered with cultural policy programs, particularly the information and public diplomacy ones, in a hard-hitting propaganda campaign of its own[2].

With the hardness of the Cold War, additional emphasis was placed on explaining America's viewpoints and objectives to the rest of the world. The US Information and Educational Exchange Act of 1948, also known as the Smith-Mundt Act, placed international overseas information activities under an Office of International Information at the Department of State. The United States Information Agency (USIA) was created in 1953. The new agency, independent from the State Department, contained all the information programs, like the Voice of America (VOA) and those promoted by the widespread posts known as the US

---

[1] Richard T. Arndt, "Public Diplomacy, Cultural Diplomacy: The Stanton Commission Revisited", in Kenneth W. Thompson (ed.), *Rhetoric and Public Diplomacy: The Stanton Report Revisited*, Lanham, MD, University Press of America, 1987, pp. 85-104. The public and cultural diplomacy are parts of the so called 'soft power'; on this subject see Joseph S. Nye Jr., "Soft Power", *Foreign Policy*, No. 80, 1990, pp. 153-172; *id.*, *Soft Power: The Means to Success in World Politics*, New York, Public Affairs, 2004.

[2] On US public and cultural diplomacy see "Rapporti culturali internazionali", *Rivista di Studi Politici Internazionali*, XXV, No. 1, 1958, pp. 59-62; Frank Ninkovich, *The Diplomacy of Ideas: US Foreign Policy and Cultural Relations, 1938-1950*, Cambridge-New York, Cambridge University Press, 1981; William R. Keylor, "La propagande comme instrument de la puissance américaine dans les premières années de la Guerre froide", *Relations Internationales*, No. 94, 1998, pp. 179-197.

Information Service (USIS)[3]. The government's educational exchange programs remained at the State Department, but two years later part of the administration of the exchange programs, their operation overseas, was assigned to USIA.

The long duel with the Soviet Union shaped American cultural diplomacy for more than 40 years. At the beginning, the main target of the US propaganda offensive was Europe, but in the subsequent years other regions became Cold War battlefields. This was particularly true for the Mediterranean region, marked by the Arab-Israeli conflict. The action to promote the American image was relevant from the 1950s, with the opening of new embassies in the Arab countries and the declaration of the Eisenhower Doctrine. The funds for US Information Service's offices in Latin America, the Far East and western Europe were diminished, in favor of those in Africa and the Middle East[4].

The US aimed to incorporate the region into a global anti-Soviet alliance, and wanted to preserve western control of Middle Eastern oil resources. It was concerned about the diminished abilities of Britain and France to exert influence over the region, and about the increasing anti-western feelings generated by the establishment of Israel.

The US propaganda was intended to expose the fallacies of Communism and to emphasize the American values of freedom and democracy. The goals included strengthening western-oriented elements, increasing awareness of the Soviet threat, building a willingness to cooperate both regionally and with the West, and driving the revolutionary pressures and nationalistic movements throughout the area, like Nasserism, into orderly channels not antagonistic to the West. The targets were varied: poor and predominantly illiterate rural populations, political and economic elites, teachers, professionals, *mullahs*, and others who were the moulders of opinion. Propaganda goals were to be achieved by controlling information and manipulating its interpretation. The tools used included financial assistance, technical cooperation, pamphlets and

---

[3]   On the USIA see Wilson P. Dizard Jr., *Inventing Public Diplomacy: The Story of the US Information Agency*, Boulder, Co, Lynne Rienner, 2004, in particular pp. 177-197. On the VOA see Alan L. Heil Jr., *Voice of America: A History*, New York, Columbia University Press, 2003, in particular on the Middle East, pp. 311-328. The Central Intelligence Agency (CIA), as part of its covert efforts to fight Communism abroad, supported a wide variety of intellectual and cultural programs overseas. See on this subject Peter Coleman, *The Liberal Conspiracy: The Congress for Cultural Freedom and the Struggle for the Mind in Post War Europe*, New York, Free Press, 1989; Frances Stonor Saunders, *Who Paid the Piper? The CIA and the Cultural Cold War*, London, Granta, 1999.

[4]   "Rapporti culturali", *op. cit.*, p. 61; see also Dizard, *Inventing Public Diplomacy...*, *op. cit.*, pp. 78, 84.

posters, magazines, radio broadcasts, books, libraries, music, movies, cartoons, and religion[5]. Actually, US diplomacy was sympathetic toward Islam, which had been seen as a natural enemy of materialistic ideologies. Following World War Two, scholars of the Middle East eagerly volunteered their expertise on Cold War issues, especially the question of whether Arab and Islamic societies were susceptible to Communist expansion. The "Islamic strategy" reflected western scholar's assumptions that a monolithic Islam could somehow be manipulated to shape the political future of the Middle East[6]. But very little attention was paid to the different meaning and importance given by Arab and Islamic culture, which hardly accepts the notion of secular state, to the concepts of liberty and democracy – partly because of their distorted application made by US governments in the region.

Meanwhile, cultural diplomacy was carried on through educational institutions, often founded and run by private organizations, in some cases religious ones. Examples include the prestigious achievements of the American universities in Cairo, established in 1919, in Beirut, where a college opened in 1866, and the "Robert College" in Istanbul, founded in 1863; or the American schools founded in: Beirut, in 1905; Istanbul, in 1911; Alexandria, in 1924; Cairo, in 1945; Tangier, Tunis, Damascus, Amman, Jeddah and Tel Aviv in the 1950s; Rabat, Kuwait City, Dhahran and Riyadh in the 1960s; Casablanca, Abu Dhabi and Sanaa in the 1970s; Muscat and Doha in the 1980s[7].

---

[5] Joyce Battle (ed.), "US Propaganda in the Middle East – The Early Cold War Version", *National Security Archive Electronic Briefing Book No. 78*, www.gwu.edu/~nsarchiv/NSAEBB/NSAEBB78. In particular, on the radio broadcasts see Muhammad Ayish I, "The VOA Arabic Service: A Study of News Practices and Occupational Values", *Gazette: International Journal for Communication Studies*, 40, No. 2, 1987, pp. 121-130. On the propagandistic attitude of the VOA's Arabic broadcasts see James Vaughan, "Propaganda by Proxy?: Britain, America, and Arab Radio Broadcasting, 1953-1957", *Historical Journal of Film, Radio and Television*, 22, No. 2, 2002, pp. 159. See also Gary D. Rawnsley, "Radio Diplomacy and Propaganda: The BBC and VOA" in *International Politics*, 1956-64, London, Macmillan; New York, St. Martin's Press, 1996.

[6] For example see: Bernard Lewis, "Communism and Islam", *International Affairs*, 30, No. 1, 1954, pp. 1-12; *id.*, *The Middle East and the West*, Bloomington, Indiana University Press, 1961, pp. 134-35. About the American Middle Eastern scholarship and its relation to a European literary tradition of writing about the Islamic world, see Edward Said, *Orientalism*, New York, Vintage Books, 1994, [1978], pp. 255-328; Douglas Little, *American Orientalism: The United States and the Middle East Since 1945*, Chapel Hill, University of North Carolina Press, 2002, pp. 9-42. See also Melani McAlister, *Epic Encounters: Culture, Media, and US Interests in the Middle East, 1945-2000*, Berkeley, University of California Press, 2001, pp. 266-277.

[7] See the pages of the US Department of State's website related to overseas schools actually in activity: http://www.state.gov/m/a/os/c1684.htm. An American school, now closed, was established also in Teheran.

Other cultural instruments were the financing of art exhibitions, concerts, archeological missions and academic and educational exchange programs. Examples include the Fulbright Program, the nongovernmental scholarship plan established in 1946 for the exchange of students, scholars, teachers and artists[8], and the American Friends of the Middle East (AFME), then America-Mideast Educational and Training Services (AMIDEAST), a private non-profit organization established in 1951, which focused on exchange programs and developments projects.

Nevertheless, the result of a cultural policy pursued mostly in a propaganda form was a feeling of manipulation among Arab populations. US public diplomatic efforts to counter Soviet propaganda in the Middle East[9] proved counter-productive, concentrating almost exclusively on broadcasting as loudly as possible its openness and love for dialogue, rather than actually engaging in it[10]. As a consequence, a sensation of subjection to US policy and culture started to spread accross the Arab world, and charges of American cultural imperialism took root in many countries.

The confirmation of the US propaganda attitude came after the fall of the Berlin Wall, when Washington failed to see a need for public diplomacy after the end of the Cold War. During the Clinton Administration the will to dismantle the public diplomacy system emerged. The cuts at the USIA's budget led to the closing of American cultural centers around the world and the downsizing of scholarship funds. In 1999 the functions of the USIA were transferred to the Department of State, with negative consequences especially in the Middle East and North Africa[11].

---

[8] Arthur Power Dudden and Russell R. Dynes (eds.), *The Fulbright Experience, 1946-1986: Encounters and Transformations*, New Brunswick, N.J., Transaction Books, 1987; Richard T. Arndt and David Lee Rubin (eds.), *The Fulbright Difference, 1948-1992*, New Brunswick, N.J., Transaction Publishers, 1993.

[9] For an example of Soviet cultural policy in the Middle East see Karen Dawisha, "Soviet Cultural Relations with Iraq, Syria and Egypt 1955-70", *Soviet Studies*, 27, No. 3, 1975, pp. 418-442.

[10] On the necessity to "provide a service from the audience's viewpoint" see Kenneth R. Sparks, *Selling Uncle Sam in the Seventies*, "Annals of the American Academy of Political and Social Science", n, 398, 1971, p. 121.

[11] Dizard, *Inventing Public Diplomacy...*, *op. cit.*, pp. 235-260. See also Kim Andrew Elliot, "Too Many Voices of America", *Foreign Policy*, No. 77, 1989, pp. 113-131; Richard Holbrooke, "The Anti-Terrorists Are Losing the Battle of Ideas", *The Washington Post*, Oct. 29, 2001; Helena K. Finn, "The Case for Cultural Diplomacy: Engaging Foreign Audiences", *Foreign Affairs*, 82, No. 6, 2003, p. 15. For some examples of the current debate in the United States on this subject see also David Hoffman, "Beyond Public Diplomacy", *Foreign Affairs*, 82, No. 2, 2002, pp. 83-95; Peter G. Peterson, "Public Diplomacy and the War on Terrorism", *Foreign Affairs*, 81, No. 5, p. 74; Kim Andrew Elliott, "Is There an Audience for Public Diplomacy?",

In the same way, British and, especially, French cultural policies were characterized by the will to promote the image of their own country, rather than the dialogue with other cultures. Like the United States, there was the need to counter the Communist propaganda, a threat for their colonial empires. Like the United States, their cultural policies were weakened by a strong foreign policy in the Mediterranean. And, again like the United States, a subsequent feeling of manipulation and cultural colonialism, aimed at the maintenance of the western influence, spread in the region. Moreover, British cultural policy was weakened by a lack of organization and coordination. Culture was not a concept that attracted enthusiasm within Great Britain. For a long time, the British government did not give particular importance to culture as an issue to export. Unlike Paris, London did not adhere to a cultural messianism and did not conceive a link between a cultural policy abroad and gains in political or commercial fields. Its military, political and economic power should have been sufficient to expand its influence throughout the world[12].

As a result, Britain did not have a cultural diplomacy as a form of coordinated government action. Importance was given to target audiences, and separate agencies were preferred to a single administration. With the end of the Second World War, the Ministry of Information was closed, a Central Office of Information was created in 1946, and some activities were reallocated to separate departments, like the Information Research Department (IRD) in the Foreign Office (FO), established in 1948. The main instruments of British cultural policy were officially independent organizations, like the British Council and the External Services of the British Broadcasting Corporation (BBC), even if both were regularly under the threat of cutbacks[13].

The New York Times, Nov. 16, 2002; Mark Leonard, "Diplomacy by Other Means", *Foreign Policy*, No. 132, 2002, pp. 48-56; Joseph S. Nye Jr., "Propaganda Isn't the Way", *The International Herald Tribune*, Jan 10, 2003; Robert Satloff, "How to Win Friends and Influence Arabs: Rethinking Public Diplomacy in the Middle East", *Weekly Standard*, Aug. 18, 2003; Alexander T. J. Lennon (ed.), *The Battle for Hearts and Minds: Using Soft Power to Undermine Terrorist Networks*, Cambridge, Mass., MIT Press, 2003; Stephen C. Johnson, "Improving US Public Diplomacy Toward the Middle East", *Heritage Lectures*, No. 838, Feb. 10, 2004.

[12] Anthony Parsons, "'Vultures and Philistines': British Attitudes to Culture and Cultural Diplomacy", *International Affairs*, 61, No. 1, Winter 1984-1985, pp. 1-8.

[13] On the British cultural policy abroad see "Rapporti culturali", *op. cit.*, pp. 53-58; Harold Beeley, "The Changing Role of British International Propaganda", *Annals of the American Academy of Political and Social Science*, No. 398, 1971, pp. 124-129; Philip M. Taylor, "Puissance, propagande et opinion publique : les services d'information britanniques et la guerre froide, 1945-1947", *Relations Internationales*, No. 55, 1988, pp. 377-394; J. M. Lee, "British Cultural Diplomacy and the Cold War:

The British Council for Relations with Other Peoples was founded in 1934 as an independent organism, with the aim to promote a better comprehension of British culture and the British way of life, pioneering the teaching of English as a foreign language and sustaining a programme of exchanges in different fields of the arts[14]. In 1940, it became a "Body Corporate", by then financed almost completely by the government[15]. Actually, it was the FO's main vehicle for cultural relations with other countries, and the instrument to promote liberal and democratic values against totalitarian ideologies[16].

Before and during the Second World War, the British cultural policy abroad, that officially refused the propaganda term and preferred that of projection[17], was the answer to the Fascist threats in the Mediterranean,

---

1946-61", *Diplomacy & Statecraft*, 9, No. 1, 1998, pp. 112-134; Philip M. Taylor, *British Propaganda in the 20th Century: Selling Democracy*, Edinburgh, Edinburgh University Press, 1999, which insists on a British model for a democratic propaganda. On the IRD and other departments see Lyn Smith, "Covert British Propaganda: The Information Research Department, 1947-77", *Millenium*, 9, No. 1, 1980, pp. 67-83; Scott Lucas and C. J. Morris, "A Very British Crusade: IRD and the Beginnings of the Cold War", in Richard J. Aldrich (ed.), *British Intelligence Strategy and the Cold War 1945-51*, London, Routledge, 1992, pp. 85-110; Richard J. Aldrich, "Putting Culture into the Cold War: The Cultural Relations Department (CRD) and British Covert Information Warfare", *Intelligence & National Security*, 18, No. 2, 2003, pp. 109-133. Another instrument of the British cultural policy in the Middle East was the British Academy, established in 1902, and since 1950 the channel for the government's support for British schools and institutes overseas, and sponsored societies, like the British Institute of Archaeology at Ankara and the British School of Archaeology in Iraq.

14 Frances Donaldson, *The British Council: The First Fifty Years*, London, Cape, 1984, pp. 16-17, 20-21. See also A. J. S. White, *The British Council: The First Twenty-five Years, 1934-1959*, London, The British Council, 1965; Philip M. Taylor, "Cultural Diplomacy and the British Council: 1934-1939", *British Journal of International Studies*, 4, No. 3, 1978, pp. 244-265.

15 Donaldson, *The British Council...*, *op. cit.*, pp. 70-71. The resources made available for the British Council's work where made available by three sponsoring departments: the Foreign Office, the Colonial Office and the Commonwealth Relations Office.

16 Christine Okret-Manville, "La politique étrangère culturelle, outil de la démocratie, du fascisme et du communisme. L'exemple du British Council, 1934-1953", *Relations Internationales*, No. 115, 2003, pp. 399-410.

17 Max Beloff, "The Projection of Britain Abroad", *International Affairs*, 41, No. 3, 1965, p. 478; Philip M. Taylor, *The Projection of Britain: Overseas Publicity and Propaganda, 1919-1939*, Cambridge-New York, Cambridge University Press, 1981 pp. 1-2; Temple Willcox, "Projection or Publicity? Rival Concepts in the Pre-War Planning of the British Ministry of Information", *Journal of Contemporary History*, 18, No. 1, 1983, pp. 97-116. See also Ruth Emily McMurry, "Foreign Government Programs of Cultural Relations", *Annals of the American Academy of Political and Social Science*, No. 235, 1944, pp. 58-60.

an area of strategic importance for the British Empire. In these years, the British Council paid a particular attention to Egypt, a country that represented a link between India and the oil fields of the Middle East. In the late 1930s, financial subsidies were given to schools and cultural centers located in Cairo, Istanbul, Jerusalem, and grants were assigned to students from the Mediterranean area[18].

In the Cold War years, the British government's strategy can be divided in two phases: (1) those that began after 1947, marked by a global opposition to the progresses of Soviet propaganda; and (2) a reduced action, due to the financial difficulties of the 1950s, which focused on the colonies and the Commonwealth countries[19]. But the grudging acceptance of the tools of cultural diplomacy and the experience of Second World War propaganda led to a preference for a political and psychological warfare[20].

In the 1950s Arab nationalism focussed the minds of British policy makers on the merits of broadcasting, cultural exchanges, teaching English, and welcoming overseas students. The Mediterranean had always held a strategic significance, related to the protection of the oil supplies and the creation of the Baghdad Pact. The propaganda effort was linked with the need to counter Nasserism's influence and that of its Soviet allies, and to conserve the last spoils of the British Empire[21]. Only the circumstances of the Middle East, in the mid-1950s, obliged policymakers to find ways of coordinating the apparatus at their disposal. Due to a lack of means, from 1954 many activities were closed and reduced in western Europe and in some Commonwealth countries, in favor of the Mediterranean[22]. And only after the Suez crisis, did the British government decided to improve systematically the projection of Great Britain abroad with relevant financial sources[23].

---

[18] Donaldson, *The British Council...*, *op. cit.*, pp. 92-93; Okret-Manvile, "La politique étrangère culturelle", *op. cit.*, pp. 403-404.

[19] *Ibid.*, pp. 406-410.

[20] Lee, *British Cultural Diplomacy...*, *op. cit.*, p. 132.

[21] On the public diplomacy effort to maintain the empire see Susan L. Carruthers, *Winning Hearts and Minds: British Governments, the Media and Colonial Counter-Insurgency 1945-1960*, Leicester, Leicester University Press, 1995. See also Charles Armour, "The BBC and the Development of Broadcasting in British Colonial Africa 1946-1956", *African Affairs*, 83, No. 332, 1984, pp. 359-402.

[22] Beloff, "The Projection", *op. cit.*, p. 480; Peter Partner, *Arab Voices: The BBC Arabic Service, 1938-1988*, London, BBC External Services, 1988, p. 89; Lee, *British Cultural Diplomacy...*, *op. cit.*, pp. 126-130.

[23] Taylor, "Puissance, propagande", *op. cit.*, pp. 379, 393.

In this region the presence of the British Council was widespread. After those opened in Egypt, in the 1930s, and Yemen, Morocco, Syria, Palestine, Jordan, Iraq, Iran, Lebanon, Turkey and Cyprus, in the 1940s, new offices were founded in: Bahrain, Israel, Kuwait and Libya in the 1950s; Algeria, Saudi Arabia, Tunisia and the United Arab Emirates in the 1960s; Oman and Qatar in the 1970s[24]. The Council's action was carried on through the: creation of schools, libraries and chairs to consti-tute a linguistic and educative offer; organization of conferences, art exhibitions, theatrical representations, projections of educational and cultural movies; distribution of prints; provision of scholarships to enable young overseas students from the Arab world, who had the potential to become tomorrow's leaders and opinion makers, to be educated in Britain. Even if the nature of the Council's activity was related more to the elites, with a long-term, non-propaganda perspective, it was nevertheless a political tool.

This was particularly true for the information instruments, like BBC's Arabic Service, which started in January 1938, as a response to the Italian radio station in Bari[25]. During the 1950s, The BBC and the Voice of America, as well as clandestine broadcasting facilities, oper-ated by the western intelligence agencies, such as Britain's grey and black radio stations based in Cyprus, sought to counter the influence of Arab, especially Egyptian, propaganda in the battle to influence popular opinion[26]. Its programs were not aimed at the elites, though many of the top people in the Arab world were among the service's regular listeners. At the end of the 1970s, BBC had a regular audience[27] of some four million adults, which at the end of the 1980s became ten million, and

---

[24] Donaldson, *The British Council...*, *op. cit.*, pp. 373-376; see also www.britishcouncil. org, that contains the British Council's *Worldwide address book*.

[25] H. Schuyler Foster Jr., "The Official Propaganda of Great Britain", *The Public Opinion Quarterly*, 3, No. 2, 1939, p. 296; Beresford Clark, "The B.B.C.'s External Services", *International Affairs*, 35, No. 2, 1959, p. 173; Partner, *Arab Voices...*, *op. cit.*, p. 17. See also Callum A. MacDonald, "Radio Bari: Italian Wireless Propa-ganda in the Middle East and British Counter-Measures, 1934-1938", *Middle Eastern Studies*, 13, No. 2, 1977, pp. 195-207.

[26] On the British radio covert propaganda see Partner, *Arab Voices...*, *op. cit.*, pp. 90-93; Gary D. Rawnsley, "Overt and Covert: The Voice of Britain and Black Radio Broadcasting in the Suez Crisis, 1956", *Intelligence and National Security*, 11, No. 3, 1996, pp. 497-522; Douglas A. Boyd, "Sharq al-Adna/The Voice of Great Britain", *Gazette: International Journal for Communication Studies*, 65, No. 6, 2003, pp. 443-454. A significant element of the radio propaganda campaign in the Arab world, quite apart from the broadcasts of the BBC, the VOA and the clandestine stations, was the bid to influence the radio stations of independent Arab states, co-opting and manipulating them; see Vaughan, "Propaganda by Proxy?", *op. cit.*

[27] Listeners who tuned in at least once a week or more often.

spread throughout North Africa and the Middle East[28]. The BBC's broadcasts represented an honest effort towards impartial activity, due to the independence enjoyed by the Corporation in terms of program content. This independence was ensured by the 1952 Licence and Agreement, even if the Corporation did its work "in the national interest"[29]. Even so, the BBC still was accused by the Mediterranean and Third World countries of cultural imperialism and propaganda[30].

French cultural policy abroad was also perceived by its end-consumers as a one-way relationship activity, and something similar to propaganda. But, unlike the American and British cultural policies abroad, it was not necessarily a consequence of the Cold War. The French believed the representation of their culture to be virtually a sacred mission, a *mission civilisatrice*, which made them consider their values and their cultural production, with a special regard to their language, as worthy of adoption by other peoples[31]. This messianism corresponded with political nationalism and, after the Second World War, cultural diplomacy, one of the few political means available, was subordinated to France's will of regaining its rank as a first-rate world power[32].

---

[28] See Bernard Bumpus, "Broadcasting and Audience Research in the Middle East", *Bulletin: British Society for Middle Eastern Studies*, 6, No. 1, 1979, p. 16; Partner, *Arab Voices...*, *op. cit.*, pp. 68, 151.

[29] Clark, "The B.B.C.'s", *op. cit.*, pp. 174, 177; Taylor, "Puissance, propagande", *op. cit.*, pp. 391-392. For the BBC's will to maintain its independence also during the Suez Crisis see Partner, *Arab Voices...*, *op. cit.*, pp. 94-112.

[30] Bumpus, "Broadcasting and Audience", *op. cit.*, p. 22; Vaughan, "Propaganda by Proxy?", *op. cit.*, pp. 159-161.

[31] Brian Weinstein, "Francophonie: A Language-Based Movement in World Politics", *International Organization*, 30, No. 3, 1976, p. 486; Mathew Burrows, "'Mission civilisatrice': French Cultural Policy in the Middle East, 1860-1914", *The Historical Journal*, 29, No. 1, 1986, pp. 109-135. See also J. Thobie, "La France a-t-elle une politique culturelle dans l'Empire ottoman à la veille de la Première Guerre mondiale ?", *Relations Internationales*, No. 25, 1981, pp. 21-40. On the principal exponents of the doctrine of the *mission civilisatrice* see Albert Salon, *L'action culturelle de la France dans le monde. Analyse critique*, Thèse de Doctorat sous la direction de Jean-Baptiste Duroselle, 3 vols, Université de Paris I, 1981 [published in 1983], pp. 294-393.

[32] For a general view of the French cultural diplomacy see also McMurry, "Foreign Government", *op. cit.*, pp. 55-56; "Rapporti culturali", *op. cit.*, pp. 68-71; Arnaldo Bascone, "La politica francese degli scambi culturali", *Quadrivio*, II, No. 5, 1962, pp. 11-50; Suzanne Balous, *L'action culturelle de la France dans le monde*, Paris, Presses universitaires de France, 1970; François Roche, Bernard Pigniau, *Histoires de la diplomatie culturelle française des origines à 1995*, Paris, La Documentation française, 1995.

Like the British, the French considered cultural relations as an instrument to strengthen the link with the colonies and the empire. But, unlike Britain, France pioneered cultural relations, and had a big tradition in cultural foreign policy with a well-organized structure. As early as 1910, French cultural diplomacy was already coordinated by a *Bureau des écoles et des œuvres françaises à l'étranger*, then by the *Service des Œuvres françaises à l'Étranger*, created in 1920[33]. French cultural instruments and denominations were copied by other countries, such as, for instance, the cultural attachés and cultural institutes.

For a long time, until the first decade of the last century, French cultural policy operated very little outside the boundaries of the Middle East and North Africa. Beginning in the 19th century, French elementary, middle and high schools were opened by private organizations. Examples include several religious institutions, such as *Œuvre des Ecoles d'Orient* (the *Missions catholiques*), founded in 1855, *Alliance israélite universelle*, created in 1860, and the secular *Alliance française*, established in 1883, and *Mission laïque française*, founded in 1902. The schools were opened mainly where there were Christian minorities, such as in Lebanon, or in French colonial communities like those in North Africa. French diplomats facilitated the establishment of these schools and the French government subsidized their operation[34]. The movement towards more examples of French cultural policy in the region grew. French high schools began educating local elites. The new *lycée* of Galatasaray in Istanbul, opened in 1868 and educated generations of French-speaking Turkish elites. The era also saw the establishment of influential cultural institutes, like the archeological school in Cairo, established in 1880; of numerous lectureships in several cities; and in Beirut, four separate faculties created between 1881 and 1913 by the Jesuits to form Saint Joseph's University[35].

---

[33] See Antoine Marès, "Puissance et présence culturelle de la France. L'exemple du Service des Œuvres françaises à l'Étranger dans les années Trente", *Relations Internationales*, 1983, 33, pp. 65-80.

[34] Burrows, "'Mission civilisatrice': French Cultural Policy...", *op. cit.*, pp. 117-135. See also Georges Ollivier, *L'Alliance israélite universelle 1860-1960*, Paris, Documents et Témoignages, 1959; André Chouraquai, *L'Alliance israélite universelle et la renaissance juive contemporaine. Cent ans d'histoire*, Paris, Presses universitaires de France, 1965; Maurice Bruézière, *L'Alliance Française : Histoire d'une institution, 1883-1983*, Paris, Hachette, 1983; André Thévenin, *La Mission laïque française à travers son histoire, 1902-2002*, Paris, Mission laïque française, 2002. Financial assistance was given also to the "Missions protestantes".

[35] Bascone, "La politica francese", *op. cit.*, p. 14; Roche, Pigniau, *Histoires de la diplomatie...*, *op. cit.*, pp. 13, 34, 280.

Even if the educational institutions attracted a very small part of the population, some of their members were well placed in government, business and journalism. At the beginning of the last century, French language was the most spoken and written western language in the Mediterranean region and widely spoken by other (non-French) foreigners in the region[36]. Following the First World War, the cultural budget for the Middle East increased to solidify French rule in the mandated areas of Lebanon and Syria[37]. After the Second World War, with the decolonization and the loss of Tunisia, Morocco and Algeria, attention was paid to technical cooperation in these countries. In 1956, the *Direction Générale des Relations Culturelles et des œuvres à l'étranger* (DGRC), established in 1945, was transformed in *Direction Générale des Affaires Culturelles et Techniques* (DACT)[38]. In the first years of the 1960s the French Government planned an expansion of the French cultural offensive and, especially, of the French language overseas. The loss of the colonial empire should have been compensated by the creation of a linguistic and technical empire, paying attention not only to the elites but also to the masses[39].

Moreover, the need to maintain an influence in the region was satisfied by several forms of foreign institutes. Foremost among them were prestigious scientific research institutes dedicated to archaeology, law, social sciences and Arab studies, like those in Rabat, Tunis, Cairo, Beirut, Istanbul, Damascus, Teheran, Baghdad, Jerusalem, and Saana. Cultural institutes and libraries were created for the local populations, with the purpose of organizing cultural manifestations and classes in French language and civilization. These cultural institutes were established in Tripoli, Tel Aviv, Ankara, Istanbul, and Teheran. These institutes became especially important in Morocco, traditionally central in the French cultural policy abroad[40], with facilities in Rabat, Tangier, Agadir, Marrakech, Meknes, and Oujda. Numerous cultural centers and missions, less important than the institutes but with the same structure and with a multidisciplinary vocation, were founded in Algeria, Cyprus, Egypt, Iran, Iraq, Israel, Palestine, Jordan, Lebanon, Qatar, Syria, Turkey, and Yemen. Finally, chairs and schools were established in Algeria,

---

[36] Burrows, "'Mission civilisatrice': French Cultural Policy", *op. cit.*, p. 110.

[37] Marès, "Puissance et présence culturelle", *op. cit.*, p. 73.

[38] Robert Frank, "La machine diplomatique culturelle française après 1945", *Relations Internationales*, No. 115, 2003, p. 331.

[39] Roche, Pigniau, *Histoires de la diplomatie…*, *op. cit.*, pp. 89-99; Frank, "La machine diplomatique", *op. cit.*, p. 332.

[40] Roche, Pigniau, *Histoires de la diplomatie…*, *op. cit.*, pp. 34-35.

Cyprus, Libya, Egypt, Jordan, Iran, Israel, Palestine, Lebanon, Morocco, Syria, Tunisia, and Turkey[41].

Thanks to a well-organized cultural policy, and despite strongly nationalistic tendencies, France had an enormous edge over the United States and Britain in spreading its language and culture in the Mediterranean, and there was little need to improve information programs[42].

Italian cultural policy had a remarkable success, too, in this region. After the birth of the Italian kingdom, particular attention had been paid to the Mediterranean, where, because of the presence of important Italian communities and, later, the Fascist imperial ambitions, Italy improved relevant cultural relations. Schools, in many cases founded and directed by missionaries, often with governmental subsidies, were opened in Egypt, Libya, Tunisia, Syria, Lebanon and Palestine, while university chairs were established in Egypt, Algeria and Lebanon[43]. There were also the important activities of the archaeological missions[44] and the private and educational *"Dante Alighieri"* society, the latter was particularly active in the North African countries[45]. The Fascist government pursued its propaganda activity with publications and the broadcasting programs of *Radio Bari*[46].

---

[41] Bascone, "La politica francese", *op. cit.*, pp. 12-38.

[42] On French success and US failure in methods of cultural diffusion in the Middle East and North Africa see Gordon Wright, "La présence culturelle des États-Unis au Moyen-Orient et en Afrique du Nord : problèmes et perspectives", *Politique Étrangère*, XXXVI, No. 5/6, 1971, pp. 565-579.

[43] See the sections dedicated to cultural institutes and schools abroad in the review *Romana. Rivista degli Istituti di Cultura Italiana all'Estero*, passim. For some particular cases see Simonetta Della Seta, "La presenza e l'opera dei Salesiani in Palestina", *Storia Contemporanea*, XX, n, 1, 1989, pp. 81-101; Marta Petricioli, "Italian Schools in Egypt", *British Journal of Middle Eastern Studies*, 24, No. 2, 1997, pp. 179-191.

[44] Marta Petricioli, *Archeologia e Mare Nostrum. Le missioni archeologiche nella politica mediterranea dell'Italia, 1898-1943*, Roma, Valerio Levi, 1990.

[45] See *Romana*, passim. For an example see Nullo Pasotti, "La presenza dell'Italia in Tunisia", *Il Veltro*, IV, No. 10-11, 1960, pp. 66-70. On the "Dante Alighieri", established in 1889, see Beatrice Pisa, *Nazione e politica nella Società "Dante Alighieri"*, Roma, Bonacci, 1995; Patrizia Salvetti, *Immagine nazionale ed emigrazione nella Società "Dante Alighieri"*, Roma, Bonacci, 1995.

[46] See Mario Tedeschini Lalli, "La propaganda araba del fascismo e l'Egitto", *Storia Contemporanea*, VII, No. 4, 1976, 717-749. In particular on *Radio Bari* see Daniel J. Grange, "Structure et techniques d'une propagande : Les émissions arabes de Radio Bari", *Relations internationales*, No. 2, 1974, pp. 165-185; *id.*, "La propagande arabe de Radio Bari (1937-1939)", *Relations internationales*, No. 5, 1976, pp. 65-103; MacDonald, "Radio Bari", *op. cit.*

After the Second World War, Italian cultural policy was not characterized by a one-way relationship linked to Cold War logic, like those of the United States and Britain, or by a civilization mission related to the diffusion of the language, like France. As a consequence of the military defeat, Italy did not have the political or economic means for an efficacious foreign policy. The post-war Italian government could draw, however, on a prestigious cultural tradition, and in 1947 it established the *Direzione Generale delle Relazioni Culturali* (DRGC). Nevertheless, the disastrous experience of Fascism and its use of nationalistic values, made it difficult for Italy to project a strong image abroad. It was not able and did not want to promote a cultural policy based only on national interests and propagandistic purposes[47].

Italy had no colonial empire to defend and, since the mid-1950s, promoted a "neo-Atlantic" policy that aimed, inside the Atlantic Alliance, to bridge the North and South in the world and to play a political and economic role in the Mediterranean. Within that framework, a cultural exchange of ideas should promote a commercial exchange. After the closures of Italian cultural institutions due to the war, and in spite of the poor financial resources, the culture activities toward the Arab world were resumed and strengthened[48]. In the second half of the century, new cultural institutes opened in Beirut, Istanbul, Ankara and Tripoli, in the 1950s; in Algiers, Tunis, Tel Aviv, Haifa, Cairo, Baghdad, and Teheran in the 1960s; in Alexandria and Rabat in the 1970s, and in Damascus just a few years ago. Italo-Arab centers of studies were also established in Tangier and Amman. The cultural institutes and centers housed libraries and organized conferences and monographic courses. They offered classes of Italian language and literature, classes of Arab language and literature, classes of history of fine arts, *Lectura Dantis*, musical concerts, theatrical representations, projections of movies, and provided scholarships for local students. The conferences and the lessons were held in Italian and Arabic and the cultural programs focused mainly on historical topics like the Roman era and the Renaissance, and on the results of the archeological missions. These subjects did not seem

---

[47]   Archivio storico-diplomatico del Ministero degli Affari Esteri (ASMAE), Gabinetto (1943-1958), b. 83 (1944-1947), posiz. 6 Ris. 2/13, Istituti e scuole all'estero – Finanziamenti, promemoria, il ministro degli Esteri Alcide De Gasperi al presidente del Consiglio Ferruccio Parri, Roma, 14 luglio 1945.

[48]   For a a general view of the Italian cultural policy in the Mediterranean see Gennaro de Novellis, "L'Italia nella cultura mediterranea", *Quadrivio*, II, No. 6, 1962, pp. 9-29; *Atti del I Convegno su: La presenza culturale italiana nei Paesi Arabi: storia e prospettive. Napoli, 28-30 maggio 1980*, Roma, Istituto per l'Oriente, 1982; *Atti del II Convegno su: La presenza culturale italiana nei paesi arabi: storia e prospettive. Sorrento, 18-20 novembre 1982*, Roma, Istituto per l'Oriente, 1984.

dangerous to the elites in the Middle East and North Africa, and they were developed with a perspective related to a common civilization in the Mediterranean and a link between western and eastern culture, and not as an expression of Italian supremacy, like for Fascism[49]. Chairs of Italian language opened in Rabat, Algiers, Tunis, Tripoli, Benghazi, Cairo, Alexandria, Beirut, Amman, Damascus, Aleppo, Istanbul, Ankara, Izmir, Jerusalem, Tel Aviv, Haifa, Jeddah, Riyadh, and Sanaa. Public and private (often religious) Italian schools offered educational programs in Cyprus, Morocco, Algeria, Tunisia, Libya, Egypt, Lebanon, Israel, Palestine, Jordan, Syria, Iran, Iraq, Turkey, Saudi Arabia, and Yemen[50]. In 1952 the *Centro per la Relazioni Italo-Arabe* was established in Rome, as an autonomous section of the *Istituto per l'Oriente*[51]. Bilateral treaties for cultural and technical cooperation were signed with Algeria, Cyprus, Egypt, Jordan, Iran, Iraq, Israel, Lebanon, Libya, Morocco, Oman, Saudi Arabia, Syria, Tunisia, and Turkey[52].

Italian cultural diplomacy had a long-term perspective aimed to influence the future leaders and moulders of the Arab world, while technical and scientific cooperation was aimed at economic and social development of the Arab countries. The public diplomacy was promoted

---

[49] On the establishment of the cultural institutes and their activities, see the specific sections related to them in the numbers of the reviews: *Informazioni culturali*; *Il Veltro*; *Quadrivio*; *Esteri* and *Affari Esteri*, passim. See also "Rapporti culturali", *op. cit.*, pp. 71-80; Ministero degli Affari Esteri, Direzione Generale delle Relazioni Culturali, *Istituzioni culturali e scolastiche italiane all'estero. 30 Marzo 1961*, Roma, Tip. Riservata del Ministero degli Affari Esteri, 1961, *passim*; *id.*, *Istituzioni culturali e scolastiche italiane all'estero. 1 Gennaio 1968*, Roma, Tip. Riservata del Ministero degli Affari Esteri, 1968, *passim*; *id.*, *La promozione della cultura italiana all'estero*, Roma, Istituto Poligrafico e Zecca dello Stato, 1996, *passim*. More specifically: "L'Istituto Italiano di Cultura di Beirut", *Informazioni Culturali*, VIII, No. 6, 1955, pp. 8-10; "La cultura italiana a Beirut", *Informazioni Culturali*, X, No. 7-8, 1957, pp. 16-18; Giuseppe Valentini, "Cultura italiana nel Libano", *Quadrivio*, I, No. 3, 1961, p. 74; "Inaugurazione del Centro Italiano di Cultura ad Algeri", *Informazioni Culturali*, XIII, No. 5, 1960, p. 14; Fernando Caruso, "L'Istituto Italiano di Cultura di Teheran", *Il Veltro*, XIV, No. 1-2, 1970, p. 184; Luigi Polacco, "La presenza della cultura italiana nella Turchia di oggi", *Il Veltro*, XXIII, No. 2-4, 1979, pp. 483-491. On the Italian archaeological missions in the Mediterranean see: "Missioni archeologiche italiane nel Mediterraneo", *Il Veltro*, XV, No. 3-4, 1971, pp. 462-466; *ivi*, XV, No. 5-6, 1971, pp. 624-626; *ivi*, XVI, No. 1-2, 1972, pp. 116-120.

[50] Ministero degli Affari Esteri, *Istituzioni culturali...*, *op. cit.*, *passim*; Carlo Cirvilleri, *Le istituzioni scolastiche educative e culturali all'estero*, Firenze, Le Monnier, 1993 [1988], pp. 65-73, 76-77, 78-79.

[51] "Il Centro per le Relazioni Italo-Arabe", *Informazioni Culturali*, VIII, No. 6, 1955, pp. 14-15.

[52] See Ministero degli Affari Esteri, Servizio del contenzioso diplomatico dei trattati e degli affari legislativi, *Accordi culturali e di cooperazione scientifica e tecnica fra l'Italia ed altri stati*, Roma, Tipografia M.A.E., 1972, *passim*.

through media outlets like *Radio Bari*, which restarted its Arabic language broadcasting in 1947, and whose purpose was not primarily propagandistic.

Actually, the sympathy with which the Italian image was received by Arab public opinion was above all the result of a cultural diplomacy based on international cooperation. For the new ruling class, cultural cooperation befit a country reshaped after the war as a medium-rank power, which could play an important role in international organizations and promoting multilateral relations. The admission to UNESCO was an essential step for Italian cultural diplomacy, which conformed its action to the purposes of peace, mutual understanding and cultural cooperation of the Parisian Organization[53]. If, for the United States and Great Britain, UNESCO was an instrument to counter the Soviet Union, and a reason of prestige for France, for Italy it was the primary tool for its cultural policy[54]. This was confirmed by the replacement of the *Istituto nazionale per le relazioni culturali con l'estero* (IRCE), the organism created by Fascism to coordinate cultural relations with nationalistic purposes, with the *Commissione nazionale italiana per l'UNESCO*.

UNESCO's initiatives aimed at the Mediterranean and the Arab world, like the educational projects for the Palestinians refugees, the campaign to save the monuments of Nubia, or the Major Project on Mutual appreciation of eastern and western cultural values, aimed to avoid a future clash of civilizations, saw an important contribution from Italy. Educational and cultural programs usually take years to produce dividends, but effective cultural policy should be measured not by the

---

[53] ASMAE, Rappresentanza italiana in Francia (1861-1950), b. 364 (1946), fasc. 3, Organizzazione internazionale UNESCO, telegr. 1554, il presidente del Consiglio e ministro degli Esteri, De Gasperi, all'ambasciata d'Italia a Parigi, Roma, 24 settembre 1946.

[54] On the attitude of these countries toward UNESCO see William Richard Pendergast, "UNESCO and French Cultural Relations 1945-1970", *International Organization*, 30, No. 3, 1976, pp. 453-483; Gail Archibald, *Les États-Unis et l'Unesco: 1944-1963. Les rêves peuvent-ils résister à la réalité des relations internationales ?*, Paris, Publications de la Sorbonne, 1993; Elhem Sayah Chniti, « La Grande-Bretagne et l'Unesco 1942-1957. 12 ans de relations entre une institution des Nation-Unies et une puissance fondatrice », Thèse de Doctorat sous la direction de René Girault, 3 vols. Université de Paris I Panthéon-Sorbonne, 1997; Lorenzo Medici, "La diplomazia multilaterale italiana nel secondo dopoguerra. Il caso dell'ammissione dell'Italia all'UNESCO", *La Comunità Internazionale*, LVIII, No. 1, 2003, pp. 69-95. On Italy see also Franco Tamassia, "La politica culturale con l'estero: rapporto sull'Italia", *Lo spettatore internazionale*, IV, No. 6, 1969, pp. 695-758; Umberto Gori, *La "diplomazia" culturale multilaterale dell'Italia. Elementi per uno studio sistematico dell'azione italiana nel quadro di una teoria delle relazioni internazionali*, Roma, Bizzarri, 1970.

immediacy of its results so much as by the durability of those results[55]. This was the choice of Italy, which preferred paradoxically to not have its own cultural diplomacy, in favor of the realization of UNESCO's principles and purposes. It is not easy to estimate the results on Arab public opinion, but even after the recent pro-US political and military choices, Italian cultural diplomatic success could be confirmed for instance, by the desire of some Gulf States, after September 11, to divert their students from US universities to Italian ones and to found Italian universities in their countries.

On the contrary, the failure of the American public and cultural policy in the Mediterranean, necessarily conducted with propaganda tools, to counter the decline of United States reputation because of American foreign policy in the Middle East, could be seen by the joy and favor shown by Arab and Islamic masses for the overthrow of the conservative and western-oriented government in Iraq in 1958, in Libya in 1969, and in Iran in 1979, by the popularity in the region of Nasserism, by the anti-US attitude of many of the Arab media even if controlled by conservative governments, by the American flags burnt during Arab and Islamic demonstrations against Israel, and especially by the fact that people who were educated and lived in the United States were among the terrorists of September 11.

---

[55] Kevin V. Mulcahy, "Cultural Diplomacy and the Exchange Programs: 1938-1978", *The Journal of Arts Management, Law and Society*, 29, No. 1, 1999, pp. 28-29.

"Keen but Raw"

Mediterranean Europe Facing New Challenges

Alberto TONINI

Università di Firenze

> Muslims and Christians speak readily of crusades and jihads. Such an agenda is very reassuring to the men and women who are stranded in the middle of the ford, between the deep waters of tradition and modernity.
>
> But we are all swimming in those waters, Westerners and Muslims and others alike. And since the waters are part of the ocean of History, trying to divide them with barriers is a futile exercise.
>
> Edward W. Said
> *The Nation*, October 22, 2001

In recent years, a new theory has emerged among the analysts of International Politics affirming that we are living "a new phase" in world politics after the end of the Cold War, and that in this "new phase" the fundamental source of conflict will not be ideological or economic. The dividing line among individuals and the dominating source of conflict will be cultural.

To give strength to this approach, the new theoretical framework invoked the theory on tectonic plates, firstly elaborated by geologists. In this theoretical framework, all civilisations follow their own path without blending into one another. At best, they slide over one another, like tectonic plates, and from time to time their collision creates fault lines which engulf reality. The fault lines between civilisations will be the battle lines of the future. This was the apocalyptic conclusion of this new theory.

Listening to the proponents of this theory, the people of Mediterranean Europe suddenly realised that they were on the edge of one of the most dangerous fault lines; or rather, they probably *were* the fault line. They decided, consciously or not, that it was necessary to react, and that it was necessary to show the rest of the world that their historical experience was not an experience of fault lines and tectonic plates. On the contrary, their experience was one of exchange, cross-fertilisation and sharing, in a process which goes beyond boundaries and enriches both sides.

Their experience is now flowing into the mainstream of the process of European integration: the Treaty on European Union was negotiated at a time of radical transformation in Europe associated with the collapse of communism and the end of the Cold War. Linked to this was the gradual disintegration of three multi-nation polities: the Soviet Union, the Federal Republic of Yugoslavia and Czechoslovakia. It is perhaps unsurprising that the European Union, as a fledgling multi-nation polity, felt the need to correct the cultural homogenising tendencies of European economic integration for sub-state nations through a number of region-related institutional developments and policies.

Traditionally, tolerant multi-nation political societies have established policies that facilitate the maintenance and development of regional cultural diversity. Sub-state nationalists identify a number of EU region-related institutional developments and policies which suggest that the EU not only recognises the underlying tensions caused by the two objectives of economic integration and maintaining cultural diversity, but have acted to offset the cultural homogenizing tendencies of European economic integration for regional and national minorities. This process has been under way for sometime, and was given increasing momentum as a result of the Treaty on European Union[1].

But how could the little keen-but-raw countries of Mediterranean Europe beat the fascinating and attractive theory of the tectonic plates, that promises to explain what global politics was likely to be in years to come? The alternative way was soft power, and the alternative practice was symbolism.

---

[1] Adam Biscoe, "European Integration and the Maintenance of Regional Cultural Diversity: Symbiosis or Symbolism?", *Regional Studies*, Vol. 35, No. 1, 2001, pp. 59-61.

I. Soft Power: a Different Approach to World Politics

Joseph Nye coined the term "soft power" in the late 1980s. According to his definition, "soft power is the ability to get what you want through attraction rather than coercion or payments"[2]. It is strictly dependent upon the attractiveness of a country's culture, political ideals, and policies. Even General Wesley Clark, of the US Armed Forces, recently pointed out that "soft power gave us an influence far beyond the hard edge of traditional balance-of-power politics"[3].

Soft power is usually set against its opposite, hard power, which implies the ability to coerce others. Hard power grows out of a country's military and economic might, and it can be very effective when pursuing national interests. However you cannot launch a war whenever you wish without alienating other countries and losing the cooperation needed for achieving peace.

After the World War II, all European countries felt the attractiveness of America's culture, political ideas, and policies: when you can get others to admire your ideals and to want what you want, you do not have to spend as much to move them in your direction. Seduction is always more effective than coercion, and many values like democracy, human rights, and individual opportunities are deeply seductive[4].

Soft power, however, is difficult to wield. This is, because many of its resources are outside government control, and their effects depend heavily on how they are perceived. Moreover, soft power usually works indirectly by shaping the environment for policy, and often takes years to produce the desired outcomes. Generally speaking, governments prefer to use hard power to achieve desired outcomes within a reasonable time, even though not all wars or economic actions produced the desired outcomes[5].

The fact that soft-power resources are awkward to wield has not prevented governments from trying. Currently, the closest competitor of the United States in soft power resources is Europe. European art, literature,

---

[2] Joseph S. Nye, *Soft Power: the Means to Success in World Politics*, New York, 2004, p. XI.

[3] Wesley K. Clark, *Winning Modern Wars: Iraq, Terrorism, and the American Empire*, New York, 2003, p. 182.

[4] Nye, *op. cit.*, pp. 40-41.

[5] Witness the length and ultimate failure of both the Vietnam War by the US Army and the Afghan War by the Soviet Army. Or the fact that economic sanctions historically produced effects in only about a third of the cases where they were tried. See Gary Hufbauer, Jeffrey Scott and Kimberly Elliott, *Economic Sanctions Reconsidered*, Washington, 1990.

music, design, fashion, food and sports have long served as global cultural magnets. Furthermore, the European Union as a symbol of a uniting Europe itself carried a good deal of soft power. The idea that war is now unthinkable among countries that fought bitterly for centuries past, and that Europe has become an island of peace and prosperity gives it a positive image in much of the world. In the late 1980s, when Eastern Europeans were asked which countries would serve as models for their future, Western Europe outranked the United States. Both the Polish and the Czechoslovak election campaigns in 1989 were marked by the slogan "back to Europe"[6]. The British historian Timothy Garton Ash has written that Europe's "soft power is demonstrated by the fact that not only millions of individuals but also whole states want to enter it"[7].

In addition to its attractive culture and domestic policies, Europe also derives soft power from its foreign policies, which often contribute to the global public good. Of course, not all European policies are far-sighted, but Europe gains credibility from its position on global climate change, international law, and human rights treaties. Moreover, Europe provides 70 percent of overseas development aid to poor countries[8].

In recent years, Europeans have also been more comfortable about using multilateral institutions than Americans. This is in part a result of their experiences in the development of the European Union; but whatever the reason, in a world where unilateralism is much criticized, the European propensity toward multilateralism makes European countries' policies attractive to many other countries[9].

All these considerations are particularly true in the case of the South-European countries. They are not economic powers, they have not commercial weight in the global trade flows, and they do not possess mass destruction weapons. But they share a long-lasting tradition of cultural and multilateral diplomacy, especially in their relations with the other shore of the Mediterranean.

Even if the major cultural shifts of history embraced the Mediterranean (East and West, North and South, Islam and Christendom), it remains the best environment to study the processes of adapting, merging, and transforming human societies.

---

[6] Rudiger Meyenberg e Henk Dekker (eds.), *Perceptions of Europe in East and West*, Oldenburg, 1992, p. 50.

[7] Timothy Garton Ash, "The Great Divide", *Prospect Magazine*, March 2003.

[8] Andrew Moravcsik, "How Europe can win without an Army", *Financial Times*, April 3, 2003.

[9] *Ibid.*

II. The Language of Symbolism in Foreign Policy

We are all aware of the strength a symbol can have, for individuals, communities and nations. A symbol is something visible that by association or convention represents something else that is invisible, and symbolism is the practice of investing things with symbolic meaning. It is generally acknowledged that symbols are a vital part of social life. Decision-makers actively engage in the manipulation of symbols and rationalise their actions through them[10].

By the word "symbolism" in foreign policy, we mean any action of which the meaning, value, or significance cannot be derived only from its concrete form. Symbolic actions derive their meanings from the beliefs and perceptions of persons, not from the actions themselves. Consequently, an action that possesses positive meaning for some persons may been irritant for others; these differences arises from different patterns of meaning, valence and systemic importance attributed to symbols.

The turmoil of the past 20 years has led many to question the alleged consensus of the rest of the world with regard to Western symbols and values. Rather than an increasingly homogeneous society, the world is now portrayed as a melting pot of ethnic groups and civilisations that did not melt. The divisions that separate ethnic and cultural groupings are sometimes superimposed with generational differences. While these problems may signal a breakdown in the consensus with regard to Western values, there is substantial evidence that this consensus can be strengthened by using the language of symbolism[11].

In the field of International Relations, a symbol is not a secondary factor, something that can be considered naïve or irrelevant. A symbolic issue can be as powerful as an economic or a political issue, but the use of symbolic language must be accompanied by a wide knowledge of the symbolic references of the recipients.

To a certain extent the same symbolic discourses can be traced around the shores of the Mediterranean, where a long history of different civilisations has left a rich legacy of symbols. The Mediterranean cultural identity is understood primarily as an awareness of diversity and a search for intercultural dialogue. As the Mediterranean clearly does not correspond to a single identity or a single culture, the language of

---

[10] Murray Edelman has offered a compelling analysis of these processes. See his *The Symbolic Uses of Politics*, University of Illinois Press, 1964; and *Politics as Symbolic Action*, Chicago, 1971.

[11] Roger W. Cobb, "Individual Orientation in the Study of Political Symbolism", *Social Science Quarterly*, Vol. 53, No. 1, 1992, p. 87.

symbolism can be a relevant source of dialogue and understanding among the multiple identities and traditions that grew and developed around this sea. Even if the use of symbolism in foreign policy usually is not given very much attention in the study of International Relations, it is possible to find many significant examples originating from Mediterranean Europe in its relations with its neighbouring countries. Some of these examples can effectively describe the strength of this practice in International Relations.

III.   First Example: The Rebuilding of the Mostar Bridge

During the last four centuries, the old bridge of Mostar had been a symbol of Bosnia's multi-ethnic society. Suleiman the Magnificent commissioned it about 100 years after the Ottoman Empire has claimed the Balkans. The elegant white-marble "Stari Most", or Old Bridge, has been a beloved landmark since its completion in 1566. The city of Mostar is named after the bridge, and means the "bridge-keeper".

The bridge united the town's Muslim and Catholic communities for nearly four hundred years: the story of the Mostar bridge was not just one of bricks and mortar, great engineering, and sublime architecture. Its story was the story of this part of Europe – its grandeur, its civilizations, its tragedies.

The 16th Century bridge was blown up during the bitter fighting in the Bosnian war between the city's Muslims and Croats in 1993. What had been the most ethnically-integrated place in old Yugoslavia was now physically divided by the river. Croats on the West bank, Muslims on the East.

The methodical shelling of the bridge symbolised something far greater than just the destruction of an architectural structure. It symbolised the destruction of the multiethnic community for which Bosnia and Herzegovina were once so equally famous. The bridge was destroyed for its symbolic value.

For this same reason UNESCO pledged to rebuild it: in 1998, UNESCO, the World Bank and municipal authorities launched a joint appeal for its reconstruction, which was answered by five donor countries – Croatia, France, Italy, The Netherlands and Turkey – as well as the Council of Europe Development Bank.

Its reopening, on July 23, was seen as the symbolic healing of divisions between Muslims and Croats. A crowd flowed over it on the day of its reopening. They all came to pay tribute to a symbol – hoping that this bridge would somehow unite the two communities so bitterly divided by the Bosnian war. Many have welcomed the bridge's rebuilding, but none is underestimating the gap that still remains between Bosnia's ethnic groups. Today, the town's Croats and Muslims largely maintain that separation, sending their children to different schools and keeping to their respective sides of the Neretva.

But many say the reopening of the bridge is at least a good starting point for restoring connections between Mostar's divided communities, together with a new Western-sponsored plan to unify the town. The new Mostar statute, imposed by Lord Ashdown, the European High Representative in Bosnia, will merge three Bosnian Muslim and three Croat municipalities and the city council into a single unit and administration, abolishing parallel power structures.

The international community has helped in this process, as have four Mediterranean countries: Italy, France, Croatia and Turkey, all aware of the power of this symbol for the past and the future of Bosnia.

The reopening of the Mostar bridge is part of a larger effort of the international community, which is aimed at rebuilding the spirit of compromise throughout former Yugoslavia. The first important achievement was the agreement on the question of succession to former Yugoslavia. The agreement was signed in June 2001 by all five former Republics – Slovenia, Croatia, Bosnia and Herzegovina, Yugoslavia and Macedonia, under the auspices of the European Union. For many years, there was no progress whatsoever on this issue. After Milosević had been ousted from power, EU representatives succeeded in bringing the five partners together, and they agreed to sign the so-called Vienna Declaration on the Succession of the Public Property of the former Socialist Federal Republic of Yugoslavia. That was the first-ever agreement made among the five former Yugoslav republics, negotiated among themselves, albeit with the help of the international community.

The second example of this change in spirit was the agreement amending the constitutions of Bosnia and Herzegovina, signed on April 19, 2002. Under the new constitutions, the ethnic groups of Bosnia-Herzegovina, their peoples and citizens are represented in both entities at all levels of government and public administration – the constitutions set exact quotas for this – and they have far-reaching group rights in the decision-making process at the entity level. This constitutional agreement represents the first major compromise reached by the political leaders of the peoples and ethnic groups of Bosnia and Herzegovina[12].

---

[12] ICG, Implementing Equality: The 'Constituent Peoples' Decision in Bosnia and Herzegovina, ICG Balkans, Sarajevo, Report No. 128, April 2002; http://www.crisisweb.org/projects/showreport.cfm?reportid_618.

These two agreements show that even in the Balkans the virtues of compromise are not totally lost on the current political elites. The Vienna and Mrakovica-Sarajevo Agreements are, probably, the first relevant examples of how a new, more contemporary political culture is about to take root in the region with the help of the international community. Since then, there have been other examples: the Ohrid Agreement that brought Macedonia back from the brink of war. The Serbian-Montenegrin negotiations on their future common status also deserve a positive mention. Both compromises were achieved at the negotiating table, with the help of the EU, but without a military intervention.

However, as well as offering political assistance, it is clear that the EU is bringing certain 'values' to the country, using its soft-power resources. Bosnia and Herzegovina will be a different country once the EU mandate ends: it will be different physically, politically and, in many ways, culturally as well. One might bemoan the fact that long-held traditions are being jeopardised, and that certain continuities and specificities of Bosnian culture could be, in a purist sense, 'tainted' by Western and non-indigenous elements. This is perhaps unavoidable: globalisation – viewed here as a vast cultural phenomenon – brings different lifestyles to traditional cultures, and they are incorporated in one way or another. Western influence in Bosnia and Herzegovina is felt in a very concrete and specific way. The international community sets the political agenda and imposes legislation, creating a specific social and political system.

That is why the partnership with Bosnian citizens, intellectuals and leaders is very important. The result must not be a Western clone in the Balkans. Ideally, the result should be a country that has found its own modern identity, and among Bosnia and Herzegovina's assets are its links to the Islamic world. It is very important that the progressive forces of Islam remain in contact with the Muslim community of Bosnia and Herzegovina and *vice versa*[13].

If Bosnia and Herzegovina is successful in coming to terms with its internal problems, it could play an important role in Europe, particularly when it comes to the issue of European Islam, which needs to be further explored.

Provided that there is a specifically European kind of Islam, which continues to adapt to and incorporate European achievements – particularly the separation between religion and state, the banner of secular societies, in which religion does not interfere in politics – Bosnia and

---

[13] Christophe Solioz, "The fate of Bosnia and Herzegovina", *Journal of Southern Europe and the Balkans*, Vol. 5, No. 3, December 2003, p. 358.

Herzegovina could make an important contribution and serve as a bridge to the greater Islamic world. A successful state of Bosnia and Herzegovina could signal inclusiveness to recent Muslim immigrants in Europe[14].

This is not an obvious task when you think of the challenges that lie ahead of Bosnia and Herzegovina, but it is important to acknowledge that finding an identity as a state implies reaching out and finding ways and means to integrate it into the region at an economic, social and cultural level. It means re-establishing links across the new borders with its neighbours. Only within this regional framework will Bosnia and Herzegovina reach the point where it can integrate with Europe and be proud of its achievements. The international community, as well, will be able to be proud of having successfully completed a massive and comprehensive intervention, unique in modern history, by relying specifically on resources deriving form soft power and symbolic discourses.

IV.   Second Example: the New Library of Alexandria

The ancient library of Alexandria, in Egypt, was a unique ecumenical effort of human intellect and imagination. Alexandria, standing at the crossroads of the main communication routes linking Africa, Europe and Asia, was in past centuries a major centre of science, philosophy and art, an intellectual meeting place for eminent representatives of the Egyptian, Greek, Persian and other cultures, where they could converse and receive mutual benefit from their contacts. It was in such a climate that the first universal library in history came into being at the beginning of the fourth century BC, having as its aim the bringing together and conservation of the writings of all nations, while, at the same time welcoming their leading scholars and thinkers. From a very early point in its history, at least one copy of every work ever written in Greek, and, subsequently, translations of the most important works written in other languages, was added to its collections.

All ships passing through the port of Alexandria were required to allow copies to be made of any scrolls they had on board, if they were of interest to the Library.

The ancient library, established in 290 BC, was open to all civilisations and systematic efforts were made to collect the best works from all over the world. The result was a mixture of all civilisations and languages, where Asian, Egyptian and Mediterranean cultures enriched the dominant culture of Hellenism.

---

[14]   *Ivi*, p. 366.

By the middle of the first century BC, the Library had in its possession 532,800 manuscripts, which were listed, filed and preserved by
highly sophisticated methods. One of its finest achievements was the
catalogue of Callimachus, a catalogue of all existing works, which not
only gave their titles but also supplied detailed information on the
authors and their works, as well an analysis of each text. This gigantic
bibliography, now lost, was for a long time the essential reference work
for Greek literature.

The Library was not destroyed by the invading Arabs, as some histories would have us believe. It was the victim of a long decline, punctuated by fires and destructions that spanned over four and half centuries:
during the co-regency of Cleopatra and her brother Ptolemy, they began
to quarrel. The conflict was resolved by Julius Caesar upon his arrival to
Alexandria in 48 BC. Caesar sided with Cleopatra and granted her the
throne. Ptolemy in a rage, accused them both of treason and led the
army to besiege the palace, in what is known as "the Alexandrian War".
Caesar sent for supplies from Rome, but was outnumbered by his enemy's fleet that controlled the harbour. To avoid a naval combat, Caesar
burnt 110 Egyptian ships in the dockyards that enabled him to occupy
Pharos, control the entrance to the harbour and establish direct communication with his main forces across the sea. The fire extended to the city
and the Great Library (Megale Bibliotheke), and approximately 40,000
books (400,000 in some sources) were burnt, with a tremendous loss in
intellectual riches and human heritage.

The Daughter Library became the principle library after the burning
of the Great Library, and it survived for many centuries up until the late
3rd century. In 312 AD, Christianity was chosen as the official religion
of the Roman Empire and state support for indigenous cults ceased,
while the Alexandrian triad of Gods (Serapis, Isis and Harpocrates) was
still prominent. The sanctity of temples was threatened, and the library
endangered due to its location inside the Sarapeum. Civil war started
between Christians and Pagans, and in 389 AD, the Temple of Serapis at
Canopus fell into the hands of Christians. In 391 AD, the Roman Emperor Theodosius prohibited any non-Christian religions, and authorized
Theophilus, the fanatical Bishop of Alexandria, to transform the temple
of Dionysus into a church. The pagan inhabitants fled to the Sarapeum
as a last refuge, but the emperor issued a decree allowing the demolition
of all temples in Alexandria. The Bishop and his followers raided the
temple and the library and completely destroyed them, turning the
building into a church and causing its final closure in 391 AD[15].

---

[15] Some scholars believe that the reason for burning the Daughter Library was not only
in pursue of pagans, but also to end the Alexandrian Church and theological studies

The new Bibliotheca Alexandrina was opened to the public in October 2002, as the result of a common effort by the Egyptian government, Unesco, and various Arab countries and Western countries. The major donor countries included a large section of Mediterranean Europe: Italy, France, Spain and Turkey.

The library will play a necessary role to further cooperation between the north and the south of the Mediterranean, as well as between the East and West. The Bibliotheca Alexandrina has adopted its collection development policy in cooperation with UNESCO and with the valuable input from national and international experts, to evolve its unique collection and functions and to avoid repetition and unnecessary overlapping with other research libraries both regionally or internationally. Since the 1990 Aswan Declaration, UNESCO and the international community have been cooperating with the Egyptian government to muster resources for implementation of the library[16].

Once again, the importance of a cultural initiative, which is also rich in symbolic significance, has led to a very effective foreign policy by Mediterranean Europe, whose results are now visible on a magnificent site, very close to the location of the Ancient Library, looking towards the bay of Alexandria and the Mediterranean.

A result that is in accordance to the idea that culture can be the most effective antidote to fanaticism and any clash of civilisation. Mrs. Mubarak, the chairperson of the library's board of trustees, emphasised the need for such institutions in these difficult times – institutions that can bring people together in the pursuit of knowledge and understanding and encourage cultures to meet and connect, rather than remaining distant or meeting in conflict. "The library will be Egypt's window on the world and the world's window on Egypt. It will be a meeting point for dialogue between ideas and cultures – an openness that we desperately need at this time, especially after the tragic events the world has recently witnessed"[17].

---

and to transfer the center of Christianity to Rome. For more details see Jean-François Mondot, "La bibliothèque aux 400 000 rouleaux", *Les Cahiers Science & Vie*, n° 76, August 2003, pp. 48-55. Patrizia Zanelli, "La nuova biblioteca di Alessandria d'Egitto: un invito al dialogo fra le civiltà", *Africa*, Vol. LIX, n° 1, 2004, pp. 135-144. Sameh M. Arab, "The ancient library of Alexandria and the rebuilding of the modern one", in http://www.arabworldbooks.com/bibliothecaAlexandrina.htm

[16] Scott MacLeod, "Recreating a Jewel", *Time Europe*, Vol. 155, No. 23, June 2000.

[17] *Al-Ahram Weekly Online*, 4-10 October 2002, No. 554.

V. Third Example: "The Roads of Friendship" by the Ravenna Festival

On the last Sunday of July 2004 the Philharmonic Orchestra of La Scala in Milan performed a concert in Syria, with an audience of 11,000 people at the Roman theatre in Bosra. On that occasion, European music was performed for an Arab audience, not only Syrians, but also Lebanese and Jordanians.

The concert was offered not to a select public, but to entire families with their children who had come from Damascus to Bosra by shuttle buses arranged for this special occasion. The concert was organised under the high patronage of the presidency of the Syrian republic and the presidency of the Italian republic, the Syrian ministries for Culture and Tourism, the Italian Chambers of Deputies and Senators, the Italian ministry for Culture, and in collaboration with the Italian Embassy in Damascus, the Syrian Embassy in Rome and the Italian state-owned television, that broadcast the event[18].

The concert in Syria was not the first experiment of this kind, but it was the last event of the music festival organized in Ravenna: in July 1997 Ravenna Festival mapped out the first of its "Roads of Friendship" by crossing the Adriatic Sea to the city of Sarajevo. The notes of Schubert and Beethoven, performed by the Orchestra and Choir of La Scala, rekindled the pride and deep sense of human dignity of a people that wanted to leave the horror and ferocity behind it and recover its lost serenity.

Nothing could better re-evoke that evening than the grateful and moving words of someone who was there, the writer Zlatko Dizdarevic: "For the first time since the day our drama began we felt with all our senses that the hope of the world is culture without frontiers. [...] Dignity restored is far more than houses rebuilt. We shall never forget it"[19].

Since then, other bridges have been built: in July 1998 the Philharmonic Orchestra, Riccardo Muti and the Choir of La Scala crossed the Mediterranean to Beirut. From Sarajevo to Beirut, a route belonging to the ancient lands of Byzantium – the crossroad of wandering peoples and of a whole mosaic of cultures – led in 1999 the Ravenna Festival to another supreme destination: Jerusalem, a city that is a symbol for the three monotheistic religions, a fascinating meeting place of different cultures. Riccardo Muti, the Orchestra and Choir of La Scala performed

---

[18] *Corriere della Sera*, July 24, 2004.
[19] *Corriere della Sera*, July 15, 1997.

Giuseppe Verdi's Requiem Mass against one of the most fascinating backgrounds of the city: the Sultan's Pool.

One year later the Jerusalem Foundation presented the Ravenna Festival's President, Cristina Mazzavillani Muti, with the "Jerusalem Foundation Award", a prize set up to celebrate the exceptional occasion created by the concert. Among the reasons behind the award, also supported by Teddy Kollek, former Mayor of the Holy City, one fully senses the gratitude and unanimity with regard to this new destination on the Festival's journey of brotherhood: "… for her great dedication in seeking peace and understanding among different nations and religions through art and culture. The Roads of Friendship project, in the context of Ravenna Festival, reflects her personal ability to overcome complex difficulties and reach people across seas and human barriers, bringing a message of peace, love and cooperation. The concert held in Jerusalem was an unforgettable expression of this ability, and a noble gesture to the City and its inhabitants"[20].

After Jerusalem, Moscow, where the Ravenna Festival 2000 was concluded at the Bolshoi Theatre in a celebration of the bond between two cities historically and culturally linked by a common Byzantine matrix, whose symbol is the mosaic. In the prestigious Moscow theatre, the Festival built a new bridge of goodwill through art and culture with a performance of Beethoven's Ninth Symphony in which the Philharmonic Orchestra and Choir of La Scala was joined for the occasion the Bolshoi Theatre Orchestra and Choir. The Hymn to Joy was a sort of supreme farewell to the century and the millennium left behind, and a salutation full of hope for the one that had just begun, in the ecstasy of this Beethoven masterpiece.

In July 2001, the route of the "Roads of Friendship" reached the cities of Erevan and Istanbul with two concerts. Although the common historical roots between Ravenna and Istanbul (formerly Byzantium) are well known, and the inimitable architecture of the Byzantine basilicas with their mosaics "glowing with gold" is still there to demonstrate it, the links between Ravenna and Erevan in Armenia, one of the most ancient historical-geographical entities in the western world, are far less known. Nevertheless, the main occasion for the Erevan concert was highly significant: the solemn celebration of the 1700th anniversary (301-2001) of the proclamation of Christianity in Armenia, the first Christian country in the world.

---

[20] See the Jerusalem Foundation web site: www.jerusalemfoundation.org/news.php?id=287.

The isolation of these ancient people, today broken up and dispersed in the diaspora, led the Armenians to gather around their symbols. All this, together with the memory of the extermination, undoubtedly gave deep meaning to the Ravenna Festival project, emphasised in the words of the Patriarch of all Armenians: "The strongest and most lasting bridges stand on cultural foundations. The language of art, and especially that of music, has no need of translators. It brings people together and makes dialogue between peoples understandable".

The "Bridge of Friendship" of the 2002 Ravenna Festival, dedicated to the theme "New York, September 11", could not but lead to Ground Zero: a wound inflicted on all humankind.

The Ravenna Festival achieved an even more "choral" and musically ecumenical event, by calling on many of the best musicians from the "traditional" orchestras that are the connective tissue of musical Europe. Not only this: many members of the New York Philharmonic joined the Musicians of Europe United (representing 11 European nations). So the idea of a musical 'bridge' thrown across the Atlantic from old Europe was louder than ever, bringing a message of solidarity with a sister nation (consisting of many peoples and races) that in itself exemplifies the meaning and possibility of peaceful and active cohabitation in a unique melting pot of cultures and ideas.

In 2003, the "Roads of Friendship" crossed over the Mediterranean once again, up to the great pyramids near Cairo. The La Scala Philharmonic Orchestra and the Ravenna Festival Orchestra, the choirs of the Accademia Nazionale di Santa Cecilia and the Maggio Musicale Fiorentino and, the Cairo Opera Orchestra and Choir, conducted by Riccardo Muti, performed music by Berlioz for the pleasure of the Egyptian audience. Muti himself explains the significance behind this unique concert programme: "The piece by Berlioz, *la Grande Symphonie funèbre et triomphale*, which is concluded with an invocation of glory to the fallen heroes, acquires a universal value if we think of all those heroes who fought for freedom in a general sense, with no distinction between race or faith. And naturally the pyramids are, more than anything else, burial places which represent the realm of eternal sleep, intended not only as a resting place for the Pharaoes, but also as an expression of a wish and hope for peace all over the world"[21].

---

[21] See the Ravenna Festival official web site: www.ravennafestival.org

VI. Conclusions

Soft power and its cultural ramifications have become no less important since September 11. Soft power is highly diffuse and empowers a wider diversity of individuals and groups – including potential terrorists – to play roles that are more significant in international relations. As argued by William Tow, those employing the "calibration of fear" to advance their political aims can choose to generate societal dislocation or chaos, to damage economic assets and infrastructure, to undermine state security mechanisms or to intensify general apprehensions by discrediting incumbent elites' inability to control or quell disruptions[22]. But soft power can also work against such strategies if sustained and patient international cooperation is nurtured as a means of supporting the continued viability of civil societies and advancing the well-being of the diverse social groups within them. How effective this process will be in our time relates to how well the western countries project their own values: embodying freedom of individual choice, while preserving a fundamental tolerance for the inevitable differences such choices will produce within democratic societies[23]. The record since the terrorist attacks on September 11 is mixed. Military tribunals and racial profiling have been applied, and are symptomatic of a dangerous tendency to stretch emergency measures for protecting democracy beyond the very limits of that political system. Yet the refusal of most people in the Islamic world to embrace radical doctrines of an anti-western nature constitutes an important sign of encouragement. Ultimately, finding a balance between the prerogatives and limitations of power will be the best means to avoid the insurgence of a new crisis.

---

[22] William T. Tow, "Apocalypse Forever? International Relations Implications of 11 September", *Australian Journal of Politics and History*, Vol. 49, No. 3, 2003, pp. 314-325.

[23] Christopher C. Harmon, "Five Strategies of Terror", *Small Wars and Insurgencies*, Vol. 12, No. 3, 2001, pp. 39-66.

Conclusion

Gérard BOSSUAT

Université de Cergy-Pontoise

L'Europe méditerranéenne a été le thème de cette belle rencontre intellectuelle internationale qui a rassemblé, sous la direction du professeur Marta Petricioli de l'université de Florence, des historiens intéressés par l'histoire culturelle de la Méditerranée, des économistes, des démographes, des politistes ou des sociologues tous capables soit de donner une explication d'ensemble, soit de faire une recherche sur un cas particulier de l'espace méditerranéen. Ce colloque, très riche par l'abondance des sujets traités, a produit encore une fois son lot de certitudes et suscité beaucoup d'interrogations sur notre héritage mais aussi sur l'avenir européen et celui de l'aire méditerranéenne si chère à nous tous.

Il m'a semblé profitable d'attirer l'attention du lecteur sur quelques points forts des différentes contributions en gardant à l'esprit une préoccupation : existe-t-il une cohérence de l'Europe méditerranéenne hors du champ politique puisqu'il n'y a pas d'unité des pays européens méditerranéens, tout en tenant compte de l'Union européenne qui rassemble beaucoup de ces pays dans un projet d'intégration. Il était impossible de ne pas tenir compte du sud de la Méditerranée en raison des interactions qui se produisent entre les polarités nord, sud et est de la Méditerranée, en raison surtout d'événements graves qui ont paru opposer le monde occidental au monde arabo-musulman. L'Europe méditerranéenne est aux premières loges de cette ligne qui définit deux cultures. Les pays concernés sont évidemment l'Espagne mais aussi la Catalogne et les Baléares, la France occitane, la Corse, l'Italie dans sa complexité avec les deux grandes îles de Sicile et de Sardaigne, Malte en position de commandement stratégique du bassin méditerranéen, les pays des Balkans, en recomposition après la période d'éclatement, la Grèce mais aussi la Turquie qui, sans être d'Europe, est un partenaire de l'Europe, Chypre enfin où deux nations se réclament encore de deux cultures souvent en conflit.

Un monde méditerranéen original

Ce monde méditerranéen est original du fait des représentations que l'Europe du nord s'en fait, de sa faiblesse politique et de sa pratique démocratique récente. La question de la diversité de l'espace méditerranéen est posée de façon récurrente et obsédante à travers la notion de polarités que l'on peut comprendre comme étant des sources d'émissions qui traversent l'espace méditerranéen. Si au temps des Phéniciens ce pouvait être les marchandises et les dieux de l'Asie et de l'Occident qui transitaient par la mer, aujourd'hui un flot ininterrompu de matières premières énergétiques proviennent de l'est et du sud et transitent sur ces routes maritimes[1].

Il est si original qu'il a fasciné les élites françaises comme des élites britanniques ou d'Europe du Nord. L'analyse passionnante qui est faite de l'idée de la Méditerranée dans l'imaginaire français à travers des auteurs du XIXe et du XXe siècle est troublante à plus d'un titre, d'une part parce qu'elle est présentée par un chercheur américain, a priori moins contraint par l'histoire qu'un Européen ne le serait, d'autre part parce qu'elle utilise des sources non seulement littéraires, mais scientifiques, les botanistes par exemple. Le fonctionnement de l'objet « Méditerranée » dans l'imaginaire français est le produit des Lumières. Le XVIIIe siècle et le XIXe siècle veulent apporter la connaissance à des pays déchus de leur antique et glorieuse civilisation. Il est aussi l'expression d'un destin français qui doit s'accomplir au sud de la Méditerranée, au Maghreb, par opposition à l'espace anglo-américain du nord-ouest et germanique au nord-est[2].

Pour la période la plus récente, l'originalité du destin politique de la Méditerranée est soulignée par l'histoire des nationalismes grec et italien. Les deux pays ont en commun de craindre les pressions du nord et ont rêvé de retrouver une influence conforme à leur glorieux passé. Les Balkans qui ont toujours été très présents dans l'histoire de la Méditerranée sont restés une zone d'influence disputée entre l'Italie et la Grèce. L'histoire de ces deux nationalismes confrontés à l'impérialisme de l'Europe du nord illustre la faiblesse politique des espaces politiques méditerranéens. Le partage méditerranéen réalisé *de facto* entre la France (Afrique du Nord et Levant) et la Grande-Bretagne (Malte, Chypre, Egypte, Palestine, Irak) a conduit l'Italie et la Grèce à ressasser leur manque de considération de la part des grandes puissances et à nourrir un sentiment d'amertume qui a conduit ces deux pays à envisager la création d'une grande Italie au temps du fascisme ou d'une grande

---

[1]   Rodolfo Ragionieri : « Mediterranean Geopolitics ».

[2]   Alexis Wieck, History Department, Columbia University, New York.

Grèce après le fascisme. On hésite sur le sens à donner à ces manifesta-tions de nationalisme survenant après l'unité (Italie) ou la libération (Grèce). Elles illustrent le modèle impérialiste en cours au XIXe siècle et la façon dont les États européens du nord comme ceux de l'Europe méditerranéenne concevaient leurs relations entre eux et avec d'autres nations non européennes. La Méditerranée a été un espace de prédation impérialiste y compris pour l'Italie et la Grèce. Leur fonctionnement ne les distingue pas des autres impérialismes européens[3] ?

La pratique de la démocratie est récente en Europe méditerranéenne (sauf en France). Elle est marquée par un héritage autoritaire intéressant à relever en Italie, Espagne et Portugal. Pour les politistes, la présence d'un secteur public important serait la marque du passé autoritaire de ces États. On doit douter cependant d'une telle assertion, puisqu'il y a eu des secteurs publics très larges en Grande-Bretagne, Belgique et France qui sont des démocraties non autoritaires. D'autres comporte-ments caractériseraient cette démocratie autoritaire : l'absence de con-trôle de l'armée par le pouvoir civil, l'utilisation en Italie d'instruments administratifs créés par le fascisme pour aller vers la modernité, la faible efficacité de la police, la présence permanente de groupes de droite radi-cale et une alternance politique difficile. En Italie par exemple, l'alter-nance s'est produite après l'effondrement radical de la Démocratie-chrétienne quasiment au pouvoir depuis de Gasperi. Sans doute faut-il préférer le terme d'étatisme comme descripteur des restes d'autorita-risme dans la démocratie représentative, caractérisé d'après un interve-nant de passivité, conformisme, cynisme et aliénation. Ces héritages sont-ils utiles pour la consolidation démocratique ? Les théoriciens de la rupture ne seront pas satisfaits mais certains estiment qu'ils le sont. Quant à en faire l'emblème de la démocratie des pays européens du sud on peut en douter, certains pays d'Amérique latine ayant aussi des régimes démocratiques teintés d'autoritarisme[4].

Des réseaux méditerranéens transculturels

Une autre thématique essentielle traverse les travaux des chercheurs : l'affrontement ou le dialogue des cultures méditerranéennes. Le géogra-phe français Elisée Reclus voyait dans la Méditerranée la source de la civilisation occidentale moderne et en a fait un objet en soi, autonome, différent des autres aires géographique adjacentes. Sa vision pose le

---

[3]   Procopis Papastratis : « *Megali idea* and *Mare Nostrum*. Aspects of Greek and Italian Nationalism ».

[4]   Leonardo Morlino: « Authoritarian Legacies and Good Democracy: Southern Europe ».

problème de l'Islam qui semble disjoindre l'héritage antique gréco-romain et judéo-chrétien. L'unité méditerranéenne existe-t-elle encore après le passage des conquérants arabes ? La présentation de la longue chaîne des historiens français et francophones interprètes de la Méditerranée, de Gautier jusqu'à Braudel en passant par Pirenne provoque la réflexion et la méditation sur les heurts de civilisations de *Mare Nostrum* à la post colonisation. La Méditerranée est-elle devenue une frontière infranchissable, un rift culturel en formation que le terrorisme islamique, les attentats de Paris en 1995, de Londres en 2005 et de Madrid en 2006 et la peur induite ne peuvent que renforcer ? Albert Camus et Augustin d'Hippone n'ont-ils plus rien à nous dire, l'art andalou est-il notre étranger, les églises byzantino-arabo-normandes de Palerme ne nous parlent-elles plus? Pourtant Braudel lui-même dans sa complexité indique qu'il n'y a pas une mais des Méditerranées que la décolonisation va révéler. Faut-il alors penser que naissent des Méditerranéens quand meurt la Méditerranée ? Les historiens et les événements posent la question de la vie en commun de part et d'autre de la Méditerranée, non plus selon le modèle de l'empire romain quoi qu'il fut tolérant envers la diversité des peuples, mais dans un espace organisé, dégagé de tout impérialisme, que seule actuellement l'Union européenne (ou des pays membres de l'Union) peut proposer. Le rêve d'un pôle original anti-américain constitué par l'ensemble méditerranéen est un avatar de cette évolution au temps de la domination mondiale des États-Unis[5].

L'exemple des juifs livournais prouve que jusqu'à une période récente un réseau trans-méditerranéen d'échanges culturels, religieux, commerciaux, familiaux existaient non pas en secret mais au grand jour et dans le cadre des institutions politiques existantes ausi bien au Maghreb qu'en Egypte, dans l'empire Ottoman ou en Italie. La présence des juifs de Livourne en Tunisie évoque le temps où, en dépit des différences de cultures, et avant la colonisation, la circulation des hommes était possible tout autant que maintenant, mais où il était normal de faire sa vie sur l'un ou l'autre rivage de la Méditerranée que ce soit en Europe ou en terre d'Islam. Siècle d'or que ce XIXe siècle pour les juifs de Méditerranée ? Sans doute. Le monde arabe avait su les recevoir et leur donner une place. Toutefois des différences d'accueil existaient entre la Maroc et le Yémen, la Turquie, la Tunisie ou l'Egypte. La thèse de Braudel et de Pirenne sur l'affrontement serait-elle démentie ? Les rabbins de Livourne parlaient arabe et échangeaient en italien, français, hébreu et espagnol. Ce milieu très ouvert était riche des traditions juives

---

[5] Alexis Wieck : « From *Pax Romana* to *Pax Americana*, 1789-1995: the Idea of the Mediterranean in the French Imaginary between Orientalism and Altermondialism ».

de Méditerranée mais aussi de celles, non juives, des pays et des cultures avec lesquels il était en relation. Peu nombreuses sans aucun doute les élites de ce milieu international et interculturel se sentaient à l'aide dans les différentes villes de Méditerranée. Le cas de Livourne semble spécial, lié aux conditions historiques de la ville et du port. L'expérience de ces juifs livournais est différente de celle des communautés juives issues de la Tunisie même par exemple. Elle est donc spécifique, mais aurait été impossible dans d'autres régions du monde européen où se trouvaient des communautés juives très nombreuses[6].

Le rayonnement méditerranéen de la franc-maçonnerie italienne après 1860 montre que le réseau des intellectuels « éclairés » fonctionnait quelque soit le type de société ou de culture et de religion. Alexandrie, Constantinople, Tunis, Le Caire, la Grèce, Smyrne ont accueilli des loges créées par des francs-maçons italiens. Ces loges se donnaient comme but de recréer un lien social et un lien politique avec la mère patrie ; elles étaient donc liées à une expatriation temporaire ou durable de commerçants, techniciens, professeurs, archéologues, mais elles surent aussi toucher les bourgeoisies locales, chrétiennes et musulmanes. Elles créèrent des structures mutualistes pour les affiliés et même les profanes. Marquées par l'esprit d'ouverture et de tolérance sociale, elles propagèrent les Lumières et luttèrent contre l'ignorance et le fanatisme. Le rôle des juifs et des commerçants italiens liés aux échelles du Levant, à l'Égypte et à la Grèce depuis des siècles (Venise et Gênes) dans leur installation hors d'Italie est avérée ainsi que la politique méditerranéenne de l'Italie réunifiée[7]. L'image de la Méditerranée que donnent ces deux exemples est celle d'un espace diversifié politiquement et culturellement, mais capable de faire vivre ensemble des communautés humaines d'origine différentes. On aimerait avoir une histoire complémentaire de marchands arabes installés durablement en Europe méditerranéenne. L'histoire de Venise devrait pouvoir répondre à cette question. La démonstration que la Méditerranée est un espace de réseaux transculturels serait renforcée si d'autres toiles pouvaient être décrites.

Les convergences en Méditerranée

Des pistes sont ouvertes par les chercheurs permettant de vérifier que dans certains domaines, il y a plus de convergences que de divergences entre la rive nord et la rive sud de la Méditerranée. Les comportements

---

[6] L. E. Funaro, « A Mediterranean Diaspora : Jews from Leghorn in the Second Half of the 19ᵗʰ Century ».

[7] Fulvio Conti : « Entre Orient et Occident. Les loges maçonniques du Grand Orient d'Italie en Méditerranée entre le XIXᵉ et XXᵉ siècle ».

démographiques comparés en apportent la preuve. On pense généralement que la fertilité se maintient au sud de la Méditerranée tandis
qu'elle s'effondre au nord. Or nous sommes surpris de constater que le
sud a tendance à s'aligner sur le nord. Il s'est donc produit récemment
une transition rapide et convergente en Méditerranée, caractérisée par le
passage d'une fertilité de 7/8 enfants par femme à moins de 3. Les
raisons en sont bien connues des démographes ou des anthropologues.
L'âge des couples au mariage a augmenté et l'accès aux contraceptifs
est plus facile pour les femmes qui, comme au nord, veulent choisir le
moment d'avoir un enfant, surtout si elles travaillent ce qu'elles com-
mencent à faire davantage qu'auparavant. Les comportements familiaux
ont changé comme ils ont changé au nord de la Méditerranée. Or les
modèles familiaux étaient proches : grande famille, solidarité et esprit de
corps, liens familiaux très solides. L'éducation à l'égalité entre les
hommes et les femmes intervient aussi dans l'alignement. Cette transition amorce-t-elle un modèle de comportement méditerranéen ? En fait
elle aligne le bassin méditerranéen sur des comportements démographiques, sinon universels, du moins propres aux sociétés éduquées et plus
égalitaires. Cette évolution témoigne que le monde méditerranéen dans
son entier entre dans une « modernité » universelle, même si l'auteur se
demande comment pourra évoluer la relation homme-femme impossible
à prédire dans la culture islamique traditionnelle[8]. Laissons-lui la responsabilité de cette conclusion, mais on voit mal des sociétés arabo-
musulmanes se couper d'un mouvement universel parce que malgré le
poids des traditions elles sont emportées par la libéralisation mondiale
qui prend la forme de voyages plus faciles, d'informations abondantes
disponibles sur les télévisons satellitaires et sur l'internet. Les évolu-
tions démographiques démontrent que la convergence Europe-
Méditerranée est une réalité. En revanche, la convergence est plus forte
entre l'Europe du nord et l'Europe méditerranéenne, donc au sein de
l'Europe entière, qu'entre l'Europe méditerranéenne et les pays du sud
de la Méditerranée, mais tous vont dans le même sens.

Dans le cas de l'évolution de l'espace rural, les paysages ruraux de
l'Europe méditerranéenne traduisent un rapport nouveau entre les ruraux
et l'espace qu'ils occupent. Le titre intriguant d'une communication –
« Pas seulement des olives et des citrons : le langage de l'agriculture » –
invite le lecteur à comprendre que désormais la campagne n'est plus
dédiée uniquement à la productions agricole pour l'alimentation, mais
qu'elle fournit des matières premières pour l'agro-industrie, qu'elle est
un marché pour les produits industrialisés, un espace tampon régulateur

---

[8] Letizia Mencarini, Silvana Salvini & Daniele Vignoli: « Mediterranean Fertility.
Similarities and Differences between the Two Shores of the Mediterranean ».

du cycle travail-chômage, qu'elle contribue à la préservation et à la protection du territoire, qu'elle offre un lieu de « thérapie » pour les urbains stressés ou vulnérables. Or ce processus est enclenché depuis fort longtemps en Europe du nord et il est décrit pas les géographes et les écologues paysagistes, spécialistes du Maghreb de surcroît[9]. Passer d'espaces agricoles à des espaces mixtes dédiés à des activités organisées autour de la demande urbaine rurale est un phénomène connu, y compris des historiens. Le modèle est présenté sous le terme de « *rural local systems* », définis par « un paysage de haute valeur environnementale, adapté à une production de qualité ». Même si la recherche est limitée essentiellement à la Toscane (Montalcino, Prato), il faut se demander si cette évolution est propre à l'Europe méditerranéenne du nord. La réponse est que la spécialisation agricole, la valorisation d'un terroir rural avec tout ce qu'il compte d'atouts gastronomiques, économiques et culturels, environnementaux, paysagers et historiques sont le propre des États européens et des sociétés économiquement diversifiées et de service[10]. La convergence du monde méditerranéen européen avec le reste de l'Europe du nord est une réalité en ce qui touche à la mise en valeur des terroirs ruraux. La comparaison avec le sud de la Méditerranée ferait apparaître sûrement de grandes différences en raison de la conservation des modes de production agricoles traditionnelles.

Quand on prend la mesure de l'emploi, la variation des taux indique que les pays d'Europe méditerranéenne se situent en moyenne en dessous du taux général d'emploi de l'UE-25 (62,9) sauf Chypre (69,2) et le Portugal (67,2). Les pays suivants se situent en dessous de la moyenne européenne : France (62,8), Slovénie (62,6), Espagne (59,7), Grèce (57,9), Italie (56,1), Malte (54,5). Il apparaît aussi que le pourcentage du PNB provenant de l'économie parallèle est plus élevé dans les pays de l'Europe du sud que dans les pays de l'Europe du nord. La moyenne de l'UE-15 étant à 18,6 %, l'Italie est à 27,1 %, la Grèce à 28,7 % le Portugal à 22,7 % et l'Espagne à 22,7 %. On pourrait tirer la conclusion qu'il y a une différence des comportements entre le nord et le sud de l'Europe. Elle existe. Mais la comparaison avec quelques pays méditerranéens non européens (Turquie (47), Maroc (40), Algérie (39)) montre que la différence des taux est énorme, bien supérieure à ce qu'elle est entre l'Europe méditerranéenne communautaire et l'Europe du nord. La différence est très grande aussi entre les pays européens méditerranéens non membres de l'Union et les pays méditerranéens du

---

9 Pierre Donadieu : « La société paysagiste », Acte Sud, 2002.

10 Luigi Omodei Zorini: « Not Only Olives and Citrus Fruits: the Language of Agriculture ».

sud : Croatie (68), Albanie (64), Bosnie Herzégovine (62)[11]. La crois-sance économique a produit davantage d'emplois dans la partie nord de la Méditerranée que dans le sud et les structures archaïques (économie parallèle) perdurent davantage dans les pays méditerranéens que dans les pays d'Europe du Nord. Toutefois l'intégration européenne tire vers le haut le taux d'emploi de l'Europe méditerranéenne, différenciant l'ensemble économique européen du sud méditerranéen.

Fausses convergences et vraies spécificités

Une manière d'apprécier les divergences-convergences au sein de l'Europe méditerranéenne par rapport au sud et par rapport à l'Europe du nord est d'utiliser d'autres marqueurs tels que les différentes formes d'ethnicismes linguistiques, culturels, familiaux. Si les comportements des minorités ethniques installées le long du bassin méditerranéen nord sont globalement identiques, il sera possible de définir un caractère proprement méditerranéen opposable aux comportements des minorités du nord de l'Europe. Pour être complet il faudrait aussi prendre en compte les comportements de ces minorités dans les pays d'Islam (Berbères, Juifs, Coptes d'Égypte, Kurdes, Arméniens). L'enquête ne peut pas aller aussi loin ici. Les minorités méditerranéennes auxquelles les chercheurs ont fait référence se trouvent incluses dans des États-nations, l'Espagne et la France, et concernent l'Occitanie, la Provence, la Catalogne française, à cela s'ajoutent les régions occitanes d'Italie (Piedmont). D'autres, très conscientes d'elles-mêmes, ont négocié leur place dans l'État-nation: c'est le cas de la région de Valence ou des îles Baléares. Enfin un dernier groupe est constitué de régions de forte conscience ethnique, fières de leur histoire et dotées d'une langue acceptée par les populations locales (pas nécessairement parlée par tous): Corse, Sicile, Catalogne et Macédoine. Mais que de différences : les Catalans ont pris le pouvoir économique dans l'État-nation, ce qui n'a pas été le cas des Corses qui pourtant sont nombreux dans le reste de la France, ni en Sicile. Les mouvements ethniques ont été revigorés dans les années 1960 par la lutte algérienne après avoir été minorés durant la seconde guerre en raison du soutien que certains ont apporté au fas-cisme, ce qui n'a pas été le cas de la Catalogne anti-franquiste. La référence à une identité méditerranéenne, opposée à l'État-nation dans lequel elles se trouvent, est-elle au cœur de leur combat? En fait un chercheur explique que cette conscience méditerranéenne s'efface ou reste floue, qu'elle est soumise aux transformations dues aux mouve-

---

[11] Marcello Signorelli: « Employment and Unemployment in a Multilevel Regional Perspective ».

ments pérennes ou temporaires de populations allogènes circulant librement dans l'État-nation dont elles font partie et dans l'Europe communautaire de la libre-circulation. Parfois, les réactions contre de prétendues invasions de la région habitée par des minorités ont facilité l'affichage d'un ethnicisme linguistique et culturel au nom de la culture menacée (arrivée de pieds-noirs d'Algérie en Corse et de Castillans en Catalogne). Acceptcrons-nous la conclusion ainsi formulée de l'auteur de cette intéressante réflexion: « Finalement nous conclurons cet article avec une référence à l'identité méditerranéenne. Le "méditerranéisme" en tant que construction culturelle peut avoir joué un certain rôle subsidiaire en donnant une sorte de modèle transnational de référence à des mouvements ethno nationalistes en Méditerranée occidentale. Aussi, la renaissance musicale et artistique qui a pris place dans les pays de langue catalane depuis la fin des années 1960 se référait souvent à la musique grecque, sicilienne ou corse comme un modèle à imiter »? Le rapport à la Méditerranée devenait le moyen de se distinguer artificiellement du voisin castillan en Catalogne ou des Français du continent en Corse, tandis que les Galiciens se réclamaient au contraire du Celtisme. « Cependant on peut aussi arguer que le "Méditerranéisme" relève plus de l'image culturelle que du modèle politique influent dans les ethno-nationalismes de Méditerranée occidentale »[12]. Ce n'est donc pas la référence à l'héritage méditerranéen pris comme un paquet culturel et historique qui motive l'ethnicisme linguistique et culturel, mais le culte des valeurs spécifiques de chaque minorité, surtout quand ces minorités ne sont pas assez reconnues dans l'État-nation dont elles partagent le destin. Il n'y a donc pas de convergence pan-méditerranéenne des diverses ethnies minoritaires, mais des situations spécifiques.

Le cas de Malte est très intéressant pour notre propos parce que le patriotisme maltais affiché dès 1590 ne semble pas se référer à un méditerranéïsme particulier. Malte est marquée par Saint Paul qui aurait fait naufrage sur ses côtes et donc par le christianisme. Malte a une langue proche de l'italien des sicilo-normands. Malte est-elle italienne alors? Les nationalistes maltais se réfèrent à l'Italie plus qu'à une solidarité méditerranéenne. Or le débat sur la langue – le choix de l'italien ou de l'anglais – illustre la nature de Malte qui s'affiche européenne par la culture, se réfère à l'empire britannique, bien qu'ancienne colonie britannique, pour la langue, méditerranéenne pour l'histoire et la position stratégique au croisement de deux polarités. « Ni Anglaise ou Italienne, ni Espagnole ou Sicilienne, ni Arabe ou Musulmane, mais d'une manière ou d'une autre contenant des traits de tous cousus ensem-

---

[12] Xosé-Manoel Núñez: « Regions, Ethnic Identities, and States in Mediterranean Europe: an Attempt at a Comparative View ».

ble, la race maltaise autant mélangée que sa langue mais avec le temps plus ou moins homogénéisée reste l'une des plus petites et toujours vivantes communautés ethno-linguistiques dans le monde, en voie de se transformer finalement en État-nation unitaire »[13]. L'adhésion récente de Malte à l'Union n'est pas une marque d'appartenance à la Méditerranée, mais le choix du peuple maltais de mieux assurer sa sécurité et son développement et d'être fidèle à son passé européen. Malte poserait plus maintenant la question des conséquences de sa situation d'île frontière de l'Union que celle de son identité que personne ne remet en cause, n'ayant pas eu à subir le poids d'un État-nation. Il est vrai que dans l'histoire, l'Ordre de Malte a été seigneur de l'île pendant des siècles et a assumé un « mandat européen » de gardien des portes de l'Europe chrétienne qu'elle peut retrouver pour le compte de l'Union européenne aujourd'hui autour des valeurs européennes partagées, « dialogue and dialectic, synthesis and eclecticism, admixture and overlap » qui, à vrai dire, pourraient bien être les fruits de l'histoire de la Méditerranée.

Les îles de la Méditerranée sont toutes originales comme le prouvent les travaux sur la Sardaigne, la Sicile et Chypre. Il manquera la Corse. Il n'y a pas de modèle unique de comportement culturel, linguistique et politique des îles de la Méditerranée. Elles ont seulement en commun d'appartenir à la Méditerranée, mais que partagent-elles d'autre ? Paradoxalement la référence méditerranéenne ne serait-elle pas une forme d'entrée dans la modernité en contestant l'ordre établi ? « L'affiliation à la Méditerranée est faible bien que récemment elle soit réapparue et fasse partie des différentes références identitaires. À l'heure actuelle, elle semble appartenir à l'histoire ancienne mais elle est un projet d'avenir. Une attention certaine est portée à cette ancienne et nouvelle forme d'identification et, pourrait-on dire, elle est mise en valeur dans le processus de mondialisation »[14]. La référence méditerranéenne n'avait pas d'intérêt quand les îles étaient l'objet des convoitises des voisins méditerranéens, elle en a une dès lors qu'il s'agit de combattre pour sa survie dans un monde global et terriblement réducteur d'originalité.

La Sicile a digéré tous ses conquérants, la Sardaigne a été divisée et ne les a pas assimilés. La langue sarde est en danger, pas le sicilien. L'histoire de ces deux îles dans le processus de l'unité italienne est

---

[13] Henry Frendo: « Pressures on Assumed Identity at the Border: Malta in Europe, Empire and Mediterraean ».
« Neither English nor Italian, Spanish or Sicilian, not Arab or Muslim, but somehow containing strains of all of these stitched together, Malta's race as mixed as its language, but one which in the fullness of time more or less homogenized as one of the smallest and still surviving ethno-linguistic communities in the world, eventually transforming into a unitary nation-state ».

[14] Daniele Petrosino: « Identity and Hybridism in Sardina and Sicily ».

différente. Leur importance géopolitique n'était pas la même non plus. Leur statut culturel a changé avec la création d'un État-nation italien. Leur importance dans le cadre de l'Union européenne est relative car l'Union s'est tournée vers l'est. Toutefois, les récentes arrivées illégales de populations immigrées sur les côtes de Sicile concernent toute l'Europe et rappellent que les îles de la Méditerranée ont un rôle essentiel à jouer dans le cadre du processus de Barcelone et de la politique de bon voisinage de l'Union.

Chypre exprime excellemment les anciennes tensions entre les mondes grec et turc. On y vit les difficultés qui ont empoisonné la relation entre l'Occident et l'Orient, entre l'islam et le christianisme, entre l'hellénisme et le turquisme. On constate donc qu'un État artificiel est invivable. Il n'y a pas d'égalité réelle entre les deux populations turque et grecque parce que les Chypriotes grecs se sentent détenteurs de l'État et que les Turcs sont, à leurs yeux, une minorité protégée. Quant à l'ancien leader turc de Chypre, Denktas, il réclamait pour les Chypriotes turcs l'appartenance totale à l'espace culturel et de pensée turc. « À cet égard l'identité chypriote est définie comme le produit d'un conflit et d'une animosité entre les identités grecque et turque »[15]. Peut-on fonder un État sur un conflit ? À l'évidence non. Seul le parti communiste de Chypre, AKEL, a essayé de créer une identité chypriote commune. La guerre froide d'une part, puis l'effondrement du communisme ensuite ont ruiné cet effort raisonnable de construction d'un État. Revendiquer une identité chypriote était donc mal venu ; revendiquer l'identité chypriote revenait à trahir « sa » nation grecque ou turque, comme pouvait paraître le faire un Sarrois autonomiste face à la RFA avant le rattachement.

Ces quatre îles au destin différent (Malte, Sicile, Sardaigne et Chypre) ont donc un rapport à la Méditerranée totalement différent, tout autant qu'avec l'Europe continentale ou péninsulaire. Elles ne portent pas le destin de la Méditerranée. Elles regardent toutes sans hésitation vers l'Union européenne.

L'attente d'Europe en Méditerranée

Le propos du colloque était de présenter la situation de la Turquie et des pays du sud sud-est européen par rapport à l'Union européenne. D'opportunes comparaisons avec les pays du sud méditerranéen intéressés eux aussi par l'Union européenne devraient balancer cette réflexion. Tous, à des degrés divers, sont en attente « d'Europe ».

---

[15] Sia Anagnostopoulou: « The Problem of Identities in the Second Half of the 20th Century. Conflict or Conversion? The Case of Cyprus ».

La Turquie est un pays méditerranéen mais pas seulement méditerranéen. L'accord d'association de la CEE avec la Turquie date de septembre 1963 et a marqué paradoxalement un recul par rapport aux possibilités qu'offrait l'article 238 CEE. Ce fut un accord *a minima*. Le rapport intime de la Turquie avec l'Occident, et pas uniquement avec l'Europe occidentale, résultait de la guerre froide et du rôle des élites turques, tournées vers Washington au nom de la sécurité que les États-Unis pouvaient apporter à la Turquie. Mais la Turquie a été un allié adroit qui comptait aussi sur Moscou après 1957 (aides limitée de Moscou). Des négociations furent engagées avec la Turquie au sein de l'OECE sur les conditions d'aide aux pays à faible développement. Sans doute pour cette raison s'était-elle tournée plus naturellement vers le projet britannique de zone de libre-échange que vers l'Europe des six. Après avoir manifesté une prudente réserve envers les six la Turquie tenta d'obtenir le maximum d'avantages économiques et commerciaux de la Communauté économique européenne. Cette relation ancienne de la Turquie avec la Communauté européenne pose le problème bien connu de l'élargissement de l'Union et de l'identité communautaire européenne[16]. La Turquie a réussi à s'inviter dans le concert communautaire européen parce qu'elle était un acteur majeur en Méditerranée et parce qu'elle était une pièce maîtresse de la sécurité du monde occidental depuis 1945. Mais est-ce une raison de l'accueillir dans l'Union européenne comme État membre ? La précipitation de l'ouverture des négociations et les promesses d'adhésion qui ont été faites à plusieurs moments ont traduit en fait le manque de travail de la Communauté sur les conséquences de cette adhésion. Les risques d'une adhésion-friction de la Turquie sont réels alors que les relations avec le sud méditerranéen, non éligible à l'adhésion sont plus clairement définies.

Le sud sud-est de l'Europe, les Balkans, appartient aussi au bassin méditerranéen et a vocation à adhérer à l'Union européenne. Il est vrai que les Européens n'ont pas eu de politique très nette jusqu'au conflit dans l'ex-Yougoslavie et qu'ils en ont adopté une seulement avec le conflit du Kosovo en 1999. Un intervenant écrit: « depuis lors beaucoup d'initiatives ont été prises par l'Union pour soutenir les pays du sud sud-est. Immédiatement après la fin du conflit entre l'OTAN et la république fédérale de Yougoslavie, en juin 1999, le Pacte de stabilité pour l'Europe du sud-est a été lancé pour faciliter la reconstruction économique des pays touchés par la guerre du Kosovo. Plus important encore, aussitôt après, l'Union européenne lançait son Processus de stabilisation et d'association pour les cinq pays du sud sud-est européen leur offrant

---

[16] Elena Calandri : « Stratégie de développement, option identitaire. La Turquie et l'Europe occidentale, de l'aide multilatérale à l'association à la CEE ».

une relation contractuelle avec la possibilité de signer un Accord de stabilisation et d'association »[17]. Le rapport avec les pays des Balkans est donc désormais bien balisé. Toutefois, il faut noter que l'Union a limité ses engagements financiers, qu'elle a imposé une conditionnalité de l'aide plus stricte que celle appliquée aux autres pays en transition et qu'elle a limité provisoirement la libre entrée des produits d'exportation les plus rémunérateurs pour ces pays. « Les élargissement futurs de l'Union européenne dépendront beaucoup de la disposition de l'Union à admettre de nouveaux membres ». Or on peut se poser des questions sur les capacités de l'Union à accepter de nouveaux entrants de cette région de l'Europe bien que la Croatie ait commencé les négociations d'adhésion avec l'Union. « Il est possible que les élargissements futurs de l'Union soient ralentis, mais il est impensable de les arrêter ». Que ce soit à travers l'exemple turc ou à travers le cas des pays balkaniques, il semble que le tropisme méditerranéen de l'Union soit limité. Pourtant il est impossible que l'Union ne développe pas une grande politique en Méditerranée soit par l'adhésion de certains pays, soit par le biais de la politique de bon voisinage, soit par l'intermédiaire d'associations privilégiées et qu'elle en reste à une zone de libre-échange. Il en va de l'avenir du dialogue des civilisations pour employer de grands mots. Mais que l'on considère l'enjeu que représente l'adhésion à l'Union de territoires peuplés de populations musulmanes et chrétiennes en Bosnie-Herzégovine. Un succès conforterait la paix en donnant l'assurance que des populations musulmanes trouveront leur place en toute égalité avec d'autres au sein de l'Union.

Comment l'Union peut-elle compter dans le monde méditerranéen sinon par des politiques culturelles hardies ? On aurait tort de considérer la Méditerranée comme un espace « européen » en dépit de l'expansion européenne aux XIXe et XXe siècle. Il est aussi américain du fait de la superpuissance des États-Unis mais aussi du fait d'une présence ancienne remontant au XIXe siècle, renforcée par les combats de guerre froide. Les États-Unis ont fait une propagande multicible en accord avec un Islam anti-communiste. Des universités américaines ont été créées à Beyrouth et au Caire, de même que de nombreuses écoles américaines. Le résultat n'a pas été à la hauteur des investissements. La politique culturelle britannique existe aussi en Méditerranée mais sans obtenir les résultats escomptés non plus. En revanche, la bonne organisation culturelle française en Méditerranée arabe a conduit, grâce aux lycées et écoles français, à cibler les élites et à exercer une influence non négligeable. Les Instituts culturels français ont diffusé certaines valeurs

---

[17] Milica Uvalic : « EU Policies towards Southeast Europe : from Stabilisation towards Integration ».

universelles propres à la culture française dans les pays du sud méditerranéen dont certains sont d'anciens territoires administrés par la France. L'influence italienne s'est manifestée aussi par le relais des missions catholiques, d'écoles, de missions scientifiques et des sociétés savantes. Cette influence a été victime du fascisme qui a « nationalisé » à outrance le message. Les programmes culturels italiens après la guerre ont été repris sur d'autres baes, s'insérant aussi dans les luttes de guerre froide : « L'Italie ne pouvait plus et ne voulait plus promouvoir une politique culturelle basée uniquement sur les intérêts nationaux et des perspectives de propagande »[18]. L'Italie veut être un pont en Méditerranée entre l'est et l'ouest, le nord et le sud. L'image de l'Italie a été favorablement accueillie dans le monde arabe. L'action culturelle italienne a été distillée en prenant appui sur l'UNESCO qui lui a donné une sorte de garantie de désintéressement alors que dans le cas de la France, l'UNESCO aura été un multiplicateur d'influence. Des États arabes ont voulu et veulent encore diversifier l'accès à l'enseignement supérieur et à la culture de leurs étudiants et les dirigent vers l'Italie. Considérant cette situation, les pays européens actifs culturellement en Méditerranée : France, Italie, Grande-Bretagne, sans oublier l'Allemagne et l'Espagne qui n'ont pas fait l'objet de recherche pour ce colloque, devraient avoir une politique commune de diffusion des valeurs européennes contenues dans le projet de Constitution européenne en alternative à l'action des États-Unis et à la mondialisation tout en prenant dans leur propre culture ce qui profite au bien de la coopération.

Quel avenir pour l'Europe méditerranéenne ballottée sur l'océan de l'histoire après avoir été le cœur de l'histoire? La question n'est pas de chercher quel destin particulier elle peut avoir – c'est une autre question – mais de saisir ce qu'elle peut apporter en termes de principes et de façons d'agir à l'Union européenne et au pays riverains de la Méditerranée. Un intervenant a plaidé pour l'Europe du *soft power*, c'est-à-dire, selon Joseph Nye, la capacité d'attirer plus que de forcer ou d'acheter, contrairement au *hard power* qui implique la force ou la corruption. L'Union européenne peut exercer ce magnétisme grâce à son art, ses littératures, sa musique, le design, la mode et l'art de la table, les sports. Du fait aussi que la guerre est impensable entre pays européens, l'Union européenne exerce un magnétisme certain et elle pratique donc sans le savoir le *soft power*. L'Europe fournit 70 % de l'assistance au développement aux pays pauvres. Or de tous les espaces de l'Union européenne, la Méditerranée est le meilleur endroit pour voir fonctionner « les processus d'adaptation, de fusion et de transformation des sociétés

---

[18]   Lorenzo Medici: « Western Cultural Policy in the Mediterranean during the 20th Century ».

humaines ». On peut discuter cette assertion, sans en nier la réalité, tout en rappelant que le processus d'intégration et donc de résolution des conflits par l'intégration a commencé entre la France et l'Allemagne le 9 mai 1950, mais il est vrai que sur l'histoire longue, au moins jusqu'au XXe siècle, tous nos auteurs ont apporté des faits montrant que la Méditerranée a été plus un espace d'échanges – sinon de convergence – que de séparation, en dépit des croisades et des guerres saintes, que cet espace a permis non pas d'arriver à une unité culturelle utopique, à une fusion, mais de faire vivre ensemble des ethnies linguistiques et religieuses différentes qui partageaient cependant un mode de vie proche généré par l'histoire, le climat, la mer et les terroirs.

Si comme il a déjà été écrit, au point d'en faire un topos de la littérature, on définit l'identité culturelle méditerranéenne par la conscience de la diversité et la recherche du dialogue interculturel – d'autres auraient parlé du voyage et pris comme héros éponyme de l'identité méditerranéenne Ulysse de l'Odyssée –, ce colloque a aussi montré la force des spécificités et l'impact de la mondialisation sur cet espace. Présenter la Méditerranée comme source de la diversité et de l'échange nous conduit directement à l'Union européenne qui a reconnu dans la diversité son bien le plus précieux puisque sa devise est « unis dans la diversité ». Toutefois, comme le pont de Mostar, la tolérance multiséculaire peut être détruite. Elle peut aussi être relevée. Mais il faut un centre de puissance capable d'agir selon ces principes. L'Union européenne l'est devenue, sans comprendre toujours qu'elle a le destin de la Méditerranée entre ses mains. Si elle réussit à établir la paix en Bosnie-Herzégovine et à faire respecter les compromis sur la Macédoine, et entre la Serbie et le Monténégro, alors elle aura réussi à faire passer dans les faits cette qualité qu'on reconnaît à la Méditerranée d'être un espace de compréhension et de liberté entre les cultures. Un tel succès « pourrait être le signal de l'intégration pour les Musulmans récemment arrivés en Europe », la Turquie devenant ou non membre de l'Union européenne.

Index

L'Europe et les Europes
(19e et 20e siècles)

Titres parus / Series Titles